D1565200

SELF-ESTEEM PROBLEMS OF CHILDREN

OF CHILDREN

PSYCHODYNAMICS AND PSYCHOTHERAPY

SELF-ESTEEM PROBLEMS OF CHILDREN

PSYCHODYNAMICS AND PSYCHOTHERAPY

Richard A. Gardner, M.D.

Clinical Professor of Child Psychiatry
Columbia University
College of Physicians and Surgeons

Creative Therapeutics,
155 County Road, Cresskill, New Jersey 07626-0317

Cover photo: Young Teen Girl Rejected by Group
© Richard Hutchings—Photo Researchers

Library of Congress Cataloging-in-Publication Data

Gardner, Richard A.
    Self-esteem problems of children : psychodynamics and
psychotherapy / Richard A. Gardner.
        p.   cm.
    Includes bibliographical references and index.
    ISBN 0-933812-26-4
    1. Self-esteem in children.   2. Self-esteem in adolescence.
    3. Child psychotherapy.   4. Adolescent psychotherapy.   I. Title.
    [DNLM: 1. Child Development Disorders—psychology.
    2. Psychotherapy—methods.   3. Self-Concept—in adolescence.
    4. Self-Concept—in infancy & childhood.   WS 105.5.S3 G228s]
RJ506.L68G37   1992
618.92'8914—dc20
DNLM/DLC
for Library of Congress   92-9573
                                                               CIP

PRINTED IN THE UNITED STATES OF AMERICA

10 9 8 7 6 5 4 3 2 1

To my
new granddaughter
Rachel Liora Rubin

Welcome to the world!
May you enjoy long life,
good health, loving relationships,
and an ample share of the
happiness that life can provide.

Other Books by Richard A. Gardner

The Boys and Girls Book About Divorce
Therapeutic Communication with Children:
  The Mutual Storytelling Technique
Dr. Gardner's Stories About the Real World, Volume I
Dr. Gardner's Stories About the Real World, Volume II
Dr. Gardner's Fairy Tales for Today's Children
Understanding Children: A Parents Guide to Child Rearing
MBD: The Family Book About Minimal Brain Dysfunction
Psychotherapeutic Approaches to the Resistant Child
Psychotherapy with Children of Divorce
Dr. Gardner's Modern Fairy Tales
The Parents Book About Divorce
The Boys and Girls Book About One-Parent Families
The Objective Diagnosis of Minimal Brain Dysfunction
Dorothy and the Lizard of Oz
Dr. Gardner's Fables for Our Times
The Boys and Girls Book About Stepfamilies
Family Evaluation in Child Custody Litigation
Separation Anxiety Disorder: Psychodynamics and Psychotherapy
Child Custody Litigation: A Guide for Parents
  and Mental Health Professionals
The Psychotherapeutic Techniques of Richard A. Gardner
Hyperactivity, The So-Called Attention-Deficit Disorder,
  and The Group of MBD Syndromes
The Parental Alienation Syndrome and the Differentiation
  Between Fabricated and Genuine Child Sex Abuse
Psychotherapy with Adolescents
Family Evaluation in Child Custody Mediation, Arbitration,
  and Litigation
The Girls and Boys Book About Good and Bad Behavior
Sex Abuse Hysteria: Salem Witch Trials Revisited
The Parental Alienation Syndrome: A Guide
  for Mental Health and Legal Professionals
True and False Accusations of Child Sex Abuse:
  A Guide for Legal and Mental Health Professionals

To my classmates
    behind whom I trailed,
    from the first grade
    to graduation from medical school.

In my attempts to achieve
    your levels of success,
    I enriched enormously
    my own fund of knowledge,
    providing me thereby with life-long
    enhancement of my self-esteem.

CONTENTS

CONTENTS

ACKNOWLEDGMENTS

I deeply appreciate the dedication of my secretaries, Donna La Tourette and Linda Gould, to the typing of the manuscript of this book in its various renditions. I am grateful to Muriel Jorgensen for her diligence in editing the manuscript. She provided useful suggestions and, at the same time, exhibited respect for my wishes regarding style and format. I appreciate the efforts of Robert Tebbenhoff of Lind Graphics for his contributions to the production of this book from the original manuscript to the final volume. I am grateful to Barbara Bernstein for her diligence in the proofreading of the page proofs. I am grateful, as well, to Chris Saucier for her thorough and useful index.

Most of all, I am indebted to the child patients I have seen over the last 35 years who have taught me much about self-esteem, the ways in which it becomes lowered, and the methods that may be utilized to enhance it. It is my hope that what I have learned from them will prove useful to others for bringing about a higher sense of self-worth.

INTRODUCTION

DEFINITION

Self-esteem is a very difficult term to define. Most of us have an intuitive feeling about what the word means, but when asked to define it specifically, most are hard put to do so. Robson (1988), in an excellent review article on the subject, concluded:

> Because it is an abstract concept, any definition of self-esteem that is more than an exercise in semantics must incorporate hypotheses based on the theoretical viewpoint of the writer, and must remain provisional pending the empirical investigation. The definition can then be modified and refined in the light of observation and experiment.

Elsewhere Robson (1989) states:

> Self-esteem is an idea rather than an entity and the term signifies different things to different people. Measuring instruments inevitably reflect the theoretical stance of the inventor and sometimes intercorrelate poorly, suggesting that they are identifying different constructs.

Beck (1967) considers an important element in self-esteem the individual's interpretation of events. His definition of self-esteem is:

> The sense of contentment and self-acceptance that stems from a person's appraisal of his own worth, significance, attractiveness, competence, and ability to satisfy his aspirations.

For the purposes of this book I will simply define self-esteem as the thoughts and feelings of regard that one has about oneself. Self-esteem can be high, or it can be low. One does well, however, to view it to be on a continuum, which can fluctuate considerably from time to time, and even from minute to minute. It does involve an appraisal of oneself, and the concept must rely on attributes, some of which are made specific in the Beck definition, e.g., one's sense of significance, competence, etc. Although Beck's definition certainly covers very important areas of consideration when one assesses one's own self-worth, there are other factors operative in self-esteem that I will be focusing on in this book. I will also use the term *self-worth* synonymously with self-esteem. Some dictionaries define self-esteem as *pride.* Pride relates to high self-esteem and is not applicable to low self-esteem. Accordingly, I will use the term *pride* as synonymous only with high self-esteem.

SELF-ESTEEM IS VERY MUCH IN VOGUE

Self-esteem considerations are extremely important when attempting to understand the psychogenic learning disabilities. During the last 15 to 20 years, schools have been particularly sensitive to the self-esteem issue and have taken it into consideration to a significant degree when devising educational programs and their assessment, especially grading systems and teachers' comments. (I will comment further on this later in this book.) Furthermore, in the last few years many formal programs of self-esteem enhancement have developed, programs in which group leaders teach individuals how to enhance their own and one another's self-esteem. Schools, business, and industry have been swept up in this wave of enthusiasm for self-esteem programs. Many of these programs are nothing more than orgies in which people compliment one another: "You're great," "You're terrific," and "You're splendid." The recipients of these compliments then chant about how they *are* great, splendid, etc. It is my hope that by the time the reader finishes reading this book, he (she) will appreciate the superficiality of these silly exercises with full recognition of the depth and breadth of the factors operative in building self-esteem.

THE COMPLEXITY OF THE PROBLEM

For many years I have seen school reports in which the school guidance counselor, psychologist, or other consultant has advised the teacher to "raise this child's self-esteem." Nothing further is said about how to accomplish this, and the report goes on to make other recommendations. When I see this comment I usually think, "I would appreciate your telling me specifically how you would go about raising this child's self-esteem." It is difficult to consider any form of psychogenic pathology without bringing in the self-esteem factor. The factors that contribute to a high sense of self-worth are multiple and complex. The approaches to helping a child with low self-esteem are also varied and complicated; the aforementioned recommendation implies that a simple solution is at hand. It is my hope that by the time the reader finishes this book he (she) will have some appreciation of the enormity of the problem. It is not my wish to produce in the reader a totally pessimistic attitude regarding helping children with low self-esteem. Rather, I hope that an appreciation of the complexity of the problem will place the reader in a better position to ascertain the *specific* factors operative in a particular child's self-esteem problem and direct his (her) attention to those areas where something might be done. And such understanding is the first step toward helping such patients.

Furthermore, I hope that the therapist will not expend significant effort trying to enhance self-worth in areas where the chances of change are extremely small. For example, a boy has a Full Scale IQ of 88. This youngster is going to have great difficulty feeling good about himself in the academic realm because of his intellectual impairments. Although placement in a special educational class may protect him somewhat from a negative comparison of himself with peers, he still recognizes that he is in a special class and is likely to be referred to by peers (overtly or covertly) as "retard" and "ment." Because of coordination difficulties, he does poorly in sports and so cannot derive a high sense of self-worth from this area. This is in contrast to other less academically oriented students who can provide themselves compensatory ego-enhancement in the realm of sports. Because of cognitive impairments in the socialization realm, the boy has few if any friends. Accordingly, he cannot enjoy the ego-enhancement that comes with being popular, or even sought after by peers. His siblings complain about how he embarrasses them when they bring friends to the home because of his atypical behavior, intrusiveness, and lack of respect for their privacy and their guests'. This too cannot but lower his self-worth. Last, although his parents may profess the same pride in him as they have for their other children, in their hearts they know that their professions of pride are a sham; rather, they go through life with a deep ache in their hearts, as they are ever confronted with the deficiencies of this child. Without this positive feedback from parents, his self-esteem is lowered even more. And it is for such youngsters especially that I would ask the aforementioned psychologist, "Would you please tell me just how one should go about raising this child's self-esteem? Would you please tell me exactly *where* I should start?"

THE UBIQUITY OF THE PROBLEM

H. L. Mencken once said that self-confidence is the delusion that others don't know how inadequate you feel about yourself (or words close to that). Once again, Mencken has confronted us with an unpleasant truth. All of us suffer throughout life with feelings of insecurity. All of us have our compensatory facades. Sometimes these are quite obvious, like the blowhard, the muscleman, the braggart, and the person who is forever attempting to obtain the praise and admiration of the world. But most of us use more subtle mechanisms for compensating for our feelings of inferiority. When a therapist says, "I am treating this man for feelings of low self-esteem," he (she) is basically saying (if he [she] were to be honest): "I am treating this man whose feelings of self-worth I would like to believe are lower than mine. I hope I am right here because, if mine are lower than his, then to be really honest about it, I may not be able to help him." In short, it is to be hoped that the therapist's basic feelings of self-worth will be higher than those of the patient he (she) is treating for these problems.

ALFRED ADLER AND FEELINGS OF INFERIORITY

Alfred Adler took issue with Freud regarding his emphasis on sexuality as the central element in the development of psychopathological processes (Mullahy, 1955). He considered feelings of inadequacy and the various methods people utilize to compensate for them to be more important factors. I am in agreement with Adler on this point. Although I believe that Adler took his theory too far—thereby repeating Freud's mistake of exaggerated emphasis on one point—he has nevertheless provided us with valuable insights into the factors that contribute to the development of psychopathology. In fact, there may not be a single psychopathological symptom that does not relate, at least in part, to the problem of feelings of inadequacy and the attempts to deal with it. More specifically, I believe that most symptoms contain, in part, an element that serves to enhance self-worth or to avoid situations that may lower it.

Examples are not difficult to find. In fact, one could randomly select any symptom and not have too much difficulty finding confirmation for this principle. Consider the common student symptom of cheating on tests. Youngsters who cheat on tests do not believe they have the capacity to get a good grade honestly (they may or may not have such ability) and fear the feeling of low self-worth they will suffer if they do poorly.

Children who bribe others for friendships do not believe they have the personality qualities that will predictably attract companions and have to delude themselves into believing that those who are "bought off" are genuinely friends. In this way they protect themselves from ego-debasing feelings of loneliness. Those who brag are generally individuals who feel inadequate; those who have the "real stuff" generally do not need to brag. Delusional grandiosity is the extreme example of this mechanism. Paranoid projections often include an element of attributing to others the self-denigratory feelings that one harbors within oneself. Considering others to be falsely criticizing is less ego-debasing than recognizing that the criticisms are self-derived and genuinely valid. Of course, there are many symptoms in which the self-esteem element plays only a small role; however, I do not know of a symptom in which it plays no role at all.

Because of the central role that low self-esteem plays in the development of a wide variety of psychopathological symptoms, it follows that anything that the therapist can do to enhance self-esteem should be therapeutically beneficial. I would go further and state that whatever a therapist can do to enhance a patient's self-esteem—in a real and genuine manner—can be viewed as therapeutic. Such enhancement of self-esteem can be considered the universal antidote of psychotherapy. I emphasize here, however, that the enhancement must be real and genuine, not specious, artificial, or superficial. Patronizing praise, compliments not directed to genuine attributes, and intrinsically condescending words of praise will ultimately be ego-debasing. Throughout the course of this book I will describe what I consider the psychotherapeutic maneuvers that can be genuinely ego-enhancing and thereby therapeutically effective.

It was indeed unfortunate that Freud reacted so harshly to anyone who would question his theories. Rather than giving consideration to Adler's ideas, and possibly even incorporating them into his own, he totally rejected Adler with the result that each of them set up their own separate "synagogues," a situation that exists to this day. We have many houses of worship in the field of psychiatry, many of which have followed in the pattern set up by Freud originally. Individuals must form their own amalgams of the various theories and come up with some composite that seems to make sense to them. (And this book is an example of my own amalgam.)

☐ ONE
SPECIAL THERAPEUTIC TECHNIQUES

In this chapter I describe some special therapeutic techniques I have developed, techniques that I have found useful in the treatment of children with self-esteem problems. It is not my purpose here to describe the wide variety of psychotherapeutic techniques that may be useful in the therapy of such children. Rather, I present here techniques that I have devised and developed and have found particularly useful in the treatment of children with psychogenic problems. My purpose here is not to discuss these techniques in detail, but rather to provide enough basic information for the reader to utilize them. Some illustrative examples are provided, but the reader who is interested in more examples does well to refer to my publications referred to in the discussion of each of the methods.

THE MUTUAL STORYTELLING TECHNIQUE

HISTORICAL BACKGROUND

The use of children's stories as a source of psychodynamic information is well known to child psychotherapists. To the best of my knowledge, this was first described in the literature (in German) by Hug-Hellmuth in 1913. (The first English translation appeared in 1921.) A fundamental problem for the child therapist has been this: How does one use the information one can derive from such stories and bring about psychotherapeutic change? This is the "great-leap-forward" question of child psychotherapy. Children's stories are generally easier to analyze than the dreams, free associations, and other verbal productions of adults. Often, the child's fundamental problems are exhibited clearly to the therapist, without the obscurity, distortion, and misrepresentation characteristic of the adult's fantasies and dreams.

A wide variety of psychotherapeutic techniques have been devised to use therapeutically the insights that the therapist can gain from children's stories. Some are based on the assumption, borrowed from the adult classical psychoanalytic model, that bringing into conscious awareness that which has been unconscious can in itself be therapeutic. The psychoanalytic literature is replete with articles in which symptomatic alleviation and even cure is described as quickly following the patient's gaining insight into the symptom's underlying psychodynamic patterns. My own experience has been that very few children are interested in gaining conscious awareness of their unconscious processes in the hope that they can use such insights to alleviate their symptoms and improve their life situation. I believe that one of the reasons for this disinterest is that the average child of average intelligence is not cognitively capable of taking an analytic stance and engaging in a meaningful psychoanalytic inquiry until the age of about ten or eleven. This corresponds to Piaget's level of formal operations, the age at which the child can consciously differentiate between a symbol and the entity that it symbolizes.

Of course, brighter children are capable of analytic inquiry at earlier ages. But even these children are generally not interested in assuming the analytic stance and delving into the unconscious roots of their problems—unless there are significant environmental factors that stimulate such inquiry. For example, the child who grows up in a home in which both parents are introspective and analytic is more likely to think along these lines. Accordingly, it is only on rare occasions that I do direct analytic work with children under the age of ten or eleven. And when this occurs, it is usually with a patient who is extremely bright and who comes from a home in which the parents have been or are in psychoanalytic treatment themselves and are deeply committed to introspective approaches to dealing with life's problems. But even in adult therapy, professions of commitment to analysis notwithstanding, most of my patients are not deeply committed to psychoanalytic inquiry. And they are generally even more resistant to analyzing their resistances to such inquiry. Hence, I rarely attempt to employ a psychoanalytic approach to the therapeutic utilization of children's self-created stories.

In the 1920s Anna Freud and Melanie Klein—both influenced deeply by Hug-Hellmuth's observation—attempted to work analytically with children, and the analysis of their stories was essential to their therapeutic approaches. Although they differed significantly regarding the interpretations they gave to children's stories, they agreed that the gaining of insight into the story's underlying psychodynamic meaning was crucial to meaningful therapeutic change. Beginning in the 1930s, Conn (1939, 1941a, 1941b, 1948, 1954) and Solomon (1938, 1940, 1951, 1955) described the same frustrations this examiner experienced with regard to getting children to analyze meaningfully their self-created stories. They were quite willing to analyze those children who were receptive to such inquiries. But for those who were not, they were equally satisfied discussing the child's story at the symbolic level. They believed that therapeutic changes could be brought about by communicating with the child at the symbolic level. For example, if a child told a story about a dog biting a cat and was unreceptive to analyzing it, they found that discussions about why the dog bit the cat and what better ways there were to handle the situation could get across important messages without producing the anxiety of analytic inquiry.

During my residency training in the late 1950s, most of my supervisors were classical psychoanalysts and considered the analytic approach to be the optimum one for the treatment of most children's psychogenic disorders. Most of the children I saw did not even consider themselves to have symptoms, the obvious preliminary step if one is to embark upon an analytic approach to the alleviation of their problems (and this is still the case today, over 30 years later). It was then that I first began to experience the frustration of children's unreceptivity to analysis. I was much more comfortable with the approach of Conn and Solomon, namely, responding to the child's self-created stories at the symbolic level. It was from these experiences that I derived in the early 1960s the technique that I subsequently called *the mutual storytelling technique*. Basically, it is another way of utilizing therapeutically children's self-created stories. It stems from the observation that children enjoy not only telling stories but listening to them as well. The efficacy of the storytelling approach for imparting and transmitting important values is ancient. In fact, the transmission of such values was and still is crucial to the survival of a civilized society. Every culture has its own heritage of such stories that have been instrumental in transmitting down through the generations these important messages.

It is reasonable to speculate that thousands of years ago, in the early days of civilized society, attempts were made to impart directly important messages necessary for people to learn if they were to cooperate meaningfully in social groups. It was probably learned quite early that direct confrontations of such messages (especially when personal criticism was involved) might not be the most effective way to get such messages incorporated into people's psychic structures. And this was especially the case when others witnessed the "corrective" confrontations. Because most such messages relate to behavior that is socially unacceptable (take the transgressions enumerated in the Ten Commandments, for example), it is likely that public confrontations caused guilt, embarrassment, and significant unreceptivity toward those who attempted to impart these communications. It is reasonable to speculate that a subsequent development involved the recognition that storytelling might be a useful vehicle for incorporating such messages in a disguised and therefore less threatening way. After all, storytelling is an ancient tradition and, up to the twentieth century, it was probably one of the most popular forms of evening entertainment.

It was in such storytelling sessions that people would relate the events of the day and, considering the fact that external sources of entertainment were limited and infrequent, some degree of elaboration of events was probably welcomed. Furthermore, it is reasonable to speculate that a certain amount of "expansion of the truth" was not seriously criticized because of the extra entertainment value that such elaboration provided. We today do not differ very much from our ancient forebears in this regard. It is reasonable to assume further that the popularity of this form of entertainment made it an attractive vehicle for the incorporation of messages that were important to impart to individuals for immediate purposes as well as for perpetuation down the generations. It was probably appreciated that one could circumvent listeners' defensiveness regarding being told about their wrongdoings by describing the transgressions of *others* and the lessons *they* learned from their departures from acceptable patterns of behavior. The basic principle was: "Of course, none of us here would ever do such terrible things. However, it's interesting to hear about others who did these things and what they learned from them." Adding violence and sex (traditionally attractive modalities in any story) enhanced their attractiveness to listeners. Ultimately, these stories became the primary vehicle for transmitting down the generations important messages necessary for the survival of the group. In fact, I would go further and state that societies that did *not* have such a heritage did not survive because they did not have this important vehicle for transmitting their values to subsequent generations.

Much more recently, with the development of written language, these stories achieved a new permanence. Our Bible is one example of such a document. The Old Testament is basically a collection of stories that were prevalent from the period around 750 BC to 250 BC. Most consider these stories to be combinations of fact and fantasy. Each individual, of course, must make a decision regarding how much of these two elements are present.

There are some who claim that everything in the Bible is completely true and others who go to the other extreme and claim that it is complete fantasy. Although people may differ regarding what they consider the fact/fantasy ratio to be, most will agree that these stories have had a profound influence on humanity and have contributed significantly to moral development and the perpetuation and survival of civilized society.

The mutual storytelling technique is in this tradition. It attempts to rectify one of the fundamental problems of storytelling as a vehicle for transmitting important messages, namely, that any story, no matter how well tailored to the needs of a particular audience, is likely to be relevant to only a small fraction of those who listen to it. After all, an audience generally consists of men and women of varying ages from childhood through old age. It is unreasonable to expect any particular story to "turn on" more than a small fraction of such a heterogeneous group. The mutual storytelling technique attempts to circumvent this drawback by using a story that is designed to be specifically relevant to a particular patient at that particular time. The stories are tailor-made to the individual and are therefore more likely to be attended to with receptivity and incorporated into the listener's psychic structure.

THE BASIC TECHNIQUE

In this method the therapist elicits a self-created story from the child. The therapist then surmises its psychodynamic meaning and then tells a responding story of his (her) own. The therapist's story utilizes the same characters in a similar setting, but introduces healthier resolutions and adaptations of the conflicts present in the child's story. Because the therapist is speaking in the child's own language – the language of allegory – he (she) has a better chance of "being heard" than if undisguised messages were transmitted. The direct, confrontational mode of transmission is generally much more anxiety provoking than the symbolic. One could almost say that with this method the therapist's messages bypass the conscious and are received directly by the unconscious. The child is not burdened with psychoanalytic interpretations that are generally alien and incomprehensible. With this technique, one avoids direct, anxiety-provoking confrontations so reminiscent of the child's experiences with parents and teachers.

The technique is useful for children who will tell stories, but who have little interest in analyzing them (the vast majority, in my experience). It is not a therapy per se, but one technique in the therapist's armamentarium. Empirically, I have found the method to be most useful for children between the ages of five and eleven. I generally do not treat children under the age of four (I find it more efficient to counsel their parents). In addition, children under the age of five are not generally capable of formulating organized stories. In the four- to five-year age bracket, one can elicit a series of story fragments from which one might surmise an underlying psychodynamic theme—which can serve as a source of information for the therapist's responding story. The upper age level at which the technique is useful is approximately eleven. At that time, children generally start appreciating that they are revealing themselves. They may rationalize noninvolvement with the technique with such justifications as "This is baby stuff" and "I don't feel like telling stories." Last, the technique is contraindicated for children who are psychotic and/or who fantasize excessively. One wants more reality-oriented therapeutic approaches such as *The Talking, Feeling, and Doing Game* (to be discussed later in this chapter); otherwise the therapist may entrench and even worsen their pathology.

Dolls, drawings, and other toys are the modalities around which stories are traditionally elicited in child psychotherapy. Unfortunately, when these story-facilitating instruments are used, the child's story may be channeled in highly specific directions. They have specific forms that serve as stimuli that are contaminating to the self-created story. Although the pressure of the unconscious to create a story that serves a specific psychological purpose for the child is greater than the power of the facilitating external stimulus to contaminate the story, there is still some contamination when one uses these common vehicles for story elicitation. The microphone connected to a video- or audio-tape recorder does not have these disadvantages; with it, the visual field remains free from distracting and contaminating stimuli. The microphone almost asks to be spoken into. Eliciting a story with it is like obtaining a dream on demand. Although there are differences between dreams and self-created stories, the story elicited by a tape recorder is far closer to the dream than that which is elicited by play material.

In earlier years I used an audiotape recorder. In more recent years I have used a videotape recorder. For the therapist who has this instrument available, it can enhance significantly the child's motivation to play the game. Although hearing one's story on the audiotape recorder can serve to facilitate the child's involvement in the game, watching oneself on television afterward is a much greater motivating force. The fantasies these instruments help engender are rarely, if ever, contaminating of the story they are designed to facilitate. But the examiner should not conclude that these instruments are crucial. They are merely devices. Long before they were invented, children enjoyed relating self-created stories. The therapist should be able to elicit stories from most children without these contrivances. Such instruments should be viewed as additional motivating facilitators and, of course, they have the additional benefit of the playback, which provides reiteration of the therapeutic messages. In earlier years many children would bring their own tape recorder, simultaneously tape the stories with me, and then listen to them at home for further therapeutic exposure. Recently, I added a second video-cassette recorder to my office closed-circuit television system. Children now bring their own videocassettes (to be found with increasing frequency in homes these days), tape the story sequences along with me, and then watch their sessions at home. Later in this chapter I will discuss in detail the utilization of the videocassette recorder in child therapy.

SPECIFIC TECHNIQUES FOR
ELICITING SELF-CREATED STORIES

I begin by telling the child that we are now going to play a game in which he (she) will be guest of honor on a make-believe television program. In earlier years I would ask child patients if they would like to be the guest of honor on the program; in more recent years I seduce them into the game without the formal invitation. I merely say, "And now we're going to play a game in which you're going to be the guest of honor on a television program." Of course, if the child strongly resists, I will not pressure or coerce. We then sit across the room from the mounted camera, and the video cassette recorder, lights, and camera are turned on. I then begin:

> *Gardner:* Good morning, boys and girls. I'd like to welcome you once again to "Dr. Gardner's Make-Up-a-Story Television Program." We invite boys and girls to this program to see how good they are at making up stories. The story must be completely made up from your own imagination. It's against the rules to tell stories about anything that really happened to you or anyone you know. It's against the rules to tell a story about things you've read about, or heard about, or seen in the movies or on television. Of course, the more adventure and excitement the story has, the more fun it will be to watch on television later.
>
> Like all stories, your story should have a beginning, a middle, and an end. And after you've made up your story, you'll tell us the lesson or the moral of your story. We all know that every good story has a lesson or a moral. Then, after you've told your story, Dr. Gardner will make up a story also. He'll try to tell one that's interesting and unusual, and then we'll talk about the lesson or the moral of his story.
>
> And now, without further delay, let me introduce to you a boy (girl) who is with us for the first time. Tell us your name, young man (woman).

I then ask the child a series of questions that can be answered by single words or brief phrases. I will ask the child's age, grade, address, name of school, and teacher. These "easy" questions reduce the child's anxiety about the more unstructured themes involved in "making up a story." I then continue:

> *Gardner:* Now that we've heard a few things about you, we're all interested in hearing the story you've made up for us today.

Most children at this point begin with their story, although some may ask for "time out to think." Of course this request is granted.

There are some children, however, for whom this pause is not enough, but will still want to try. In such instances the child is told:

> *Gardner:* Some children, especially when it's their first time on this program, have a little trouble thinking of a story. However, I know a way to help such children think of a story. Most people don't realize that there are *millions* of stories in everyone's head. Did you know that there are millions of stories in your head? (The child usually responds negatively.) Yes, right here between the top of your head and your chin [I touch the top of the child's head with one finger, and the bottom of his (her) chin with the another finger], right between your ears [I then touch the child's two ears], inside your brain, which is in the center of your head, are millions of stories. And I know a way how to get out one of them.
>
> The way to do this is that we'll tell the story together. In this way, you won't have to do all the work by yourself. The way it works is that I start the story and, when I point my finger at you, you say exactly what comes into your mind at the time that I point to you. You'll see then that your part of the story will start coming into your brain. Then after you've told the part of the story that comes into your mind, I'll tell another part, and then I'll point to you. Then we'll go back and forth until the story is over. Okay, here we go. (The reader will note again that I did not ask the child if he (she) wished to proceed, rather I just "rolled on.")
>
> Okay, here we go (I now speak *very slowly*). Once upon a time . . . a long, long time ago . . . in a distant land . . . far, far away . . . far beyond the mountains . . . far beyond the deserts . . . far beyond the oceans . . there lived a . . .

I then quickly point my finger at the child—jolting him (her) out of the semi-hypnotic state that I have tried to induce by this "introduction," which basically says nothing. It is a rare child who does not offer some associative word at that point. For example, if the word is "cat," I will immediately say, "And *that* cat. . . . " and once again point firmly to the child, indicating that it is his (her) turn to tell more of the story. I follow the next statement provided by the child with, "And then. . . ." or "The next thing that happened was. . . ." Or, I will repeat the last few words of the patient's last sentence, with such intonations that continuation by the child is implied. Every statement the child makes is followed by some connective term supplied by me and indicates to the child that he (she) should provide the next statement. At no point do I introduce any specific material into the story. The introduction of such specific phrases or words would defeat the purpose of catalyzing the child's production of his (her) *own* created material and of sustaining, as needed, its continuity.

This approach is successful in eliciting stories from the vast majority of children. However, if it is unsuccessful, it is best to drop the activity in a completely casual and nonreproachful manner, such as: "Well, today doesn't seem to be your good day for storytelling. Perhaps we'll try again some other time."

While the child is relating the story, I sometimes jot down notes (usually just key words). These help me analyze the story and serve as a basis of my own. When the child completes the story, I then elicit its lesson or moral. In addition, I may ask questions about specific items in the story. My purpose here is to obtain additional details that are often helpful in understanding the story. Typical questions might be: "Is the dog in your story a boy or a girl, a man or a woman?" "Why did the horse do that?" or, "Why was the cat so angry at the squirrel?" If the child hesitates to provide a lesson or a moral, or states that there is none, I will usually reply: "What, a story without a lesson? Every good story has some lesson or moral! Every good story has something we can learn from it."

Usually, after completing my responding story (some details of this process will be described below), I will ask the child to try to figure out the moral or the lesson of my story. This helps me ascertain whether my message has been truly understood by the child. If the child is unsuccessful in coming forth with an appropriate lesson or moral to my story, I will provide it. Following the completion of my story, I generally engage the child in a discussion of its meaning to the degree that he (she) is capable of gaining insight and/or referring the story's message to himself (herself). Many children, however, have little interest in such insights, and I do not press for them. I feel no pressure to do so because I believe that the important therapeutic task is to get across a principle, and that if this principle is incorporated into the psychic structure (even unconsciously), then therapeutic change can be brought about.

FUNDAMENTALS OF STORY ANALYSIS

Obviously, therapists are in no position to create a story of their own unless they have some understanding of the basic meaning of the child's story. The greater the familiarity with the child, the greater the likelihood the therapist will be in the position to do this. Also, the more analytic training and experience a therapist has, the more likely he (she) will be able to ascertain correctly the meaning of the child's story.

First, I try to determine which figure(s) in the child's story represent the child himself (herself) and which symbolize significant individuals in the child's milieu. Two or more figures may represent various aspects of the *same* person's personality. There may, for example, be a "good dog" and a "bad dog" in the same story, which are best understood as conflicting forces within the same child. A horde of figures, all similar, may symbolize powerful elements in a single person. A hostile father (or one viewed as hostile by the child), for example, may be symbolized by a stampede of bulls. Malevolent figures can represent the child's own repressed anger projected outward, or they may be a symbolic statement of the hostility of a significant figure. Sometimes both of these mechanisms operate simultaneously. A threatening tiger in one boy's story represented his hostile father, and the father was made more frightening by the child's own hostility, repressed and projected onto the tiger. This is one of the reasons why many children view their parents as being more malevolent than they actually are.

Besides clarifying the particular symbolic significance of each figure, it is also important for the therapist to get a general overall "feel" for the atmosphere of the story. Is the ambiance pleasant, neutral, or horrifying? Stories that take place in frozen wastelands or on isolated space stations suggest something very different from those that occur in the child's own home. The child's emotional reactions when telling the story are of great significance in understanding its meaning. An 11-year-old boy who tells me, in an emotionless tone, about the death fall of a mountain climber reveals not only his anger but also the repression of his feelings. The atypical must be separated from the stereotyped, age-appropriate elements in the story. The former may be very revealing, whereas the latter rarely are. Battles between cowboys and Indians rarely give meaningful data, but when the chief sacrifices his son to Indian gods in a prayer for victory over the white man, something has been learned about the boy's relationship with his father.

I then ask myself: "What is the main pathological manifestation in this story?" or "What is the primary inappropriate or maladaptive resolution of the conflicts presented?" Having identified this, I then ask myself: "What would be a more mature or a healthier mode of adaptation than the one utilized by the child?" I then create a story of my own. My story generally involves the same characters, setting, and initial situation as the child's story. However, very quickly my story evolves in a different direction. The pathological modes are not utilized, although they may be considered and then rejected by various figures in the story. Invariably, a more appropriate or salutary resolution of the most important conflict(s) is achieved.

In my story I attempt to provide the child with more *options* for dealing with the problems and conflicts depicted in the child's story. The communication that the child need not be enslaved by his (her) psychopathological behavior patterns is crucial. As mentioned, if therapy is to be successful, it must open new avenues not previously considered by the patient. It must help the patient become aware of the multiplicity of options that are available to replace the narrow, self-defeating ones that have been selected.

On occasion, the therapist will be confronted with a dilemma regarding the utilization of the child's protagonist in his (her) responding story. For example, if the child depicts himself (herself) with a figure that is intrinsically denigrating or ego-debasing, such as a worm or a skunk, the therapist may have to make a decision regarding the utilization of this same figure in the responding story. To use it is basically to communicate to the child that it is a justifiable representation of himself (herself). To discard it, and replace it with a less deprecating figure, circumvents the ego-debasing implications of its utilization but robs the therapist of an important element whose removal detracts from the attractiveness and even the effectiveness of the responding story. To the degree possible, the therapist wants to maintain the same characters and the same scene. We must appreciate that we can only understand the meaning of a small fraction of the story's elements. When we remove or replace a "protagonist" or even a "prop" from the "stage" we risk the removal of important psychological material. The more we do this, the more we veer "off track" and the less the likelihood our story will be meaningful to the child.

In such situations I generally choose to preserve the child's protagonist, its negative elements notwithstanding, because I believe that the benefits of maintaining this figure far outweigh the drawbacks of its removal. However, in order to circumvent somewhat the detrimental effects of its preservation, I generally quickly add certain positive elements intrinsic to the figure. For example, with regard to a skunk I might quickly add that the skunk generally doesn't smell, and that the odor it does emit is a protective device that has survival value. The worm too has the assets of flexibility of movement and ability to crawl into small places. I cannot say that this compromise is completely without its drawbacks and that via its utilization I have completely removed untoward effects of the symbol. Every good medicine has its untoward side-effects, and therapeutic techniques are not exceptions to this principle. It behooves the therapist to know clearly what the drawbacks of the therapeutic instrument are and to mimimize their detrimental effects as much as possible. It is hoped that the advantages of the technique's utilization will far outweigh its risks.

After I have completed my story, I attempt to get the patient to try to figure out its lesson(s) or moral(s). If the child states that the story has no lessons, then I might somewhat incredulously respond: "Why, every story has at least one lesson or moral. I want to see how good you are at trying to figure out at least one of the lessons or morals for this story. Every story teaches us something." It is preferable that the child at least try to surmise the lesson or the story, but if the child cannot, then I present one or more lessons or morals. (It is nowhere written that a story must have only one lesson or moral.) My lesson(s) attempts to emphasize further the healthier adaptations I have included in my story. If, while telling my story, the child exhibits deep interest or reveals anxiety, then I know that my story is "hitting home." I know then that I am on the right track, and that I have ascertained correctly the meaning of the story and have devised a responding story that is relevant. The anxiety may manifest itself by jitteriness or increased activity level. If the child is bored, it may mean that I am off point. However, it may also be a manifestation of anxiety, and the therapist may not know which explanation is most relevant.

There are therapists who might take issue with my approach here, claiming that it is antitherapeutic to provide communications that produce tension and anxiety in a patient. I am in disagreement. Effective therapy involves the patient's tolerating some unpleasant emotions, such as tension and anxiety. Adequate functioning in life requires a certain degree of tolerance for the unpleasant and therapy—being a microcosm of life—should follow the same principle. What is contraindicated is exposure of the patient to overwhelming feelings, feelings that may produce psychological trauma and decompensation. Therapists who "pull back" too quickly when a patient manifests tension and anxiety are not only depriving their patients of these important maturing experiences, but may be joining with the patient's defenses against dealing with important therapeutic material. Patients recognize that operations are painful, but they are willing to tolerate the pain because of the ultimate benefits to be derived from the procedure. And psychotherapy is similar. I let the patients' reactions tell me whether I am going "too far" with my confrontations (even symbolically provided via storytelling). When playing the mutual storytelling game, excessive anxiety will result in children's refusing to play or in the inability to provide self-created stories. In short, my usual suggestion to therapists is that they push a *little* too far, rather than pull back too quickly.

Following the completion of my story and its moral, I usually try to engage the child in a discussion of our stories. For the rare child who is interested in gaining insight, we will try to analyze our stories. For the majority there may be a discussion along other lines, and these are usually at the symbolic level. In earlier years, when I used the audiotape recorder, children were sometimes interested in listening to the tape. In subsequent years, after I began using the videocassette recorder, interest in reviewing the program increased. Viewing the program made possible a second exposure to the messages I wished to impart. And, as mentioned, I have recently purchased a second videocassette recorder— which enables the child to bring his (her) own tape and replay it at home. This not only provides the opportunity for reiteration of the therapeutic messages, but also serves to entrench the therapist-patient relationship.

CONCLUDING COMMENTS

I have described the basic rationale of the mutual storytelling technique. I do not claim to have invented a new method of treatment. The principle is an ancient one, and many therapists have no doubt utilized the method. I believe that my main contribution lies in having written articles on the subject and having formulated more specific criteria for analyzing and creating stories. The utilization of the method in the treatment of a wide variety of psychiatric disorders of childhood is discussed in a number of other publications of mine (Gardner, 1968; 1969d, 1970b,c; 1971a,b; 1972b,c; 1973b,c; 1974a,b,c,d; 1975a,b,c,d; 1976; 1979b,c; 1980b; 1981b; 1983b; 1986a; 1988b). A comprehensive description of the details of utilizing the technique (with regard to story analysis and the therapist's story creations) is provided in my full-length text on the subject (Gardner, 1971a). Others have reported utilization of the technique as well (Arnott and Gushin, 1976; Aust, 1984; Gabel, 1984; Mabee, 1986; Nickerson, 1975;

Oudshoorn, 1979; Schooley, 1974; Stirtzinger, 1983; Strom, 1987; Hoffman and Wizansky, 1989).

DRAMATIZED STORYTELLING

Children call us "talking doctors." Many of us do not fully appreciate the significance of this epithet, especially with regard to its implication that our therapeutic approach is a relatively narrow one. The most potent mechanism for modifying behavior is the experience. The old proverb, "A picture is worth a thousand words," is well known. I would add to this, however, that "An experience is worth a million pictures." To the degree that the therapist can provide experiences, to that degree will he (she) be able to bring about clinical change. This hierarchy of the efficacy of the various forms of learning is well epitomized by the following comparisons. Let us take, for example, the experience of reading a play. Reading the play is purely a visual experience, both at the level of reading the written page and the visual imagery that is engendered by such reading. It is primarily an intellectual experience, although some emotions may certainly be engendered. Let us compare this with attending a theatre and observing the play being acted. It is likely that the individual will be more affected by the play because an auditory modality of input has now been added to the visual experience associated with reading the play. If one becomes an actor in the play, then one is even more likely to remember its messages. The reason for this is that one is now adding physical action to the visual and auditory modalities of input. With each additional modality, there is a greater likelihood that the story will have an impact. However, the emotions being exhibited in the play are feigned. No matter how convincing the actor is, the emotions are still turned on and off in accordance with the dictates of the script. The actor is still play acting. Compare this with emotions that are caused by an actual experience. Here, the reactions are engendered by reality and are even more likely to be recalled in the future. To the degree that we provide our patients with experiences—as opposed to relatively sterile insights—to that degree we improve our chances of helping them.

Because the therapeutic situation may not allow us to provide our patients with as many natural and uncontrived experiences as we would like, we do best to provide them with every possible encounter that comes as close to them as we can. Although play-acting does not have as much "clout" as an actual experience, it may be a superior form of interaction and communication than merely talking—and this is especially true for the child. Just as the mutual storytelling technique was developed from the observation that children naturally enjoy both telling and listening to stories, the idea of dramatizing them arose from my observation that children would often automatically (and at times without conscious awareness) gesticulate, impersonate, intone, and enact in other ways while telling their stories. I found that when I introduced such theatrics myself, the child became more involved in my stories and receptive to their messages.

Whereas originally I introduced the dramatic elements *en passant*, that is, in the process of telling my story (just as the children tended to do), I subsequently formalized the process by inviting the child to reenact our stories as plays following our telling them: "I've got a great idea! Let's make up a play about our stories. Who do you want to be? The wolf or the fox?" At times I would invite the mother and even siblings to join us. (We often have the problem of having a shortage of available actors.) We see here another way in which mothers can be useful in the child's treatment. (A little encouragement may be necessary at times to help some mothers overcome their "stage fright.") Of course therapists themselves must be free enough to involve themselves in the various antics that are required for a successful "performance." They must have the freedom to roll on the floor, imitate various animals, "ham it up," etc. They have to be able to be director, choreographer, writer, and actor—practically all at the same time. They may have to assume a number of different roles in the same play, and quickly shift from part to part. Such role shifts do not seem to bother most children or reduce their involvement or enjoyment. Nor do they seem to be bothered by the therapist's "stage whispers," so often necessary to keep the play running smoothly.

Younger children, especially those in the four- to six-year age group, who may not be inclined to tell well-organized stories, will often improve in their ability to relate them when the dramatic element is introduced. Others, who may have been initially unreceptive to or too inhibited to freely tell stories, may do so after the enjoyable dramatic elements are utilized. The experience becomes more fun and the children tend to forget their reservations. In this younger group, as well, the strict adherence to the pattern of the child's first telling a story and then the therapist's telling his (hers) may not be possible or desirable. A looser arrangement of interweaving stories and plays back and forth may be more practical and effective.

Children generally enjoy television (a statement that I'm sure comes as no surprise to the reader). Even more, children enjoy seeing themselves on television (something a child rarely has the opportunity to do). Therapists who have available a camera and video cassette recorder can provide children with an immensely beneficial therapeutic modality. Making a video cassette recording of a therapeutic experience increases significantly the likelihood that children will expose themselves to reiteration of the therapeutic communications. In the 1960s, when I first developed the mutual storytelling technique, the child and I would often listen to the audio tape recording of the mutually told stories. In the late 1960s, I began encouraging children to bring to the sessions their own audio cassette recorders (a practice initiated by a child) and to listen to these stories at home afterwards.

Around 1970 I purchased a closed-circuit television system and began making videotapes of our stories, both the standard interchanges as well as those that were dramatized. Around 1980 I purchased a standard home video cassette system and camera. This enabled me to lend the videotape to those children who had such an instrument at home. In the last few years, I have added a second video cassette recorder and invite children to bring their tapes to the office. This enables the child to watch at home the various therapeutic interchanges that we tape. Of these, probably the most valuable are those in which dramatizations occur because this ensures even more that the child will listen to the tape and profit from what is contained therein. A number of clinical examples to be found in this book will demonstrate the use of mutual storytelling dramatizations. Elsewhere (Gardner, 1981a, 1986a) I have provided clinical vignettes with verbatim descriptions of such dramatizations.

MUTUAL STORYTELLING DERIVATIVE GAMES

INTRODUCTION

During the first few years of utilization of the mutual storytelling technique, I found some children to be inhibited with regard to their freedom to create and verbalize stories. Accordingly, I began to think of other ways that could be useful in facilitating children's providing me with such material. Recognizing that children enjoy immensely playing board-type games, especially those in which there is a competitive element, a series of games was devised. These games involve traditional board-game materials, such as dice, reward chips, and playing pawns. The introduction of the reward chips serves to enhance children's motivation to provide projective material. Whereas in the mutual storytelling technique no rewards are provided, in these games token chips are given, and the winner (the person who has accumulated the most reward chips) receives a prize.

The games included in the category of mutual storytelling derivative games are: *The Board of Objects Game, The Bag of Toys Game, The Bag of Things Game, The Bag of Words Game, Scrabble for Juniors, The Feel and Tell Game, The Alphabet Soup Game,* and *The Pick-a-Face Game.* They all involve the child's utilization of a figure, object, or word as a point of departure for first making a comment and then telling a story. The child receives one chip for making a comment (an easier but less revealing response) and two chips for telling a story (a more difficult, but more revealing response). Also, the child receives an additional reward chip for telling the lesson or moral of the story. The therapist plays similarly and, of course, the therapist's responding stories are designed to introduce healthier modes of adaptation and resolution than those used by the child. Last, but certainly not least, prizes are available for the winner. It is beyond the purpose of this book to describe these games in detail. They were first described in my publication *The Psychotherapeutic Approaches to the Resistant Child* (Gardner, 1975a). An update and elaboration of these descriptions was provided in my *The Psychotherapeutic Techniques of Richard A. Gardner* (Gardner, 1986a).

Although reward chips are given, it would be an error for the reader to conclude that these games represent a kind of *behavior modification*. These games share with behavior modification the use of reward chips, but the similarity ends there. In behavior modification one uses rewards in order to change behavior at the manifest level. Behavior therapists differ with regard to their views about the presence or absence of unconscious processes and whether, if present, they play a role in symptom formation. But they are in agreement in not generally giving significant attention to unconscious processes in the therapeutic process. Many take the position that the symptom is basically the disease and its removal represents a cure.

My use of chips in these games serves an entirely different purpose. I am using them to reward the child for providing self-created free associations and stories for psychotherapeutic use. My utilization of reward chips is based on the belief that unconscious processes do exist and that the understanding of them (especially by the therapist) plays an important role in the therapeutic process. In short, I am using reward chips for the elicitation of psychodynamically meaningful material, material derived often from unconscious processes. Behavior therapists, in contrast, use reward chips to change behavior at the manifest level. We share in common the use of reward chips, but we use them for entirely different purposes.

It would be an error, also, if the reader were to conclude that I have absolutely no conviction for behavior modification. This is not the case. One cannot deny the importance of positive and negative reinforcement in human development. One of the primary reasons why children are "good" is that they hope to gain the affection and love of their child rearers; and one of the main reasons why they inhibit themselves from being "bad" is their fear of loss of such affection. When two-year-old Johnny decides not to run into the street, it is not because he is aware that he may be endangering his life; rather, he restricts himself from doing so because of his anticipation that significant caretaking individuals will react with strongly negative feedback and even painful physical responses (a slap on the backside or a not so gentle wrenching of his arm) if he does so (Gardner, 1990). The experimental rat presses the bar in order to obtain food pellets and will drop down to the random level of bar pressing frequency if the pellets are permanently withdrawn. So ubiquitous is this pleasure-pain principle that one could argue that behavior therapy is basically nature's form of treatment. In part, I agree that it is. However, the human brain is so complex and sophisticated that other mechanisms, beyond pain and pleasure, are operative, and so more sophisticated methods of psychotherapy are warranted when psychological disorders are present. This does not mean that we must choose between the two. Rather, we can combine both approaches.

Furthermore, I generally prefer to utilize behavioral modification techniques in the context of my psychotherapeutic program. I consider their isolated utilization to be somewhat artificial and sterile. For example, one could help an agoraphobic woman desensitize herself to her fear of open places by suggesting that she force herself to tolerate increasingly the fears that she experiences when she sets forth from her home. This would basically be the traditional behavior modification approach. One might even try to quantify the times of exposure on a chart while pointing out to the patient her progressive improvement. My own approach would be to focus on what I consider to be the primary factors that are contributing to the agoraphobia, factors such as excessive dependency on the people with whom she lives and fears of asserting herself as an adult in a world of adults. This would not preclude, however, my encouraging desensitization and some kind of more informal assessment of her progress. Even the staunchest subscribers to the psychoanalytic theory would not dispute the value of desensitization. The crucial question is whether one believes that one can get a significant degree of symptomatic alleviation over a long period by merely focusing on the removal of the agoraphobic symptom. I believe that one is not likely to achieve long-term improvement by behavior modification techniques alone. Even if one does, I would still consider the therapeutic work to have been only partially completed, because the underlying factors that have contributed to the formation of the symptom have not been dealt with.

The mutual storytelling derivative games also make use of the competitive element. Basically I am using competition to enhance the child's motivation to acquire chips. There are some readers who probably would take issue with me on this point because of their belief that competition is basically a dehumanizing experience that we would do best to dispense with entirely. Obviously, I do not share this view. I think that one must differentiate between healthy and unhealthy competition, between competition that is humane and competition that is inhumane. In healthy competition one strives to win, but one still has respect for one's opponent. In unhealthy competition, the primary purpose is to degrade and destroy one's opponent for a variety of pathological purposes such as hostility release, compensation for feelings of inadequacy, and self-aggrandizement. At any particular time there are thousands of people working in laboratories—hoping someday to win a Nobel prize. Although only an extremely small fraction of these individuals will attain their goal, most would agree that society is a better place because of the existence of the prize. And one could say the same thing about a wide variety of other awards in the arts, sciences, and other fields of endeavor—awards that have served to enhance human motivation and striving toward excellence. If not for healthy competition, we might still be living in caves. If not for unhealthy competition, many people who reached premature death might have lived longer lives.

When using these games, the therapist should keep in mind

these differentiations and do everything possible to keep the competition at a healthy level. Ideally, the patient and therapist will be so swept up in the game that both will forget whose turn it was and who is to get the reward chip. But even when this ideal is not reached, the therapist should strive to make the game so exciting that the child will frequently forget that it was his (her) turn. When the child does appear to be more interested in acquiring chips than providing psychodynamically meaningful material, the therapist should discourage such preoccupations with comments such as: "Wait a minute. Don't throw the dice yet. I haven't finished giving my answer," "Hold on, I'd like to ask you a question about what you've just said," and "That's a very good beginning for your story. Now let's hear the middle and the end of your story. Every story has a beginning, a middle, and an end."

The general principle I follow when playing these games is that the child receives one chip for making a statement and two for telling a story. The statement option is introduced for children who are so restricted that they cannot relate a self-created story. As mentioned, the material so elicited should be used as a point of departure for various kinds of psychotherapeutic interchange. Often, the therapist may wish to respond with a story that is created to address itself to pathological manifestations in the child's story. For some children one might want to discuss the child's story at the symbolic level with comments such as: "Why did the cat run away from the rabbit?"and "Was there something else the cat could have done, something better than running away?" The rare child who is interested in an introspective inquiry might be asked: "Is there anything in your story about the three squirrels that is like what's happening in *your* house?"

As mentioned, it is not my purpose here to describe the mutual storytelling derivative games in detail. In the course of this book I will occasionally make reference to these games and they will be included in some of the clinical vignettes. My experience has been that these games enhance children's motivations to tell stories and are especially useful for children who are too inhibited or resistant to tell self-created stories spontaneously.

THE STORYTELLING CARD GAME

The Storytelling Card Game (Gardner, 1988b) is my latest contribution to the mutual storytelling derivative games. Of the numerous games in this category, I consider it to be the most predictably effective for eliciting self-created stories from children. I am not completely sure why this is the most popular and most efficacious of all the mutual storytelling derivative games. Like the others, it has been designed to be attractive to children. Like the others it includes a mildly competitive element, reward chips, and a prize. It differs from the others in that the child takes a much more active role in creating the scene that becomes the focus for the child's projections. Whatever the reasons, I strongly recommend the instrument to the reader and have found it an excellent complement to *The Talking, Feeling, and Doing Game* (Gardner, 1973d) (to be described later in this chapter).

One can consider there to be a continuum from deeply unconscious material to material that is in conscious awareness and readily accessible for cognitive scrutiny. The dream probably represents the best example of unconscious material; an accurate description of an observed reality is an example of cognitive. Pure mutual storytelling, unaffected by the contaminants of play material, is close to the dream end of the continuum. The mutual storytelling derivative games, affected as they are by external stimuli, represent a shift toward the conscious end of the continuum, but are still very much on the unconscious side. In contrast, *The Talking, Feeling, and Doing Game* elicits primarily conscious material (although some of the cards do elicit some degree of unconscious material). *The Storytelling Card Game*, then, as a mutual storytelling derivative game, can be viewed as an instrument that complements *The Talking, Feeling, and Doing Game* as a therapeutic modality.

EQUIPMENT

The equipment (Figure 1-1) consists of 24 picture cards of which 20 depict a scene that is free from either humans or animals and

Figure 1-1

four are blank. All cards, including the blank ones, are numbered in the lower right corner. The cards portray common scenes: living room, classroom, kitchen, library, bathroom, backyard, meadow, etc. Fifteen human figurines are provided, depicting people from infancy to old age. The arrow spinner board is divided into 16 sectors on which the arrow may come to rest. Ten sectors provide for winning or losing chips, either with the bank or the other player. The other six sectors instruct the player to select one from four specific picture cards from the stack of 24 and throw the die, e.g., "Select card 5, 6, 7, or 8 and throw the die." A die and tray of reward chips (the bank) are also provided.

BASIC FORMAT OF PLAY

The game begins with each player taking five "free" reward chips from the bank. These provide each with a "cushion" for any losses that may be incurred early in the game, before the player's personal treasury is enriched by chips acquired from storytelling. The spinner arrow is the central element in the game play. Each player in turn spins the arrow and follows the instructions indicated in the sector on which the arrow comes to rest. When the spinner comes to rest on one of the ten sectors involving chip gain or loss, the player wins or loses chips as indicated. Such activity is of little psychotherapeutic value, but it does enhance the child's excitement and involvement in the game. When the arrow comes to rest on one of the six sectors indicating card selection, the player selects one from the group of four cards indicated by the spinner and then throws the die. The number indicated by the die is the maximum number of figurines the player may choose from the array provided. Only one die is used in order to ensure that the number of figures chosen will be six or less, the usual number of people in a family. If two dice were to be used, it is likely that many of the throws would entail the child's using a larger number of figurines, beyond the number of people found in most families. And this might reduce the psychotherapeutic value of the stories so elicited. Once the figurines have been placed on the card, a reward chip is given. If the player can tell a self-created story about the picture, two more reward chips are given. Finally, if the player can tell the lesson or moral of the story, an additional chip is earned. The story so elicited then serves as a point of departure for a wide variety of psychotherapeutic interchanges between the therapist and patient. The winner is the player who has acquired the most chips when the game is over.

TECHNIQUES OF PLAY

Although the players alternate turns, it is preferable that the patient spins first ("You're the guest, and guests go first"). This practice enables the therapist to obtain uncontaminated material from the child. If the therapist tells a story first, the material he (she) provides may contaminate the child's subsequent responses.

The Creation of the Child's Picture

When the spinner arrow instructs the child to select one from four specific cards and to throw the die, the therapist does well to instruct the child to spread out all four cards, review them carefully, and then select one of them (Figure 1-2). This is preferable to the child's quickly selecting a card. Choosing one card in a relaxed fashion, with full opportunity to inspect all four,

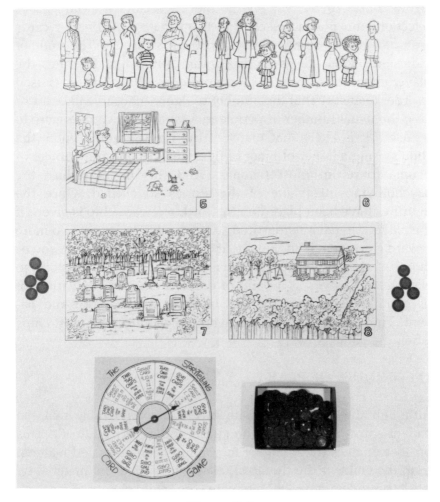

Figure 1-2

increases the likelihood that the card chosen will be relevant to the child's psychological processes. If the child selects the card simply on the basis of the number, before even seeing the four cards ("Oh, I'll take number 5. That's my lucky number"), the examiner should not respect the request; rather, the child should be required to inspect the cards carefully before making the selection.

Following the selection of the card, the player throws the die. The number so obtained indicates the *maximum* number of figurines the player may take from the array of 15 provided. This allows the player some flexibility regarding the number of figurines chosen and is thereby less constrictive of the projections than would be the case if the player were required to take the exact number of figurines indicated by the die. Here too, the figurines should be spread out and the child encouraged to give thought to the selection. If the child chooses the figurines rapidly, it is less likely that the choices will reflect the most relevant psychological issues. The figurines are then placed on the picture selected and the player receives one reward chip (Figure 1-3). The child should be instructed to lay the figurines down on the picture card and not attempt to stand them up. They are not designed to be utilized in this manner and attempting to do so will generally waste time (and possibly damage the figurine, if an attempt is made to bend it). The player is also free to place the figures in any arrangement desired.

The Creation of the Child's Story

Next (and this is the most important part of the game), the player is required to tell a story about the picture so created. When first introduced to the game, the therapist might say something to the child along these lines: "Now I want to see how good you are at making up a story about the picture you've just made. The rules of the game are that the story must be completely made up from your own imagination. It can't be about anything that really happened to you or anyone you know. It can't be about anything you've read, seen on television, or videotape, or in the

Figure 1-3

movies. It must be completely made up from your own imagination." If the game is being videotaped (an extremely valuable enhancement of the game's efficacy), then the therapist might add, "Naturally, the more interesting and exciting the story, the more fun it will be to watch on television afterwards." If the therapist suspects or concludes that the story so elicited is "lifted" from other sources, he (she) does well to remind the patient that stories must be completely made up from the player's *own* imagination and they cannot be taken from other sources ("places"). Telling the child that the rules require that only stories the child creates himself (herself) will be rewarded with chips from the bank can enhance the child's "honesty." Upon completion of a self-created story about the picture formed, the player receives two more reward chips.

Eliciting the Lesson or the Moral of the Child's Story

Last, if the player can tell the lesson or the moral of the story, an additional reward chip is given. Younger children, who might not understand the meaning of the words "lesson" and "moral," might be asked, "What do we learn from this story?" If the child claims that the story has no lesson or moral, the therapist does well to respond somewhat incredulously, *"Every* story has a lesson or moral. I'm sure you're smart enough to figure out what the lesson or moral of this story is." The lesson or moral assists the therapist in ascertaining which of the various themes that may be included in the story is likely to be the most important to focus on. Accordingly, a player can obtain up to four reward chips for each story.

The Therapist's Response To the Child's Story

After the patient has completed his (her) story, the therapist may use the child's story as a point of departure for a wide variety of possible therapeutic interventions, e.g., a responding story in which adaptations are introduced that are healthier or more judicious than those utilized by the child (mutual storytelling technique). Other examples of therapeutic intervention would be discussion at the symbolic level ("Do you think that biting was the best way for the dog in your story to deal with that problem?"), general discussion ("Let's talk some more about the problem the boy had in your story, the problem of dealing with bullies"), or psychoanalytic inquiry ("Is there anything in your story that's like what is happening at home with you and your parents?"). It is important for the reader to appreciate that the responses presented herein are only suggestions and the game allows for great flexibility regarding the therapist's own individual style of responding to the child's stories.

The Therapist's Responding Story

If the therapist chooses to tell a responding story at that point (one based directly on the child's story), he (she) may well request that the child "help" the therapist tell the story in order to incorporate the child's own resolutions and adaptations. If, however, the child's contributions reflect psychopathological patterns, the therapist should not include such in his (her) story, but present the healthier alternatives. The therapist might want to discuss these pathological contributions provided by the child or merely make a comment that he (she) would prefer a different course for the story to take. The therapist then takes two reward chips for his (her) story and may also reward the child with one or two chips for his (her) contribution(s) (if "deserved"). The therapist's obtaining chips for providing a responding story encourages the child to respond similarly to the therapist's stories. When the therapist completes the story, he (she) should ask the child to try to "figure out" the moral or the lesson, rather than immediately providing the moral or lesson himself (herself). In this way the child's involvement is elicited even further and the therapist can ascertain whether or not the child appreciates the story's fundamental message(s). If the child provides a reasonably good moral, a reward chip is given; if not, the therapist then provides a lesson and takes the reward. Both can receive reward chips for the moral if each can provide a good lesson. (It is nowhere written that a story must have only *one* lesson or moral.)

In sum, the therapist is entitled to a maximum of three chips for a responding story (two for the story and one for the moral or lesson). Because the therapist has not created the picture, he (she) is not entitled to the one chip provided the child for forming a picture with the card and figurines. The child, however, may earn extra chips by providing meaningful contributions to the therapist's story and moral. The therapist does well *not* to take chips for his (her) contributions in discussions emerging from the child's story, but should judiciously award chips to the child for meaningful and therapeutically useful contributions to and remarks about the therapist's story.

The therapist may respond in any of the other aforementioned ways to the child's story or say nothing at that point and incorporate the information so gained into his (her) subsequent responses during the course of the game. Whatever the nature of the therapist's response(s), an attempt should be made to play at a slow pace and discourage the child's providing quick responses in order to obtain chips. When played properly, both players are so engrossed in the stories and discussions that chips play a relatively minor role in the therapist-patient interchanges.

The Therapist's Initiated Story

When the therapist is the player directed by the spinner board to select one from four cards and then throw the die, he (she) might display the four cards and ask the child to make the selection ("Can you please help me pick a card?"). In this way the card selected is more likely to relate to issues relevant to the child. After the die is thrown, the therapist might enlist the child's assistance for selecting figurines and even allow the child to make the decision regarding which ones are chosen, how many (up to the maximum), and where they should be placed on the card. Such participation by the patient increases the likelihood that the picture created will be relevant to issues pertinent to the child. However, if the therapist has a particular theme in mind, he (she) might choose the card and determine the figures to be selected. The therapist does well to utilize both methods of picture creation.

When the therapist tells a story, he (she) should create stories that either are based on the child's previous stories (with the introduction of healthier themes) or incorporate other themes considered therapeutic. Just as was the case when the therapist tells a responding story, here too while telling his (her) story, the therapist should try to engage the child's involvement, be receptive to the child's contributions to the telling of the story, and invite the child to try to "figure out" the lesson or moral of the story.

If, in spite of the therapist's courtesy that the "guest goes first," the spinner does not come to rest on a sector requiring storytelling until the therapist's turn (first, second, or third time around), the therapist will then be in the position of having no immediately preceding material on which to base a story. In such situations he (she) might tell a story relevant to the child's clinical problems or topics focused on in the previous session (properly disguised by symbol and/or metaphor). If the therapist is concerned that such a story might be too contaminating of the child's subsequent responses (a reasonable consideration), then he (she) might tell a more neutral story concerning issues relevant to practically all children, but not particularly related to the child's problems, e.g., tolerating fears, enduring present frustrations for future rewards, self-expression, self-assertion, the value of practice, etc.

The Child's Response to the Therapist's Story

The therapist's story may serve as a point of departure for a variety of possible responses by the child, e.g., a responding story, discussion at the symbolic level, general discussion, and psychoanalytic inquiry. The therapist should encourage responses along these lines, but if the child chooses to go on and take his (her) next turn, this should be respected. It is hoped that the therapist's stories and responses will become incorporated into the child's psychic structure and affect subsequent responses and stories. Even more important, it is hoped that the messages the therapist transmits will contribute to psychotherapeutic change — which, obviously, is the purpose of the game. Again, it is important to emphasize that the child should be discouraged from racing ahead simply to acquire more chips; rather, a slow pace is encouraged in order to get as much therapeutic "mileage" from each interchange.

Ending the Game

The play time is not fixed; rather, it is determined by the therapist's judgment regarding how rich the interchanges are and the time available during the session. When the play time is ended, the player with the most chips is declared the winner and receives a prize. Prizes are not provided as part of the game equipment. Traditional gum-ball machine trinkets will often serve well and can be readily purchased from supply houses and manufacturers of such materials.

INDICATIONS AND CONTRAINDICATIONS

The Storytelling Card Game is indicated for the wide variety of psychogenic problems for which children are brought to treatment. It is contraindicated for children who are psychotic and/or those who are significantly involved in fantasy. For such children the game might entrench their problems because it encourages further fantasizing. Such children do much better with more reality-oriented games such as *The Talking, Feeling, and Doing Game*.

The game is designed to be used in individual psychotherapy only. It would be injudicious for the therapist to use it in a group therapy situation because the first child's picture configuration and story is likely to contaminate the responses of the other children in the group. The best projections are made on a blank screen. Although there is some contamination of the screen by the picture card and figurines, at least the screen has been created to a significant degree by the individual who provides the projection. In contrast, if the game is used in a group therapy setting, the card screen (even when blank) is likely to be contaminated by the story provided by a previous child.

AGE RANGE

The game has proved most useful for children between the ages of four and eleven. Children below four are not generally appreciative of the give and take of standard board-game play, do not wait their turns, and are not generally capable of providing the kinds of structured stories, i.e., with logical sequences, that are the optimum kinds to elicit for the purposes of therapy. Children of four and five may, however, provide story fragments that may still prove useful. Under these circumstances the therapist should try to surmise specific psychodynamic themes running through the child's story fragments. The upper age limit of eleven has been derived from empirical observations that youngsters beyond this age generally begin to appreciate that their self-created stories reveal personal information. They thereby become defensive and excuse themselves from play or refuse to participate, with rationalizations involving their belief that the game is only for younger children.

MODIFICATIONS

It is important for the reader to appreciate that the instructions here should be considered as guidelines. Actually, the game allows for great flexibility and the therapist does well to consider his (her) own modifications and innovations. Presented here are a few that the therapist may find useful.

To provide flexibility of figure choice, the instructions allow the child to use fewer figurines than the number indicated on the die. However, the examiner does well occasionally to permit the child to take a greater number of figurines than the die indicates — in order to enhance even further the potential variety of responses. Such expansion of the rules is especially justified if the request is not only reasonable but allows for the creation of a story that probably would be more meaningful than one created with a more limited number of figurines. Although allowing the child to take extra figurines should be judiciously permitted — because of the potential psychodynamic value of the stories thereby elicited — it would be an error to encourage the practice by using two dice. The "busy" stories created with many figures are less likely to focus on the specific intrapsychic and intrafamilial themes most often contributory to the psychopathological process. Accordingly, if the child routinely asks for extra figurines, then it is likely that pathological processes are operative — especially resistance to dealing with guilt-evoking and anxiety-eliciting material. Although the therapist would certainly want to understand the reasons for such pathological utilization of the figurines, he (she) might still want to restrict the child to work within the maximum number provided by the die.

The game has been designed to elicit psychotherapeutically meaningful material from children who are resistant to discussing directly their difficulties. Accordingly, it is especially useful for resistant and uncooperative children. Occasionally a child will be so threatened by storytelling that he (she) will refuse to play the game. Such inhibited children may still be engaged in a modification in which the child is not required to tell a story, but merely provide a statement about the picture created. Although such a statement will not generally provide as much psychodynamically meaningful material as a story, it can nevertheless provide the therapist with some useful information. This is especially the case if a particular theme pervades the various statements the child makes. Generally, it is judicious to reward only one chip for a statement rather than two, in order to enhance the child's motivation to tell stories. Also, because the statement does not usually have a lesson or a moral, the child is further deprived of the more remunerative opportunities provided by a story and lesson.

Some children are so resistant and/or inhibited that they might not even be able or willing to provide a statement. The therapist does well not to simply "give up" on such children, but try another modification. Specifically, the therapist might continue playing the game and provide stories himself (herself), without requiring of the child similar participation. Of course, the child will still be required to spin the spinner and is given the opportunity to acquire or lose chips when the spinner arrow comes to rest on one of the ten sectors indicating such transactions. Although the child may not avail himself (herself) of the opportunity to acquire chips through storytelling, such a child might listen to the therapist's stories (always based on material relevant to the child) and derive some therapeutic benefit from such listening.

GENERAL DISCUSSION

The stories elicited in the context of *The Storytelling Card Game* are likely to be closer to issues relevant to the child's problems than those elicited from traditional picture cards utilized in many diagnostic projective instruments, e.g., *The Thematic Apperception Test (TAT)* (Murray, 1936), *The Children's Apperception Test (CAT)* (Bellak and Bellak, 1949), and *Roberts Apperception Test for Children* (Roberts, 1982). Generally, the scenes portrayed in these instruments, although sometimes vague, include a specific number of figures, each of whom is readily identifiable regarding sex and approximate age. Although there are a universe of possible responses to each of the scenes provided in these standard instruments, the pictures utilized in *The Storytelling Card Game* provide the opportunity for a greater universe of possible responses because the child has the option of deciding the sex, approximate age, and number of figurines (1 to 15) to be included in the picture. Furthermore, the child determines the arrangement of the figures, and this too increases the variability of the responses when compared to traditional projective cards in which the relative positions of the figures affects the kinds of stories that will be elicited. Because the child himself (herself) creates the picture, rather than the creator of the drawings utilized in standard diagnostic projective instruments, the picture is more likely to tap the particular issues that are relevant to the child patient at that particular point. Last, *The Storytelling Card Game* provides four blank cards, reducing thereby the potential contamination of projections provided by traditional picture scenes. If all 16 of the sectors were to involve storytelling, the game would be too high-pressured because every spin would require a self-created story. This potential problem is obviated by utilizing only 6 of the 16 sectors for storytelling and using the others for gaining or losing chips.

Besides the chips, other elements in the game enhance the likelihood that the child will provide self-created stories for the examiner. Spinning the spinner engenders excitement as the child hopes that the arrow will come to rest on a sector that will provide reward chips. The examiner should note that the ten sectors that are *not* involved in storytelling result in the gain or loss of *one or two* chips. In contrast, the six sectors that involve storytelling allow for the potential gain of *four* chips. Accordingly, the child is more likely to hope that the spinner will come to rest on one of the storytelling sectors. Throwing the die also enhances interest and excitement, as the child generally hopes to obtain a high number in order to have the opportunity to utilize more figurines.

The game's mildly competitive element also enhances the child's involvement because of the prospect of winning the game and acquiring a prize at the end. Therapists are sometimes concerned about the potentially ego-debasing effects of competitive games in therapy, especially if the child loses frequently. *The Storytelling Card Game* is so structured that this potential risk is reduced significantly. Specifically, if each player were to take every opportunity to get as many chips as possible during every turn, then the winner would be determined by pure chance. The likelihood is that over the course of the game, the spinner will come to rest on both high- and low-yield sectors, and this should ultimately even out. Furthermore, if the child avails himself (herself) of the opportunity to earn extra chips by contributing to the therapist's stories and other responses, then the likelihood is that the child will win and that the potentially ego-debasing effects of losing will be obviated. However, as mentioned, when the game is played properly, the therapist and child are so absorbed in the stories and other interchanges that little attention is paid to who has more chips and who ultimately wins.

FINAL COMMENTS ON THE STORYTELLING CARD GAME

Although designed to serve as a psychotherapeutic game, *The Storytelling Card Game* can also be used as a valuable diagnostic instrument. I am not referring to its use in providing diagnostic classifications, but to its value in providing examiners with information about underlying psychodynamics. When so utilized, the child is first provided with card #1, then asked to select one or more figurines from the array, and place them on the picture. The examiner then asks the child to tell a story about the scene thereby created. This procedure is then repeated with cards

2, 3, etc. Generally, the examiner does well not to use all 24 cards in one sitting, but to spread the examination over two to three meetings. *The Storytelling Card Game* differs from traditional projective diagnostic instruments in that the children create their own pictures – thereby providing purer and more idiosyncratic projections.

The game may serve as an excellent companion to *The Talking, Feeling, and Doing Game*. *The Storytelling Card Game* taps primarily unconscious material. In contrast, *The Talking, Feeling, and Doing Game* is likely to elicit material more conscious in nature. Therefore, the two together provide the therapist with the opportunity to obtain material over the wide range from conscious to deep unconscious. Accordingly, the therapist does well to alternate the games, both within sessions and between sessions. Last, and most important, the use of these games should of course not preclude direct discussion with the child, work with parents and family, and other therapeutic modalities.

CONCLUDING COMMENTS ON THE MUTUAL STORYTELLING DERIVATIVE GAMES

I consider the mutual storytelling derivative games to be valuable therapeutic instruments. Although they are basically quite similar to one another with regard to the "rules," they are generally not considered so by most children (especially younger ones). The situation here is similar to that which is found in children's games in general. Many board games are basically identical with regard to the fundamental rules of play; the differences are the figures and equipment that are utilized when playing the seemingly different games. Accordingly, children are used to this sort of thing and generally do not object to these similarities in the derivative games. They are generally less valuable than pure mutual storytelling because the fantasy created with "Dr. Gardner's Make-Up-a-Story Television Program" is essentially completely free of external contaminations. These games should then be viewed as instruments of second choice. It is preferable for the therapist to be presented with a free self-created fantasy that is told into the atmosphere. Although the external facilitating stimuli here do provide some contamination, my experience has been that the pressure of the unconscious to project fantasies relevant to issues meaningful to the child at that particular time are far more powerful than the capacity of the external facilitating stimuli to provide significant contamination.

The mutual storytelling derivative games are generally useful for children from about the age of four (the earliest age at which I treat) to about eleven. At that age, children begin to appreciate that their stories are revealing of underlying psychodynamic processes over which they are likely to feel anxiety and/or guilt. Accordingly, most will then refuse to play the game with rationalizations such as "This is a baby game" and "I'm not in the mood to play those kinds of games." This is one of the reasons why I devised *The Talking, Feeling, and Doing Game*, which I will be discussing in detail in the next section. Another reason for the game's development was that there were some children who were still not providing me with psychologically meaningful material, even though I presented them with one or more of these games. *The Talking, Feeling, and Doing Game* proved useful not only in eliciting material from these more resistant children but by extending, as well, the upper age limit for obtaining useful projective material that could readily be utilized in therapy. I found that I could engage most children up to the age of 14 or even 15 with *The Talking, Feeling, and Doing Game,* five or six years after the mutual storytelling technique and its derivative games were no longer therapeutically useful.

THE TALKING, FEELING, AND DOING GAME

INTRODUCTION

The mutual storytelling technique proved useful for facilitating children's telling self-created stories and providing other fantasy material that was of value in therapy. There were, however, children who were not free enough to tell stories using the relatively unstructured format of "Dr. Gardner's Make-Up-a-Story Television Program." It was for these children that the derivative games were devised. However, there were still some children who were so inhibited, constrained, or resistant that even these more attractive modalities did not prove successful in getting them to reveal themselves. It was for these children that *The Talking, Feeling, and Doing Game* (Gardner, 1973d) was devised. This game proved useful for engaging the vast majority of such children. In addition, for children who were free enough to reveal their fantasies, it proved useful as *another* therapeutic modality.

THE BASIC FORMAT

The game is similar in appearance to the typical board games with which most children are familiar (Figure 1-4). It includes a playing board, dice, playing pawns, a spinner, a path along which pawns are moved, reward chips, and cards that are drawn from the center of the game board. This familiarity, as well as the fact that it is a *game*, reduces initial anxieties and attracts the child to the therapeutic instrument.

To begin the game, both the therapist and the child place their colored pawns at the START position. Each player takes five chips from the bank. These serve as a buffer if there are any losses prior to the acquisition of chips. They also give the child a little "taste" of the rewards that can be acquired in the course of the game. Alternatively, the patient and the therapist throw the dice and move their pawns along a curved path of squares that ultimately end at the FINISH position. For younger children, one die can be used. A pawn can land on one of a number of squares: white, red, yellow, SPIN, GO FORWARD (a specific number of squares), and GO BACKWARD (again, a specific number of squares). If the pawn lands on a white square, the player takes a Talking Card; on a yellow square, a Feeling Card; and on a red square, a Doing Card. If the pawn lands on SPIN, the player spins the spinner and follows the directions. Generally, these provide gain and loss of chips, or forward and backward movement of the playing pawn. Similarly, landing on GO FORWARD

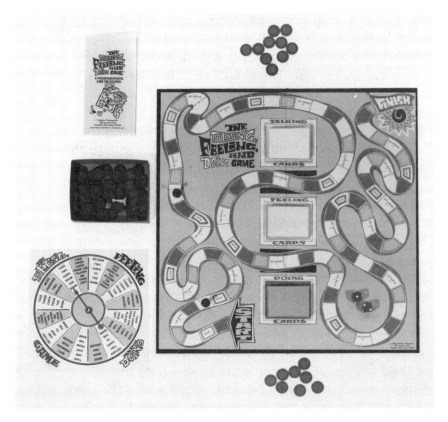

Figure 1-4

or GO BACKWARD squares results in movement of the pawn. The spinner and movement squares are of little, if any, psychological significance. They are included to ensure the child's fun and relieve some of the psychological pressure associated with a high frequency of drawing only the aforementioned three types of cards.

Of course the core of the game is the directions and questions on each of the cards. As their titles imply, the Talking Cards instruct the player to make comments primarily in the intellectual and cognitive area. The Feeling Cards focus primarily on affective issues. The Doing Cards usually involve playacting and/or some kind of physical activity. The child is given a reward chip for responding to each of the cards. Although token reinforcement is provided, the game is by no means a form of behavior modification. Positive reinforcement is not being given for behavioral change at the manifest level. Rather, the child is being reinforced for providing psychodynamically meaningful material for psychotherapeutic utilization. The child's and the therapist's responses are used as points of departure for psychotherapeutic interchanges.

There is no actual time limit for the game. Both the therapist and the patient play similarly, and each responds to the cards. The first player to reach the FINISH position receives five extra reward chips. The second player continues to play until he (she) also reaches the FINISH position. If the game is interrupted prior to one player's reaching the FINISH position, the player who is closest to that position receives three extra reward chips. The therapist should discourage the child's active competition for the acquisition of chips. Rather, the game should be played at a slow pace, and each response should serve as a point of departure for psychotherapeutic interchange.

There are 104 cards in each stack. I always randomize them and have never "stacked the deck" with specific cards that I hope the child will draw. The cards are so designed that any card will be relevant to any player. About five percent of the cards are so simple and nonthreatening that just about any child will respond. These are basically included for the extremely fragile child who would be threatened by the cards that touch on basic problems of living. These simpler cards ensure that the child will get chips and thereby remain motivated to participate in the game. The most liberal criteria are used when deciding whether or not a child should be given a chip for responding. Again, the therapist wants to do everything possible to draw the child in and maintain interest. Some typical low-anxiety cards: "How old is your father?" "What's your lucky number? Why?" "What is your telephone number?" "What is your address?" "What's your favorite flavor ice cream?" "What's your favorite smell?" "Make believe you're blowing out the candles on your birthday cake." "Make a funny sound with your mouth. If you spit, you don't get a chip."

The remaining questions and directions are far richer psychologically and are at the "heart" of the game. These are not as anxiety provoking as a request to make up a story that will reveal free fantasies; however, they provide highly meaningful therapeutic material. Some typical cards: "All the girls in the class were invited to a birthday party except one. How did she feel? Why wasn't she invited?" "Everybody in the class was laughing at a girl. What had happened?" "A boy has something on his mind that he's afraid to tell his father. What is it that he's scared to talk about?" "What's the worst thing a boy can say to his mother?" "Suppose two people were talking about you, and they didn't know you were listening. What do you think you would hear them saying?" "What things come into your mind when you can't fall asleep?" "If the walls of your house could talk, what would they say about your family?" "Tell about something you did that made you proud." "What's the worst thing that ever happened to you in your whole life?"

TECHNICAL AND THERAPEUTIC CONSIDERATIONS

The child's responses are usually revealing of the psychological issues that are most relevant to him (her) at that point. The questions and instructions cover the wide range of human experiences. The material elicited is likely to be relevant to the factors operative in bringing about the child's disturbance. The questions are designed to direct the child's attention to the basic life conflicts that are being resolved in inappropriate and maladaptive ways by the symptomatology. They direct the child's attention to the basic life conflicts that are at the foundation of psychopathological processes (Gardner, 1986a). As mentioned, each response should serve as a point of departure for therapeutic interchanges. The therapist should not merely provide the child with a chip and then race on with the game to see who can reach FINISH first. Rather, the therapist tries to get "as much mileage" as possible from each response, using his (her) discretion when deciding how much discussion is warranted for each patient. Highly defensive and resistant children will not be able to tolerate the kind of in-depth discussion in which the healthier child can readily participate.

The therapist answers the same questions as the child. The greater the therapist's knowledge of the child's problems, the more judicious will be his (her) responses. Obviously, it is not the therapist's role to provide answers relevant to his (her) *own* life problems. Rather, the responses should be designed to provide therapeutic messages pertinent to the child's difficulties. I always respond honestly. Often I will provide a response that will relate to an experience of mine in childhood that is relevant to the patient's problems. Children generally enjoy hearing about the events of their parents' lives that occurred at that time in the parent's childhood that corresponds to the age of the child at the time of the conversation. Such discussions draw children closer to their parents. The same principle holds in therapy. Such revelations, then, can contribute to a deepening of the therapist-patient relationship. As mentioned, a good relationship is crucial if therapy is to be successful. Without it, there will be little receptivity to the therapist's messages and practically no identification with him (her).

Many therapists, especially those with a classical psychoanalytic orientation, may take issue with the freedom with which I reveal myself. They would argue that I am contaminating terribly the therapeutic field ("blank screen") and making the patient's free associations practically useless. I am in full agreement that such revelations contaminate the patient's free associations. I am not in agreement, however, that the classical approach is without its drawbacks. It does indeed provide the so-called blank screen for the purest projections. However, the acquisition of such information is done in a setting that, I believe, is antitherapeutic. It creates a distance between the therapist and the patient that compromises the development of a good therapist-patient relationship. The patient's thoughts and feelings about the therapist become distorted and divorced from reality. The situation increases the likelihood that the patient will develop delusions about the therapist and will idealize him (her). It will widen the gap between them as the patient comes to view the therapist as

perfect. We can love most those whom we know nothing about —
but such love is more delusional than real, based as it is on a
paucity of information. The benefit of purer free associations is
more than counterbalanced by the losses associated with a
compromised therapist-patient relationship and the antitherapeutic experience of the patient's comparing himself (herself)
negatively with the therapist. *The Talking, Feeling, and Doing Game*
provides therapists with the opportunity to reveal defects in a
noncontrived and nonartificial setting. They thereby become
more human to the patient, and this is generally salutary for the
therapist-patient relationship. In addition, my revelations are not
those that would compromise my own privacy and that of my
family. Even with these restrictions, there is enough that has
gone on in my life to provide me with a wealth of potential
information for revelation.

I uniformly answer all questions. Some highly defensive
children, however, may find it difficult to do so. Sometimes, I will
inform such children that failure to answer the question will
result in their not getting a reward chip, and this will lessen the
likelihood that they will win the game. Some children are
motivated by this "threat" and try to respond to the card. On
occasion, a child will refrain from answering most cards but still
involve himself (herself) in the game. Many of these children
listen attentively to my responses and, I believe, gain thereby
from the game. Although I am working here in a partial vacuum
because I am not getting as much information from the child as is
desirable, my knowledge of the child's history and background
provides me with enough information to give responses to the
cards that are meaningful to the child and pertinent to his (her)
problems.

The question is sometimes raised about winning and losing
when playing therapeutic games with children. *The Talking,
Feeling, and Doing Game* obviates this problem. It may not be
immediately apparent to the therapist that the main determinant
as to who wins the game is *luck*. If each player answers each card,
the determinant as to who wins the game is the dice. If a player
obtains many high throws, then he (she) will reach FINISH earlier

and thereby acquire fewer chips. If a player obtains a larger number of low throws, more chips will be acquired when going from START to FINISH. Because low and high throws average out for each player, wins and losses also average out over the course of treatment.

Although *The Talking, Feeling, and Doing Game* was originally devised to engage resistant children in therapy, it has proved useful for less defended children as well. In fact, it has proved to be the favorite therapeutic activity of the children in my practice. Many other therapists have informed me that this has been their experience as well. This therapeutic boon is not without its drawbacks, however. One danger of the game is that it will lure the child (and, unfortunately, the therapist) away from utilizing techniques that are more likely to elicit "deeper" psychodynamic material. Dealing with this material is also important in therapy. Accordingly, the therapist should not injudiciously "respect" the child's wishes to devote the entire therapeutic experience to this technique. This problem has been partially obviated by the introduction of *The Storytelling Card Game*, because of its capacity to both attract the child and elicit unconscious material. *The Talking, Feeling, and Doing Game* is generally useful for children over the age of five or six, the age at which they begin to appreciate the give-and-take structure of board games. At that age, of course, the therapist may have to read the cards to the child (or read along with the child), but this is not an impediment to meaningful play. Whereas the mutual storytelling technique and its derivative games are generally not useful above the age of 11, one can get a few more years' mileage from *The Talking, Feeling, and Doing Game*. My experience has been that it can be useful up to the age of 14 or 15. It can be especially valuable, then, for younger adolescents who are too old and defended to tell self-created stories, but too young to talk freely about their problems (such as is often the case for children in their mid-teens and older).

Although primarily designed to be used in the one-to-one therapeutic situation, the game can be used in child group therapy as well (preferably for small groups of three to five children). When so utilized the therapist can use a child's response as a point of departure for group discussion. The game is particularly useful in child group therapy because it provides intrinsic structure in a situation that traditionally tends to become unstructured (the children tend to become playful, rambunctious, distracted, etc.). In addition, it facilitates discussion of problems in a setting in which such conversations are usually difficult to accomplish because of the reticence of most children to engage in them. One can use it for this purpose in a number of ways. One way I have found useful is to have the first child respond to a card and then get input from each of the other players about the first player's response. Each of the other participants, of course, receives a chip for his (her) contribution. The second child may now answer the same question or choose his (her) own card. In this way I go around the board, involving each child in the responses of the others. When utilizing the game in this manner, the therapist can choose whether to participate as a player or as the group leader. I generally prefer to take turns myself for the sake of "egalitarianism" as well as the desire to gain the therapeutic benefits to be derived from my revelations about myself.

The game can also be useful in selected family therapy situations. Generally, unsophisticated and/or uneducated parents may welcome the game as a catalyst for family discussion; more sophisticated and/or educated parents will generally not need such assistance in their family therapy work.

Generally, the material elicited when utilizing the mutual storytelling technique is closer to pure dream and free fantasy than that revealed in *The Talking, Feeling and Doing Game*. The "Make-Up-a-Story Television Program" is so structured that there are no specific stimuli around which the stories are told. Traditional play materials such as dolls and puppets, although valuable and frequently effective catalysts for story elicitation, contaminate the story and tend to "draw" the child's projections into specific directions. The cards in *The Talking, Feeling, and Doing Game* are similarly contaminating. However, I believe that the "push" of the unconscious material to be released in a form specific for the child's needs at that particular time is far stronger than the "pull" of the evoking stimulus and its power to significantly alter the projected material. Accordingly, the "channeling" of the projections is not very significant.

CONCLUDING COMMENTS

The popularity of *The Talking, Feeling, and Doing Game* has been a great source of gratification. It has become standard equipment for the child psychotherapist, and many therapists consider it vital in their work with children. Over the years I have received many letters in which therapists have expressed gratitude for my introduction of the game. I have even had the dubious compliment, on a few occasions, of plagiarized versions being introduced. These, to the best of my knowledge, have never enjoyed similar popularity. (One such plagiarizer lost motivation to continue marketing the game after a letter from my attorney "reminding him" of the consequences if he did not cease and desist.)

The Talking, Feeling, and Doing Game is not without its disadvantages. All good drugs have their untoward side effects. In fact, it is often the case that the more powerful the drug, the greater the side effects. One of the main drawbacks of *The Talking, Feeling, and Doing Game* is that it may be *too* enticing to both the patient and the therapist. It is seemingly an easy therapeutic modality. Many therapists, I am certain, play it without fully appreciating its complexities and how difficult it can often be to utilize it properly for therapeutic purposes. The child, too, may find it attractive because it seemingly protects him (her) from talking about more painful subjects directly. It should not be used as the only therapeutic modality because it will deprive the therapist of some of the deeper unconscious material that can more readily be obtained from projective play and storytelling. In short, therapists should not be tempted into using the game throughout every session; they should do their utmost to balance the therapeutic activities with other modalities. As mentioned, *The Storytelling Card Game* can obviate significantly this drawback.

I have also found the game particularly useful in the treatment of children with neurologically based learning disabilities. Its utilization for this purpose is described elsewhere (Gardner, 1973b, 1974c, 1975c,d, 1979c, 1980c,d). For further articles on the game's general utilization I refer the reader to book chapters of mine on the subject (Gardner, 1983c, 1986c). Throughout this book I will be providing numerous examples of the game's utilization in the treatment of children with psychogenic learning disabilities.

It may be of interest to the reader to learn that since the introduction of the game in 1973, I have not come across one article in the psychiatric and psychological literature in which the game's utilization is described and/or studied. In late 1989, a thorough computer search of the literature did reveal one reference in the "Idea Exchange Column" of an educational journal (Poppen, 1975). Considering the fact that the game has become standard equipment in most therapists' offices, I find this paucity of articles surprising. I still do not know whether I should feel flattered or disappointed.

PARENTAL PARTICIPATION IN THE CHILD'S TREATMENT

For many years I practiced in the traditional manner and saw my child patients without their parents. Usually the mother rather than the father was available to bring the child and then sit in the waiting room. However, I did not strictly refrain from involving her in the treatment. I would intermittently bring her in to discuss certain issues with the child, and also had occasional separate sessions with her and/or the father. In my initial evaluation, I would see the mother and father, both individually and together. In addition, during the initial evaluation, I would also have a session or two with the child and the parents together, and even occasionally bring in one or more siblings. However, the basic therapeutic program after the initial evaluation was that the child and I were alone in the room. As is true of most trainees, I automatically accepted as optimum the methods of treatment used by my teachers and supervisors. I believed that being with the child alone was crucial to the development of a good therapist-patient relationship, and that to the degree that I brought third parties into the room, to that degree I would compromise our relationship. In addition, I believed that it was very important to have a confidential relationship with the child, a relationship in which he or she would have the security of knowing that I would not reveal to the parents anything he or she told me.

Over the years I became increasingly dissatisfied with this procedure. When something would come up in a session that I thought would be important for the mother to know about (nothing particularly confidential), I would bring her in and, in the last few minutes of the session, quickly give her a run-down of what had happened and then would make some recommendations. Most often this was done hurriedly; however, on occasion, we would run overtime because I considered it important that she fully understand what had happened in the session and what my recommendations were. My usual experience was that the mother had little conviction for the recommendations, primarily because she had not been witness to the situation that brought them about. When I started keeping the mothers in the room for longer periods, I found that the children generally did not object and, in addition, the mothers had greater conviction for my recommendations because they had been witness to the situations that had brought them about. They not only had the opportunity to observe directly the events that resulted in my suggestions, but they had ample time to discuss them with me in detail. This resulted in their much more frequently and effectively carrying out my recommendations. To my surprise, the children did not express any objections. They had not read the books that I had read—books that had emphasized the importance of my seeing the child alone and the crucial role of the confidential relationship.

In this section, I discuss in detail the ways in which I utilize parents in the treatment of children. I generally refer to my approach as *individual child psychotherapy with parental observation and intermittent participation*. Although this title may appear cumbersome, it states exactly what I do. In addition, I will often indicate to the parents that they are my *assistant therapists*. This designation communicates the point that their active participation in the therapeutic process will be utilized.

Before discussing the ways in which I use parents in the child's therapy, it is important for the reader to learn about my views on confidentiality in treatment, especially in the treatment of children. I will describe my position on confidentiality, therefore, before I present descriptions of the ways in which I enlist the aid of parents in the child's treatment.

THE ISSUE OF CONFIDENTIALITY AS IT RELATES TO THE PARENTS' PARTICIPATION IN THE CHILD'S TREATMENT

Many therapists believe that the active involvement by a parent(s) would significantly compromise the child's confidentiality, and this, they believe, is crucial if there is to be meaningful therapy. I believe that such therapists are placing too much weight on confidentiality. The parent is coming primarily for treatment, whether the patient is a child or an adult. The patient is not coming primarily for the preservation of confidentiality. I believe that to the degree that the preservation of the confidentiality relationship serves the ends of treatment, to that degree it should be respected. If it is a choice between confidentiality and doing what is in the best interests of the patient therapeutically, then, I believe, the therapeutic indications should be given priority over the confidences. One must not lose sight of the primary aim of therapy: to do what is in the best interests of the patient. In order to describe my position more specifically, I will consider the confidentiality issue as it pertains to the treatment of the adult, the adolescent, and the child. Although there are differences with regard to confidentiality in these three areas, there are basic similarities that hold for all three categories.

Confidentiality in Adult Therapy

If the adult is to have a successful therapeutic experience, he or she must have the feeling that the therapist will not disclose to others what is revealed during the course of treatment. Otherwise, the freedom to reveal will be significantly compromised—to the point where therapy may become meaningless. Most therapists would agree, however, that there are certain situations in which strict adherence to confidentiality may be antitherapeutic. Such is the case when there is a strong suicidal or homicidal risk. Basically, when a human life is at stake, concerns about confidentiality are reduced to the point of being trivial. If the patient is suicidal, it behooves the therapist to enlist the aid of family members and close friends to do everything possible to protect the patient. This usually involves their active participation in hospitalizing the suicidal patient. It would be unconscionable, in my opinion, to "respect" such a patient's request that the suicidal danger not be divulged to the nearest of kin. Similarly, when there is a homicidal risk, the therapist should do everything possible to warn the potential victim. When a patient in treatment raises the issue of confidentiality, I will openly state that he or she can feel secure that I will not reveal what is divulged—with the exception of situations in which there is a homicidal or suicidal danger. In most cases, the patient is thereby reassured that confidences will not be divulged because neither of these eventualities seems likely. On occasion, however, a depressed patient will be told that I might divulge the suicidal danger. In such cases I will reassure the patient that everything will be done to avoid such disclosure. However, I inform the patient that there might be an occasion in which I might divulge the suicidal risk, if such divulgence might prove lifesaving. Interestingly, most patients are not upset by this. Some healthy part of them appreciates that they could conceivably "go crazy," and that at such a time they might impulsively commit a self-destructive act that could cause irreparable damage and even death. My position provides reassurance that should such a situation occur, some healthy and stabilizing intervention will take place. My experience has been that this is usually reassuring.

In recent years there has been a number of cases in which litigation has centered on this issue. Psychiatrists were sued for malpractice because they preserved patients' confidences, and there was a resultant suicide or homicide that could conceivably have been prevented. The usual defense was that the therapist was respecting the patient's confidentiality and acting in the highest ethical traditions of the medical profession. Even in former years, I did not subscribe to this view. It is not in the highest ethical tradition of the medical profession to sit by and do nothing when there might be a suicide or homicide taking place. It is in the highest interests of the medical profession to protect human life. Fortunately, the courts and ethical committees in medical societies are shifting in the direction of supporting divulgences in such cases. This is a good trend.

Confidentiality in Adolescent Therapy

It is not uncommon for me to have the following conversation with an adolescent.

> *Patient:* Everything I say to you is just between me and you. Right? You'll never tell my parents anything I tell you. Right?
> *Therapist:* Not right.
> *Patient:* You mean you're going to tell my parents everything I tell you?
> *Therapist:* No, I didn't say that either.
> *Patient:* But my friend goes to a shrink, and his shrink told him that everything they speak about is strictly confidential, and his shrink says that he'll never tell my friend's parents anything about what goes on in a session.
> *Therapist:* Yes, many psychiatrists work that way. But I don't. Let me tell you how I work. As long as you don't do anything dangerous, to either yourself or others, you can be quite sure that what we speak about here will be held strictly confidential. I'm in full appreciation of the fact that it's important that you have the feeling that what we talk about is strictly confidential. However, there are certain exceptions. And these exceptions hold for anyone, regardless of age. My policy is the same for all. It's not just for

teen-agers. It's the same whether you're 5 years old or 85 years old. The basic policy is this: As long as you're not doing anything dangerous, you can be sure that I won't reveal what you tell me. However, if you're doing something that's dangerous, I reserve the right, at my discretion, to reveal to your family whatever I consider important to reveal to help stop you from doing the dangerous thing. I may need their help. What do you think about what I've said?

At that point the patient may ask me to tell him or her what things I would reveal. I will not then provide "food for thought." I do not wish to give the youngster suggestions for various forms of antisocial and/or self-destructive behavior that may not have entered his or her head. Rather, I ask the adolescent to tell me what things he or she might do that might warrant such divulgence. I may then use this as a point of departure for a therapeutic inquiry. However, I do have a "list." It includes: heavy use of drugs (not occasional use of marijuana), heavy use of alcohol, dangerous driving (especially when under the influence of drugs or alcohol), criminal behavior, and for girls, a desire to have an out-of-wedlock child (occasional sexual intercourse is not a reportable item). I also impress upon the adolescent the fact that should one of these dangerous situations arise, I will not automatically discuss the problem with the parent. Rather, I will exhaust all possibilities of discussion with the patient and the adolescent group before divulging the risk. Usually, such discussions are enough. However, when they are not, the youngster usually knows beforehand that I am going to divulge the information.

There is another aspect of the confidentiality issue in adolescence that warrants comment. The parents have a reasonable right to know whether there is a significant risk of dangerous behavior. When this issue is broached, generally in the initial evaluation, I will tell them that they should know that "no news is good news," that is, that I will divulge dangers to them, and if there are no such divulgences, they can feel assured that no great risks are imminent.

I am fully appreciative of the fact that the adolescent needs a special, separate relationship with the therapist. This is part of his or her developmental need to establish a separate identity from that of the parents. This autonomy is necessary if the adolescent is to grow into an independent, self-sufficient adult. Active participation by the parents in the adolescent's therapy can compromise this goal. However, the goal can still be achieved with some participation on the part of the parents. Occasional joint sessions in which the youngster is seen along with the parents need not interfere with this goal. There can still be a significant percentage of sessions devoted to the adolescent alone, and the confidential relationship can also serve the purpose of enhancing separation and autonomy. The potential divulgence of a dangerous situation also need not interfere with this sense of autonomy so important to the adolescent's development.

Confidentiality in Child Psychotherapy

By child psychotherapy I am referring to the treatment of children between the ages of about four and ten. In my opinion, the confidentiality issue has little if any place in the treatment of most of these children. There are many therapists who will say to such children something along these lines: "Whatever you tell me here in this room is just between you and me. I promise I'll never tell your mother or father what you tell me. You can trust me on that." Many children might wonder exactly what the therapist is referring to. They know of no great secrets that they want to keep from their parents. And this is especially the case for younger children. The parents know quite well that the child is soiling, stealing, lying, truant, and so on. They, more than the child, are aware of these problems, and it is they who initiated the treatment. So the statement must be confusing and even irrelevant to many children.

In addition, the statement sets up a structure in which there are "we" (the therapist and the patient) and "they" (the parents). "We" and "they" can easily become "we" versus "they." And this concept can introduce schisms within the family. The family has enough trouble already; it does not need an additional problem brought about by the therapeutic program. The system also impedes open communication. Generally, communication impairments contribute to the development of and perpetuation of psychopathology. The confidential relationship with the child is likely to increase the communication problems of the family. The thrust of the therapy should be to encourage open expression of the issues that are causing people difficulty. A conspiracy of silence usually serves only to reduce communication and defeats thereby an important therapeutic goal.

The therapist should attempt to create an atmosphere in which there is an open pool of communication – an atmosphere in which all things pertinent to the child's treatment are discussed openly with the parents. I do not make any statements about this. I do it as a matter of course. I make no mention of the confidentiality. If the child says to me that he or she does not wish me to tell his parents something, I will get very specific about what it is he or she wishes me not to divulge. Almost invariably it is an issue worthy of being discussed with the parents. Usually, the child fears repercussions that are unreal and exaggerated. Encouraging the child to express to the parent(s) the forbidden material, either in my presence or at home, is usually therapeutic. It can teach all concerned that the repression (unconscious) and suppression (conscious) of thoughts and feelings is likely to perpetuate problems, whereas civilized discussion is the best way to resolve family problems.

A boy, for example, will say to me that he doesn't want me to tell his parents something. On further inquiry the issue almost invariably is one that should be discussed with the parents, and the child's fears of what will happen if such information is disclosed are unrealistic. Encouraging the child to express to the parents(s) the forbidden material, either in my presence or at home, is usually therapeutic. It can teach all concerned that the repression (unconscious) and suppression (conscious) of thoughts and feelings is likely to perpetuate problems, whereas civilized discussion is the best way to resolve family problems. The therapist can serve as a catalyst for such expression, and his or her presence can make the atmosphere a safer one for the child to first make such revelations.

There is an aspect of S. Freud's famous Little Hans case (Freud, 1909) that is pertinent to my discussion here. During the one joint session that Freud held with Little Hans and his father, Hans expressed some hostility toward his father that he had not previously revealed. I believe that it is unfortunate that Freud did not direct his attention to this in his report of the case. I would speculate that the reason why Hans had not expressed the hostility previously was that he was afraid to do so because of fears of his father's retaliation. However, in the presence of "Professor Sigmund Freud," a man of whom both the patient and his father were in awe, Hans could safely reveal his anger because of his awareness that his father was not likely to react with severe punitive measure in Freud's presence. I suspect that Hans's having had the living experience that his father would react to his hostility in a civilized manner made it easier for him to express his resentments elsewhere. And this, I believe, was a contributing factor to the alleviation of his symptoms. Later in this chapter I will discuss in greater detail this and other aspects of the Little Hans case.

Classical psychoanalysts, in particular, are strict adherents to the confidentiality principle. It is they, more than other therapists, who make it a point at the outset to emphasize to the child that they will respect confidences. It is of interest that Freud did not consider confidentiality to be an important issue in his treatment of Little Hans. Hans's father was the therapist and Freud was the supervisor. When reading the transcript of the treatment, one observes that Hans revealed just about every intimacy one can imagine a child might have: bowel movements, urination, masturbation, interest in observing his mother's toilet functioning, sexual fantasies toward his mother, and so forth. If he were indeed hiding material that a child might be afraid to reveal, I would find it hard to imagine what such material might be. Little Hans knew that his father was revealing their discussions to Freud. In the one joint session that Freud had with Hans and his father, there was open discussion of these intimacies. Classical analysts often point to the case of Little Hans as the proof that Freud's theories of infantile sexuality, the Oedipus complex, and castration anxiety are valid. Libraries have been written on these theories—which are supposedly proven by the Little Hans case. However, the structure of Freud's therapeutic program is often ignored by the same psychoanalysts. They do not utilize the parents as assistant therapists (as did Freud), and they enter into a strictly confidential relationship with the child (which Freud did not do). In both cases, I believe, they do the child and the family a disservice.

REASONS FOR PARENTAL AMBIVALENCE REGARDING A CHILD'S TREATMENT

Parental involvement in a child's treatment is at best tenuous. Although parents may profess commitment to the therapeutic process, there are many reasons why they are generally quite ambivalent and their mixed feelings about the treatment may interfere significantly with its progress and even result in their prematurely terminating therapy. In this section I discuss some of the more common reasons for impaired parental commitment to the therapeutic process. An understanding of these factors can be useful in increasing the likelihood that the therapist will be able to engage the parents more successfully and thereby increase the likelihood of the child's involvement in treatment. Some of the more common ways in which parental resistance exhibits itself are lateness to the sessions, canceling sessions for frivolous or weak reasons, forgetting to follow through with the therapist's recommendations, complaining to the child about treatment (its cost, time commitment, etc.), and withholding payment (one of the most predictable ways to ultimately bring about a cessation of treatment).

One of the most important reasons for compromised parental commitment to therapy is the financial privation that it often involves. This is especially the case when the child is in private treatment. Whereas the parents may agree initially to commit themselves to the cost of the treatment, when the bills start coming they often have a change of heart and remove the child prematurely from treatment or support the child's resistances, which are inevitably present. There is also a time commitment in that the parent who brings the child (more often the mother) will generally think of better ways of spending her time than bringing the child to a therapist. If she has other children and cannot afford housekeepers, then bringing the child to treatment may become an additional burden. Here again, these extra pressures compromise her commitment to the therapeutic process.

Most parents experience guilt when the therapist advises them that the child need treatment. They consider it proof that they somehow failed in the child's upbringing (Lippman, 1962). A common way that parents assuage such guilt is to rationalize withdrawal of the child from treatment. This is done either overtly or covertly. After all, if they can justify removing the child from treatment, especially if they can believe that he (she) does not need it, they thereby absolve and even obviate their guilt. Therapists should tell such parents that they appreciate that at every point in the child's development the parents did what they considered to be in the child's best interests (usually the case) and that through misguidance and/or unfortunate circumstances, and/or the unavoidable effects of their own difficulties, their child developed psychiatric problems. Furthermore, the therapist does well to advise such parents that, at the present state of our knowledge, we do not understand all the factors that contribute to a child's psychiatric difficulties. Thus, even if they themselves had no psychiatric problems, and even if there had been no detrimental circumstances, and even if they had assiduously followed the best available advice, their child might still have developed difficulties (Kessler, 1966). Moreover, they must be helped to appreciate that innate temperamental factors may be contributing significantly to the child's problems (Thomas et al., 1963). My experience has been that a discussion of these factors can often be useful in reducing parental guilt and thereby increasing the likelihood that they will support the child's therapy.

Many parents become jealous of the child's intimate relationship with the therapist and may act out such feelings by undermining the treatment. They may consider themselves the ones who did all the "dirty work": they changed the diapers, took the child to pediatricians at all hours of the night, and made the hundreds of other sacrifices necessary for successful child rearing. Yet the therapist is "the good guy" who is viewed by the child as benevolent, kind, and sympathetic. Often the parents are threatened by the anxiety-provoking revelations about themselves that inevitably emerge during the child's treatment, and the desire to avoid these can contribute to their impaired commitment to the process.

One of the most effective ways of reducing parental guilt and the resistances that emerge from it is to have the parents participate actively in the child's treatment. Parents who believe that they are somehow at fault in causing the child's disorder can assuage their guilt by actively contributing to the therapeutic process. They are thereby helping "undo" what they have "done." By working closely with the parents, the therapist is more likely to develop a good relationship with them. The child will sense the parents' feelings about the therapist and will then be more likely to develop such involvement himself (herself). When parents have a good relationship with the therapist, they are more comfortable expressing resentments and disagreements. The failure to express such differences and complaints is one of the most common sources of parental resistance to the child's treatment and removal of the child from it.

Therapists who believe that it is their role to protect child patients from the indignities suffered at the hands of their parents are likely to alienate parents. The preferable position should be one of impartiality. The therapist should be viewed by all family members as someone who criticizes the parents when such criticism is warranted and, similarly, criticizes the child, again when such criticism is warranted. His (her) criticisms, however, should be benevolent, and he (she) should not "keep score" regarding who is getting more or less. The therapist takes the side of neither parent nor child; rather, he (she) supports the side of healthy behavior regardless of who exhibits it.

Another common source of parental resistance to treatment derives from the situation in which the parent may not genuinely want the child to be relieved of his (her) presenting symptoms, despite protestations to the contrary. The child's problems may play an important role in the family equilibrium. For example, the overprotective mother may want her child with separation anxiety disorder to stay at home, and the parent may undermine the therapist's efforts to get the child back to school (Gardner, 1984). Parents of delinquent youngsters often gain vicarious gratification from their children's antisocial acting out (Johnson, 1949, 1959; Stubblefield, 1967). Parents may ostensibly want their child to do better academically but, unconsciously, may undermine the treatment because they fear that the child will surpass them educationally and socioeconomically.

It behooves therapists to appreciate these and the multiplicity of other factors that may contribute to parental undercommitment to the therapeutic process and even removal of a child from treatment. The therapist should try to detect these compromising factors during the initial evaluation and deal with them at the outset. Otherwise, they may cause a compromise in and even a cessation of the therapy. I discuss below the specific ways in which parents can be utilized in the child's treatment. Such utilization has many benefits for the child's treatment and is one of the predictable ways to obviate, circumvent, and avoid the aforementioned potential compromises in the child's therapy.

WAYS IN WHICH PARENTS (USUALLY THE MOTHER) CAN BE USEFUL IN A CHILD'S THERAPY

Gradually my procedure evolved into the position of informing the parents that they would be my therapeutic assistants in the child's treatment. Recognizing that it would most often be the mother who would be bringing the child, I invited the father to feel free to attend, without any prior notification, any session when he was available. My experience has been that this occurs from 5 to 10 percent of the time. For ease of presentation I utilize the term *mother* when I refer to my therapeutic assistant. However, it should be understood that fathers are available on occasion to serve in this role. My usual procedure is to have the mother come into the session with the child at the outset, and then to keep her in the room as long as I consider it warranted. This ranges from five to ten minutes to the full session.

The mother can be useful in a number of ways. The younger the child, the less likely that he (she) is going to be able to recall many of the important events that occurred since the last session. This is especially the case if the child is seen only once a week. My usual experience is that when I ask a child at the outset what has gone on since I saw him (her) last, there is no response. It is almost as if the child were frozen in ice or transfixed in space since the previous session. Knowledge of these events is often vital for the understanding of many of the child's therapeutic productions. The mother, almost invariably, is a ready source of this important information. The more knowledge the therapist has about the child, the greater will be his (her) capacity to respond with a meaningful story utilizing the mutual storytelling technique. These stories, like dreams, often relate to important events that have occurred in the day or two prior to their creation. The child is often not in touch with these events, nor will he (she) readily provide them. Many mothers, when hearing the child's story, offer these vital data. It is important for the therapist to appreciate that the mother knows the child far better than he (she). Although not trained as a therapist, her hunches about the meaning of a story may be better than the therapist's—regardless of the number of years of psychoanalytic training the therapist has had. In the post-story discussion period, as well, the mother's input can prove most valuable.

When analyzing the child's dream the mother's assistance can also be invaluable. The child may include in the dream a figure who is entirely unknown to the therapist. The therapist certainly should obtain as many associations as possible from the child. This, of course, is the best way of ascertaining exactly what the dream figure symbolizes for the child. However, most children provide only a paucity of associations to their dream symbols, and the mother's input can be extremely valuable. She can ask the child leading questions about the figure, and she can often be a better interrogator than the therapist because she has some hunches about what may be important. And, when this fails, her specific and direct comments about the dream figure can often provide the therapist with useful information for understanding the dream.

The presence of the mother in the room enables the therapist to observe mother-child interactions that would not have otherwise been seen. The mother's observations of the ways in which I handle the child, especially when he (she) is being difficult, can be useful to her in that it provides her with a model for handling these situations herself. (I am not claiming that I always handle every situation in the most judicious fashion. However, I believe that I do so more frequently than most of my patient's parents.)

The effects of parental participation on the treatment are important and may be even more important than the specific way in which a parent can be useful to treatment. Whereas originally I was taught that such participation would compromise my relationship with the child, my experience has been just the opposite. It is hard to have a good relationship with someone who is a stranger, and whose only or primary contact is the monthly bill. Not only is such a situation likely to produce some alienation, but the paucity of contact increases the likelihood that negative distortions and misinterpretations about the therapist will not be corrected. Having the mother in the room provides her with the opportunity to air her grievances, express her resentments and disappointments, ask questions, and so on. This is the best way to prevent or resolve such problems. Both parents' feelings toward the therapist are extremely important in determining what the child's feelings will be. A parent's animosity toward the therapist frequently, if not invariably, will be picked up by the child. If there is a dispute between the therapist and the parents, the child will have a loyalty conflict. Most often he (she) will side with the parent. After all, the parents are providing the food, clothing, and shelter; they are the ones who are with the child the remaining hours of the week. The child knows where his (her) "bread is buttered," and it is extremely unlikely that the child will, over a period of time, basically support the therapist's position when it is in conflict with the parents'. Accordingly, anything that can improve the relationship between the therapist and the parents is likely to strengthen the tie between the therapist and the patient.

Parental participation can strengthen the therapist's relationship with the parents in other ways. Seeing the therapist "in action" enables the parents to know firsthand exactly what is going on in the sessions. They are not left in the dark about the therapeutic procedure. In the traditional method, parents are ignorant of what is going on, and this can be a source of irritation and alienation. This is especially the case when the parents are paying for the treatment. When they know what they are spending their money for, they are less likely to harbor negative distortions and criticisms. Of course, if the therapist is spending significant amounts of time with traditional play therapy—which is much more play than therapy—then the parents may have a justifiable criticism and may reasonably consider themselves to be wasting their money. The play techniques that I describe in this book are, I believe, much more *therapy* than play. I believe that one of the main reasons child therapists often hesitate to allow parents to observe them is that they are basically ashamed of what they are doing.

Parents most often feel ashamed of the fact that they are bringing their child for treatment. No matter how much the therapist may try to assuage their guilt, they generally feel that they were at fault. And even though the therapist may initially say to the parents that they did their best and that they should not feel guilty, he (she) then proceeds to ask questions that are basically designed to elicit information about what the parents did wrong. And the acquisition of this vital information cannot but entrench and enhance guilty feelings. The facts of the matter are that the parents did make mistakes, or else the child would not have developed psychogenic difficulties. As benevolent as were their motivations, as dedicated as they may have been to the child-rearing process, they were indeed deficient in certain areas and that is why the child is coming for treatment. Platitudes and gratuitous reassurances regarding the inappropriateness of such guilt are not likely to work. One way of genuinely reducing such guilt is to invite the parents to be active participants in the therapeutic process. In this way they become directly engaged in reducing and alleviating the very problems that have brought about their guilt. And the working-together process produces a sense of camaraderie with the therapist that also entrenches the relationship with him (her).

In the field of psychiatry, people like to give labels and names. I am often asked what I call this therapeutic approach. It is not family therapy because it is rare for all family members to be present. In addition, when I do have family sessions, they are primarily during the diagnostic phase. While I do practice family therapy in certain situations, that is not what I am describing here. It is more than parental counseling, which is also part of my therapeutic process, because the parent is actively involved in the child's treatment. The name that I use for the method is *individual child psychotherapy with parental observation and intermittent participation*. Although this name is somewhat cumbersome, it describes accurately what I do. It focuses primarily on the child and the techniques that I utilize are primarily designed for child therapy. Accordingly, it is a form of individual child psychotherapy. However, there is parental observation in that the parent (usually the mother) observes directly the therapeutic process. In addition, she actively participates to the degree that it is warranted during the session. To date I have not come up with a better name for this procedure.

I wish to emphasize again that the presence and participation of the parents do not usually compromise the therapist-patient relationship with the child—although this goes against what I had been taught, and this goes against what many still believe. The basic determinant of the relationship between the therapist and the child is their own personalities. A healthy mother does not believe that her relationship with her first child will be significantly compromised by the appearance of the second or third. No competent therapist would advise a parent to have only one child, lest the relationship with the first be compromised by the appearance of a second. No healthy mother strictly excludes the father's presence on those occasions when she is with her child, with the argument that it will compromise her relationship with her son or daughter. It is not the presence of one or a few others in the room that is the primary determinant of the relationship between two people. The relationship depends more on qualities that exist within and between the two of them. Therapists who strictly adhere to the traditional view may be providing the child with an antitherapeutic experience. This view expresses, both explicitly and implicitly, the notion that exclusivity is crucial for a good relationship. This can only engender possessiveness, egocentricity, intolerance for sharing, excessive dependency, and other untoward reactions.

SITUATIONS IN WHICH THE PARENTAL PRESENCE IS CONTRAINDICATED

It would be an error *always* to involve a parent throughout all of the sessions. In my view, this would be substituting one inappropriate therapeutic procedure for another. Those who strictly refrain from parental involvement are providing their patients with what I consider to be a significantly compromised form of treatment. Similarly, those who would strictly adhere to the opposite, that is, insist that a parent be present in every session—throughout the session—are imposing an equally rigid and, on occasion, antitherapeutic treatment procedure. What I am suggesting is that the therapist have the flexibility to tailor each therapeutic program to the particular needs of the patient. Most, but not all, patients do best with active parental participation. However, there are some children for whom the parental participation is contraindicated. And it is these situations that I discuss here.

First, there is the issue of the child's age. I generally do not treat children below the age of about four. There is no strict cutoff point at the fourth birthday. There are children who are younger than four who are psychologically older than four, and these may be good candidates for treatment. And there are children who are older who still might not be candidates for direct therapy. But generally, it is around the age of four that the average child becomes a potential candidate for a meaningful therapeutic endeavor. Prior to that age my therapeutic focus is primarily on work with the parents, with intermittent interviews with the child, both alone and with the parents. I want to establish familiarity and groom the child for treatment if the counseling does not prove to be adequate to relieve the problem(s).

At about the age of 11, children may start revealing confidences that should not justifiably be communicated to the parents. (As I will discuss later, below that age I do not believe that most children have a significant amount of material that warrants the special confidential relationship so frequently utilized by many therapists.) Also at about the age of 11, many children begin to appreciate that their projected fantasies are revealing of their own problems, and they may become defensive about utilizing such techniques. In fact, children at this age generally consider traditional play therapy approaches to be beneath them. Accordingly, after the age of 11 or thereabout a high degree of parental involvement in the treatment may be contraindicated. Again, there should be no sharp cutoff points here. It depends upon the child's maturity and the nature of the information being discussed.

When an overdependent child is in a symbiotic relationship with an overprotective mother, the therapist would not want to utilize the mother to a significant degree in the therapeutic process. To do so might only entrench the pathology. Such a child needs "breathing space" and the freedom to develop a separate relationship—separate from that which he (she) has with the mother. To actively involve the mother in the treatment may defeat this goal. However, this does not mean that the mothers of such children should be strictly excluded from all aspects of the child's treatment. No harm is done, in my opinion, by having the mother come in during the first few minutes of the session in order to apprise the therapist of the events that have occurred since the previous session. In addition, she can be kept in the waiting room to be "on call" should her further participation be warranted. (This is standard procedure for me. I do not support a mother's going shopping or attending to other activities while the child is being seen. I emphasize to her the importance of her being available, at a moment's notice, during the session. And this can only be accomplished by her remaining in the waiting room.) Even when a child is suffering with separation anxiety disorder, some active participation with the mother can be useful. Here, again, one would not want to keep her in the room for significant amounts of time.

There are some parents who are so psychologically fragile that they cannot tolerate the criticisms and other forms of negative feedback that would be directed toward them during the therapeutic session. This is especially the case for parents who are psychotic or borderline. Such a parent may be so defensive that he (she) would not be able to handle many of the therapeutic revelations, even though expressed symbolically. Were the parent to sense the underlying meaning of a hostile symbol, it could be ego-debasing and precipitate psychological deterioration. Such a parent's exposure to the child's therapy could be considered cruel and would be likely to alienate significantly both the parent and the child. Any benefits that the child might derive from the parent's presence might be more than offset by the compromise of the therapist-patient relationship that such exposure might result in. In addition, such benefits might also be obviated by the parental psychiatric deterioration and its resultant compromise of parenting capacity. This is not a common situation, but I mention it because it does occur.

There are parents who are extremely hostile, and such hostility might be exhibited toward the therapist. No matter how hard the therapist tries, such parents never seem to be satisfied. No amount of explanation or discussion seems to reduce the hostility. Yet, such parents may bring their children. When they are invited to participate actively in the child's treatment, they may use the opportunity to collect ammunition, for example, "Is this what I'm spending all my money on?—to hear you tell those stupid stories?" "How is answering questions about whether or not he touches his penis going to help him obey me at home?"

"My husband is right: psychiatry is a lot of bullshit!" Such parents tend to "cramp my style" when I am working under their observation and scrutiny. I have the feeling that everything I am doing is going to be used as ammunition against me. Attempts to discuss their negative attitudes have often proved futile. Accordingly, I have found it in the child's best interests to have such parents sit in the waiting room. Although I am deprived of their input, such loss is more than counterbalanced by the enhanced efficiency of the individual therapeutic process with the child. It is the lesser of the two detrimental alternatives. Therapy, like life, often boils down to such a choice. If there were a better option, I would utilize it. So I work under these compromised circumstances.

One might ask the question: "What about the overbearing mother who is always intruding in the child's therapy? Shouldn't she be kept out of the room?" My answer to this question is: "Not so quickly." Let us take, for example, the following situation. I am in session with Jimmy and his mother. I ask Jimmy a question. His mother answers. At that point I consider myself to have a golden opportunity for a meaningful therapeutic interchange—an opportunity that would have not been possible had the mother been out of the room. At that point I will say to Jimmy, "Jimmy, what just happened?" Jimmy may respond, "You asked me a question." And I will respond, "And what happened then?" Hopefully, Jimmy will respond, "My mother answered you." To which I will respond, "Right! And what did you do?" Jimmy may answer, "I didn't do anything." To this I will respond, "Yes, Jimmy, that's right. You didn't do anything. But I believe that you had certain thoughts and feelings when your mother answered my question and didn't give you a chance to answer it yourself. What exactly did you think at the very moment she answered? Exactly what were you feeling at that time?" Here, of course, I will try to get the child to express the thoughts and feeling that he must have had about his mother's intrusiveness. It is generally easier for the child to express this in the therapist's presence. The child recognizes that the therapeutic situation reduces the likelihood that the mother will react with severe punitive measures in the therapist's presence. The child may fear that there will be "hell to pay" when he (she) gets home, but the child also knows that there will be at least some protection in the consultation room. If the therapist can encourage such expression during the session and use it as a point of departure for a therapeutic approach to the mother's intrusiveness, it will have served a very useful purpose in the child's treatment.

As mentioned, the richest therapy is that which provides experiences. When the parent is in the room, there is a much greater likelihood that significant experiences will take place. The therapist should view such experiences as golden opportunities, to be grabbed onto and milked to their utmost. They are the most meaningful aspects of the therapeutic process, and they should be cherished. Accordingly, I do not quickly remove intrusive parents from the room. I can conceive of the possibility of a parent being so compulsively intrusive that I would not have the opportunity for such interchanges, and that no living space would be provided for the child. However, this has not yet occurred, and I have been successful in utilizing the situations in which the intrusiveness was exhibited as a step toward a reduction of the problem.

This same principle is operative in the more common situation where the child is fearful of expressing hostility toward a parent, hostility engendered by a wide variety of parental deprivations and maltreatment. In a session in which there is the therapist's implied protection, the child can be most comfortable in first expressing his (her) resentment. Having done so under protected conditions, the child will generally feel more comfortable doing so outside of the session.

I had an experience a number of years ago that demonstrates this point quite well. A boy repeatedly complained to me in sessions that his father insisted that he finish every morsel of food at every meal. His father would be extremely angry at him if he did not eat every speck of food. I asked him if he had expressed to his father the resentment he felt over this. The patient stated that he was afraid to do so. I knew the child's father in that I had interviewed him on a couple of occasions during the evaluative process and, in addition, had seen him on two occasions in joint session with the mother and the child. I knew that he was not as punitive as the patient viewed him to be, and that although he was indeed insisting that the child finish all the food on his plate, he would not have reacted anywhere nearly as violently as the patient anticipated. Accordingly, I felt comfortable encouraging the child to express his resentment. I would not have done so had the father been more punitive. In that case, I would have tried to work more directly with the father himself.

Each week I encouraged the child to express his resentment and told him that I would be asking him in the next session what had happened. Each week he returned with some excuse: "Oh, I forgot to tell him this week." "I was very busy this week." "I had a lot of homework to do this week." I knew that this could go on for months and contribute to the perpetuation of the symptomatology that was a derivative of the pent-up hostility the child was feeling. Accordingly, I had a family session during which I encouraged the child to express his feelings about the mealtime situation. He hesitantly did so and had the *living experience* (again that important concept) that his father did not react as punitively as he had anticipated. We all recognized that he was expressing his anger in a safe situation, with the implied protection of the therapist. However, it was following that session that he became freer to express his resentments in other areas and to assert himself more generally. Had I not brought the father into the room, it might have taken a much longer time to achieve this result.

A rarer, but nevertheless very important situation in which the parent's presence is generally contraindicated is the one in which the parent is suffering with an incurable disease. If the parent is openly discussing the disease, then the parental involvement can be salutary for both the child and the parent. However, if the parent is using denial and other related défense mechanisms as a way of dealing with his (her) reactions to the illness, then participation in the child's therapy can be detrimental to the parent. One would not want to have such a parent exposed to the child's working through his (her) reactions to the inevitable death of the parent. Such exposure can be cruel and inhumane. Having the parent there will probably lessen the likelihood that the child will reveal his (her) true feelings because of the appreciation (depending upon the child's age, sophistication, and intelligence) that his (her) revelations may be detrimental to the parent.

CLINICAL EXAMPLES

Freud's Case of Little Hans (The Boy Who Feared Horses)

Here, I present as a clinical example my analysis of Freud's case of Little Hans. Although all the other case examples in this book are derived directly from my own clinical experience, I have chosen to discuss Freud's case of Little Hans here because it lends itself well to demonstrating some important points made in this chapter as well as other sections of this book. However, I will only focus on certain aspects of the case that pertain to issues focused on in this chapter: confidentiality and the utilization of the parent (in this case the father) in the child's treatment. For those readers who may not be familiar with the details of the case, and for those who may wish to refresh their memories, I present this brief summary:

> At the age of four-and-three-quarters Hans developed the fear that if he went out into the street, a horse might bite him. Accordingly, he dreaded leaving his house and preferred staying at home with his parents and sister Hanna, who was born when he was three-and-a-half. He was especially fearful of a horse's falling down, "making a row" with its feet, and possibly dying. Large dray horses, especially those pulling heavy wagons, were particularly frightening, as were horses with black muzzles around their mouths and flaps around their eyes.
>
> Freud did not conduct the analysis; rather, he instructed the father in the analytic method. The latter conducted the treatment and brought back to Freud detailed notes of his interchanges with his son, and these are recorded verbatim in the article. Freud saw the boy only once during the four months of therapy. The

interview with the child and father together took place a little less than three months after the onset of the phobia.

Freud considered Hans's symptoms to be manifestations of oedipal difficulties. The horse symbolized his father, who he feared would castrate him (bite off his penis) in retaliation for his incestuous wishes toward his mother. Horses with black muzzles and flaps around their eyes were particularly reminiscent of his father, who had a black mustache and wore glasses. His fear that the horse might fall down and die was a reaction formation to his wish that his father would die—thereby leaving him the uncontested possessor of his mother.

Freud was presented with a child who exhibited neurotic symptoms. There were many ways in which Freud could have involved himself with his little patient. As mentioned, he had no guidelines. From all the possible alternative methods, he chose to have the father serve as therapist. It would have been more consistent with his previous pattern for Freud himself to have seen the child. Freud (1909) gives us his reason for this dramatic departure:

> No one else, in my opinion, could possibly have prevailed on the child to make any such avowals; the special knowledge by means of which he was able to interpret the remarks made by his five-year-old son was indispensable, and without it the technical difficulties in the way of conducting a psycho-analysis upon so young a child would have been insuperable. (p. 149)

It is of interest that Melanie Klein, Anna Freud, and the child psychoanalysts who followed them—although basically accepting the Freudian theory (the differences between them notwithstanding)—did not generally utilize the parents in the treatment process. In fact, at the present time most classical child analysts, although they may get a history from the parents, confine their treatment exclusively to the child. They recognize that involvement with the parents may have therapeutic benefit; but the greater such involvement, the less they consider the treatment to be justifiably called psychoanalysis—which they consider to be the most definitive, reconstructive, and therapeutic form of therapy for those patients for whom it is the indicated treatment. Yet there is no question that Freud considered Hans to have been psychoanalyzed. A strange paradox.

Many therapists (not only classical child analysts) do not involve the parents directly in a child's treatment because they believe that disclosure of the child's revelations to the parents would compromise the therapy. Many hold that having the parents present in the session would restrict the child from freely expressing important material. Many believe that it is important to establish a special relationship with the child that is "all his (her) own." The preservation of the child's confidentiality is looked upon as an important prerequisite to effective treatment. From the outset this is communicated to the child. At the first meeting he (she) alone is brought into the therapist's office (most often with tremendous anxiety and resistance) while the parent or parents are left in the waiting room. One purpose of this separation is to communicate this special relationship at the onset. In addition, the child is often told, quite early in treatment, that what is said to the therapist will not be revealed to the parents.

Although Freud was a strong proponent of confidentiality for his adult patients, there were no such considerations for Little Hans. His deepest and most humiliating secrets were to be directly revealed to his father, the person with whom one would think he would be the most hesitant to discuss them. There is little evidence that Hans felt the need for confidentiality or that the therapy was an "invasion of his privacy." There is little reason to believe that Hans's treatment was in any way compromised or otherwise interfered with by his being asked to reveal himself to his father. Even in Freud's one interview with Hans, the father was present. Yet, the more ardently and strictly the classical child analyst adheres to the Freudian theories, the less the likelihood he (she) would have such an interview.

Most therapists, regardless of their therapeutic orientation, would not instruct a parent in the therapy of his (her) own child. First, to be a therapist requires many years of exacting training and experience. Because parents (with rare exception) have not had such training, they are ill equipped to conduct such therapy, and to teach them to treat their own children would be a disservice to the patients. In addition, the child's parent cannot have the objectivity the therapist must have toward the patient if the therapy is to be successful. Yet Freud seems to have ignored these considerations. Stone, in his novel on Freud (Stone, 1971), states that Hans's father was one Max Graf, a graduate in jurisprudence, a doctorate in music, and an editor. He was one of the members of Freud's weekly discussion group and therefore had some familiarity with psychoanalytic theory. Neither Freud nor Stone described him as having had any previous experience as a therapist. But even if he did, Freud did not believe that he would be sufficiently impaired by lack of objectivity to disqualify him as an effective therapist (which he apparently proved to be).

Whereas the theoretical conclusions that Freud came to in his work with Little Hans have often been too literally and even rigidly adhered to, the implications of Freud's mode of conducting the analysis have been largely ignored by the classical analysts. And this, I believe, has been most unfortunate.

Had Little Hans been working with Freud alone (with Freud having no therapeutic contact with the parents and his "respecting" Hans's right to confidentiality) and had Freud encouraged him to discuss his sexual and hostile feelings with his parents, I believe it would have taken Hans far longer to do so. In the single interview with Freud, Hans was encouraged to talk about these matters, and there was, I believe, the implied protection by a man who had already achieved formidable stature in Hans's eyes. Even prior to this interview, Hans knew that everything he said could be brought back for Freud's consideration, and in this way too Hans was reassured (from what had been communicated to him about Freud) that he would get Freud's benevolent protection. Furthermore, I believe that the repeated discussions of the anxiety-provoking material with the father served to desensitize Hans to them in a way that would not have been accomplished as quickly had Freud himself seen the boy alone. Hans repeatedly had the *living experience* that the terrible retaliations he anticipated from his father did not occur.

Four months is a very short time for an analysis. One of the reasons for its short duration was, I believe, the intensive experience that Freud provided to the child with his father; the father was the person whom the horse symbolized in the first place–the person to whom Hans had to learn to desensitize himself, as well as the person with whom he had to work out the other problems he had in his relationship. This experience was a significant (and largely unappreciated) element in Hans's cure. *Hans was afraid of horses, and Freud had Hans work with the "horse."* Whether Freud did this by choice, hunch, intuition, or chance, we will probably never know. It is indeed unfortunate that Freud did not tell us more of the reasons for his decision (if there were any). If his followers had heeded this aspect of the case as diligently as the more theoretical aspect, the whole course of child psychoanalysis might have taken a different path.

What factors, then, were instrumental in bringing about Hans's cure? The most important, I believe, was the improvement in Hans's relationship with his father. To conduct the analysis, the father assiduously noted all of Hans's comments that he considered relevant. This new attention and interest was a potent antidote to his previous deprivations and traumas. The analysis provided Hans with the opportunity to have the *living experience* that his father was more benevolent than he had believed and that his father did not, in fact, retaliate for Hans's hostility in the way that he had feared. This was most rapidly and conveniently accomplished via Freud's choice of the father as the child's therapist. To go further with this, I believe that the psychoanalytic experience–working together in it–provided the father and son with a new intimacy that they probably did not previously enjoy. Mutual revelation of inner feelings, in a benevolent setting, invariably brings people closer together. For a boy who was suffering some deprivation of affection in his relationships with his parents, this experience was clearly therapeutic. I do not think that *what* was said (in fact, the father made some hostile comments and a number of analytic blunders) was nearly as important as the experience of spending time alone together in a mutually enjoyable and productive endeavor. Regarding this issue, Freud (1909) stated, "The only results of the analysis were that Hans recovered, that he ceased to be afraid of horses, and that he got on rather familiar terms with his father as the latter reported with some amusement" (p. 285). Freud described Hans's improved relationship with his father as a fringe benefit of the treatment; I consider it a crucial contributing factor to the cure.

Another critical factor in Hans's cure relates to his relationship with Freud. The parents' admiration of Freud, which must have been formidable, could not but have been transmitted to Hans. He was repeatedly told that Freud was going to cure his phobia; therefore, the suggestive element, I believe, was strongly operative (although Freud denied this). In addition, the single interview with Freud must have had a powerful influence on the boy, observing as he had the awe and respect his parents had for "the Professor." It is reasonable to assume that everything that had that happened during this interview (Freud, 1909, pp. 184-185) must have considerably affected Hans. These suppositions are well substantiated by Hans's comment to his father upon returning home: "Does the Professor talk to God?" (Freud, 1909, p. 185). Hans's fantasies of Freud's omnipotence and omniscience were reinforced during the interview by Freud's statement to him:

> Long before he was in the world, I went on, I had known that a little Hans would come who would be so fond of his mother that he would be bound to feel afraid of his father because of it; and I told his father this. (Freud, 1909, p. 185)

Following the interview, Hans expressed to his father his amazement that "he can tell all that beforehand" (Freud, 1909, p. 185). It is reasonable to assume that all that Freud told Hans, either directly or through his father (but especially directly), was received with greater receptivity and was held onto more tenaciously than if he had been in treatment with a more mortal and fallible therapist.

Also, there was uniform agreement between the father and Freud. At no point did Freud describe any differences of opinion between himself and the father. Only on the question of whether Hans should be told about vaginas and sexual intercourse was there the faintest possibility raised of the father's not following through with Freud's suggestions. Other than this possible exception, the father dutifully followed all of Freud's advice. Few therapists enjoy such cooperation on the part of a parent. More often than not parental jealousies, resentments, and other neurotic problems interfere with our work and place the child in the position of being torn between us and the parents—no matter how hard we try to establish a good working relationship with them. Hans had no such conflicts—and this, I am sure, was one of the reasons why his therapy proceeded so rapidly. However, such cooperation on the father's part was not without its drawbacks and dangers. His credulous attitudes caused him to transmit many communications that were not valid or relevant to Hans (Gardner, 1972d). Hans, however, got better in spite of this misinformation. In addition, the father did not serve for Hans as a good model for independent thinking and healthy self-assertion, so slavishly dependent was he on every one of Freud's words.

I think the most important thing that happened in the interview was Freud's making it easier for Hans to express his angry feeling toward his father. Freud (1909) stated:

> I then disclosed to him that he was afraid of his father, precisely because he was so fond of his mother. It must be, I told him, that he thought his father was angry with him on that account; but this was not so, his father was fond of him in spite of it, and he might admit everything to him without fear. (pp. 184-185)

Soon after this comment Hans reported that his father had hit him. Hans had unexpectedly butted his head into his father's stomach, and the latter had responded with a "reflex blow with his hand" (Freud, 1909, p. 185). Hans had not previously mentioned this incident, and the father then "recognized it as an expression of the little boy's hostile disposition towards him" (Freud, 1909, p. 185). It is reasonable that Freud's comments not only made it easier for Hans to express his hostility toward his father but made him feel less guilty about his anger. He was able to test his father's reaction in Freud's presence and thereby gain Freud's implied protection from any retaliation on his father's part. Such an experience, I believe, made it easier for Hans to express his hostility in subsequent situations when Freud was not present—contributing thereby to Hans's cure. Three days after the interview Freud described the *"first real improvement"* (Freud, 1909, p. 186) in Hans's phobia.

I do not believe it an oversimplification to state that all psychogenic symptoms are, in part, the result of a lowering of one's self-esteem and that, in a misguided and often self-defeating way, they attempt to enhance compensatorily one's feelings of self-worth. Therefore, helping a patient improve self-esteem is one of the most predictable ways to alleviate psychopathological symptomatology. There were a number of things that happened to Hans that enhanced his feelings of self-worth and in this way contributed to his cure. The improved relationship with his father (especially the greater attention he was receiving) must have made him feel better about himself. There is a self-deprecatory element in guilt ("How terrible I am for these thoughts, deeds," etc.). With an alleviation of the guilt Hans felt over his hostility toward his parents came a corresponding enhancement of his self-worth. Lastly, the attention that Hans was getting from the famous Professor must have also made him feel very important. The reader who is interested in reading further my comments on the case of Little Hans might wish to refer to my article on the subject (Gardner, 1972b). Therein I discuss other aspects of the case, aspects that go beyond those discussed in this chapter, namely, confidentiality and the use of the father in the child's treatment.

The Case of Jack ("Daddy, please take me fishing")

The way in which a mother served well as an assistant therapist is well demonstrated by the case of a boy whom I will call Jack. He was six when he entered treatment. The chief complaint was stuttering. I consider stuttering to have a strong neurophysiological basis; however, I also believe that psychogenic factors can affect the stuttering in that in tense situations the stuttering is more likely to be worse. Accordingly, my psychotherapeutic approach with such patients is to make every attempt to reduce their tensions in the hope that the benefits to be derived from such reduction will ameliorate the stuttering symptomatology as well. I therefore explore other areas of difficulty, especially those that may produce tension and anxiety. In Jack's case, such difficulties were not hard to find. He was significantly inhibited in asserting himself, especially with his father. He was particularly fearful of expressing resentment toward his father and expected dire repercussions for such expression. His father, unfortunately, was very insensitive to Jack. However, he would not have responded with the terrible punishments Jack anticipated. In those situations in which Jack squelched his anger, his stuttering would predictably increase. Jack's anger-inhibition problem was so profound that he was generally viewed as a "model child" by his teacher, parents, and the parents of his friends.

One Monday afternoon (the day is pertinent) Jack began the session with his mother (whom I had learned could be an extremely valuable "assistant therapist"). He said that he had nothing much to talk about and asked if he could draw something with crayons. Suspecting that he had something important to "say" with this medium, I readily agreed. First he drew a blue pond. Then he drew grass and trees around the pond. Lastly, he drew some fishes in the pond and then put down the crayon. When I asked him if the picture was finished, he replied that it was. I then asked him to tell a story, and he stated, "A boy went fishing there, and he caught a few fish." When I attempted to get him to elaborate upon the story, he flatly denied that there was anything more to the story. I told him that I considered him an excellent storyteller, and that I was sure that he could do better. Again, he stated that there was nothing more to the story. When I asked him if there was anything else he could add to the picture, he again stated that the picture was completed. I noted that there were no figures in the picture, either human or animal, and suspected strongly that this had some significance. However, it would have been antitherapeutic to suggest that he place figures in the picture, in that this would have been a significant contaminant to the purity of his fantasy.

I turned to Jack's mother and asked her if she had any ideas regarding the meaning of Jack's picture and "story." She responded strongly in the affirmative, and then turned to Jack and began an inquiry. She first asked him if he recalled what he had asked her on arising the previous morning, which was a Sunday. Jack had no recollection. Upon further urging he did recall that he had asked her to ask his father to take him fishing. She then asked him what her response was, and Jack replied, "You said that Dr. Gardner said that it's a bad idea for you to be my messenger boy, and that if I wanted to ask Daddy something, I should ask him myself." The mother agreed that this was what happened, and then asked him to continue telling what had taken place. Jack replied, "I asked Daddy if he would take me fishing, and he said that he wouldn't take me now, but that he would take me later." In the subsequent inquiry by the mother it was revealed that for the next five hours Jack repeatedly asked his father to take him fishing, and the father repeatedly said that he would do so, not then but later. Finally, by midafternoon, Jack's father told him that it was too late to go fishing.

The mother then described how Jack's stuttering immediately became more severe. Whereas earlier in the day the stuttering had been relatively mild, it became so bad following this final rejection that Jack was practically unintelligible. And the increased severity was still present when I saw him the following day. The picture and its associated story now became completely understandable. It clearly represented the fantasy that had existed in Jack's mind throughout the previous day. There was a pond that he hoped to visit. The story about the boy who went fishing represented his wish that he had gone, but he never did. Given the egocentricity of the six-year-old, if he is not there fishing, then no one is there—thus the conspicuous absence of human figures. In this situation, I decided not to tell a responding story but to use the picture and the associated inquiry with his mother as the point of departure for further discussion.

I then asked Jack what his thoughts and feelings were after what had happened with his father the previous day. Jack denied any resentment at all over the rejection. He reiterated his father's statement that it was really too late, in such a way that it was clear that he considered his father's excuse to be justified. I responded incredulously that I could not believe that there wasn't even a little bit of anger over what had happened. In the ensuing discussion Jack did admit to some anger and then we went on to discuss what he feared would happen if he were to express his resentment. I reassured him that his father, although insensitive at times, was not the kind of person who would be as punitive as Jack anticipated. I then suggested a joint session with the father in which the whole issue could be discussed.

In the following session Jack hesitantly and with some fear did express his disappointment over his father's rejection the previous Sunday. The session proved to be a meaningful one and was the first of a series in which Jack *had the experience* that expressing resentment did not result in the terrible consequences he had anticipated. If Jack's mother had not been present in the session, I would not have known what the picture meant, and we would not have then gone on to the series of meaningful and therapeutically useful discussions that focused on issues that were at the core of Jack's anger-inhibition problem.

The Case of Howie (Nude Bathing in New Zealand)

Howie came to treatment at the age of eight with chief complaints of severe tics of the face and occasionally of the shoulders. No verbal tics were ever present, and I did not consider him to be suffering with Gille de la Tourette's syndrome. In addition, there was a stuttering problem. He was an extremely tense boy and the combination of tics, stuttering, and tension was interfering with his properly attending to his school work. He could not state exactly what distracted him while in the classroom, but he found it extremely difficult to concentrate there. At home, as well, he was always "on edge" and would "fly off the handle" at the slightest frustration or provocation.

By the time five minutes had passed during my initial interview with Howie and his parents, I had a fairly good idea about an important contributing factor to Howie's symptoms. His mother was the most sexually seductive woman I have ever encountered off the movie screen. Not only did her perfume precede her into the room, but her breasts were so propped up that they might more probably be referred to as torpedoes. So prominent were they that the rest of her body appeared almost as an afterthought that trailed after them as they entered the room. They seemed to me to defy the laws of gravity. Just about every movement, every gesture, and every vocal intonation oozed sexual seductivity. In accordance with the important therapeutic principle that the therapist should attend to distracting stimuli that appear to be interfering with what are ostensibly the issues under consideration in the interview, I recognized immediately that a likely cause of Howie's symptoms was the anxiety he was suffering over the sexual excitation he was constantly exposed to in the presence of his mother. His tics and other tension manifestations related to his fears of expressing directly his sexual thoughts and feelings. (I did not know at that time how great these fears were and what the special situations were in the household that made these formidable.) Were I to have had a deeper therapeutic relationship with the family, I would have brought the mother's sexual seductivity up at that point. However, I considered it more judicious to suppress my distraction and proceed with the interview (as best I could).

In the course of my evaluation I learned that Howie's mother considered herself to be "liberal and modern" with regard to the undressing situation in the home. Specifically, she did not consider it unnatural to undress in front of her children and husband. She also considered it "natural" to take baths and showers with Howie and/or his sister. When I suggested to her that this might be sexually titillating to Howie, she scoffed and accused me of being old-fashioned.

Howie's parents both complained about the fact that Howie's mother was frequently propositioned by men. Typically, she would report the experience to her husband, who invariably would go into a raging fit with threats such as, "I'll kill the bastard," "Just wait till I lay my hands on that son of a bitch," "I'll cut off his balls," and "There ought to be laws that can get guys like that thrown in jail." The parents had described how on a number of occasions they had been invited to dinner parties where a man would make sexual advances toward the mother. Typically, Howie's mother would respond with a loud shriek: "How dare you make sexual advances to me. Imagine, a married man, and your wife is only standing a few feet away!" Needless to say, the room was generally completely silent by the time she reached the end of this little speech. Invariably, Howie's father would go into one of his fits and on a few such occasions physically assaulted the man who had made passes at his wife. As might be expected, Howie heard about what had happened and on many occasions was witness to his father's outbursts of rage and threats.

As mentioned elsewhere (Gardner, 1968, 1986a) I believe that when children exhibit oedipal symptomatology, there are very often specific family influences that are likely to produce the oedipal constellation of symptoms, specifically sexual titillation by the mother and/or castration threats by the father. Howie had an extremely seductive mother. He had a father who literally threatened to kill those who had illicit sexual designs on his wife and to "cut off their balls." Howie could not but place himself in the category of those who were not only titillated but who risked being castrated and/or murdered for their sexual excitation. It was no surprise that Howie was an extremely tense boy who stuttered and ticked. His situation and symptoms certainly warrant being viewed as oedipal.

Early in therapy I recommended that Howie's mother discontinue the practice of undressing in front of and bathing with him. She was most unreceptive to my recommendation. However, she finally agreed to follow my recommendation with the response, "Well, you're the doctor." My experience has been that this comment invariably reveals lack of conviction for compliance. In the following session Howie's mother described how she had "really" followed my advice. She had gone to the bathroom to take a shower and made sure to tell Howie that he was not permitted to come into the bathroom. However, when she got out of the shower she realized that she had "forgotten" to bring in a towel. Accordingly, she called to Howie and asked him to bring a towel into the bathroom, but warned him that he should cover his eyes with his hand and be very sure not to look through the slits between his fingers. Unfortunately, I was totally unsuccessful in my attempts to get his mother to appreciate the seductivity of what had gone on. She merely accused me of "having sex on the mind all the time, just like all men." She also told me that she had heard about psychiatrists who find a sexual interpretation to everything and she was beginning to suspect that I was like the rest of them.

One day, early in treatment, Howie came into the waiting room and his tics were significantly worse. When I asked what had happened the mother replied, "I can't understand it, Doctor. He was perfectly fine until he came to this office." It is not uncommon for therapists to be accused of making symptoms worse. I replied by asking the mother exactly when things got worse.

She replied, "I don't know, Doctor. He was fine while we were riding over here in the car. And he was fine when we got into your waiting room. It happened while we were sitting down there waiting for you." I then asked her what she and Howie were doing while waiting.

She responded, "We weren't doing anything, Doctor. We were only reading a magazine together. It was *Time* magazine." I asked her to bring in the magazine and I sat the two of them down on the couch and requested that they try to reconstruct the situation as carefully as they could. I asked them to try to recall the exact page where they had started reading the magazine together, to go through the pages one at a time, and try to recall the discussion that ensued. The magazine was brought in; they sat down together and began perusing the magazine.

Finally, after four or five minutes, Howie said, "Mommy, I think you said something funny when we were looking at this picture." He pointed to a *Qantas Airlines* advertisement in which was depicted a beach scene. The advertisement read: "It is not generally known that Australia and New Zealand have among the most beautiful beaches in the world. Call your travel agent. *Fly Qantas.* Come and see for yourself." I then asked exactly what the conversation was around this advertisment.

The mother responded, "I don't think anything happened, Doctor. All I said to Howie was, 'I wonder whether they have nude bathing there in Australia and in New Zealand?'" Again, my attempts to get Howie's mother to appreciate that she was introducing sex into a situation where others would not have had a sexual association proved futile. She again accused me of being a sex maniac.

As the reader might expect, my efforts to help Howie failed completely. Both the mother and the father had too great an investment in the mother's seductivity to give it up so quickly or easily. It was the mother's primary source of attention and ego enhancement. Over many years this woman had devoted significant time and energy to perfecting her seductive skills and talents. In addition to providing her with an inordinate amount of attention, her seductivity served as a hostile outlet. She tantalized men and not only rejected them herself but could rely upon her husband to attack them as well. For her husband, having such an attractive wife was a source of enhancement. In addition, having a wife whom other men appeared to prefer in preference to their own wives was also a source of pride. And his wife's complaints about those who propositioned her provided him with an outlet for his own pent-up hostility. After a few months' treatment the family discontinued therapy and informed me that they were going to find another psychiatrist – one who "didn't have so much sex on his mind." I wished them luck in their quest for such a psychiatrist.

The Case of Walter ("Stop touching the walls")

Walter was referred for treatment at the age of ten because of a touching compulsion. Specifically, he felt compelled to run his hands along walls as he walked past them. The movements were executed with his finger tips in the vertical direction. Not only was he compelled to perform these motions indoors, but outdoors as well. Accordingly, his finger tips would often become irritated to the point of bleeding and in recent months many had become callused. In the classroom, as well, Walter was compelled to touch the walls. The compulsion was so strong there that he could not restrain himself from getting up out of his seat during lessons and going over to the side of the room to touch the walls. And this of course interfered with his learning in school. He was getting poor grades in spite of high intelligence. He was also the subject of ridicule in the classroom because of this symptom, so much so that at times he would resist going to school entirely. I had never before encountered this particular symptom (and I never have since, for that matter).

By the time we reached the end of my two-hour consultation with Walter and his parents, I still did not have the faintest idea why Walter had this unusual compulsion. As we stood near the door making the next appointment, at which time I was going to explore the matter further, the reason for the compulsion immediately became apparent. As the four of us stood talking, Walter was stroking his mother's breasts with both hands. The movements were identical to those used when he executed his compulsive ritual. The parents appeared to be completely oblivious to what was going on and carried on the conversation as if nothing unusual was happening.

In accordance with my belief that it is very important to give serious consideration to certain therapeutic "distractions," I interrupted the conversation and asked the parents if they had noticed anything unusual going on while we were talking. They both replied in the negative — even though Walter was still stroking his mother's breasts. I then directed their attention to what was happening and the mother laughed and said, "Oh, he does that all the time. It doesn't mean a thing." The father agreed that this was a common occurrence but considered it harmless.

As is clear, Walter's symptoms certainly could be explained along oedipal lines. It is clear, as well, that there was obvious maternal seductivity that was a primary contributing factor. In Walter's case, the therapy proceeded well. I did not have too much difficulty impressing upon the parents the relationship between Walter's symptoms and the mother titillating him. The mother did not have difficulty complying with my suggestion that she no longer permit Walter to caress her breasts. Within a week there was a marked reduction in the symptomatology. The parents had some sexual problems (as the reader might have guessed), and I was successful in effecting some improvement in that area. And this, of course, lessened the mother's need to gain her gratifications from her son. Walter had other problems as well, and these were dealt with successfully, so that by the end of the five months of treatment he was asymptomatic.

The Case of Tara ("Your brother's in heaven")

The way in which the educational element and parental involvement can combine to effect dramatic improvement in a child's symptoms is well demonstrated by the case of four-year-old Tara, who was referred because of phobic symptoms of about six months' duration. When Tara was two, her brother Kevin (then 16) was found to be leukemic. During the next one-and-a-half years, Tara's mother was swept up in the care of her older child. Her mother's involvement in the care of Kevin was so extensive that little time was left for Tara. Tara was never told that her brother's illness would be fatal; at the time of his death she was simply told that he had gone to heaven, where he was very happy. The family was European, and the father had been temporarily assigned to his organization's office in the United States. At the time of Kevin's death, the family returned to their native country for the burial. Unknown to Tara, her brother's body was in the cargo compartment of the airplane. When they arrived in their native country, Tara was quickly sent to stay with friends while her brother was buried.

Upon returning to the United States, Tara began exhibiting the symptoms that ultimately brought her to treatment. Whereas previously she had attended nursery school without difficulty, she now refused. When the doorbell rang, she panicked and would hide under the bed. Whereas previously she enjoyed visits at the homes of friends, she now refused to go. She seemed comfortable only when she was close to both of her parents and would scream hysterically if they left. Although her parents had told her that Kevin was in heaven, she repeatedly asked questions about her brother. Apparently she was not satisfied with the answer her parents had given her. Observing Tara to be so upset by her brother's absence, the parents decided to destroy most of his personal possessions and stored away the remainder.

My inquiry with the patient confirmed my initial speculation that Tara's symptoms were the direct result of the way in which the parents had handled Kevin's death with regard to her. From Tara's viewpoint, people, without explanation, could suddenly disappear from the face of the earth. Accordingly, there was no safety because one never knew why such disappearances occurred. It might be that someone came to the door and took children away; or perhaps it occurred at nursery school; or maybe one was abducted from the homes of friends and relatives. No place was really safe. In addition, there was no point in trying to get explanations from one's parents as to how such disappearances occur, because their answers would also prove unsatisfactory.

With this speculation regarding the origin of Tara's symptoms, I asked the parents what their genuine beliefs were regarding the brother's whereabouts. Both claimed that they had no conviction for any type of existence in the hereafter and their religious convictions were not particularly deep. They said it was their view that telling Tara that her brother was buried in the ground would be psychologically deleterious. I told the parents what I considered to be the source of their child's problems. I explained to them that although their explanation was benevolently motivated, I considered it to be doing her more harm than good. I suggested that they return home and tell Tara exactly what they believed happened to their son—as simply and as accurately as possible. I suggested that they give her one of her brother's few remaining mementos and tell her that it would always be hers. Although initially reluctant, they finally gained some conviction for my suggestion and decided to follow my recommendations.

I then explained to them the psychological importance of mourning and described how Tara had been deprived of this important salutary experience. I suggested that they encourage Tara to ask the same questions that she had asked in the past and to recognize that the repetition of these conversations was an important part of the mourning and working-through process. Furthermore, I suggested that they slowly urge her to face once again the various phobic situations and to reassure her each time that she, unlike Kevin, would not be taken away. I suggested that they impress upon her the fact that Kevin was sick and that he died of physical illness. She, however, was well, and there was no reason to believe that her death was anything but remote.

Within one week, there was a dramatic improvement in Tara's condition. After having been told about the true circumstances of her brother's death, Tara cried bitterly. As I had suspected, Tara repeatedly questioned her parents during the next few days, and this time the parents responded in detail and with patience. She was given a picture of her brother, which she carried around at all times and proudly showed to friends and relatives. With such presentations, she would once again discuss in detail her brother's death. Concomitantly, there was a marked diminution in all of her fears. Within a week she was again attending nursery school without difficulty. She no longer cowered at the ringing of the doorbell and once again began visiting friends. Moreover, she experienced only mild fear when her parents went out at night. No further sessions were scheduled, and the parents were advised to contact me again if there was a need for further consultation. Six months later, I learned through the referring colleague that Tara had remained asymptomatic.

This case demonstrates well the value of education in treatment and how active participation by parents can be extremely useful in child therapy. Although seeing Tara alone might have ultimately brought about the same alleviation of her symptoms, I believe that active work with the parents and my "educating" them caused the therapy to proceed much more rapidly than it would have had I seen the child alone.

The Case of Mack (The Baseball Hall of Fame)

Mack entered treatment at nine-and-a-half because of disruptive behavior at school and home. There was a basic organic deficit characterized by hyperactivity and impulsivity. His father had left the home about one year previously and was most unreliable regarding his visits. When he was home he was frequently condescending toward Mack. And the anger Mack felt in response to these indignities was being displaced onto siblings, peers, his mother, and his teacher.

Near the middle of his eighth month in treatment, Mack spoke about his father's visit to the home that previous weekend. Although he tried to speak enthusiastically, it was quite clear that he was forcing the impression that the experience was pleasurable. Mack's mother, however, related how he had followed his father around all weekend "like a puppy dog." She stated that it was pathetic to see how Mack would not resign himself to his father's lack of interest. She described how whenever Mack would try to elicit his father's attention or interest, he would be responded to with a "shut up" or "don't bother me." Mack became upset by what his mother said and denied that there was any validity to it.

He then described two dreams. In the first he was in a hotel in Cooperstown, New York, the site of the National Baseball Museum. (Mack was an avid baseball fan.) There he was trying to get into a cable car of the kind seen in San Francisco. The patient could not figure out the meaning of the dream. He did describe, however, a pleasurable experience at Cooperstown with his mother and teenage siblings a week previously but could provide no further associations. Mack's mother then offered further information. She described how the whole family had gone to San Francisco when Mack was about five and this had been one of the high points of his life. This occurred long before his father had left the home, and Mack often referred to the experience with great pleasure. The meaning of the dream then became clear. In response to the frustrations that he had experienced with his father the previous weekend, Mack was dreaming of a return to happier days with his father in San Francisco. The more recent experience with his mother in Cooperstown was marred by his longing to regain the joys of the San Francisco trip with his father (as symbolized by his trying to get on the cable car). In his dream, he was not successful in getting onto the cable car. This reflected his appreciation, at some level, that his father could no longer provide him with the kind of gratifications he had given him in the past.

Had the mother not been in the room I would not have understood the meaning of this dream. Its analysis is a good example of the vital role that a parent can play when actively participating in the child's therapy. Both the mother and I agreed that the aforementioned interpretation was valid. When it was presented to Mack, he admitted that it might be possible, but I did not get the feeling that he accepted our explanation with much conviction.

Mack then went on to relate his second dream. In it he was walking to school with a classmate and they were going to be late.

There was a bus ahead and Mack wanted to run and catch the bus. His friend, however, was resistant to the idea. The dream ended with neither boy reaching the bus. Rather, there was a confused discussion regarding whether they should have boarded it. Again, Mack was unable to ascertain the meaning of the dream and I, myself, could offer no specific suggestions. Mack's mother, however, stated, that in her opinion, buses appeared to be the symbol of Mack's father. When he lived at home, Mack's father commuted into New York City and returned each day in a bus to the suburban New Jersey home where the mother and children lived. Especially when he was younger, Mack would often ask if his father was on a passing bus. With this information the dream became clear. It reflected Mack's ambivalence about joining his father. On the one hand, he desperately wants to catch up to the bus (as symbolized by Mack's pursuing it); on the other hand, he does not anticipate acceptance by his father or gratifying experiences with him and so lags behind (as symbolized by his friend's [Mack's alter ego] resistance to such pursuit).

Again, when Mack was offered this explanation for the dream, he passively accepted its interpretation, but I did not feel that I was "hitting home." However, I did have the feeling that there was some receptivity, that some seeds were planted, and subsequent experience bore this out. Had Mack's mother not been present, these advances would have been much more slowly achieved.

Final Comments on Parental Participation in the Child's Treatment

I believe that the traditional practice of seeing children alone, while mothers are in the waiting room, seriously compromises therapeutic efficacy. My experience has been that children's treatment proceeds much more rapidly when there is active participation by parents. I believe that thousands (and possibly even millions) of hours have been wasted by having mothers sit in waiting rooms reading magazines while their children are being seen alone by their therapists. In many cases such therapy is basically a waste of time. I am referring here to therapy that is primarily play. If the parents are paying for this, they are paying for a very expensive playmate. But even when the therapy is providing the child with a richer experience, it is still not as efficient or as effective as it might have been if there were more active parental involvement. Throughout the rest of this book, I will be describing the ways in which parental participation has been useful in children's treatment.

CONCLUSIONS

In this lengthy chapter, I have summarized the most important techniques I utilize in the treatment of children. Because many of these are not "mainstream," I considered it important to go into some detail so that readers will be in a better position to utilize these techniques in the course of their work. Probably the least controversial of my methods is *The Talking, Feeling, and Doing Game,* which, I am pleased to say, has become standard equipment for therapists. Therapists who are strongly committed to the psychoanalytic approach have had certain reservations about the mutual storytelling technique and its derivative games because of my belief that it is not crucial to facilitate the patient's gaining conscious insight into unconscious processes. Rather, I consider it important to get the message across and to communicate basic principles. For children this is more effectively done via the utilization of symbols and metaphors. Although I am certainly not against helping children gain insight into the underlying psychodynamic processes that contribute to the development of their symptoms, I do not have a strong need to do so. I view the gaining of insight to be the "frosting on the cake" and it is more important to get across a point by using those approaches that provide experiences and symbolic communications. But even more important than such educational and experiential aspects of therapy is the establishment of a good relationship within the context of which the child has experiences that bring about therapeutic change. Elsewhere (Gardner, 1986a) I have elaborated in detail on this important aspect of treatment.

Probably the most controversial aspect of my therapeutic approach is the active utilization of parents. It is my hope that hesitant readers, after reading my rather lengthy discussion, will have a more receptive attitude toward using parents as their "assistant therapists" in the course of their work.

# TWO
REFLECTED APPRAISALS
A CORE SELF-ESTEEM ISSUE

REFLECTED APPRAISALS

I believe that deprivation of parental affection—overt or covert—
is a primary etiological factor in the vast majority of (if not all) forms
of psychogenic pathology. One of the most predictable results of
such deprivation is the child's lowered sense of self-worth. Here
I discuss one specific way in which low self-esteem develops in
infancy as a result of such deprivation. Harry Stack Sullivan
introduced the term *reflected appraisals* to refer to the process by
which young children assess themselves. Having no guidelines of
their own, children derive their first self-images from their
parents' appraisals. The young child basically subscribes to the
dictum: "I am what my parents say I am." The parents' assessment criteria for the child—what is good, bad, right, and wrong—
become the child's. Having no other criteria to utilize for the
assessment of self-worth, the child uses those that are available.
As the child grows older and makes friends, he (she) enters other
homes and goes to school. New criteria are thereby introduced;
distortions in the self-image, which may have been derived from
the parents, can be modified. In healthy development, two main
processes take place: 1) increased experience and further modifi-

cations produce greater accuracy and realism in the self-image and 2) decreased reliance on the environment and increased respect for inner convictions result in self-esteem being determined less by the capriciousness of external events and more by the tried and tested internal criteria for ascertaining self-worth. However, this earlier experience of "reflected appraisals" is so deep and lasting that children whose parents are significantly rejecting may never be able to gain a full feeling of self-worth and, as a result, may spend their lives futilely utilizing a variety of psychopathological mechanisms to bolster their low self-esteem.

A four-year-old girl comes into the house crying to her mother, "Johnny called me stupid." The judicious mother replies (while kissing away the child's tears), "He's the stupid one, not you. He's stupid if he calls you stupid. You're not stupid; you're very smart. You're four years old and you know all the letters of the alphabet. You can write your name, you can call people on the telephone, and you know all the different coins. You're not stupid, you're smart. He's stupid, and silly if he can call you stupid. I think you should tell him that *he's* stupid if he calls *you* stupid." This is the optimal response. Not only is the mother contradicting the criticism but providing the child with *specific* criteria to assess her own self-worth. Merely to advise the child to ignore the criticism, or to respond with a similar one, is not too useful. The response, "If he calls you a name, then you call him a name back," has some value, but it does not get to the core of the problem. The basic issue is whether or not the child warrants a criticism regarding intellectual capacity. To say that the criticism is unwarranted does not go far enough. The parent has to point out to the child the exact reasons why the criticism is unjustified. To say to the child that she is not stupid may result in the child's internalizing the statement. However, when specific examples of high intelligence are identified, it is much more likely that the self-appraisal of high intelligence will be incorporated into the child's psychic structure.

Following such a mother's articulate and sensitive response, the child may go out and say to her tormenter: "My mother says I'm very smart. I'm four years old and I know all the letters of the alphabet, and I can write my name, and I can use the telephone. I know all the different coins. You're stupid if you call me stupid." Then, while sticking out her tongue, the child says, "So there!" It is to be noted that the child's response begins with "My mother says. . . ." She is appealing to the authority of her mother here and hopes that her message will be given extra clout by invoking her mother's wisdom on these points. Furthermore, her reiteration of her mother's message serves to incorporate these criteria for the assessment of self-worth into her own psychic structure. If she grows up in a healthy fashion, these criteria will be incorporated and then she will not have to refer to her mother when responding to similar criticisms in the future.

What can be done if the child in this situation indeed has lower-than-average intelligence? I would recommend this response: "Yes, it is true that you have more trouble than others learning things in school. But you're still very good in swimming and other things. You're also very good with your hands and can throw a ball very far. I think he's cruel and mean for calling you that name, just because you have trouble with certain things. I think you should tell him that he's being mean and cruel if he calls you such a name." In this case the mother is also attempting to provide her child with accurate criteria for self-judgment. It would be misguided benevolence to deny the intellectual deficiency to which the other child was probably referring. Had the mother denied the deficit, it would set the stage for confusion and the development of various psychopathological processes. The mother would be wise, as well, to point out genuine areas of competence that could serve to enhance the child's self-esteem.

In both of these cases, the child's sense of self-worth is being determined by the reflected appraisal. It is to be hoped that these children will give consideration to what others say about them, but will utilize their ever-growing repertoire of criteria for assessing self-worth. The failure to do so will leave them at the mercy of all those who might criticize them. And the older people are, the more credibility they should be giving to their internal self-assessment criteria. Because we can never be completely acceptable to everyone, we must invariably be exposed to disapproval. If we indiscriminately accept all criticism as valid, we will detest ourselves. Parents must help children understand that they are not exactly what others may consider them to be; parents should help them appreciate that, no matter how hard they try, there will always be those who will dislike them. Children must be helped to ask themselves questions about *who* the criticizers are, whether or not their opinions are worthy of respect, what their motivations might be for providing such criticism, whether they are benevolently or malevolently motivated, and whether they are accurate or inaccurate. This is certainly a difficult goal to achieve. None of us ever completely achieves it. However, to the degree that we do, self-esteem will be less dependent on the vicissitudes of life and the capriciousness of others and more dependent on our continually expanding and modified set of internalized criteria. I sometimes find helpful in achieving this goal the story "The Pussycat and the Owl" in my book *Fables For Our Times* (Gardner, 1981a).

Relevant here is the riddle, attributed to Abraham Lincoln: "If you call a tail a leg, how many legs does a dog have?" The usual answer here is "Five." Lincoln's answer: "No, the correct answer is four. Calling a tail a leg doesn't *make* a tail a leg." Although young children will certainly not appreciate this riddle, the message is a wise one and could serve them well when they become old enough to appreciate its significance.

In the child-rearing process parents should help their children enrich their sets of criteria for judging their self-worth. They should help children look to their own opinion, to those of their parents, and to those outside the home. Children should learn to consider with receptivity, but not with gullibility, the opinions of those whom they respect. They should learn to accept what seems reasonable to them and reject what does not. They must be helped to recognize that their parents as well may have their distortions and their fallibility. Parents should be comfortable enough to reveal these deficits as they naturally manifest themselves in the course of the child's growing up. And each parent should judiciously describe the other parent's fallibilities as well.

(In my discussion of perfectionism, later in this book, I discuss the issue of parental fallibility/infallibility in greater detail.)

EXCESSIVE DEPENDENCY ON THE OPINIONS OF OTHERS

Children who grow up with an exaggerated sense of dependency on the opinions of others develop a common psychological problem. As adults they may subscribe to the dictum: "If someone criticizes me, they are right." A correlative of this is also often present: "I must always be cautious not to do or say anything that might make another person angry at me, because if someone does get angry at me, I will feel terrible." There are millions to whom these dicta are guiding principles of life. They are continually fearful of asserting themselves or revealing anything that might irritate or alienate another. They follow the principle: "If they reject me, I must be objectionable." They become timid, inhibited, and limited human beings—continually fearful of asserting themselves and expressing their opinions. They may be viewed as friendly, flexible, and ingratiating; but they may also be viewed as spineless, passive, and easily exploitable.

Excessive dependency on the opinion of others can affect a child's academic performance. One manifestation of the problem is fear of criticism from those who are less successful academically. Better students invariably become the focus of criticism. Although they may enjoy the admiration and emulation of their peers, they also are subject to criticisms that often stem from jealousy. Although we are taught as children that the loser in any competition should be a "good sport" and congratulate the winner, the advice causes the loser to suppress the anger that must be present after a hard-fought race (regardless of the area of competition). We would do better to sanction an expression (in a civilized way) of resentment of the winner that is inevitably present in the nonwinner. Then both winners and losers would be more comfortable with the hostility.

Some children reduce their efforts because they fear that if they are academically successful they will suffer the alienation of their classmates. Such children must be helped to appreciate that they are compromising themselves significantly and may be giving up more promising futures for a little more present popularity and that this is a terrible price to pay to gain a few more "friends." They must develop "thick enough skins" to tolerate these criticisms.

Most children who slow down their academic efforts in order to avoid jealous criticism may grow up into adults who react similarly in the competitions of adult life. The psychodynamics are similar to those involved in the depression that some people feel after obtaining a long sought-after goal. For example, the president of a large company, whatever esteem he (she) may enjoy, is usually the object of much inappropriate and displaced hostility. Presidents, governors, and mayors have traditionally been considered to the cause of all the woes of their constituents. A factor involved in this animosity is the frustration of the craving and demand to be provided with a simple solution to complicated problems in the hope that a single individual may be able to implement that solution. Our leaders invariably disappoint us in this regard because of the impossibility of the demands that were being made upon them in the first place. One element in this hostility is the jealousy and resentment that the nonsuccessful feel toward the successful. Individuals who finally find themselves occupying these high offices may find the hostility directed toward them intolerable. In some cases they slow their pace as they get higher. Others decline the honor. And others quit or acquire a convenient illness that provides an excuse for them to withdraw from the lofty position. Some do so poorly that they get demoted back to a position where they will be less subjected to criticism. A few even kill themselves. In the latter group, a significant factor is the belief that they are as unworthy as their detractors claim them to be. These individuals exhibit to an extreme degree the dependency problem that involves reflex acceptance of the opinions of others, especially criticisms.

CLINICAL EXAMPLE

Martin, a seven-year-old boy, was referred because of generalized apathy, lack of involvement with peers, and disinterest in school in spite of high intelligence. His mother was an extremely angry woman who stated during the first session: "Doctor, my father died when I was two and I have no memory of him. I grew up with my mother and two older sisters. I don't know anything about men and boys. To me they're like strangers from another planet. I can't relate to them. My daughter I can relate to. We're on the same wavelength. I can understand her. Although I know nothing about men, I do know one thing about them and that is that I *hate them all.*" Very early I found the mother to be a bitter, self-indulgent woman who used biting sarcasm as a primary mode of relating to men. She told me about a series of male therapists she had seen—either for herself or her son—and she had only critical things to say about each of them. I could not help thinking while she was talking that my name might soon be added to the list and be mentioned with an equal degree of denigration to the next therapist. (This prophesy soon proved to be true.) The patient's father was obsessively involved in his work, was frequently absent from the home on business trips, and when home had practically no interest in his son. He had a passive-dependent relationship with his wife and served as a scapegoat for her.

In the first session, Martin told this story:

> Once upon a time there was a bear. He was trying to get some honey from a beehive. He got it from the beehive. He went home with it. The bear ate the honey.

I considered the beehive in the story to represent Martin's mother. She is the source of honey, that is, love; but this love is covered with stinging, poison-injecting, potentially painful contaminants. Seeking affection from her inevitably exposes one to her venom. In the story the bear easily acquires honey from the beehive, without any interference at all by the bees. This is an atypical element in the story that is our best clue to its meaning. Typically, bees do not sit silently by while bears put their paws in their beehives and gobble up their honey. Rather, they usually sting the bear in the obvious hope that it might retreat. The absence of this reaction by the bees in Martin's story is a statement of his wish that his mother's hostility not manifest itself when he attempts to obtain love and affection from her. In short, the story reveals his wish to gain her love without being traumatized by her malevolence.

The story epitomizes well, in a few words, the mother's basic personality pattern and her relationship with the patient. It is an excellent example of how a child's first story may reveal core problems. Because the mother's psychopathology was deep-seated and because she had absolutely no interest in entering into treatment herself, I considered her prognosis for change to be extremely poor. However, even if she exhibited motivation for treatment, under the best of circumstances it would have taken many years to bring about reasonable changes. By that time Martin might be an adolescent or even an adult. I considered it antitherapeutic to tell a responding story that would provide Martin with any hope for a dramatic change in his mother's personality, either in the present or the future. Specifically, it would have been antitherapeutic and even cruel to provide him with a story that encouraged him to hope that his mother would give him pure love, uncontaminated by her anger. Accordingly, I told Martin this story:

> Once upon a time there was a bear. This bear loved honey very much. There was a beehive nearby, but he knew that the bees were not always willing to let him have some. Sometimes they were friendly, and then they would give him a little bit. Other times they were not, and he knew then that it was wise to stay away from them or else he would get stung. When the bees were unfriendly, he would go to another part of the forest where there were maple trees which dripped sweet maple syrup. When the bees were friendly, he would go to them for honey.

In my story I attempted to accomplish two things. First, I tried to help Martin accept his mother as she really was at that time—someone who could, on occasion, provide him with some affection but who, at other times, could be punitive and denigrating of him. In my story I advise him to resign himself to the situation and to take her affection when it becomes available, but not to seek it otherwise. Second, I attempted to provide Martin with alternative sources of gratification by suggesting that there are others in the world who can compensate him somewhat for his mother's deficiency. This is an important therapeutic point. It is unrealistic to expect patients to resign themselves to giving up an important source of gratification if one does not, at the same time, offer some kind of compensatory satisfactions. Martin might not be able to have the bees' honey at times, but he certainly could have some sweet maple syrup as a reasonable substitute. My response here is a good example of the important therapeutic principle that when one tries to take something away from a patient, one does well to give him (her) something else as a substitute. Otherwise, the attempts at alleviation—even of a presumably noxious psychopathological symptom—may prove futile. All symptoms, their alienating qualities notwithstanding, still provide patients with pathological gratifications and so they are not easily dispensed with—despite the patients' stated desire to do so.

One week later, Martin told this story:

> *Patient:* Once there was a bear in the woods——
> *Gardner:* A bear in the woods——
> *Patient:* Who was going to get honey, so he went to a beehive and he wrecked it and took out all the honey.
> *Gardner:* To a beehive and he wrecked it?
> *Patient:* Yeah. and then he——
> *Gardner:* And then he what?
> *Patient:* Brought it home and then he ate it. I think that's all.
> *Gardner:* That's all? That's the whole story? What's the lesson of that story? What do we learn from that story?
> *Patient:* That bears get honey from beehives.
> *Gardner:* Okay, come on now. You can give us a better story. Let's hear a better story.
> *Patient:* Once there was a pig and he got some straw. [Martin, at times, mumbled to the point of being inaudible.]

Gardner: The pig got what?

Patient: Straw. And he took the straw and he built a nest in the yard.

Gardner: He built a nest?

Patient: Yeah. And then he went into the mud.

Gardner: He went into the what?

Patient: The mud.

Gardner: The mud. Okay.

Patient: And then he went to the other pigs and told them to get some straw. And then they all had a nest and then the baby pigs came and hided under them.

Gardner: And then the baby pigs came and what?

Patient: Hided under them.

Gardner: Hid under the—

Patient: Yeah pigs. Under the big pigs.

Gardner: Hid under the big pigs. Yeah, then what happened?

Patient: And then the men, they gave them some corn. And then they got washed and washed them off. That's the end.

Gardner: The men washed them off. What's the lesson of that story?

Patient: That pigs get corn.

Gardner: Pigs get corn. Okay. All right. Thank you very much.

The first story is, of course, related to the story sequence of the previous week. The honey in the beehive symbolizes his mother's love, which, although sweet, is carefully guarded. The acquisition of it exposes Martin to her poisonous sting. The bear is the patient, himself. I had advised Martin to seek the honey when the bees (his mother) were receptive to his requests, but when they were not, to go to the maple trees in another part of the forest, that is, to others who are more likely to provide affection. His response here was to tell a story in which he ignores my advice and even more adamantly tries to extract love from his mother: he wrecks the beehive and takes out all the honey.

When urged to tell a second story, Martin related one that reflects his extreme dependency cravings as well as his very low opinion of himself. The nest of straw where he is fed corn reveals his return-to-the-womb fantasies, but he depicts himself as a pig wallowing in mud—a clear statement of his feelings of self-loathing. Elements in the story suggest sources for these feelings of worthlessness: his mother's lack of affection makes him feel unlovable; trying to extract love from her, against her will, only makes him feel worse about himself; regressive fantasies, however gratifying, rob him of the ego-enhancing satisfactions of growth and mastery.

Interestingly, the mother is also depicted as a pig—the baby pigs are nested under the big pigs—whereas the father, as represented by the men, not only provides affection—corn—but also washes him off as well. The father is seen, in other words, as someone who can cleanse Martin of his feelings of low self-worth.

With this understanding of Martin's stories, I told mine:

> Once there was this bear and this pig. And this bear's main desire in life was to go and get honey and sit and do nothing. And this pig's main desire was to build a nest in the mud and sit there and have people feed him corn. And everybody felt that these two animals were kind of lazy. And the kids used to call them babies 'cause they never wanted to do anything for themselves. They just wanted to hang around and be taken care of. And then when the other pigs and the bears grew up and were able to do something for themselves, this pig and this bear weren't able to because they were kind of lazy and never got used to doing things for themselves. And so they ended up quite unhappy and sad, whereas the other pigs and bears who would think for themselves and learned how to do things for themselves were much happier.
>
> And the lesson of that story is: It may be nice to be taken care of, but there has to come a time when you have to do things on your own.
>
> The end. What did you think of that story.?
> *Patient:* Fine.
> *Gardner:* Did you like any special part of it?
> *Patient:* Yes.
> *Gardner:* Which part?
> *Patient:* When they were feeding him the corn.
> *Gardner:* I see. Okay.

In my story, I combined elements of both of Martin's stories and attempted to help this boy enhance his self-esteem. I say help him enhance his self-esteem because the job is primarily his. He has to do the things that will make him feel better about himself. He has to correct his distortions; I can only guide and advise. He is told that peers will respect him less if he acts like a "baby." The implication is that their values may very well become his and that behaving in an infantile manner cannot but cause him to lose respect for himself. In addition, the ego-enhancing value of mastery and growth are emphasized: "The pigs and bears who would think for themselves and learned how to do things for themselves were much happier." I did not reiterate the theme of substitute gratifications in my story. His reaction against it had been so strong—wrecking the beehive to prove me wrong—that I decided to hold off with that advice until he was more receptive to it. Unfortunately, Martin increasingly resisted treatment, and I finally recommended a trial with another therapist. As far as I know, the parents did not seek further help.

Martin's comment that the part of my story he liked the best was "When they were feeding him the corn" was a clear manifestation of his need to deny the growth-encouragement aspects of my story and to gratify his deep-seated dependency fantasies. This pressure to withdraw into fantasy, which at times approached a psychotic level, and the associated denial of reality stimuli were significant elements in the failure of Martin's therapy.

☐ THREE
THE FEELING OF BEING NEEDED

Feeling genuinely needed contributes to one's sense of self-respect. One of the criteria I utilize to determine if seriously depressed people are suicidal is whether they have the deep conviction that no one in the whole world would miss them if they were dead. If this is the person's feeling, whether delusional or not, it speaks for greater morbidity and suicidal risk. Although children are dependent and need their parents far more than their parents need them, if they are to have a healthy feeling of self-esteem, they must feel that their loss would be painful to their parents. (Healthy children in a loving home do not think about their parents' reactions to their loss; this is often a source of concern to the emotionally deprived child.)

Children's feelings that they can engender warmth in their parents contribute to their sense of being needed. The younger child feels elated when he (she) can make others laugh. The girl who, as "mother's helper," sets the table and the boy who helps father change an automobile tire are filled with pride by the knowledge that they are contributing members of the family team. When playing games with children, adults do better for both themselves and their children if they select a game that is enjoyable to both. When an adult finds a game tedious but continues to play through obligation, the child becomes aware at some level that he (she) is not really needed as a challenging adversary. The child senses the adult's boredom and lack of interest through the latter's impatience and easy irritability, and the game then becomes a trying and depressing ordeal for the child. The sham can be ego-debasing. When the adult genuinely enjoys the game, the child appreciates that he (she) is needed and enjoyed. Sensing the adult's involvement and pleasure, the child feels useful and desirable, and winning a hard-fought game can provide even further ego-enhancement (Gardner, 1969c, 1986b).

In adolescence, especially, parents do well to look for situations in which the youngster will be genuinely needed. Prior to the 20th century people basically became adults at the time of puberty. Few were educated, and it was rare for people to be educated beyond the age of 12 or 13. One went out into the world to work at that time and married soon thereafter. Helen of Troy was 12, and Juliet 13. People had their children during their teens, became grandparents in their early thirties, and soon thereafter died. And that was it. Adolescents today do not have the opportunities to gain the ego-enhancement that comes from meaningful work and childrearing that was the case for their ancestors. The problem is that there are few areas of competence that adolescents have in which they exceed their parents. There are, however, youngsters who do indeed have such skills and knowledge. Youngsters, for example, who know more about computers than their parents can not only teach them in a meaningful way, but can enjoy an enhanced sense of self-worth as a result of their superior position. A few years ago I saw a cartoon in which a young boy was standing by his desk on which was a computer. His arms were crossed over his chest and his facial expression was one of determined anger. At the door was his father who was imploringly asking, "You know, it wouldn't kill you if you would come over and help me with my computer." At the high school level most children are learning things that their parents either do not know or have long since forgotten. Looking to the youngster as a source of information and genuinely being interested in what is being taught cannot only enhance parents but, more importantly, enhance the youngster's sense of self-worth. And this can contribute to an enhancement of the youngster's motivation in school. A youngster who is studying vocabulary words for an examination may be able to teach a parent a few new ones. In such situations parents do well to respond: "Gee, I never knew the meaning of that word. Thanks!"

These sources of feeling needed apply to children in a relatively affluent culture. Children in an economically deprived culture or in a society where they are *actually needed* to contribute to the economy may derive additional gratifications in this area (provided the strain of labor is not excessive and the economic deprivation not formidable). In many Israeli *kibbutsim*, for example, children of five are already members of the labor force. They are required to perform light tasks commensurate with their age. These are not token assignments but active and meaningful contributions. Although child labor laws have protected children against shameful exploitation (and I am not suggesting their repeal), they do deprive children of the opportunity to gain ego-enhancement from work that is genuinely needed in society. There are very few opportunities in affluent Western societies for children under 14 to work in jobs in which their contributions are genuinely needed. Newspaper delivery and babysitting are hardly vital but can provide the child with a small measure of the enhanced self-respect that comes from playing a useful role in one's society. Children as young as nine and ten can perform many useful jobs at home and can often participate meaningfully (in a limited way, of course) in many parents' occupations. Children of this age are capable of delivering messages, transporting light packages, stacking, sorting, and performing many other simple jobs. Parents who encourage, stimulate, and require such participation provide their children with a healthy experience indeed.

Most teachers are appreciative of this phenomenon in the classroom. They know the sense of ego-enhancement that comes when a child is given certain responsibilities in the school. The person who is chosen to take a message to the principal's office, be in charge of the blackboards, direct cleanup, or perform other managerial or administrative tasks often stands a little taller.

☐ FOUR
PARENTAL PRIDE IN THE CHILD, HEALTHY AND UNHEALTHY

HEALTHY PRIDE

The sense of pride that loving parents have for their children is generally appreciated by the children and contributes to their feelings of self-worth. This is related to the phenomenon of reflected appraisals. This is the phenomenon referred to by many great figures in history who consider their relationships with their mothers (more often than with their fathers) to have been an important motivating force in their accomplishments. Alexander the Great, Thomas A. Edison, Sigmund Freud, and Douglas MacArthur are some well-known examples. Healthy parents, as well, are *slightly* delusional about their children and tend to distort their perceptions of them in directions that minimize the children's deficiencies and exaggerate their assets. In moderation, the children profit from these distortions because they provide a counterbalance to the unfair criticisms that they, like all of us, are exposed to in life. People who love us are esteemed, in part, because of their benevolent blindness to our faults and their readiness to recognize admirable qualities that others seem oblivious to. Children whose parents do not have this sense of pride in them are less likely to be proud of themselves, and this will play a contributing role in their developing low self-esteem problems.

Grandparents, especially, can provide children with the positive feedback and pride that can enhance their self-worth. Grandparents can provide the kind of unadulterated praise and love that parents often are not capable of. After all, the grandparents do not have to change the diapers, get up in the middle of the night, and subject themselves to all the privations and sacrifices involved in childrearing. They get the frosting on the cake, unadulterated by the resentments and frustrations engendered in parents throughout the course of the normal childrearing process. And children need this kind of adulation to serve as a buffer for the inevitable rejections and criticisms (warranted and unwarranted) to which all individuals are subjected.

Although I usually see children along with their parents in my first consultative interview, there are occasions that warrant my seeing the parents alone at first. (A custody evaluation is an example.) In such interviews, I will often ask the parents if they have a photograph of their children to help me envision the individuals who are the central focus of our conversation. I consider the failure to have one as a slight compromise in parental commitment and pride. If the photograph is produced, I look for manifestations of pride when being told about the picture. It is not simply the smiles, the statements, and the gestures; it is more a matter of the emotional quality and the sense of pride that I am looking for. I view its absence as a parental deficit.

Another manifestation of healthy parental respect is comfort with occasional exaggeration and duplicity. The reader is probably aware that a repeated theme in my work is that dishonesty (even though well meaning) often causes more problems than it is designed to prevent. There are times, however, when parental dishonesty, judiciously utilized, is in the child's best interests, and full honesty in these situations could be detrimental. For example, when a boy proudly displays a picture he has drawn, it is cruel for a parent to comment on its artistic merits in accordance with adult standards. To say, "It's beautiful" is, in a sense, untruthful; but in another sense it is not. What is beautiful is the total experience of the child's proudly showing the picture and the child's warm glow of pride. If the adult's enjoyment and pride are added, they will be appreciated by the child and will add to his (her) sense of enhanced self-worth.

Similarly, a five-year-old girl's older sister has just proudly announced that she has lost a tooth and that she is going to put it under her pillow to see what the "tooth fairy" will leave her during the night. The younger girl, after a short period of pouting and squelched tears, pulls each of her teeth to see if one of them might possibly be loose. She then goes over to her mother and, while tugging one of her teeth, imploringly asks, "Is this tooth loose?" Only the most inhumane parent would not answer, "Well, a *little* bit." Children's self-esteem grows on such fabrications, used judiciously and in moderation. To deprive the child of them is to undermine self-confidence as well as his (her) relationship with the parent.

UNHEALTHY PRIDE

The parents' complaint that their child isn't learning in school does not necessarily mean that they are fully involved in the child's learning process. Sometimes the parental interest is minimal or is ambivalent. (The noncommitted elements may even be unconscious.) Children reflect and comply with their parents' real, even though unexpressed, attitudes; and the parent with a basically healthy investment in education will transmit this to the child, either overtly or covertly. One child comes home from school, proudly displays his (her) work, and is given enthusiastic support and praise; another is ignored or receives only a perfunctory reply. The response, "very nice," to a child's report card can be said in a number of ways. It can convey pride, enthusiasm, and genuine pleasure with the child's accomplishment. Or, it can be said in such an offhanded manner that the child gets no feeling at all that the parent is genuinely pleased. Such a deadened response to the child's efforts only dampens enthusiasm for learning.

The family atmosphere that is probably most conducive to

the child's learning is one in which the parents themselves are genuinely curious and get great pleasure from the acquisition of knowledge. Observing parents to be deriving so much enjoyment from learning, children want to join in the fun and get some of these pleasures themselves. In homes where there is very little, if any, intellectual curiosity, the child's desire to learn, to discover, and to master the unknown becomes atrophied.

Some parents consider any defect in their children to be a reflection of deficiencies within themselves, and they deny a child's faults in order to protect their own self-esteem. Some parents with this problem will find it very difficult to admit to themselves and others any deficiencies within their children. They may recognize that a child has performed an unacceptable act, but believe that the good parent always sticks up for the child, no matter how obvious it may be that the child has misbehaved. They fear that admitting a child's transgression to an outsider will cause the child to lose faith in them as parents and will undermine the child's relationship with them. These are the parents who, when confronted by a neighbor with a transgression, will explain: "My Joey would never do such a thing." Such parents are depriving their children of important knowledge about themselves—knowledge necessary for an accurate view of their self-worth. Furthermore, they are depriving them of important information necessary to function adequately in the world.

There are parents who contribute to a child's feeling of low self-esteem by disparaging those who are successful. When their children do not compete successfully, they are told that others' rewards are undeserved, that they are due to good luck, or that they are the result of special favors and influences. The teacher is described as having "pets," and little Jamie never seems to be one of them. Or Sarah has the worst string of bad luck with her teachers. Joey's primary problem in school is that he's too honest, the others cheat on examinations, and he wouldn't stoop that low. Or, the child's consistently low marks are explained by, "The teacher really doesn't like him. She really has it in for him. There's nothing he can do to satisfy her." In all of these explanations for their children's failures or deficiencies, the children's own inadequacies, which may have contributed to the poor performance, are not even considered. Sullivan (1953) describes the consequences of such parental attitudes:

> If you have to maintain self-esteem by pulling down the standing of others, you are extraordinarily unfortunate in a variety of ways. Since you have to protect your feeling of personal worth by noting how unworthy everybody around you is, you are not provided with any data that are convincing evidence of your having personal worth; so it evolves into "I am not as bad as the other swine." To be the best of swine, when it would be nice to be a person, is not a particularly good way of furthering anything except security operations [loosely: a constellation of psychological mechanisms that protect one from anxiety and feelings of low self-worth].

Parents, then, who protect their children from justifiable criticisms by deprecating others do not orient their children toward looking to their own deficits as possible contributing factors to their difficulties. The child, thereby, becomes less equipped to function adequately and so becomes even more insecure. Their self-esteem becomes lowered rather than enhanced because they are not provided with the information requisite to compensating for their deficits. By not being apprised of their deficiencies, they do not take the first step toward rectifying them.

Last, there are children who do indeed have genuine accomplishments over which their parents can have pride; however, the parents, because of problems are their own, may not appreciate the child's accomplishments and may have the need to disparage the youngster. An example of this would be the parent who continually says to the child: "You'll never amount to anything." One factor that may be operative in such a comment is parental competition with the youngster. The parent is basically jealous of the youngster's accomplishments and so has to downgrade him (her). The likely outcome of this program of denigration is that the youngster will fulfill the parental prophesy and actually end up "amounting to nothing." This self-defeating attitude in the youngster may contribute to poor academic performance, and even academic failure. Sometimes this happens literally; other times the youngster "feels like nothing," even though there may be accomplishments that demonstrate otherwise.

THE PRIDE OF PARENTS OF CHILDREN WITH NEUROLOGICALLY BASED LEARNING DISABILITIES

Parents of children with neurologically based learning disabilities are not likely to have the kinds of pride that can be so useful in bringing about a child's feelings of high self-worth. An important source of pride for parents is a child's performance in school. And I am not confining myself here only to the academic realm; rather, I am including extracurricular activities such as sports, music, dramatic performances, positive teacher feedback, and other school activities. The child with a neurologically based learning disability is not as likely to provide parents with a sense of pride in the child's accomplishments. The likelihood is that the child will do poorly academically. Accordingly, the parents cannot have a genuine sense of pride in this central area of the educational process. Their professions of such pride are not likely to "work" because the child senses, at some level, that they are not genuine. And this is especially the case if there are siblings who are receiving genuine expressions of parental pride. Some children who do poorly academically can still gain a strong sense of parental pride in the realm of athletics. In fact, there are some parents for whom good performance in sports is more important than high academic attainment. The youngster with a neurologically based learning disability is likely to have coordination problems that preclude significant success in this realm. The child has few if any friends and this too can interfere with the parents' pride. And so on, down the line, the whole list of esteem-enhancing activities that are part of the school program are not potential sources of accomplishment for such a child and, by extension, deprive the parents of areas to focus on that can give them pride in the youngster.

CONCLUDING COMMENTS

Pride, like other emotions, has an infectious quality. The vibrating heartstrings in the parent, associated with their pride in the child, is likely to produce similar vibrations in the youngster's heart and result in an enhanced sense of the child's self-worth. This positive feedback increases the child's motivation to exhibit further desirable behavioral manifestations or to provide further accomplishments for the parents in order to engender in them a further sense of pride. And so there is an upward spiraling that can contribute to significant accomplishments by the child, both in the school and elsewhere.

 **FIVE**
PLEASURE-PAIN, GUILT, AND SHAME AS THEY RELATE TO SELF-ESTEEM

THE FIVE STAGES IN THE DEVELOPMENT OF THE CONSCIENCE

Elsewhere (Gardner, 1988), I discuss in detail the five stages that I consider to be operative in the development of the internal guilt-evoking mechanisms (conscience). In the first stage, the genetic-neurological substrate, the basic neurological patterns are laid down. Embedded in these neurological structures are the circuits in which social information regarding the subsequent stages will be stored. There is great variation among individuals regarding the degree to which they have such brain substance and its receptivity for such messages to be embedded in the psychic structure. In the second stage, the imprinting stage, the earliest attachment responses are induced by ongoing opportunities for affection, attention, and tender loving care provided by significant individuals in the child's environment. Without such imprinting for positive attachment to caring individuals the child is not going to be motivated to learn what is being taught during subsequent stages because the acquisition of such knowledge does not result in the reward of affection and attention from such significant individuals. Here I focus on the relationships between the last three of these five phases and self-esteem, with particular focus on the ways in which impairments at each of these three levels can produce self-esteem problems that impact on a child's school adjustment. In the *pleasure-pain stage*, children deter themselves from those acts that are considered unacceptable by significant figures in their environment from the fear that pain, physical and/or emotional, will ensue. Physical pain may take the form of a spanking or other types of corporal punishment. Psychological pain may result from the withdrawal of parental affection, threats of rejection, denigration of the child, isolation, and a wide variety of disciplinary and punitive measures. All of these techniques are likely to be associated with a lowering of the child's feelings of self-worth.

In the *shame stage* children deter themselves from unacceptable behavior because of the expectation that significant figures will be critical if they were to observe the child engaging in such behavior. It is as if the child imagines himself (herself) surrounded by a circle of adults, all of whom are pointing their fingers at the child and saying, "Shame on you." Feelings of shame are inextricably associated with feelings of low self-esteem.

In the *guilt stage* the anticipation of pain and shame is internalized. No external figures are involved in deterring the child from performing those acts that are generally considered unacceptable by society. Rather, complex internal psychological mechanisms operate with the result that children can be relied upon to deter themselves from engaging in unacceptable behavior. In guilt there is a feeling of lowered self-worth because one has thoughts and feelings associated with the desire to perform the unacceptable act(s), or one may have already indeed perpetrated it (them). There may also be an anticipation of pain or shame if significant figures find out what the child is thinking or has done. When the guilt stage is reached, society can relax its vigil somewhat in that individuals can often (but certainly not always) now be trusted to restrain themselves from engaging in the unacceptable behavior.

In all three of these stages, if successfully employed, children will suffer with feelings of low self-worth. I would not suggest, however, that we dispense with pleasure-pain, shame, or guilt. Without exposure to these deterrents to unacceptable behavior, there can be no civilized society. Without them the world would become a predatory place where each individual preys upon the other and there are no restraints, either internal or external, to prevent such exploitation and brutalization. It is only when these mechanisms are utilized to excess that individuals become crippled psychologically. When used in a humane and reasonable fashion, they help create an individual who can tolerate the unpleasantness of occasional feelings of lowered self-esteem. The healthy individual will have so many positive and enjoyable feelings in compensation that these undesirable feelings will not be overwhelming.

FEELINGS OF LOW SELF-WORTH ASSOCIATED WITH THE PLEASURE-PAIN STAGE

The extreme example of low self-esteem resulting from detrimental pleasure-pain experiences is the physically abused child. Such children typically exhibit many manifestations of feelings of low self-esteem (Green, 1980). They do not enjoy playing with their toys or experience pleasure in other areas. Their weak attachments to human beings deprive them of pleasure in human relationships. They are often depressed and apathetic. They are hypervigilant in their encounters with others, ever expecting trauma. Probably one of the most dramatic examples of this phenomenon is their routinely flinching when approached by an adult, far more predictably than what one occasionally sees in normal children (especially when they are startled). These children appear forever startled by adult approaches. By the mechanism of reflected appraisals, their view of themselves is quite low. In fact, this is one of the hallmarks of the disorder. The mothers of these children typically do not involve themselves in the bonding process in the early years of the child's life. Never being loved, they feel unloved. Earlier in this chapter I discussed how low self-esteem results from milder forms of rejection and withdrawal of affection. Such children can be said to be suffering from psychological abuse. The child who suffers from physical abuse experiences an even greater loss of self-worth.

FEELINGS OF LOW SELF-ESTEEM ASSOCIATED WITH THE SHAME STAGE

The child who is exposed excessively to shame-engendering criticisms is likely to suffer with feelings of low self-esteem. Crying is a behavioral manifestation over which some children (especially boys) are likely to suffer with exaggerated feelings of shame. The notion that it is unmanly to cry is a deep-seated one in our culture ("Boys don't cry"). Although the proscription is less rigid for women, the woman who cries may still be considered more immature or hysterical than the one who can hold back her tears. The tradition is an unfortunate one because it does not provide proper respect for innate responses. Those who adhere to the principle unnecessarily deprive themselves and their children of an emotional outlet, the inhibition of which contributes to the formation of psychological disorder(s). One of the effects of the prohibition against crying is that the child who spontaneously bursts into tears is made to feel humiliated, and consequently self-esteem is lowered.

The crying proscription may even be extended to a child whose parent or grandparent has just died: "Be brave, don't cry" or "Big boys and girls don't cry." Children who are not exposed to such misguided admonitions may very well be exposed to subtler discouragements of the expression of their feelings: "Mary is taking it so well" or "He's holding up beautifully." Mourning involves a piecemeal desensitization to the pain one feels over the loss of a loved one. Each time one thinks of the deceased, the pain becomes a little more bearable. Each time one cries, one feels a little less pained over the loss. To inhibit these reactions (which are innate) is to prevent a healthy psychological restoration. The persistence of such pent-up emotions prevents the sense of well-being necessary to feeling good about oneself. In addition, if the child feels humiliated and embarrassed over the tears, an even further lowering of self-esteem is suffered. Elsewhere (Gardner, 1977, 1979a) I have discussed in detail some of the psychological problems that result from children being discouraged from expressing their emotional reactions to death, especially the death of a parent.

Children do well, therefore, to see their parents, especially their fathers, cry in appropriate situations. Parents who run into another room so their children will not see them cry make it less likely that their children will have a healthy attitude toward crying. Our children learn much from their imitation of us. If the adult is free to cry when the situation warrants it, the child is more likely to act in a similar way.

As mentioned, engendering shame in children is crucial for the survival of a civilized society. Oriental societies utilize this mechanism more frequently than western societies (where guilt presumably is the primary mechanism of deterrence). Parents who do not induce enough shame in their children are likely to produce psychopaths; parents who produce too much shame in their children are likely to engender in them a wide variety of psychopathological processes. Children with not enough shame may exhibit behavior problems in the classroom. Those with too much shame may be fearful of reading aloud, asking questions, and participating in extracurricular activities in which they are exposed to others (such as sports, dramatic performances, and recitals).

FEELINGS OF LOW SELF-ESTEEM ASSOCIATED WITH THE GUILT STAGE

As mentioned, an intrinsic element in guilt is the feeling of low self-worth associated with the knowledge that one has entertained ideas and impulses that are generally unacceptable in one's milieu. Some children are made to feel that they are the first persons in the history of the world to utter certain thoughts and feelings. Believing that the ideas that spontaneously and uncontrollably appear in one's mind are among the most abominable in the history of the human race invariably makes one feel terrible about oneself. Such attitudes are particularly common over sexual and angry feelings. The lowered self-esteem, which is part of the guilt children feel over certain ideas and urges, is primarily the result of parental attitudes, although it can be modified by the child's exposure to other influences.

Healthy parents recognize that there is no thought that is foreign to any human mind. They help their children accept the most heinous and despicable ideas as natural and understandable under certain circumstances. They teach their children to express such thoughts and feelings when appropriate and to suppress them when not. They teach them effective and civilized expression of such thoughts and feelings, not inappropriate self-censorship and self-denigration. They reassure their children that not only do many other children have similar thoughts and feelings, but they themselves have also had and still have the same kinds of ideas and emotional reactions. In this way they may counterbalance some of the widespread social and cultural attitudes that engender unnecessary and inappropriate guilt and the lowered self-respect intrinsic to it.

EFFECTS OF CONSCIENCE ABNORMALITIES ON CLASSROOM LEARNING

The kinds of conscience-development problems discussed in this section relate primarily to children who are subjected to excessive pain, shame, and guilt evocation during the three phases focused on here. They develop "hypertrophied" fear, shame, and guilt mechanisms with resultant significant compromises in their feelings of self-worth. And this is likely to have repercussions in the classroom. Children with low self-worth are likely to lack confidence and are unlikely to pursue their academic careers with an attitude of optimism and expectation of success. Deprived children feel unloved and do not anticipate that their parents will admire and praise them for their school accomplishments. They may transfer their anticipation of pain and rejection from their parents to their teachers, and may therefore be compromised significantly in their capacity to learn from and identify with those who instruct them. There are many children, unfortunately, who do not have enough shame and guilt. This may contribute to a wide variety of antisocial behaviors seen in school.

PSYCHOTHERAPEUTIC APPROACHES

The primary purpose of psychotherapy for children with problems in this realm is to increase guilt and shame for those who have too little and to decrease these feelings for those who have too much. There are therapists who believe that one should never do anything to increase the guilt or shame of a patient. On a number of occasions, when showing a tape to an audience, people have said to me: "Why, you're trying to make that child feel *more* guilty!" To which I respond: "Yes, that's exactly right. The problem with this child is that he doesn't have *enough* guilt. In fact, I will go further and say that there are more people in this world who need *more* guilt than people who need *less* guilt. Because Sigmund Freud felt that he had to reduce the sexual guilt that his hysterical patients had is no reason to expand this principle to include all the people who will ever go into treatment. The therapist should assess each patient and decide at which point on the guilt continuum the patient is and whether or not more or less shame and guilt is necessary."

A useful bibliotherapeutic technique for helping children find the proper point on the guilt and shame continuum—ranging from its absence to an inordinate degree—is my *The Girls and Boys Book About Good and Bad Behavior* (1990). The same book has chapters on self-esteem and pleasure-pain that can also be useful in this regard. Numerous vignettes are provided that link self-esteem, pleasure-pain, shame, and guilt. For example, in presenting the concept of shame I state:

> Shame is a special kind of feeling of low self-esteem. To feel shame two things must happen. First, you must do or say something that you know is wrong or bad. And second, people who are important to you—like your parents, for example—must see you doing the bad thing or learn that you have done it. When

these people see you doing the bad thing, you feel ashamed of yourself. And when you think about how disappointed these people are with you—because of the bad thing you have done—you may feel shame. It is almost as if the person is standing in the middle of a circle of people—all of whom are pointing at him or her—and saying, "Shame, shame on you. You should be ashamed of yourself." Shame lowers feelings of self-worth. When you feel ashamed of yourself, your self-esteem gets lower.

My presentation of the concept of guilt:

Guilt is another kind of feeling of low self-worth. People may feel guilt after *doing* things that they have learned are bad or wrong to do. People may also feel guilt after having *feelings* that they have learned are bad or wrong to feel. And people may feel guilt after thinking *thoughts* that they have learned are bad or wrong to think.

When you have guilt, the disappointed person is not any of these other people. When you have guilt the disappointed person is *you yourself*. You feel bad about yourself for what you have thought, felt, or done. Therefore, you can feel guilt when you are all alone. Even at night, when you are all alone in your room, when there is no one around to see you, you can feel guilt. Even when you hide under the covers, you can feel guilt. In this way guilt lowers feelings of self-worth.

In the ensuing material a number of topics are covered related to ways of dealing with guilt, e.g., saying you're sorry (both when you don't mean it and when you mean it), getting punishment, confessing, and providing compensation to the person who was harmed by the unacceptable act. Throughout, the emphasis is on how the implementation of the suggestions will impact on the individual's feelings of self-worth.

When a patient tells me, "I feel lousy about myself," I generally ask, "Are you doing anything that would make anyone else feel lousy about himself if he were doing the same thing?" Often, after some thought, I get an affirmative answer. The child may be cheating on tests, stealing, or lying excessively; and if he has anything approaching a normal conscience, he will feel guilty about these acts. Intrinsic to guilt is self-hatred: "What a terrible person I am for doing all these horrible things." The child in such a situation might be told, "As long as you do those things you're going to find that you'll feel lousy about yourself. I think you'll see that if and when you can stop, you'll feel better about yourself." If the child can be encouraged to take positive action and restrain himself from engaging in the esteem-lowering behavior, then one of the elements contributing to his low self-worth will have been eliminated. However, since the elements contributing to low self-esteem are many and complex, their alleviation is generally not brought about through simple maneuvers or words alone. Rather, action in a number of areas *over time* is usually necessary if meaningful changes are to take place.

I sometimes refer to this approach as the "ball-is-in-your-court principle." Here the problem is thrown in the patient's lap. They are basically told that as long as they continue involving themselves in the unacceptable behavior, their self-esteem will be low and they will suffer the psychological consequences of such feelings of low self-worth. The child who cheats on tests is not going to get the same feelings of high self-esteem as the one who achieved high grades honestly. Such children are helped to appreciate that in their "heart of hearts" they know that they really didn't deserve the high grade. The child who lies has to be helped to appreciate that there are many consequences of lying that are ego-debasing: the fear of disclosure, the rejection of those who have learned about the deceits, etc. The effects of this behavior on self-esteem are described allegorically in such stories as "The hundred-dollar lie" in my *Stories About the Real World, Vol. I* (Gardner, 1972a) and "The Fox and the Big Lie" in my *Fables for Our Times* (Gardner, 1981a).

CLINICAL EXAMPLES

Many of the cards in *The Talking, Feeling, and Doing Game* provide the therapist with the opportunity to communicate messages related to the shame/guilt issue.

Question: What is the most selfish thing you ever did? Make believe you're doing that thing now.

Response: Well, the most selfish thing I ever did was a long time ago—it was right after the Second World War—it was in 1947, when I was 16 years old. It was very hard to get jobs after the Second World War. All the war factories were closing down, and many people were fired from their jobs. They didn't need so many people anymore to make tanks and guns and things like that. And all the soldiers were getting out of the Army. And everybody was also getting out of the Navy and Air Force. There were millions of people trying to get jobs. Well, I finally got a job selling magazines to the wives and mothers of soldiers who had been in the war. I told the people how important it was to buy the magazine because it would help the veterans, the people who fought in the war. After working a few days, I found out that this magazine was kind of phony. A lot of people weren't getting the subscriptions they were paying for, and I felt very guilty about what I was doing.

I was preying on people's sympathy. I was saying that this was very important for the parents and the wives of soldiers who were killed or who had fought in the war, and it was a kind of phony organization. I didn't realize it when I got the job, but after I started working I realized it, and I soon quit. But I felt very guilty, and I think I worked a day or two too much because I needed the money so badly that I stuck with it awhile, but then my guilt overcame me and I quit the job. It had been a selfish thing to do. Sometimes when people are hungry, when they need money a lot, then they do things that they would never want to do. I was ashamed of myself when I did that. Do you want to say anything about that?

The Talking, Feeling, and Doing Game provides therapists with the opportunity to reveal their own deficiencies in a noncontrived and natural way. This lessens the likelihood that the patient will idealize the therapist. It makes the therapist a more real human being. It lessens the likelihood of the development of the unfavorable comparison in which the patient views the therapist as perfect and views himself (herself) as a bundle of psychopathology. The particular incident was chosen because it demonstrates how guilt can be useful in preventing a person from engaging in antisocial behavior. This is the kind of response I provide for patients who do not have enough guilt over their antisocial behavior. My hope is that the vignette will contribute to the development of a slightly stronger conscience.

* * *

Question: Tell about something you did that you are ashamed about?

Response: I had an experience many years ago, when I was a medical intern, that was very embarrassing. It was so embarrassing that I still remember it clearly to this day. An intern is a young doctor just out of medical school. Well, one Friday morning the resident, the doctor who was my boss, told me that I should prepare a speech about one of the patients whom I was treating. He told me that I was to give the talk the first thing the following Monday morning. He told me to look over the patient's present and past charts as well as to study all the old X-rays. The patient had been sick for many years, and there was a lot of material to cover. He told me that it was important that I do a good job because this was the biggest conference of the month and all the doctors in the hospital would be there. The hospital had over 200 doctors, and it was a very important conference.

Anyway, Monday morning I got to the hospital and started to work with my patients. I noticed that none of the other doctors was there and wondered where everyone was. Suddenly, the telephone rang and I answered. It was the resident. He was very upset and he asked me why I wasn't at the conference. I was so surprised and shocked that I almost fainted. I realized that I had totally forgotten about the conference! I had prepared nothing! I was sick to my stomach. I immediately grabbed that patient's chart, the first two X-rays that I could find, and rushed to the conference room.

What I should have done was to publicly announce that I was unprepared and to express my apologies. However, I tried to get away with it. I tried to go through the chart and give a speech about the patient, when I had very little information. I didn't lie or anything like that. I just tried to take a little information from one place and a little from the next, but it didn't hang together. Finally, one of the older doctors who organized the conference interrupted me and suggested that we discontinue the conference. I was humiliated. But I was also relieved. I certainly learned an important lesson that day. And I have never again forgotten to prepare a speech. That event took place many years ago, and although it was painful and embarrassing, I learned an important lesson.

The request to "Tell about something you did that you are ashamed about" again requires the therapist to reveal an area of deficiency. In the vignette that I selected, I also provide a message about preparing things in advance, thinking ahead, and thereby protecting oneself from humiliation. This message is likely to be of some relevance to most youngsters in treatment.

# SIX
SATISFACTION WITH ONE'S BODY

BODY CONFIGURATION AND ATTITUDE

In physically healthy people there is basically no particular body part or group of parts that is intrinsically good or bad, beautiful or ugly. Such judgments are generally "in the eye of the beholder." Shakespeare's *Hamlet* said it well: "There's nothing either good or bad, but thinking makes it so." One's assessment of the desirability or undesirability of one's body is determined in early years by parental attitudes. And the parental views generally reflect those of the society in which the child is born. Those whose body parts or features, although completely normal physically, do not conform to what is considered ideal by their particular culture may find themselves at a significant disadvantage. For example, although things have certainly progressed in recent years, black people are still subjected to significant degrees of prejudice in the United States and other parts of the world. It is quite common for black mothers, at the time of birth, to inspect their children carefully in order to make some assessment of how dark their skins are. For many mothers, the lighter the child's skin, the happier they will be. This is not simply related to the awareness that the child with lighter skin may have an easier life; it also relates to the mother's having "identified with the aggressor" and taken on the values of her persecutors. Early in life, the darker children who have been exposed to such parental assessments, in accordance with the principle of "reflected appraisals," are going to view themselves as unworthy.

In the adolescent period, especially, minor variations from the norm are generally considered particularly shameful. Breast size is a good example. In the 1920s, flat-chested women were all the rage, and well-endowed females did all they could to de-emphasize their bosoms. Since that time, bustiness has been in vogue, and it is now the less-endowed who feel inadequate. Many techniques have been devised to correct their "defect": injection of silicone, surgical implantation of plastic material, and even transplantation of fatty tissue from the buttocks. As young girls approach puberty, they eagerly await the development of these particular organs with an interest that goes far beyond their involvement in other bodily changes that are simultaneously taking place. "Training bras" may be purchased in anticipation of the great day when the breasts will appear, and wearing padded bras and "falsies" may be the only way the youngster may feel comfortable in public if her peers develop earlier or more abundantly.

"Nose jobs" are also in vogue at the time of this writing. In the area in which I live (northern New Jersey), these operations are especially common among Jewish girls who are led to believe that there is something intrinsically ugly about Jewish noses and that to have a nose like a Gentile girl will enhance their popularity. Short men wear "elevator shoes." Tall women slouch and wear flat shoes. Adolescent boys compare genitalia to determine whose are larger, and the less "well hung" may avoid locker rooms to protect themselves from the humiliations they anticipate there.

There is nothing innate about any of these feelings of shame and dissatisfaction with one's own body. All are culturally determined and transmitted through the parents from one generation to the next. All reflect an inappropriate dissatisfaction with one's body and contribute to a person's feeling of low self-worth. All start in childhood. During the 1960s and early 1970s, there was a trend among youth to counter these insidious and hypocritical attitudes. There was a greater sense of pride in one's body, less shame, less covering, and less artificiality. There was more pride in the body one was born with and less concern with how it compared with the average or some supposed ideal. "This is my body," the young people boasted, "and if you don't like it, there's something wrong with you." One manifestation of this trend was not to wear a bra because it changed the natural shape of the breast. (I have no doubt, however, that this practice served seductive purposes as well.) Young black women no longer tried to straighten their naturally kinky hair, lighten the color of their skin, or de-emphasize the thickness of their lips. Unfortunately, there has been some recent regression with regard to these advances. This factor is still operative in lowering children's self-worth.

BODY SATISFACTION AND ACADEMIC PROBLEMS

A lack of respect for one's body may contribute to academic difficulties. Children who are ashamed of their bodies may hesitate to go to school because of their fear of exposing what they consider to be their unacceptable appearance. Children are exquisitely sensitive to the criticisms that others may have about their bodies, and they are ever concerned about "looking different." Such preoccupations in school can compromise academic performance. In extreme cases it can contribute to refusal to go to school and truancy. Adolescents are even more concerned with their differences from others than younger children. It is well known that they are slavishly dependent on wearing the exact same uniform as their peers, their professions of independent thinking and individuality notwithstanding.

BODY SATISFACTION AND PSYCHOTHERAPY

Adolescents typically spend many hours with one another talking about the similarities and differences between their own features and body characteristics and those of others. They need constant reassurance that their appearance is not atypical. A discussion of this particular area can contribute to their involvement in treatment where discussion of oneself is a central focus. Psychotherapy, if it is to be going well, inevitably involves a significant amount of narcissistic gratification for the patient, as both therapist and patient focus primarily on everything the patient says and does. This is a source of ego-enhancement for all patients, regardless of age. However, adolescents, narcissists that they are, enjoy such individual attention even more than younger and older patients, and therapists do well to recognize this point when trying to find "handles" to serve as points of departure for psychotherapeutic interchanges. Therapists of adolescents do well to appreciate that if they reach a lull in the session, they do well to shift the conversation to the adolescent's appearance. It is likely that the youngster will then become a more enthusiastic participant in the discussion. If appearance is playing a role in the youngster's reluctance to go to school, then this conversation serves as a route to a central problem. But even for youngsters whose appearance is not interfering with their school attendance and performance, the conversation is likely to lead to therapeutically useful material.

 # SEVEN
SATISFACTION WITH ONE'S ETHNICITY AND HERITAGE

INTRODUCTION

There are youngsters, especially members of minority groups, who are subjected to various forms of prejudice—overt and covert. The anger engendered by racial slurs, rejections, and taunting may contribute to antisocial behavior, which may exhibit itself in school and result in academic difficulties. Furthermore, accepting as valid the criticisms of others may contribute to feelings of low self-worth, which also can contribute to poor school performance. This is especially the case for youngsters who agree with their persecutors that their heritage is indeed something to be ashamed about. Such youngsters may try to hide their identity and "pass" as a member of what they consider to be the more desirable group.

GENERAL THERAPEUTIC CONSIDERATIONS

Youngsters who are ashamed of their heritage often have parents with similar attitudes, and the therapist does well to look into such influences when this kind of shame is present—shame that can contribute to generalized feelings of low self-worth. When

139

these parental influences are present, it is crucial that the therapist work with the parents as well if the problems that generate from the prejudice are to be solved. I will focus here on youngsters who agree with their persecutors that their ethnic background is something to be ashamed of and have parents who have, either overtly or covertly, communicated this message to the patient (the usual case).

First, the therapist must interview the parents and find out exactly what their own feelings are about their ethnic background. Such inquiry will be easier if the therapist is of the same heritage as the parents. However, therapists who have any shame over their own heritage—whether it be the same or different from that of the parents—are ill equipped to deal properly with this problem. The principle is no different from the one in which therapists who have never been married are providing marital counseling. Such therapists justifiably lose credibility with patients who are seeking advice for their own marriages. It is the same principle that compromises childless therapists in their psychotherapeutic work with children.

The therapist must attempt to help the parents (and by extension the youngster) appreciate that there is absolutely no good reason to consider one ethnic group superior (or inferior) to another. I often try to get across this message by using selected vignettes. One involves asking the patients (from here on, when I use the word *patients,* I will be referring to the parents and/or the youngster) to envision a globe of the earth and imagine the various streams of migrations—both within and between continents—that have taken place over the history of the human race. They then do well to view the migrations of their own ancestors and trace these as accurately as they can, pinpointing as well as they can the various times in history when the migrations took place. I then point out to them that these migrations generally occurred because of one or more kinds of persecution: political, religious, racial, etc. The therapist might join in and trace his (her) own heritage in a similar manner. It is useful to point out that it was extremely rare for the landed aristocracy to remove themselves voluntarily and unilaterally. It was generally only in response to some threat or some hope of bettering one's life situation that the migrations took place. Few sailed away on their yachts. Most were ducking bullets and spears or threats of imprisonment, persecution, or starvation. Emphasizing this point can help the patients feel less atypical about their own heritage.

The therapist might ask the parents why they (or their forebears) came to the United States. Generally they will describe some kind of persecution or privation. The family should then be asked why the United States was chosen from approximately 150 other countries on earth that could have been selected. Most often one will receive an answer related to this country as a land of opportunity, greater freedom, etc. Or the family may say that this country, with all its deficiencies, is still the best place on earth to live. The therapist does well, then, to point out that the United States did not achieve this status by pure chance; rather, there were very specific factors in our history that contributed to our enjoying this reputation. And one of these factors relates to the waves of immigrants who came here from all over the earth. Each generation had its own ethnic make-up. One could get more specific and talk about the early English, Spanish, and French settlers in the 15th through 18th centuries. The people who came here then were looking for various kinds of religious and political freedom—just like the forebears of the patient. One could then proceed into the middle 19th century and talk about Irish and German settlers and the late 19th and early 20th centuries and describe Jewish, Italian, and Slavic immigrants. One can then move up to the late 20th century and talk about the recent influx of Asian people to the United States. All of these immigrants shared in common not only their persecutions and privations abroad but their desire to work hard and enter into the American mainstream. Pointing out that the patient's family is part of this grand plan can help reduce feelings of inferiority.

The family should be helped to appreciate that just as one's heritage is nothing to be ashamed of, one's heritage is also nothing to be proud of either. This may come as a surprising statement to many readers. I think it is important to differentiate between identity and pride. By identity I refer to the identification of and with one's own particular ethnic group and predecessors. By pride I refer to the quality of feeling proud of something. I believe that one can feel pride over some accomplishment, especially one that was attained after great effort. However, I do not believe that the feelings of pride that one may have about one's identity work particularly well toward enhancing feelings of self-esteem. After all, nothing was done to achieve any goals here. Rather, one's ethnic identity relates merely to the way the genetic dice fell and where one's position is in the long trains of global migrations. If one had to take a test in heaven — and only the highest scorers were to be allowed to go down to earth and join a particular ethnic group — then there might be something to be proud of. Otherwise, the "assignment" has nothing to do with pride. It has something to do with *luck* in that the assignment can be unlucky or sometimes lucky.

Many people try to enhance their pride in their heritage by pointing out illustrious individuals who are members of their ethnic group. This doesn't work very well for enhancing self-respect. The same group fails to point out an equal if not larger number of individuals who certainly have not distinguished themselves or even contributed to the betterment of their people. I am of the Jewish heritage and so I can speak with greater knowledge (and safety) of the manifestations of this problem in this particular group. Many Jewish people point with pride to famous Jews such as Albert Einstein, Sigmund Freud, Felix Mendelssohn, Baruch Spinoza, Benjamin Disraeli, Golda Meir, etc. My views on this practice: Einstein should certainly be proud of his accomplishments in that few individuals have made such formidable contributions to our knowledge of the universe. His parents have some right to be proud of their input into their son's growth and development. And some of his teachers as well. However, such pride should not extend to everyone else in his synagogue. I, personally, did absolutely nothing to contribute to Einstein's successes and therefore do not deserve any of the enhanced sense of self-worth that came his way. If I attempt to enhance my self-worth by warming myself in his sunshine, it will do me little good. In fact, it might do me some harm because I will be trying to bolster my self-esteem with a maneuver that is basically specious and thereby ego-debasing.

In the 1960s blacks realized that they were making a terrible error by joining with their persecutors and agreeing with them that there was something to be ashamed of in being black. Accordingly, they began to proclaim that they were *proud* to be black. Black is not ugly. "Black is beautiful," they proclaimed. I see no point to all of this. It just won't work. Black is intrinsically neither ugly nor beautiful. Just like every other phenomenon in this world, whether one likes it or dislikes it, whether one thinks it beautiful or ugly, depends upon the "eye of the beholder." Shakespeare's Hamlet said it well: "There's nothing either good or bad but thinking makes it so." By extension, being black is neither something to be proud of nor something to be ashamed of. It is just one of the various skin colors that human beings possess.

The family has to be helped to appreciate that anyone who persecutes or thinks less of them because of their ethnic background has some derangement in thinking, "has a screw loose in his (her) head." In addition, if those who are persecuted believe that there is something wrong with them, then they too have defects in their thinking and have "screws loose in their heads." Viewing the persecutor as having a cognitive deficit can help the persecuted react with greater equanimity. The youngster and parents have to be helped to appreciate that there is something wrong with those who are prejudiced against them. Youngsters who retaliate in kind with ethnic slurs have to be helped to appreciate that they are lowering themselves and that they will not thereby enhance their self-worth. At appropriate times they should be helped to ignore the taunters and appreciate that the taunters have defective thinking. If they feel compelled to respond, they should be helped to do so in a way that addresses itself to the absurdity of the ethnic slur and to communicate the message that there is something strange and odd about the thinking of the persecutor—so perverse that the comments cannot be taken seriously.

I have found other comments to be helpful in this area. For

example, in recent years most large cities have witnessed a massive influx of a wide variety of ethnic groups. In some cities each school district is required to provide ethnic and language classes for every minority group whose representation exceeds a specific number of youngsters. Once this number has been reached, the educational system provides after-school classes in which the children are taught about the history and language of their ethnic group. Some school systems hold yearly festivals in which all the ethnic groups participate, generally in their own clusters. But there is significant intermingling.

Many ethnic groups provide their own cultural programs. If the family has not joined one, they should be encouraged to find one in their area, especially for the youngster. Such experiences help the children feel that, although different, they are in no way inferior. The family has to be helped to appreciate that being different does not mean that one is inferior. Nor does it mean that one is superior. I cannot emphasize the latter point strongly enough. The fact that one is the object of another's prejudice does not preclude the same family's being biased against others in different ethnic groups. In fact, bias generally goes both ways. If the family members view their skin color or facial characteristics as bad or ugly, they have to be helped to appreciate that such an attitude exists in the eye of the beholder and that there is absolutely no intrinsic quality that is either good, bad, right, wrong, beautiful, or ugly. In certain African tribes women's necks are stretched with a series of collars and their bodies are scarred. This is considered beautiful. In some societies obesity is viewed as beautiful and in others anorexia is the turn on. What probably is beautiful is the healthy human body. It is truly a marvelous creation and to be ashamed of it is certainly sad. If the therapist is successful in helping the family members develop healthier views about their heritage, the anger in the youngster should be reduced and this contribution to antisocial acting out and school refusal diminished.

It is important for the therapist to appreciate that ethnic prejudices and rivalries tend to become dramatically reduced from generation to generation. Newly arrived immigrants still have vivid recollections of the "old country" and strong psychological ties to their heritage. Their children, having been born and raised in the United States, have fewer such ties and are likely to be much more strongly committed to American society and values, their strong involvement and exposure to their heritage notwithstanding. In the adolescent period, especially, parents may "flip out" when their children date members of other ethnic groups. Some do this as a manifestation of adolescent rebellion, in that it is predictably going to provoke the parents and provide other hostile gratifications. Marrying outside the clan, and then producing "biheritage children," significantly attenuates the "pure" ethnic bonds. But even those who marry within their ethnic group do not generally have the same deep commitment to the perpetuation of their heritage as do their immigrant parents. By the second generation the commitment to their heritage becomes even more attenuated as the youngsters truly mix into the American mainstream. By that point the attitudes and behavior (although not the appearance) of the descendants of the various ethnic groups may be indistinguishable from one another, and one gets only a hint of heritage from the name (which also may become anglicized into mainstream American by that point, either by decision or marriage). When working therapeutically with such families, it is important to identify the generational level and point out the inevitability of history. Parents who are strongly committed to a full perpetuation of their heritage on new soil must be helped to appreciate that their task is likely to be an impossible one and they should stop trying to buck the course of history.

In the course of discussions on this point, I might relate my own experiences: I grew up in New York City, in the southwest section of the Bronx. My neighborhood was primarily Jewish and Irish Catholic. Unfortunately, there was significant animosity between the two groups. I recall quite well gangs of youngsters coming down the hill from the Irish-Catholic section chanting, "The Jews caused the war" (World War II) and "Franklin Delano *Rosenfeld* caused the war" (again World War II) and "The Jews killed Christ." Sometimes we fought back, but more often we fled in terror. Of course, there were other ethnic groups in the Bronx at that time, especially Italians, Poles, Germans, Spaniards, Blacks, and Protestants of northern European heritage. At that time if, for example, an Irish Catholic were to marry an Italian Catholic, both families would have fits and go into deep mourning. Disowning a youngster for such an act of family disloyalty was not inconceivable.

Over the half-century since my childhood, the children and grandchildren of my neighborhood inhabitants in the Bronx have moved elsewhere, especially to the suburbs surrounding New York City (in New Jersey, Westchester, and Connecticut). In the community where I live, Tenafly, New Jersey, there is a Catholic church. Worshiping together are Irish, Italians, Poles, Germans, Hispanics (from central and South America, the Caribbean, and Spain), Blacks, Chinese, Japanese, Koreans, Filipinos, Indians, and an assortment of other ethnic goups. Intermarriage is commonplace (especially among those of the same race, but not yet between those of different races). As far as I can tell, the people cooperate well and there is little significant interethnic rivalry. Once a year they hold an "International Festival," a dinner dance at which booths are set up and the fare of each of the ethnic groups is served. I have always found this to be a heartwarming occasion. In addition, the school conducts a United Nations Day every October 24th, on the anniversary of the founding of the UN. Children come in costumes reflecting each one's heritage. There are films, slide shows, and discussions about various ethnic groups throughout the world. Guests from the United Nations address the children. Furthermore, they eat an international lunch cooked by school mothers and collect food and money for the United Nations Children's Fund. The main emphasis is that all children, regardless of heritage, race, color, creed, or religious belief, are united together in the "family of God."

A few years ago I had two experiences in my practice, one right after the other, that demonstrate well this process of reduction of ethnic commitment from one generation to the next.

I had a 13-year-old girl of Syrian background in treatment. Although she was born in the United States, her two older siblings were born in Syria, as were her parents. They were of the Moslem faith and had been actively involved in wars with Israel. The youngster entered treatment because of peer problems and academic underachievement. One day the mother called me, quite upset, and asked for an emergency appointment. She told me on the telephone that the girl was hysterical because of a recent problem involving her relationship with a girl in her class. When I saw them the next day, both were quite upset. The problem was that my patient had not been invited to this classmate's Bas Mitzvah (Jewish rite of entering adulthood) and she felt terribly rejected. I immediately asked whether they thought this related to any prejudice against people of Arabic heritage, and they both immediately denied that this was the case, pointing out that other non-Jewish children had been invited. We then explored other possible explanations for her failure to be invited: there were only a limited number of possible invitations, or the Bas Mitzvah girl was not a close friend, or perhaps my patient had done things to alienate her classmate. Of interest here is that this event took place at a time when the patients' forebears in the Middle East were in a state of undeclared siege with Israel, and they were still literally killing one another. My patient and her parents couldn't have cared less about what was going on on the other side of the globe; their main concern was that the youngster had not been invited to the Bas Mitzvah.

Uncannily, about a week later, the whole scenario was again replayed by another 13-year-old patient of mine, this time a boy of Egyptian heritage. The family came to the United States from Egypt when he was one year old, and he and his parents were very upset because he had not been invited to a neighborhood boy's Bar Mitzvah. Once again, there was an ethnic history related to a recent war with Israel, and absolutely no concern about what was going on on the other side of the world. What was of concern was the invitation to the Bar Mitzvah. In both of these cases we see parental commitment to the movement of their children into the mainstream of American life. They could not care one iota about history, heritage, and past wars (even those in the recent memory of the parents).

In my work with the family I may tell them that although I myself was subjected to various prejudices throughout my life (the persecution by the Irish Catholic youngsters in my childhood being only one example), I have found that in the course of my work as a psychiatrist that all people, regardless of their heritage, are basically the same. All people essentially want the same things for themselves: physical health; family; financial security; and children who will be physically healthy, well educated, and who will grow up to be independent individuals capable of forming families of their own. They want the opportunity to work, and they want the opportunity to have reasonable amounts of leisure and recreation. Over the years I have treated patients from a wide variety of ethnic groups who have all proven this particular principle repeatedly. In the course of such work, my own prejudices have become reduced significantly. (I did not say eliminated entirely. I do not believe that there is anyone who is completely free of prejudice, especially when one is programmed to be so in childhood.) In the course of such a discussion, I will tell the family that my second wife is Irish-Catholic. The moral of the story: The best way to reduce prejudice is to marry someone from the initially hated or feared ethnic group!

I recognize that some therapists, especially those with a classical psychoanalytical orientation, would take issue with my revealing to patients such personal matters about my private life and would consider such divulgences to be a serious therapeutic contaminant to blank-screen projections. I am in agreement that such divulgences do indeed affect blank-screen projections. However, I believe that the negative effects of this contamination are more than outweighed by the benefits to be derived from the strengthening of my relationship with my patients that results from some divulgences. These disclosures reveal me to be a human being who has personally known the suffering of persecution and the pains of divorce. Revelations such as these also, I believe, enhance patients' interest in therapy, especially when dramatic elements are to be found in the vignettes. They follow the old principle (mentioned throughout this book) that therapeutic communications are far more effective when presented in the format of allegory, metaphor, anecdote, personal experiences, etc. Therapy, more than anything else, should be a human experience, and such divulgences contribute to the attainment of this goal.

Mention has been made of the fact that those who are the object of prejudice are not usually free of prejudice themselves. Bias is ubiquitous and prejudice is the other side of the coin from ethnic chauvinism. In fact, I believe that those who have pride in their heritage (a quality that I have already criticized) are intrinsically saying that their particular ethnic line is superior to that of others. It is a short jump, then, from ethnic pride to more overt forms of prejudice. As mentioned earlier, in the section on reflected appraisals, those who try to enhance their own sense of self-worth by denigrating others are not likely to be successful. To see others as low-lifes cannot work to enhance self-esteem because the condescending party is not enhancing esteem by the utilization of specific qualities that can genuinely work to increase one's sense of self-worth. Accordingly, the therapist does well to explore aspects of prejudice in those families who are complaining that they themselves are discriminated against. It is beyond the scope of this book to discuss in detail the therapeutic approaches to this aspect of the problem. Prejudice has many psychodynamic factors that should be understood and dealt with in the course of treatment. One aspect of such therapy, however, is providing the patient with living experiences with members of the hated group. This can often work more effectively than intellectual understanding of the psychodynamic factors operative in the prejudice.

One of the most important accomplishments of former president Jimmy Carter was his bringing about some degree of rapprochement between Egypt and Israel. All agree that the breakthrough here was his meetings with Premier Menachem Begin of Israel and President Anwar el-Sadat of Egypt at Camp David. The meeting took place in September 1978 and lasted 13 days. I suspect strongly that during the course of their numerous and lengthy meetings, they did not devote themselves entirely to formal discussions. Rather, there must have been times when they relaxed and "let down their hair." I suspect that it was during these periods that they engaged in discussions about their families, their children, their grandchildren, and personal experiences of their lives. It was then that they had the living experiences that reduced significantly their animosity toward one another, and they came to see each other as humane individuals, not people whom they wished to kill. Thus, I believe that the most important factors operative in bringing about the reduction of hostilities between the two men, and by extension their nations, had less to do with intellectual processes and formal negotiations, than it did with the basic human relationship that the two men developed over the course of this intense experience.

Carl Rogers, during the later years of his life, devoted himself to bringing together world leaders in the hope that they would reduce their prejudices and hostilities by coming to know one another as human beings who had the same basic goals in life. Unfortunately, he was not successful with this very humane, although impractical, plan.

CLINICAL EXAMPLE

I recall one patient whose mother was of Caucasian, northern European heritage and whose father was born in Brazil. The boy was occasionally considered to be Puerto Rican, and this was a source of great shame to him. His general response was to deny vehemently that he was Puerto Rican. His hope was that if everyone were to become convinced that his father was Brazilian, all would be well with him. He had to be helped to appreciate that his way of dealing with the problem involved a basic agreement with his persecutors that being Puerto Rican was something to be ashamed of. He had to be helped to appreciate that there is no ethnic group that is intrinsically superior or inferior to another, that they are just different. He had to be helped to appreciate that those who viewed him as less worthy because of his skin color, whether it be the result of his Puerto Rican, Brazilian, or any other racial background, were misguided in their thinking and cruel. This issue had played a role in his school avoidance problem. His incorporating the aforementioned principles into his psychic structure helped him significantly toward becoming more comfortable attending school and dealing with those who teased and ridiculed him because of his skin color.

EIGHT
COMPETENCE

THE CRUCIAL RELATIONSHIP BETWEEN COMPETENCE AND SELF-ESTEEM

I cannot imagine genuine self-esteem existing without competence in some specific area. One cannot esteem oneself in a vacuum; one can only have esteem for specific qualities. In addition, the qualities that are esteemed must not be easily acquired. If they are genuinely to work, they must have been acquired through effort over time. One must be proud about something specific; one can't be proud of something in a vacuum. A child who has not gained genuine competence in major areas of functioning in the formative years is going to be a prime candidate for the utilization of maneuvers that seemingly enhance competence in a quick way, but basically do not work.

During the elementary school period, a child may gain a sense of high self-worth by being a good student or by perfecting skills in athletics. Others gain competence in artistic pursuits. Others are highly social, gain friends, and enjoy recreational activities. The healthiest children, of course, derive self-esteem from many of these activities. A child who reaches adolescence without having gained significant competence and esteem enhancement (the two go together) from *any* of these pursuits may resort to drugs to provide feelings of high self-worth quickly and easily. Narcotics not only desensitize the youngster to the pain associated with the recognition of inadequacy in all these areas but also provide a sense of euphoria that is associated with a feeling of high self-worth. The drawbacks, of course, are that the drug will inevitably wear off, leaving the individual with the same feelings of inadequacy. Furthermore, it is extremely unlikely that one will compensate for these deficiencies while under the influence of drugs. The two-year-old boy who builds a tower of blocks beams over his accomplishment. His sense of mastery is ego-enhancing. The mother who says, "What a beautiful tower you've built!" directs her compliment to the product of his labors, raises further his feelings of self-worth, and increases the likelihood that he will build again. In contrast, the mother who responds, "You're going to be a great engineer someday, and we'll be proud of you; the family will be famous," uses the child's accomplishments for her own self-aggrandizement, lessens his pleasure and feelings of competence, and makes it less likely that he will derive ego-enhancing gratifications from building.

The general principle that the most meaningful praise directs itself to the product of the child's labors is an important one. It genuinely says to the child: "You have every right to feel good about yourself for what you have accomplished." Parents who try to use their child's attainments for their own ego-enhancement rob the child of some of the gratifications of the attainment. Such a parental attitude may be a contributing factor to some children's loss of incentive to work and learn.

Parents who, under the guise of helping their children with their homework, actually do it for them or point out their mistakes so that their children can be assured of handing in perfect papers, are seriously undermining their children's self-confidence. Such children cannot possibly enjoy a feeling of mastery if they have not indeed "mastered" their subjects. A few poor grades do far more for such children than all their A's in homework. Low marks may mobilize them to learn on their own; high marks, especially when obtained by their parents, may cripple them educationally. The preferable attitude for parents to take is to view their children's homework as a matter between the children and their teachers. They should be available to help their children try to figure things out, but not to do their homework for them or to provide so much input that the children are not challenged. The parental assistance should stimulate effort and encourage enthusiasm. The aim of the parental contribution should be to help their children learn how to help themselves. The old proverb is important enough to repeat: "Give a man a fish, and you've given him a meal. Teach a man *how* to fish, and you've given him a meal for life." This should be the guiding principle for parents who are helping their children with homework. It could also be a guiding principle for teachers and school administrators.

The father who makes models for his son so that they "look better" is sabotaging the child's attempt to gain a feeling of self-confidence. The mother who cannot allow her daughter to cook her own rather mediocre cookies and intrudes so that they "come out better" robs the child of an important growth experience. Such children may become psychologically paralyzed: they become incapable of performing up to their age level in many areas. They cannot help but compare themselves unfavorably with their peers, and they inevitably suffer from feelings of inadequacy.

Relevant to this important principle is the anecdote about the Texan who comes to New York City. He has a ticket for a concert at Carnegie Hall, but has never been to the city before and doesn't know how to get to Carnegie Hall. Accordingly, he approaches a little old lady with whom the following interchange takes place:

> *Texan:* Excuse me, ma'am. Can you please tell me how I can get to Carnegie Hall?
> *Little Old Lady:* Sonny, if you want to get to Carnegie Hall, you've got to practice, practice, and practice!

Without practice there is no accomplishment. Without practice there is no competence. And without competence there is no self-esteem. The point is also well demonstrated by a newspaper clipping I read some time around 1970. A man in Toronto submitted a painting to an art contest and was awarded second prize. Upon receipt of the award, he announced that his submission was nothing more than a piece of cardboard that he had found in his garage on which he had wiped his paintbrushes. Whatever pleasure the man may have gained from this deceit (and I am in full agreement that the judges deserved what they got), he could not have the same kind of enjoyment as someone who had genuinely labored to obtain the same prize. The somewhat nebulous criteria for what constitutes "great art" allow international recognition for people who could not but wonder, at times, whether what they are producing is really worth all the fuss that the art world is providing and all the money that their productions are attracting. People like Michelangelo and Rembrandt, I strongly suspect, did not have these concerns.

Adolescents who take drugs do so, in part, to desensitize themselves to the massive feelings of self-loathing they suffer because they have few if any areas of competence or skill. The euphoria they may experience in the early stages of the addiction provides a compensatory sense of self-worth. To try to wean such youngsters from the drug—without providing them with some rehabilitative program in which they can gain a sense of proficiency and mastery—is futile. Many are addicted to alcohol for similar reasons. Alcoholics Anonymous helps, in part, because it provides the alcoholic with a sense of competence in helping other alcoholics abstain. In small towns, when the members run out of alcoholics to help, they often revert to drinking again because they no longer have the opportunity to engage in an activity that provided them with their greatest source of ego-enhancement.

PURSUIT AND THE WORK ETHIC AS THEY RELATE TO COMPETENCE

As mentioned, if competence is to successfully enhance self-worth, it must be acquired through effort over time. There is hardly a school child who has not been asked to memorize these lines, which Thomas Jefferson wrote in the Declaration of Independence:

> —We hold these truths to be self-evident, that all men are created equal, that they are endowed by their Creator with certain unalienable Rights, that among these are Life, Liberty, and the pursuit of Happiness . . .

Yet, there is hardly a child who thinks seriously of the significance of the word *pursuit* in this passage—a word that is vital to its understanding. Jefferson might well have written "Life, Liberty, and Happiness," but he was wise enough to know that no one can be guaranteed the right to happiness, something that exists at best only for short periods and under very special circumstances.

Dr. Geoffrey Osler, a New York City neurologist and a gifted teacher, once suggested that Jefferson should have written "Life, Liberty, and the happiness of Pursuit." Osler's position, which I support, was that the *process of pursuit* of a goal provides our greatest happiness. In the *attaining process* and in the short period around the time of *attainment*, we enjoy the greatest happiness in life. Although life may allow us many periods of happiness, it cannot provide us with a chronic state of happiness. For the sake of completeness (but not, by any means, for the sake of poetic beauty), one could combine what Jefferson and Osler said and guarantee to all men the right to Life, Liberty, the pursuit of Happiness, and the happiness of Pursuit. In short, all should be given the freedom and opportunity to enjoy the happiness that can come from pursuing one's goals as well as the happiness that comes with their attainment.

The more arduous the pursuit, the greater the sense of enhanced self-worth that comes with the attainment of the goal. The greater the challenge, the greater the difficulty, the greater the risk of failure—the greater the feelings of self-worth when the obstacles are finally overcome. The mountain climber who reaches the top of Mount Everest is both psychologically and physically "on top of the world." Climbing smaller mountains are less of a challenge, and therefore provide less ego-enhancement. Pleasure and excitement along the pursuit route can also increase the ego-enhancement that one experiences upon attainment of the goal. The fantasies of success along the way also play a part in enhancing self-worth, and parents can introduce children to this process very early in life. For example, one parent tells a child about a forthcoming fourth birthday party a day or two in advance. Another tells the child a few weeks in advance, and the two together enjoy the excitement of selecting the guests, purchasing the invitations, mailing them out, excitedly waiting for the mail to see the responses, and finally making the preparations before the party. The two children have very different experiences with their parties, the latter obviously getting more pleasure and ego-enhancement than the former.

An experience I had in medical school demonstrates this point quite well. As some patients appreciate, there is a very strict hierarchy among the doctors who care for patients in the hospital. And this is especially the case in hospitals affiliated with medical schools. Generally, students do not participate in direct patient care until their third year of medical school (although there are a few isolated exceptions). The third-year medical student is indeed "low man (woman) on the totem pole." These students generally "do all the dirty work" (and I leave it to the imagination of the reader to speculate what such assignments might involve). Next up the ladder is the fourth-year student, who gets a little less of the dirty work and has a little more responsibility. But fourth-year students do not have their medical degrees, and they must work under the careful supervision of more senior people. Next is the intern, who just recently acquired an M.D. degree, may not have a license to practice medicine, and still must work under careful supervision—even though he (she) has more responsibilities than the medical students. Next on the ladder is the junior resident, who has more responsibilities than those below him (her) but still not as many as those above. Next is the senior resident, and then there could be a third- and fourth-year resident, and then a chief resident—depending upon the number of years of training required by the particular specialty. Above this small army are the attendings, divided into the categories of assistant attending, associate attending, and attending. The attendings are not generally involved in direct patient care but supervise and advise the residents, interns, and students.

The incident that comes to mind here occurred on July 1st of the year I began as a third-year student. This is the traditional transition date when each individual moves up one notch on the ladder. On this particular day, on a medical ward, a new second-year resident began his duties as the primary direct-care physician for a ward of approximately 20 people—lined up in two rows of 10 beds on each side. As he entered the ward, with those beneath him trailing behind, he stood at the entrance to the ward, raised up his arms in front of him, and proudly stated: "Mine, mine, all mine!" These patients were now "his" and they were in his domain. He had worked many years to achieve this goal, committed himself assiduously to the work ethic, and was now enjoying the strong sense of high self-worth associated with his accomplishment. We do best for our children to impart to them that life is never perfect. Life inevitably has its frustrations, its struggles, and its grave disappointments. It can also provide, for those who are willing to work for them, intense periods of gratification and even happiness. And a central element in such happiness is an enhanced feeling of self-worth. If we are successful in imparting this view to our children, we will lessen the likelihood that they will suffer with ego-debasing disillusionments about themselves and others.

PSYCHOTHERAPEUTIC APPROACHES TO COMPETENCE ISSUES

Basic Therapeutic Considerations

It behooves therapists, when treating children with self-esteem problems, to encourage them to develop their interests and talents. Without proficiency in genuine skills, feelings of competence can at best be unstable. Children must, however, be discouraged from pursuits in which they have not demonstrated particular aptitude. The boy with a neurologically based learning disability, with an associated coordination deficit, would suffer deep humiliations in a sports-oriented summer camp. The asthenic child can be reassured that many boys on the football team wouldn't stand a chance against him at chess.

Children who cheat on tests do not have, or do not believe they have, the competence to be successful in their studies. They do not seem to appreciate that reaching a goal dishonestly cannot provide the same degree of satisfaction or the same sense of accomplishment as coming by it honestly. They do not seem to appreciate that the gratifications they may derive from the attainment are generally more than counterbalanced by the inner feeling of shame that accompanies the knowledge that the high grades were not genuinely earned. When I learn in treatment that a child is cheating on school examinations, I will often say, "You really can't feel good about yourself having gotten this high mark by copying." In addition, I might remind the child that it is likely that classmates have observed the cheating, and this certainly is not going to increase his (her) popularity. And low popularity cannot be associated with high self-worth.

Generally, when a child tries to cheat when playing a game with me, I will comment that it is no fun for me to play with a cheater and that I will only continue to play as long as the rules are followed. Having the *living experience* that the cheating may threaten the continuation of an enjoyable experience, as well as lessen the affection the child enjoys from someone who is respected, can serve as an effective and realistic deterrent. Furthermore, I might ask the child whether he (she) plays the same way with peers and, if so, to consider the possibility that this may be one of the reasons he (she) has so much trouble keeping friends.

The reader should note that in such situations I do not appeal to higher ethical and moral principles when attempting to modify a child's behavior. Rather, I direct myself to the child's sense of expediency and to other considerations relevant to his (her) everyday experiences. In my philosophy of things, the cheater is not being watched by someone up there who is keeping a careful record and will see to it that someday children will be punished for all their transgressions (either in this life or after death). I therefore do not use such appeals to help the cheaters see the errors of their ways. I can, however, appeal to more mundane considerations that are not only more effective in helping the child with this difficulty, but also avoid the additional difficulties introduced when one appeals to the Almighty for help in solving a problem. To be reminded that cheating makes one feel lousy about oneself and may cause one to lose friends is honest, direct, and relevant to the child's life in the present. To invoke the wrath of God, hell's fires, and other forms of eternal damnation may scare the child out of cheating, but it may scare him into other things far worse.

Children who have few if any friends are likely to suffer with feelings of low self-esteem. Such children may find that "philanthropy" can gain for them an amazing degree of popularity. Doling out candy, money, small toys, and other gifts may make the difference between spending a lonely afternoon in the house and being one of the gang, if only as a follower. Such children often resort to stealing money from parents and siblings to support their charitable enterprises. Although purchasing friends in this way may temporarily relieve such children's loneliness and the associated feelings of worthlessness, they inwardly know that their friendships are specious, that they are dependent upon continual bribery, and that they are being exploited. Such awareness inevitably lowers feelings of self-worth.

It is important for therapists to impress upon such children that they are being taken advantage of and that those who play with them only for a price are not true friends. More important, these children must be helped to rectify those patterns that are alienating their peers in the first place and to replace them with modes of relating that will attract genuine friends. This will bring about the enhancement of their feelings of self-worth and lessen the likelihood that they will have to resort to bribing, a specious and compensatory method for self-esteem enhancement.

The mutual storytelling technique can provide the therapist with many opportunities to transmit messages related to the relationship between competence and self-esteem. When utilizing the technique, one can impart messages that encourage the acquisition of genuine proficiency, expose as spurious the ego-gratifications that are based on fantasy, and help the child clearly differentiate between patronizing flattery and genuine compliments. In addition, playing the game itself provides the child with genuine creative gratifications. While making up a story, the child demonstrates ingenuity, creativity, originality, and on occasion a sense of humor. These experiences also enhance self-worth.

Mark, a nine-and-a-half-year-old boy, was referred for treatment because of disruptive and hyperactive behavior in the classroom. At home he was difficult to manage and frequently uncooperative. Particular problems existed with regard to Mark doing his homework. He frequently refused to do it, and his parents' warnings and threats regarding the consequences of his not doing homework proved futile. He generally subscribed to the life philosophy: "I'll worry today about today, and I'll worry tomorrow about tomorrow." Another dictum by which Mark lived was: "I'll cross that bridge when I come to it." His parents' concerns and warnings about the future repercussions of his inattentiveness to his school work were continually of no avail.

Investigation into the background of Mark's difficulties did not reveal factors that I was certain were playing a role in his difficulties. The one factor that I considered possibly operative was the fact that his father had made significant contributions in his field, and Mark probably had the feeling that he could never reach his father's level of competence and renown. He didn't want to confront the fact that he might not achieve his father's level of competence. This reaction, however, was inappropriate because, if it were indeed justified, then all the children of distinguished contributors would end up academic failures. There are still many things to be done in this world and many ways of achieving a sense of competence. Furthermore, one need not be a superachiever or well known to lead a gratifying life.

During his second month of treatment Mark told a story that lends itself well to being divided into three parts. Accordingly, I will present each of the parts separately and describe what I considered to be its meaning.

> *Patient:* Well, once there was this farmer and he liked to plant all kinds of crops, and he raised chickens and cows and horses. He like to work out in the garden. He liked to feed the chickens and get their eggs.
>
> One day he took an egg out of underneath a chicken and the chicken bit him. And he didn't know what to do because the chicken never bit him before. So he sold the chicken to a man and this man got mad and he sold the chicken to another man. And this person that he sold the chicken to got mad and said he didn't want it. So he gave it back to him and that man gave it back to the farmer. And then that chicken died so he was kind of glad.

Generally, the protagonist of a story represents the patient. In this case, the patient depicts himself as a farmer. The other "protagonist" of this first part of the story is the chicken. The chicken lends itself well to representing a female in that it is the layer of eggs—the origin of life and a source of food. In this case, I considered the chicken to represent Mark's mother. This speculation is further supported by the fact that the chicken bites the farmer. I considered the biting to symbolize the mother's harping on Mark to do his homework. Mark would like to get rid of the chicken, that is, "get his mother off his back." But Mark, like all other human beings, is ambivalent in his relationship with his mother. A part of him would like to get rid of her, and yet another part of him recognizes that to do so would be a devastating trauma. The chicken, then, goes back and forth between Mark and two prospective purchasers. Selling the chicken involves some comfort with duplicity on Mark's part in that the farmer does not inform the buyer of the chicken's alienating defect (biting), which caused him to sell it. The buyer, presumably after being bitten himself, similarly exposes the bird to a third person.

The latter, equally dissatisfied, returns the chicken to the second who, in turn, gives the unwanted creature back to the original owner.

Having learned that one cannot so easily rid oneself of people who irritate us, the farmer utilizes a more expedient solution: the chicken conveniently dies. This solution, often resorted to in inferior novels, provides a quick solution to a complex problem. It is generally not particularly adaptive in reality because those who hound, persecute, and otherwise make our lives miserable generally do not die so conveniently. In fact, they often appear to live longer than those who treat us benevolently.

In addition, we are not told why the chicken suddenly decides to bite the farmer. All the farmer had done was to take an egg (equals love). The farmer is portrayed as innocent, as not having done anything to provoke this hostile act on the chicken's part. There is no consideration of the possibility that the farmer may have contributed to the chicken's behavior by some provocation or negligence, as is so often the case in reality. This segment of the story is also a statement of Mark's desire to solve the problem with the biting chicken (equals mother) by hostile acting out rather than by civilized discussion. Now to return to the second part of Mark's story.

> So he went along with his farming and when he was planting his crops—you know corn—in his cornfields, he found like a little, whatever you want to call it, stone. And he kept it because it was kind of pretty. So when he was keeping it, he kept it in his dresser, you know. And every time when he went out to work in his crops, he had the stone with him. He would put it in his pocket and every year he held that in his pocket the crops would come up just the way he wanted them to, and when he didn't have it with him something went wrong. So he always had the stone with him. And then he thought that it was a magic stone.

Here, the farmer finds a magic stone that brings him good fortune as long as he keeps it in his pocket. He need only keep the stone in his pocket and his crops will flourish; failure to do so causes them to "grow wrong." I considered this part of the story to be a manifestation of Mark's life philosophy that he need not exert any effort; things will somehow work out. He need not show any forethought or planning; somehow all will go well. He need not put in any effort to accomplish things in life, especially learning in school. He utilizes the magic stone to counteract the insecurity engendered in him by parental threats and to suggest that at some level he is fearful that things will not work out. The magic stone provides him with the power to bring about a favorable outcome without any effort on his part. Again, this is a maladaptive response to his school difficulties. And now to the third and last part of Mark's story. I include here the post-story discussion, which is also important if the therapist is to be certain about the meaning of a child's story.

And then one day when he was riding along in his wagon pulled by a horse, it went across the bridge and the wheel came off, you know. And the bridge started to crack. So he grabbed the stone and put it in his pocket and then just got up and walked across to the other side. And then he took the horse to the other side with him and the bridge fell out, you know. As soon as he took it [the stone] out of his pocket the bridge fell into the river. So he had to go and tell the people about it so they could put up a sign so nobody else could run into it. They put up a sign that said, "Bridge Out." And the townspeople paid to put up a new bridge.

And when the man found out that he lost the stone, he was very unhappy and like he didn't tell anybody ever that he had the stone. So one time he was walking along in the same spot that he found the crop. He found the stone again. And he always had good luck forever on.

Gardner: Tell me something. Is it true that it was because the man had taken the stone out of his pocket that the bridge fell down?

Patient: Yes.

Gardner: And that if he had kept the stone in his pocket the bridge would not have fallen down.

Patient: Right.

Gardner: What about the wheel of his wagon? Would that have broken had he kept—

Patient (interrupting): Well, the wheel broke and the weight of it pushed and cracked the bridge.

Gardner: I see, but it was because he didn't have the stone that the bridge fell down?
Patient: Right.
Gardner: And what's the lesson of that story?
Patient: If you've got something you believe in, you should try to hold on to it, like you know, not try to lose it. If you really believe in it don't you know, fool around with it.
Gardner: Okay.

Here, the farmer is riding a wagon. The wagon lends itself well to symbolizing an individual's feelings about his (her) ability to move along life's course. It is analogous to the automobile in this regard. A man, for example, has a repetitious dream in which his automobile is just sitting there with all four tires deflated. The dream is a statement of his sense of impotency with regard to his capacity to move along life's course. A neurologically impaired girl has a dream that she is driving her father's car and each time she puts her foot on the brake, the car doesn't stop. The dream reveals her feeling that she cannot "put the brakes on" her thoughts, feelings, and actions. In Mark's fantasy the wheel of the wagon "came off." This is a statement of Mark's sense of instability. It probably reflects his awareness, at some level, that his failure to work in school is compromising his capacity to move along life's course. Furthermore, it may relate to his parents' warnings that if he does not "shape up," his future will be a bleak one.

But it is not only the wheel that comes off; the bridge itself "started to crack." This is a statement of an even more profound sense of insecurity in Mark. The supporting structure under the wagon is also weak. The wagon on the bridge symbolizes Mark's view of his capacity to move along life's course. After all, the bridge connects one point to another and facilitates such progress. If the bridge breaks, one is stopped (at least temporarily) from moving along life's path. In short, the breaking of the wagon's wheel and the falling of the bridge depict Mark's belief that his world is falling away from under him. His difficulties at school and at home were interfering with his gaining a sense of competence in coping with life. In both the academic and behavioral realms he was not acquiring the talents and skills necessary if one is to feel confident and cope well with reality. In compensation for his feelings of inadequacy in these areas, he provides himself with a magic stone that protects him from the dangerous results of his incompetence. Furthermore, the magic stone fantasy is consistent with his life philosophy that somehow things will work out.

In the post-story discussion, I questioned Mark in order to be certain that I understood completely the facts of his story. If the therapist is not completely clear about the incidents in the story, he (she) is ill equipped to analyze it. And, of course, any stories that the therapist creates that derive from an incorrect rendition of the child's story are likely to be completely off point and of little or no therapeutic value. Just as Mark's story lent itself well to being divided into three segments, I divided my responding story into three segments, each of which corresponded to one of the patient's. This was the first of the three segments of my responding story:

> *Gardner:* Now I'll tell my story. The title of my story is "The Chicken and the Stone."
> Once upon a time there was a farmer and this farmer had a chicken and this chicken would lay eggs. And one day he went over to the chicken to get an egg, and the chicken bit him. He got very angry and he thought, "I know what I'll do. I'll get rid of this chicken. I'll sell this chicken to someone else." He also thought, "Maybe it will die. Then I won't have any problems with it."
> So another man came along and he said, "Would you like to buy a chicken?"
> And the man said, "Well, tell me about this chicken. Is she a good chicken? Is she kind? Does she bite?"
> The farmer said, "Well, she may bite."
> "Look," the man said, "I don't want a biting chicken."
> And the farmer didn't know what to do because there he was stuck with this chicken. He said, "Gee, I wish this chicken were dead."
> The second man said, "Look, here you have a chicken that's biting. You want to get rid of her. You want her to die. Is that the only way you know how to solve a problem with a biting chicken? You know, you can't solve life's problems by killing off or selling

off the people who are bothering you. You've got to work it out with them. You can't get rid of people so easily and you can't even get rid of biting chickens so easily. So I suggest that you try to figure out some way of solving this problem with the chicken.

Well, he talked to the chicken. (In my story this chicken talks.) And he found out that there were things he was doing that were bothering that chicken and that's why the chicken bit him. And when they were able to settle that problem, and he stopped doing the things that bothered the chicken, the chicken stopped biting him and then the chicken continued to lay many more eggs and he then no longer wished to get rid of the chicken, to sell her, and he no longer wished that the chicken were dead.

Whereas the first buyer in Mark's story gullibly buys the chicken without asking questions, in my story he inquires about the chicken's habits—especially whether she bites. I attempted thereby to communicate that buyers in reality may not easily be taken in by the seller's duplicity. I hoped to let Mark know that one doesn't easily get away with lying and in this way lessen his tendency to lie in order to achieve his ends. The farmer then tells the truth about this defect in the chicken. My hope here was that this honesty would serve as a model for the patient. Thwarted in his attempts to get rid of the malevolent chicken, the farmer expresses the wish that it die. Again, reality considerations reign and the chicken remains very much alive. At this point the buyer becomes more directly the transmitter of my healthier communications and adaptations. He advises direct inquiry into the difficulties in the farmer-chicken relationship in the service of resolving them in ways more civilized (discussion rather than hostile acting out) than those already attempted by the farmer.

Accordingly, the farmer invites the chicken to express his grievances ("In my story this chicken talks") rather than act them out with biting. The chicken does so and the problems are resolved. Because the patient's story did not specify the nature of the chicken's sources of irritation, I made only general reference to them. Had I wished to get more specific, I would have first asked Mark *why* the chicken bit the farmer. The information so gained could have served to provide me with specifics for my story. But I already had so much information to work with by the time Mark finished his complete story that I decided not to add any more material. Overloading can reduce the child's receptivity to the therapist's stories. My main message then was that if someone is hostile toward you, rather than trying to get rid of him (her) by separation or death, try to work out the problem through civilized inquiry and nonviolent action.

Whereas in Mark's story the potential purchaser refuses to buy a biting chicken, and then goes his way, my purchaser conducts an inquiry and provides advice. This is a common maneuver that I utilize in the mutual storytelling technique. It is one of the ways in which I provide my therapeutic messages. I wear many guises. Sometimes a passerby stops to watch the action and then, without any invitation on the part of the protagonists, enters into a discussion with them in the course of which he dispenses advice. Sometimes, unbeknownst to the participants, a "wise old owl" has been sitting on a bough of a tree watching the activities below. Then, at some judicious point, he (she) interrupts the proceedings and starts pontificating. Again, there is full attention and receptivity to everything the owl says. The protagonists "hang on every word." Sometimes I use a teenager for this purpose. The reader does well to recognize the value of the teenager in the treatment of young children. There is no one in the world who possesses more omniscience than the teenager. He knows everything and is in no way modest about his vast storehouse of knowledge of the world. The reader might be interested to learn that in the 30 years or so that I have been utilizing this technique, not once (I repeat *not once*) has the recipient of such gratuitous advice ever responded with a comment such as: "Listen, Buster, I would appreciate your not butting into our business. If I wanted your advice, I would have asked for it. And until that time comes, I'd appreciate your keeping your trap shut."

Now onward to the second part of my responding story, which, as mentioned, directs its attention to the second segment of the child's.

Now, one day this farmer was working in his cornfields and he found a very pretty stone. It was very shiny and very pretty.

And he said, "I wonder if this is a magic stone. I'd sure like to have a magic stone. My crops haven't been doing too well lately. So he rubbed the stone and he hoped that the crops would do better. But nothing happened. The crops were still poor.

But one day he was in town and he was in a general store buying provisions, and the owner of the store noticed that the farmer was rubbing the stone and holding it in his pocket. And he said, "What are you doing there?"

The farmer said, "Oh, that's my magic stone. That gives me luck."

He said, "Has it ever given you luck?"

The farmer replied, "Well, no, but I'm hoping it will make my crops better."

And the man in the store said to him, "Well, I never heard of a magic stone." He said, "What are you doing with your crops? Are you using any fertilizers and things like that?"

The farmer said, "Well, not really. I really don't believe too much in them. It's a lot of extra work putting in those fertilizers and it costs money.

And the man said, "Well, I think that the reason why your crops aren't doing well is that you're not taking care of them well enough. You're not putting in fertilizers." And he asked the farmer some other questions about what he was doing and it was clear that the farmer was not doing everything that he could. And the man in the store said, "Instead of rubbing a magic stone, I suggest you get to work on your farm and start taking good care of your crops. I think there's a better likelihood that they'll do well than if you rub a magic stone."

And the farmer thought about what the man had said and he decided to try him out. So he got the fertilizer and he started to work harder on his crops, and sure enough that year he had a better crop than he had ever had before. Well, although the farmer was impressed with what the storekeeper had said, he wasn't fully sure that the stone still wasn't magic.

In my responding story, the magic stone is not effective in improving the farmer's crops. No matter how much he rubs it, the crops remain weak and malnourished. My advice to utilize more realistic and predictably effective methods is transmitted through the owner of the general store. As I am sure is obvious to the reader, this is another one of the disguises that I utilize in my responding stories. The farmer is receptive to this advice and, although it works, he still does not give up hope that his stone will perform magic. We are generally more attracted to easy and quick solutions than to difficult and complex ones, and the farmer is not immune to this human frailty. It will take a more dramatic proof of the impotency of his stone to convince him of its worthlessness in controlling natural events. (See part three of my story below.)

The transcript does not provide the reader with information about the boy's facial expressions and gestures while I told my story. While relating the second phase of my story, the patient began to blink. I considered this a manifestation of the tension I was arousing in him with my statement that his fantasies of a magic solution to his problems were not going to be realized. Furthermore, he placed his right hand in a seemingly strange position, namely, as if he were holding a stone in it. His arm was flexed at the elbow and his fingers so positioned in cup-like fashion that he could very well have been holding a stone. I believe that his gesture was unconscious, and it reflected his need to "hang on" to the stone that I was symbolically taking away from him. It certainly provided me with confirmation that my story was indeed "hitting home" and touching on important issues.

I then continued and related the third part of my story:

> And on his farm there was a bridge that was somewhat old and weak, and he used to look at it and say, "I wonder if I should fix it up one of these days. Nah, I'll rub my stone. It will keep it going." So he used to rub his stone every time he'd pass that bridge in order to keep the bridge solid. But one day as he was riding his wagon across the bridge, a wheel broke and his wagon fell down and sure enough the bridge broke as well, even though he had his magic stone in his pocket. And there he was in the water—his horse jumping around very scared, the wagon broken even more than it had been, the farmer sitting in the water all wet, and his wagon broken even more, and the bridge completely crushed. And there he was with the magic stone in his pocket! And as he sat there, he realized that this stone really wasn't magic. Finally it took *that* to make him realize that it wasn't magical and that there's no such thing as magic. And after that he decided to

build a new bridge. He threw away the stone and he built a new strong bridge, and that was the end of his belief in a magic stone. And do you know what the lesson of that story is?

I interrupt the transcript here before the post-story discussion, which begins with the patient's response to my request that he provide the moral of my story. As is obvious, in my story I again attempt to drive home the point that the magic stone will not work. Just as the patient's third segment is basically a restatement of his second, in that in both the magic stone is used to assuage tension (induced by his parents' threats) and perpetuate his life philosophy that all will go well even if he doesn't put in effort, my third segment is basically a restatement of my second. Here, while I related my story, the patient involved himself in even more dramatic gesturing. Specifically, at the point where I described the farmer sitting in the water, after the bridge had broken through, the patient spontaneously began to rub "water" off his thighs. He then resumed the gesture of holding the stone. However, at the point where I described the farmer's throwing away the stone, the patient, without any prompting on my part, engaged in a stone-throwing maneuver. I wish to emphasize to the reader that there was no suggestion, either overt or covert, by me that the patient dramatize or in any way gesticulate the elements in my story. His spontaneous involvement in this way was confirmation that he was swept up in my story and that my message was being incorporated into his psychic structure.

As is my usual practice, rather than tell the moral myself, I generally ask the patient what he (she) understands to be the lesson of my story. In this way, I can often determine whether my messages have been truly understood, because a correct statement of the moral requires a deep appreciation, at some level, of the story's fundamental meaning.

This is the interchange that followed my question about the story's moral:

Patient: Don't count on something else to do your work for you.

Gardner: Right! That's one lesson. That's the lesson with the magic stone. What's the lesson of the part with the chicken and the egg and the biting?

Patient: You should fix your own problems now if you can, or else somebody else will fix them for you.

Gardner: Well, *that* and if you have a problem with someone, it's not so easy to get rid of the person.

Patient: Try to figure it out.

Gardner: Try to figure it out with them. You can't kill them off, you can't sell them generally. Human beings are not like chickens. You can't just sell them or kill them so easily. If you try to, you know, you'll get into a lot of trouble. So the best thing is to try to work the problem out with the person. The end. Wait a minute. I want to ask you something. Do you want to say anything about this story?

Patient: No.

Gardner: Did you like it?

Patient: Yeah.

Gardner: Any particular part?

Patient: The part where he found the stone and it was pretty and shiny.

Gardner: Uh huh. Any other part?

Patient: No.

Gardner: Did you learn anything from this story? Did this story-teach you anything?

Patient: No.

Gardner: Not at all?

Patient: Well, yeah.

Gardner: What does it teach you?

Patient: Well, you should kind of figure out your own problems and don't count on other people to do stuff for you.

Gardner: Okay. What about magic? What does it say about magic?

Patient: Magic—well, if you've got a magic stone make sure it's *really* a magic stone and then go counting on it. (laughs)

Gardner: Do you think there are such things as magic stones?

Patient: No. (laughs)

Gardner: I don't believe so either.

Patient: You can keep them as a good luck charm—as a pretty piece, but not as a magic stone.

Gardner: Do you think a good luck charm *really* brings good luck?

Patient: Hhmmm, not really.

> *Gardner:* I don't think so either. No. Okay. So that's the end of the program today. Goodbye boys and girls.

It is unrealistic for the therapist to expect that a single confrontation or story, or any other single experience in therapy, is going to bring about permanent change. Those who have conviction for time-limited therapy believe that this is possible, and they will attract patients who are gullible enough to believe this as well. If such rapid changes could indeed take place, Mark might very well say to me something along these lines: "Dr. Gardner, you're right. There's no such thing as magic. You've convinced me of that today. I can promise you that I will never again believe in magic. Now let's go on and talk about my next problem."

There are, of course, patients who say things along these lines. It is one of the more common forms of resistance and/or methods for ingratiating oneself to the therapist. In the real world, the world in which there is no magic, the best one can hope for at the outset is to introduce an element of ambivalence regarding the patient's belief in magic. And this is what I believe occurred here. The post-story discussion reveals some discomfort on Mark's part with my message, but also some receptivity to it. In ensuing stories there were statements of negation of magic ("There's no such thing as a magic stone"), which is not yet a manifestation of complete "cure" of the problem. True "cure" comes when there is no mention of magic at all. Doing and undoing is not the same as never having done at all. Mark did reach the point, however, about three or four months later, at which magic did not appear in any form whatsoever in his stories. It was then, I believe, that he reached a healthier level with regard to this problem.

* * *

Gavin, a six-year-old boy, came to treatment with chief complaints of poor school performance, disinterest in playing with other children, and generalized apathy. The patient's father had inherited a well-established business, and although in his thirties, he was basically a weak and inadequate person who was still quite dependent on his own mother. He had married an attractive woman because of the enhanced esteem he anticipated he would enjoy from such a beautiful wife. She was sexually inhibited, self-involved, and quite vain. Neither parent was deeply involved emotionally with the patient.

During his first session, Gavin told the following story. As mentioned, a first story in treatment, like the first dream in treatment, can be a rich source of information about a patient's underlying problems.

> Once I climbed a tree and fell down and then a bird flew down. It was pretty big and it lifted me up back into the tree. I fell down again. And that time it didn't lift me up, so I had to climb up myself.
> Then I went inside my house and said, "Ma, how come— Mommy, how come I always fall down from the tree?" And my mother said because the branches break too much.

The story clearly reveals Gavin's concept of his parents and his relationship to them. The father, as represented by the tree, cannot provide him with support. Each time he climbs the branches—the father's outstretched arms—they break and he falls to the ground. The bird—the mother—also attempts to hold him up, but she, too, is unsuccessful.

Accordingly, I told Gavin the following story:

> Once upon a time there was a boy and this boy loved to climb trees because when he was up at the top of a tree, he could see far away and he really felt big. Well, one day he was climbing a tree and the branch broke and he fell down. He got very upset and he thought: "I'd better be careful. Next time I climb a tree, I'd better test the branches and make sure that they are strong."
> Well, the next day he was trying to climb a tree and it looked all right and then he tested some of the branches and they weren't too strong, so he said: "Well, I'd better stay away from that tree." Then he got another idea: "I'll get a ladder." And he got a ladder and he climbed up the ladder and in this way he didn't have to step on the weak branches and he still got to the top.

Well, this boy gradually grew up and he found that he was so tall that he didn't have to stand on trees after a while because he could see what he wanted without it.

And the lesson of that story is that if a tree you want to climb has a weak branch, test it first. And if it won't hold you, then get a ladder. But know this also: everybody grows up and then they are big enough to see many things without having to climb trees.

In my story I attempted to help Gavin gain from his father the support that he was capable of providing by testing the branches. I encouraged him to use his own resources—the ladder—when his father was unable to gratify the child's needs. I also tried to offer him the hope and consolation that as he grew up he would be capable of doing more on his own and would thereby suffer less from the frustrations, feeling of impotence, and low self-worth engendered by his parents' inadequacies.

The Talking, Feeling, and Doing Game

There are many cards in *The Talking, Feeling, and Doing Game* that enable therapists to address themselves to competence problems. Whereas the mutual storytelling technique utilizes primarily *unconscious* communications, *The Talking, Feeling, and Doing Game* uses primarily *conscious* messages in the therapeutic interchanges.

* * *

Question: You've just written a book. What are you going to call it?

Response: First, before telling you about the title of the book and what's in it, I'd like to tell you how I feel when I have just finished writing a book. It's a very good feeling. Writing a book is a lot of hard work. It really feels great when it comes from the printer and I can look at that book and say: "Isn't that great. I wrote that book." It makes me feel great, just to look at it.

Now, with regard to the title of the book, let's say it's a book called *Trying to Help Children with Their Problems.* Notice that I said *trying* because psychiatrists can't be sure that they can help children with their problems. They can only try. The child must try as well. Children who don't try usually don't get help with their troubles.

Now, with regard to what I say in the book, the most important thing I would say would be that changing things is very hard. Sometimes it's scary. If you try to change things, you may often find that things get better. If you don't try to change things, they'll usually remain the same. I also say that people who believe that there are no troubles usually continue having them, whereas people who don't hide from the problems are more likely to change them.

First, I discuss with the child the ego-enhancement that comes from writing a book. Although it is a long labor, it is a "labor of love," and there is great ego-enhancement that comes after its publication. I then emphasize the importance of effort in the therapeutic process. Finally, I encourage desensitizing oneself to frightening situations and point out the self-defeating results of the utilization of denial mechanisms.

* * *

Question: Name three things that can make a person happy.

Response: I would say that one thing that could make a person happy is to do something very well. The person has learned how to do it well and can do it well. It's taken a lot of practice, but it makes an individual feel very good when he or she can do something very well after trying hard over a long period to learn how to do it. That would be one thing that would make a person happy.

A second thing—this would be for a parent—is to have a child who is getting the kinds of good feelings that I described first, that is, if you have a child who has a certain thing that he or she is interested in and has learned how to do well and has become accomplished in that particular thing. That can make a parent happy.

And the third thing: If a person takes care of his or her health, then it can help make the person feel good.

Feelings of competence and high self-esteem are intimately connected. Here, I not only provide this message for the child but elaborate on the further feelings of self-worth that come from the positive feedback from significant figures such as parents.

* * *

Question: Compare any two things in the whole world.

Response: I'm going to compare two boys. One has studied hard for a test and is taking it in the classroom. I'm going to compare him with another boy, who watched television the night before and who didn't study. The second boy is copying answers from the paper of the first. Both of them get an A on the test. I'm going to compare the feelings they have about their high grade. The first boy is proud of himself and when he goes home he tells his mother and father that he got an A. The other boy knows in his heart that he didn't really deserve the high grade. He doesn't particularly feel proud of himself because he knows that there is nothing to be proud of over getting an A when you've cheated. He doesn't show the paper to anybody. When his mother asks him what he got on the test, he tells her the high grade. When she praises him, he feels uncomfortable. He knows that he's cheated and that he didn't deserve the A. He also feels bad about himself for having lied to his mother.

The response obviously is applicable to the child who cheats on examinations at school. As mentioned, my approach to such symptoms focuses on the feelings of lowered self-worth that are often felt by such children. Unfortunately, there are many children with very weak consciences who suffer little if any guilt over such transgressions. Such a response may not prove particularly useful for such children. It does, however, introduce them to the phenomenon—a phenomenon that may have been totally outside their scheme of things. I also mention the lowering of self-esteem that is a concomitant of short-cuts and duplicitous ways of achieving a goal.

* * *

Question: A boy was laughing. What was he laughing about?

Response: This boy was not only laughing, but he was cheering. He was just jumping up and down with joy. He had just gotten his eighth grade report card and learned that he had gotten into three honors classes in the ninth grade. He was very happy. He had worked very hard in order to make the honors classes and had hoped that he might make one or two of them. But he didn't think that he would get into *all three*. He was very proud of himself and couldn't wait to get home and tell his parents. His teacher had written a note on the report card that said: "Robert, I am very proud of you. Good luck in high school." He was also very happy that he knew that, when he applied to college, having been in three honors classes would look very good on his record, and this would help him get into the college of his choice. And so he ran home from school laughing and singing all the way. It was really a happy day for him. What do you think about what I said about that boy?

This is the kind of response I provide for youngsters with low academic motivation. My purpose here is to enhance their school interest by demonstrating the joys and ego enhancement that are the potential benefits of such commitment to the educational process. Although the primary focus here is on the enhanced feeling of self-worth that comes from academic achievements, mention is also made of the further enhancement that comes from parental pride and reinforcement.

* * *

Question: What's the best story you ever heard or read? Why?
Response: Of all the books that I ever read when I was young, the one that I remember to have been the best was the one describing the life of Thomas A. Edison. As you probably know, Thomas A. Edison was one of the greatest inventors who ever lived. Although he wasn't the only man to work on these things, his inventions were important—giving us the electric light bulb, the phonograph, and the moving picture camera. He was a poor boy who grew up in Ohio. He was a very hard worker and was an extremely curious person. He was immensely interested in how things work.

He had a laboratory near his home in New Jersey, and it is said that he would sometimes work most of the night on his inventions. He loved learning about how things work, and he loved trying to figure out better ways of doing things. To this day, people all over the world use his inventions. To this day, he is remembered as having given humanity some of its greatest inventions. He must have really felt great about himself because of all the good he did for people all over the world. It was mainly his curiosity and his hard work that did these things both for himself and for others. It was Thomas A. Edison who said: "Genius is 1 percent inspiration and 99 percent perspiration." Do you know what that means?

Edison epitomized the gratification and fame that can come to someone who is strongly committed to the work ethic. I emphasize here the great benefit that can accrue to others from the efforts of a strongly motivated person. My aim is to engender some desire on the youngster's part to view Edison as an admirable figure worthy of emulation and inspiration. Obviously, one such message is not going to achieve this goal. However, the seed is planted, and with reiteration over time it is quite possible that Edison will become incorporated into the youngster's psychic structure and join with other introjects to serve as a model for identification and emulation.

COMPETENCE AND EXTERNAL REINFORCEMENTS

In the previous section I focused on the internal reinforcement that comes from gaining competence. There are those who claim that this should be enough and that efforts that focus on external rewards are somehow less worthy. My views on the subject are epitomized in the comment made by the boy who demonstrates proudly to his mother that he can now ride his bicycle without using his hands. His exclamation, "Look, Ma, no hands!" demonstrates some vital psychological principles. As he rides his bicycle, he is clearly proud of his accomplishment; not only can he ride his bicycle, but he can do so without using his hands. His hard-earned skill in so delicately balancing his bike is a genuine source of ego-enhancement to him. Real accomplishments and genuinely desirable attributes are the bedrock upon which feelings of self-worth are built. Without this foundation, feelings of security are at best shaky and are more likely pretense and delusion.

An additional element of psychological import in the boy's

boast relates to his need to communicate his accomplishment to his mother and to the implied anticipation of her praise and admiration. The long-sought-after attainment, the ego-enhancing deed, no matter how great a source of satisfaction it may be, cannot provide us with full gratification unless we can share the accomplishment with others and win some praise or other positive feedback. And the mother is the prototype of all future praisers.

Compliments not ultimately associated with concrete accomplishments can be ego-debasing. "What a fine boy" or "Aren't you a nice girl," stated when one cannot think of anything specific to compliment a child about, makes many children squirm. They sense that they are being "buttered up," and they are insulted as well, because the comment implies that the speaker thinks they are stupid enough to be so taken in. At some inner level the child responds, "The only reason he calls me a 'nice boy' is he can't think of anything *really* good to say about me." The net result of this is that a compliment designed to be ego-enhancing turns out to be ego-debasing. And this is the case with all patronizing and gratuitous compliments; they produce the opposite effect than what they were designed for. In contrast, when a youngster is told: "You play the piano beautifully. It's a pleasure to listen to you. You must play for Grandma and Grandpa when they come next Sunday. I know they'll thoroughly enjoy listening to you," or "What a good cake you baked," or "Great, a home run," the child stands a few inches taller.

The ideal attitude toward potential admirers should be to appreciate that one's primary source of pleasure and ego-enhancement can only be derived from the productive act itself. We should recognize that the praise of others can only be of incidental importance in this regard. It should not be our primary concern; it should not be our primary motive for initiating the activity; nor should we need praise so much that we are willing to engage in odious pursuits to attain it. Rather, the admiration and esteem of others should be the fringe benefit of our accomplishments. We need expertise in bike riding (and the adult derivatives of such childhood accomplishments) to provide us with genuine self-worth, and we need an admiring mother (and her surrogates in adult life) to give us further support, encouragement, and ego-enhancement.

The world is a far better place for such secondary sources of ego-enhancement. At the very time the reader is reading this paragraph, there are thousands (and possibly tens of thousand) of people in various parts of the world who are working diligently in the hope that some day they may win a Nobel prize. The vast majority are aware of the fact that the likelihood of their achieving this goal is remote, but its very existence enhances their efforts and provides immeasurable benefits to humanity. Actors and actresses are working for their Oscars. Television people aspire to win the coveted Emmy award. And there are the Pulitzer prizes, Olympic gold medals, Book-of-the-Month Club selections, and a host of other ways in which we praise and reward accomplishment. In school, as well, these external rewards are important. Grades and academic awards are the most common manifestations of this practice. Those who would do away with them are depriving children of important incentives.

Many years ago I saw a cartoon that demonstrates this point quite well. It depicted a golfer on a golf course. In the first picture he hits the ball way up into the air. In the second picture we see the ball falling directly into the cup. A hole in one! In the third picture he is jumping up and down with glee. In the next picture he looks to his right and sees no one. In the next picture he looks to his left and sees no one. By this time his facial expression has changed from joy to disappointment. In the last picture he is walking off the golf course, bag of clubs on his back, with a hang-dog, depressed expression. One can only imagine that if there were a squirrel or a bird who could share his joy with him and provide him with a well-deserved compliment, he would welcome it.

Whereas there are those who go to the extreme of scoffing at the value of external reinforcement, there are others who emphasize it too much. Many behavior modification programs are a case in point. In many such programs the child is routinely positively reinforced for good grades and negatively reinforced for bad grades. The negative reinforcement may take the form of removal of positive reinforcement. Such emphasis may result in the child's losing sight of the ego-enhancement that comes from the primary accomplishment. Furthermore, the world is not going to provide such external reward consistently. Accordingly, it ill equips the child to adjust adequately to adult life. Following graduation, the child may not continue learning for the inner gratification that it may provide because he (she) has never experienced it. Parents who set up a system in which the child, for example, gets a dollar for every A are also placing too much emphasis on external rewards. The ideal educational program focuses primarily on the internal gratifications and the enhanced sense of self-worth that come from learning. It places only limited focus on the external reinforcements.

PSYCHOTHERAPEUTIC APPROACHES TO EXTERNAL REINFORCEMENT ISSUES

General Psychotherapeutic Considerations

Many therapists are quite free with compliments. They consider them important to the course of treatment. I am particularly conservative with regard to compliments. I consider many therapists to be "going overboard" with them and, I believe, they do their patients more harm than good as a result of their free and often ingenuous use of them. There is no place in treatment for the backslapping, hail-fellow-well-met type who looks for every opportunity to compliment a patient, no matter how superficial and even meaningless the praise. As mentioned, the older the patient, the more likely he (she) is going to appreciate the meaninglessness of these compliments and find them patronizing and ego-debasing. They recognize that if there were genuine areas of competence to focus on the therapist would do so, and this substitute just "will not work." Accordingly, I am quite judicious with regard to bestowing compliments on my patients, regardless of age. However, when I do provide a compliment, it is based on a genuine accomplishment or an admirable behavioral

manifestation. Because they come so infrequently, they are trea-
sured by the patients and they are, I believe, more likely to be
genuinely ego-enhancing.

The Talking, Feeling, and Doing Game

This game can provide messages related to primary and
secondary reinforcement to learning. These vignettes from *The
Talking, Feeling and Doing Game* demonstrate how it may be used
to encourage academic pursuits for primary and secondary gratifications.

> *Question:* Make believe you're picking up an envelope that
> you find while walking down the street. There's a note inside, but
> no name on the front. You open it up. What does the note say?
> *Response:* Well, the note is from a teacher to a boy and it says,

> Dear Joey,
> I want to congratulate you on your very fine work during the
> last quarter. You certainly have improved. It's quite clear that
> you've been studying very hard. Your marks have gone up
> considerably. I am sure that you must be very proud of yourself on
> your fine performance. I'm certainly proud of you and I'm sure
> your parents, as well, are proud of you.
>
> > Your teacher,
> > Mrs. Jenkins
>
> That's what the note says.

My aim here is obvious. Patients to whom I provide this response
rarely receive such comments. My hope is that they will be
envious of the fantasized boy in my response who enjoys such a
comment.

* * *

> *Question:* Make up a lie.
> *Response:* Jimmy (substitute patient's name) is one of the
> proudest boys in his class. He's proud about his high marks, which
> make him feel very good—especially after he's worked a long time.
> He got mainly A's. He feels proud when a teacher compliments

him on a job well done. And he feels proud of himself when his parents get excited about his good grades.

One could argue that this response "rubs salt in the child's wounds." Although it might have this negative effect, it can also raise the child's appreciation of the pleasures to be gained by dedication to academic pursuits. It is only in the ensuing discussion that one can ascertain its effect on the child.

* * *

Question: What's something you could say that could make a person feel good?

Response: One thing you could say that could make a person feel good is to compliment the person on an accomplishment, that is, on something he or she did very well. For example, if a boy worked very hard making a model airplane, and it turned out very well and looked very good, then I'd say to him, "That's a beautiful job you did!" That would make him feel very good about himself. Or, for example, if a girl started the school year as a very poor student and then improved significantly, she would also feel very good if someone complimented her on her accomplishment. If, for example, she was spending a lot of time in the early part of the year goofing off and fooling around, then she wouldn't feel very good about herself. Let's say that she then begins to study much harder. After a lot of work over time, the teacher might say on her report card: "Congratulations, Sarah, you have really improved. Whereas you were once a pain in the neck because you never tried hard or did your homework, now it's a pleasure to have you in the classroom. It's a pleasure to be your teacher. You've really come a long way. Keep up the good work." Now that's the kind of thing that would make the girl feel good about herself. What do you think about what I've said?

When I congratulate a patient on an accomplishment, I generally focus my attention primarily on the deed or the act and direct the youngster's attention to the good feeling he (she) must be experiencing over the accomplishment. I secondarily mention other people who may be pleased over the patient's accomplishment and/or external rewards, such as high grades, certificates, awards, honors, etc. Also included here is the notion that hard work is necessary if one is to enjoy these benefits.

FURTHER COMMENTS ON COMPETENCE AND SELF-ESTEEM

I introduce my next point anecdotally. Many years ago I visited my son Andrew's junior high school in association with a parent-teacher's meeting. The parents made the rounds of the various classrooms that their children were attending and met with their teachers. I was quite pleased with Andy's teachers, but the one who impressed me most was the shop teacher. This was basically the message he gave to the group of parents:

> I want to tell you, first, that I don't know very much about theories of teaching. In fact, to be absolutely honest, when I go to teacher's conferences, I really don't understand what they're talking about at faculty meetings when they speak about educational psychology and philosophy. But I can tell you this: when a kid makes something here in the shop—something that he can be proud of—it really makes him feel good. (These were the days when there were no *hers* in shop class.) For example, if a kid makes a tree sign with the family name on it, and nails it up on a tree outside his house, he really feels good every time he walks down the path to his house and sees *his* sign there. It really makes him proud. If a kid makes a little lamp—I have one here (it looks like a water pump and every time you pull down the handle, a chain that is attached to it turns on the light)—he really feels good about himself when he sees that lamp sitting there in the house and when he sees people using it, it really makes him feel good about himself. . . .
>
> And let's say I have a kid who is shy and timid. What I do is make that kid a *monitor* for the whole row. It's his job to be sure that no boy leaves his row without cleaning up completely. His job is to inspect that row before anyone can leave, and he inspects every kid's work bench to be sure that it's completely spic and span before that boy has permission to leave the room. And the monitor works under my authority. When I give a shy kid this kind of job, it really makes him stand taller. It makes him feel better about himself. . . .

I want you to know that I run a tight ship here. In order to pass my course you've got to produce. Also, I've got to run a tight ship here because we have a lot of equipment that could be dangerous. We have electrical saws and drills here that could literally kill someone. So safety is *number one* here; I can't be lax in this room. The safety monitors, too, know that I mean business and there will be absolutely *no* horsing around in this shop. There is absolutely no running here. If a kid runs I boot him out for the day. And there's no wise-guy back talk either. These kids have got to know that I'm boss around here and that I won't put up with any wise-ass characters. . . .

Although some of this shop teacher's colleagues had Ph.Ds, I believe that he knew more about educational philosophy than most of them. This man was one of the most admired teachers in the school. He was the one, more than others, whom graduates would return to visit. This man knew about self-esteem and healthy ways to help youngsters deal with the inevitable feelings of low self-worth with which adolescents (like all people) suffer. He knew that competence and hard work are very valuable antidotes to feelings of low self-worth and provide healthy self-esteem. He knew that vigorous self-discipline—when humane and reasonable—is also ego-enhancing. This man was "building character"—something we don't hear much about these days. I am convinced that this man probably did more good for his junior-high-school students than most of the other teachers in that school. Years later, most of the graduates, I am convinced, remembered little of what they had learned in their academic subjects; but I believe that the living experiences that this man provided his students probably contributed to lifelong personality changes of far greater educational value.

As mentioned, we are living at a time when the self-esteem issue is very much in vogue. There is a plethora of books on the subject, and both schools and industry are hopping on the bandwagon. The encounter groups of the '60s and '70s are now being replaced by group meetings, the purpose of which is to provide ego-enhancement for the participants. Typically, the members are provided with a list of compliments to bestow upon one another and themselves. People repeat in litany-like fashion,

"I am a good person" and "I am special." In response to a canned compliment a participant is taught to respond, "I affirm you for being a good friend." Little is said about competence, diligence, and discipline. You are not what you do; you are what you and others say you are. This "stroking" is believed to bring about enhancement of self-worth. It doesn't matter what you do (or don't do); what's important is what you say about yourself and what others tell you about yourself. Talk about failures is nonexistent. Making distinctions between good, better, and best are also avoided. Everybody is equal, all are good, all are great, all are splendid. All are wallowing in nostrums. These gimmicks do not work. Phyllis Schlafly, president of the Eagle Forum (a politically conservative group whose politics I am generally not in agreement with), made this statement about the influence of the self-esteem cult on our educational system: "Instead of teaching them how to read, they are teaching kids to feel good about being illiterate." On this point, I am in 100 percent agreement with Ms. Schlafly.

NINE
COMPETITION

HEALTHY VS. UNHEALTHY COMPETITION

Competition and competence have some degree of overlap. In recent years, competition has been viewed by many educators and psychologists as a detrimental influence on personality development. Particular emphasis is given to the fact that those who lose in a competitive activity will suffer with low feelings of self-worth. I believe that this is a misguided view. I believe that proper discrimination has to be made between healthy and unhealthy competition. Success in competition can enhance self-esteem. We should not deprive those who succeed from the ego-enhancement that comes from that success, even though those who lose may experience lowered feelings of self-worth. Furthermore, healthy individuals do not suffer psychologically traumatic feelings of low self-worth when they lose; nor do healthy individuals turn into egomaniacs when they win. In healthy competition there is respect for one's competitor and the appreciation that it's "not the end of the world" if one loses.

In healthy competition one puts the competition into proper perspective and recognizes that it is of secondary importance to the primary *activity* (sports, art, writing, debate, etc.) into which the competitive element has been introduced. In unhealthy competition the primary aim is to degrade, humiliate, and even slaughter one's opponent. Denigrating and even destroying the opponent is "the name of the game." Certainly, we could very well dispense with unhealthy competition; but we should preserve healthy competition and make every attempt to derive what benefits we can from it. If not for healthy competition, we might still be living in caves; if not for unhealthy competition, many people would not have suffered severe physical and psychological trauma, and even premature death.

THE FUTILITY OF TRYING TO DISPENSE WITH COMPETITION ENTIRELY

Many schools in recent years have tried to remove competition entirely. There are "noncompetitive" schools and "noncompetitive" camps. I place the word *noncompetitive* in quotes because I do not believe that they genuinely can be so. I believe such attempts are naive and predictably will fail. When students in these situations still demonstrate competitive strivings, in spite of the allegedly noncompetitive atmosphere, the administrators claim that these children have been so imbued by society to be competitive that their own attempts to provide a healthier atmosphere have proven futile. I disagree. I believe that competitive strivings are locked into the genetic structure of the human animal. All other forms of life are in active competition for survival. Darwin said it well: "Survival of the fittest" is the basic law of evolution. One need just sit in one's favorite spot and look around and think about what's going on and one will see immediately how competition is one of the fundamental principles of nature. As we sit on the seashore admiring the beauty and peacefulness of the scene, we know quite well that the seagulls are not flying around for our aesthetic gratification. Rather, they are looking for food in order to survive. Throw some bread crumbs toward them and they will flock around, viciously competing with one another for the food. Or they will make a nose dive into the ocean in order to pluck whatever little fish is unfortunate enough to have been viewed from above. And the fish there are not floating around simply for the benefit of the seagulls. At the same time that they are avoiding being cannibalized by the bigger fish, they are looking around to cannibalize the little ones. And so it goes up and down the animal kingdom. Plants compete in other ways, but competition is nevertheless the rule of the world.

Although we humans need not utilize our competitive strivings in the service of murdering one another, we certainly have residua of such strivings that can be put into healthy channels. The ego-enhancement that comes from winning the race, reaching the top of the ladder first, or excelling over others in a wide variety of humane and civilized endeavors can be an important source of human enhancement, and, if directed in healthy ways, a source of great social benefit. We need not destroy one another, or even be insensitive to one another, in order to gain the physical and psychological benefits to be derived from a civilized utilization of the genetically programmed competitive strivings that exist within all of us.

One patient of mine attended a Quaker school that prided itself on being noncompetitive. Even the coaches were warned that the youngsters should be encouraged to play games for the fun of it and not to concern themselves with winning or losing. Unfortunately, this created problems when the Quaker school was playing against other schools in various sports. In these schools, just the opposite was occurring, namely, the youngsters were being imbued with a "fighting spirit" and were being encouraged by their coaches to "get in there and win." An adolescent patient of mine was on the schools's basketball team and described this pep talk given by the coach:

> Now listen you guys. What I'm telling you now is just between us. I don't want you to breathe a word of this to the people upstairs in the classrooms. When you get out there on the court, I want you to wipe up the floor with those guys. I want you to burn their asses off. I want you to beat them into the ground.

Although one might take issue with this coach's use of

language, and although one might say that he is going a little too far, I believe that his is basically the healthier approach to competitive sports. I am not saying that only fiercely competitive sports are healthy. I certainly believe that one can engage in sports "just for the fun of it," without concerning oneself with who wins or loses, and still gain healthy competitive and ego-enhancing gratifications. I also believe, however, that fiercely competitive sports can be psychologically healthy too – if put in proper perspective. Encouraging these boys to play their best in their basketball games is not encouraging them to be fiercely competitive in any other aspect of their lives, nor does it necessarily teach them to be insensitive to their opponents and/or all human beings whom they may encounter.

An excellent example of many of the principles presented in this section on self-esteem is to be found in Holmes's (1964) book on adolescent psychotherapy. Dr. Holmes has graciously given me permission to quote the following material from his book.

> At the outset I had very few doubts about how the recreational therapy program should work. Miss B, who was then in charge of girls' "RT," proposed that they all be required to attend a weekly swimming class, and I confidently advised her that this would be unwise. "All people," I explained, "have an inherent phylogenetic dread of water," and we could logically expect this to be pathologically exaggerated in mentally ill persons. (The reader will understand that the recollection of this incident worked upon me a distinctly emetic effect.) Swimming was declared an optional activity and failed after several weeks of trial because none of the girls attended.
>
> A similar plan for instructing the boys in the fundamentals of various physical skills was proposed by Mr. K, director of "RT" for the boys. I pointed out to him the need for emphasizing the recreational aspects of this activity, and further urged that competition and score-keeping be omitted in order not to intensify the low estimation in which our patients already held themselves.
>
> The "RT" staff strove conscientiously to carry out the program as it had been precisely and asininely defined, but in spite of their best efforts the patients refused to cooperate. They were scornful, rebellious, and utterly perverse in their refusal to have

fun while discharging their pent up aggressive energy. It was all very disappointing, and once again I reminded myself that one could hardly expect more from sick, delinquent youngsters. They were told they needed the exercise, and we tried to convince them of the therapeutic value of having a good time. Although they were rather casually required to attend the regularly scheduled daytime "RT" sessions, individual patients who were unusually "threatened" by fear of physical injury or competition were frequently excused.

A few months after the opening of the service, I began to hear disturbing reports from several of the boys about how things were being changed in "RT." Jerry, a 15-year-old delinquent boy, explained in persuasive detail his reasons for refusing to attend the activity any longer. He explained that it wasn't fun any more. For the past three weeks, five days per week, they had done nothing but figure-eight basketball drills, shooting practice, and running laps. Mr. K, Jerry observed, was a "mean bastard" who gave them neither praise nor respite. He was routinely requiring each boy to run an additional lap for each deliberate "mistake" made during drill and was holding them overtime, making them late for dinner whenever the entire group lagged in completing the day's exercises.

Calisthenics, deep knee bends, and push-ups were required for warming up at the beginning of each hour. And to make matters even worse, Mr. K had started coming up on the ward before each period for the applying of firm, personal, though unobtrusive pressure on each of the boys to attend.

It was a grim picture indeed, and in light of Jerry's proved capacity for revising reality to suit his convenience, there was little reason to believe it could possibly be true. I spoke with Mr. K about it, and he modestly confirmed every detail of Jerry's account. It seemed to me that no great harm had been done, so I advised him to "ease up on the patterning approach and get back to recreation."

But, as it developed, there are some things too great for the human soul to endure—cruelty to children being one of them. Mr. K stood firm and courageously defended his approach without benefit of theoretical rationale. He simply insisted that "it's better for them."

We called in the head nurse, and she confirmed my suspicions that for the past several weeks the number of complaints from the boys about the "RT" sessions had increased markedly. However, she also noted that attempts to refuse the activity had fallen almost to zero. I decided to see for myself, and it was immediately apparent that Jerry had understated his complaints. After they had finished their grueling workout, I finally saw what I had long since despaired of ever seeing. The boys left the gymnasium perspiring, panting, and bone-weary. They complained lavishly and in chorus. They were bright-eyed, square-shouldered, and flushed with pride in the aftermath of battle. The evidence was incontestable.

From that moment on, "cruel regimentation" became the official guiding policy, and "recreation," in this area at least, gave way to physical education.

Explaining the psychological rationale for this paradoxical reaction was a simple matter, after the fact. Mr. K was advised to proceed according to his own judgment, with the added assurance we would be happy to provide the theoretical explanations for his successes after he had accomplished them.

Since then problems centering around the "RT" program have been isolated and infrequent occurrences. The physical education program, like the school, functions without a respectable rationale which can dignify it as therapy. The boys follow a year-round schedule of coaching in tackle football with full equipment, basketball, boxing, baseball, and track. Each of these endeavors requires *many consecutive weeks of monotonous drill, all without a prospect of immediate reward*. When they have acquired sufficient skill and strength to qualify for competition the boys are forthwith subjected to the "threat" of winning or losing. The approach has provided them with an *earned and well-deserved* sense of masculine accomplishment.

The physical education program for the girls also emphasized the teaching of physical skills, although it is not nearly as demanding as for the boys. Basketball, swimming, volleyball, modern dance, and choral music are stressed. Periodic courses in some of the fundamental do's and don't's of hairstyling, cosmetics, clothing, bearing, and posture are also included.

Despite their symphonic complaints the patients are as a group more dedicated to these activities than are the staff. They understand and readily accept the idea that intercurrent psychological symptoms are insufficient cause for their failing to fulfill this obligation to themselves.

Knowing how to deal well with competition is crucial if one is to survive in the real world of adult life. And teaching children healthy competition is one of the goals of the educational system.

Schools, in recent years, appear to have lost sight of their important role regarding competition. In many schools grades are dispensed with, comments that compare one child to another are considered *verboten,* and a whole system of euphemisms has sprung up, the purpose of which is to protect children from the allegedly ego-debasing effects of competition. The fact that some people's self-esteem is lowered when they do poorly is no reason to deprive those who do well of the ego-enhancement that comes from accomplishment. It is a disservice to the high achievers because they are deprived of the enhanced self-esteem that comes from their accomplishment, and depriving them of this positive feedback might very well lessen their motivation to keep up their high levels of attainment. And depriving the less successful of information about their poorer standing deprives them of the opportunity to correct their deficits and possibly to move into areas where they could become more successful.

PSYCHOTHERAPEUTIC CONSIDERATIONS

Many child therapists have traditional board games available for utilization in therapy with children. I am very dubious about the basic therapeutic value of most of these instruments. I am not claiming that they have no therapeutic benefit at all; only that they are of limited therapeutic value and that most of the other instruments and approaches described in this book are much more efficient. One cannot deny that, while playing a traditional competitive board game with a child, many aspects of the child's personality will be revealed without the child's appreciating what is happening. A child's reactions to winning and losing, how competitive a child is, if a child is prone to cheat, if a child plays aggressively or passively, and if the child shows forethought and planning may be revealed in the course of playing the game (Gardner, 1969d, 1986a, 1986b). Games may also be fun and therefore therapeutic in their own right, in that pleasure is generally therapeutic. These benefits notwithstanding, the disadvantages of the utilization of these games generally far outweigh their advantages. The actual time during which useful information is being gained about the child often represents an extremely small fraction of the therapeutic session. The rest of the time is just spent playing a game. When most of the other instruments described in this book are utilized, there is often a higher frequency of meaningful material provided.

For many therapists the utilization of traditional competitive board games is essentially a "cop out." They require little therapeutic talent or skill, and the therapist can rationalize that useful therapy is being accomplished when, in actuality, all the therapist is doing is whiling away the time. Obviously, more uncooperative and inhibited children are likely to be engaged by such instruments. The hope of some therapists is that after some period spent on this relatively low-key activity, the child will be groomed for deeper, more introspective treatment. The danger of such an approach is that after many months, and even years, this goal may never be reached (the usual situation). Other more predictably successful resistance-reducing approaches (mentioned throughout this book) might have been utilized with a better chance of a positive therapeutic outcome. Play therapy should be much more *therapy* than play. The use of these games is often much more *play* than therapy (Gardner, 1986a).

The mutual storytelling technique and its derivative games, as well as *The Talking, Feeling, and Doing Game,* share in common the utilization of competition. They differ from the aforementioned traditional games in that embedded within the game structure are mechanisms that enhance the likelihood that the child will provide meaningful psychotherapeutic material. The likelihood of obtaining such material from the aforementioned traditional games is very small. The therapeutic benefits are peripheral and incidental to such traditional board games. The therapeutic benefits of the games I describe in this book are central to them. Recognizing that children enjoy immensely playing board-type games, especially those in which there is a competitive element, this series of games was devised. These games involve traditional board-game materials, such as dice, reward chips, and playing pawns. The introduction of the reward chips serves to enhance children's motivation to provide projective material. Whereas in the mutual storytelling technique no rewards are provided, in these games token chips are given, and the winner (the person who has accumulated the most reward chips) receives a prize.

Although reward chips are given, it would be an error for the reader to conclude that these games represent a kind of "behavior modification." These games share with behavior modification the use of reward chips, but the similarity ends there. In behavior modification one uses rewards in order to change behavior at the manifest level. Behavior therapists differ with regard to their views about the presence or absence of unconscious processes and whether, if present, they play a role in symptom formation. But they are in agreement in not generally giving significant attention to unconscious processes in the therapeutic process. Many take the position that the symptom is basically the disease and its removal represents a cure.

These games make use of the competitive element. Basically, I am using competition to enhance the child's motivation to acquire chips. However, as is obvious, the purpose of the game for the therapist is not to acquire chips, but to facilitate the elicitation of psychodynamically meaningful material for psychotherapeutic utilization. Children, however, may very well believe that the purpose of the game is to "win" and to accumulate as many· chips as possible. I am happy to have them believe that, especially because if they realized what was really happening, they might not provide me with important therapeutic material. When playing these games the therapist should do everything possible to keep the competition at a healthy level. Ideally, the patient and therapist will be so swept up in the game that both will forget whose turn it was and who was to get the reward chip. But even when this ideal is not reached, the therapist should strive to make the game so exciting that the child will frequently forget that it was his (her) turn.

If the child does become excessively competitive, then this behavior should become a point of departure for a psychotherapeutic interchange, whether directly verbal or within the context of the game per se. These games, then, provide the therapist with vehicles for providing competitive messages within the context of the game, as well as providing children with living experiences (in the course of the actual game playing) that can teach them healthier utilization of competition. If the child, for example, while playing *The Talking, Feeling, and Doing Game,* steals a couple of chips or moves the playing piece a few spaces forward, I might say, "You know, it's no fun to play with someone who cheats. If you're going to cheat I'm not going to play this game with you." This comment provides this child with the living experience that cheating is alienating and that doing so might result in a discontinuation of what might otherwise have been a pleasurable activity. For the child who was receptive to some further, more insightful discussions, I might say, "I wonder whether you do this with the children who come to your house? Do you think this is one of the reasons why they don't want to play with you?" The comment here directs itself to the child's symptomatic behavior at the manifest level. It does not go into any of the underlying psychodynamics for the cheating, psychodynamics that are very likely to deal with self-esteem problems. For the rare child who is analytically oriented, I might try to enter into a discussion in which these underlying factors might be discussed.

Clinical Example

The way in which the mutual storytelling technique was useful in the treatment of a child with problems related to competition is demonstrated by this vignette.

Linda came to treatment at the age of seven-and-a-half with the chief complaint that she was refusing to go to school; when she would go, it was only after much coaxing and sometimes bribing by her parents. There was no evidence for a separation anxiety disorder in that she had absolutely no fear of going to school. There was a deliberate passive-aggressive quality to her refusal, and this obstructionism exhibited itself in other areas of her life as well. For example, she often did not answer when spoken to; rather she sat motionless with a blank stare. Linda was not autistic, however; the unresponsiveness was clearly obstructionistic. She resisted cooperating in the home in many areas. She refused to eat at times and would not go to sleep when her parents requested that she go to bed. She was ever fighting her parents when they requested she participate in household chores.

A problem that was a significant source of irritation and alienation to both teachers and classmates was her practice of "splitting hairs" over minor issues. She would frequently point out the smallest errors made by her friends and family. She was a bright child, but was clearly using her intelligence as a weapon. Because she was only seven-and-a-half, she did not have the repertoire of information to do this successfully in more sophisticated areas. Accordingly, she focused on everyday and matter-of-fact issues. And, when she detected an error, or even suspected that an individual had made an error, she was quick to denigrate the person and correct them in a condescending way. Her peers were so put off by this that she had no friends, but she did not realize that it was this pattern that was alienating them. This was a pattern of her father's as well, and he was similarly denying its alienating effect. He was a bright man and he considered his alertness to other's defects a sign of intellectual superiority. Last, Linda had an aloof quality that further alienated her peers. Linda told this story while playing the mutual storytelling game during her third month of treatment:

> *Patient:* Once upon a time there was this king who wanted to be very famous, so he decided to conquer a lot of places so he could rule over a lot of lands so people would like him. The people didn't like to have that king. The people didn't like the king because he conquered so many places. The king thought they wanted him to conquer more places and then they would like him and so he conquered many more places, but they still didn't like him. And he got mad because the people wouldn't—um—didn't like him and he decided to—um—he said that they would have war and whoever won—if he won—he and his army won—the people would have to kind of do what he said because . . .
>
> *Gardner* (interrupting): This is a war between him and his army on one side and the people on the other?

Patient: Yeah.

Gardner: Okay. And if he won the people would have to do what he said.

Patient: And so they had a war, but he had conquered so many places and all the people wanted to get rid of him and all the people together were more than he and his army so those people won. And so the king decided to think of another way to make himself famous so the people would like him because he wanted to make himself famous. So he uh—I have to think of some more?

Gardner: Uh hmm.

Patient (after a short pause): He decided there was a person who was famous. He got him and said he would kill him so then he would be famous instead of the man. The people didn't let the king kill the man and so, well, the king found out it was no use trying to make himself famous. So he had another war and this time he got more people on his side, and the king even got his army on his side, but the people won the war again. So he decided to quit trying to make himself famous. And that's the end.

Gardner: And the lesson?

Patient: The lesson? I don't know if there's a lesson in this story.

Gardner: What could the lesson be now? This story, like all stories, has a lesson.

Patient (after a long pause): I can't think of it.

Gardner: Well, what was this king trying to do?

Patient: To make himself famous.

Gardner: Why was he trying to make himself famous? How was he trying to accomplish this?

Patient: He made war and he threatened the people, and he . . .

Gardner: And what finally happened to him?

Patient: He couldn't become famous.

Gardner: Because he lost the wars.

Patient: Yeah and the people didn't let him kill the man.

Gardner: I see. He hoped by killing this man who was famous that he would become famous.

Patient: Yeah.

Gardner: Hmmm.

Patient: This man was famous.

Gardner: I see. Then how would he become famous by killing a famous man?

Patient: Hmmm. He said like if he killed a famous man he would be famous in place of him.

Gardner: I see. What does the word *famous* mean to you?

Patient: What it means is what it means.

Gardner: Well, what is famous? Let's say there was a boy who did not know what it meant or a girl and they said to you, "What does famous mean?" What would you say?

Patient: Well, like people knew him and said he was great. He was great.

Gardner: People think you're great. Okay. Well, thank you very much. That was a very good story. Now it's time for my story.

I believe that the story reveals Linda's attempts to enhance her feelings of self-worth. The king, who of course symbolizes Linda, wants to be well liked. He wants to be famous and he tries various maneuvers to bring about this state of affairs. He tries conquering people, but this doesn't bring about the esteem that he wants. It brings about defeat and it incurs the further hatred of the defeated. He then plans to kill a famous man and in some way replace him; but this plot is thwarted. The story ends with the king's resigning himself to the fact that he is not going to be famous.

The story reflects Linda's situation in that she, like the king, tried to gain attention and enhanced self-worth by putting other people down by splitting hairs or by trying to point out their errors on minor points. It revealed some awareness on Linda's part that this maneuver was not going to work very well, that people were not going to allow her to subjugate them, and that even if she were to succeed in subduing others, it would still not gain her love and affection. However, her repertoire did not include other options for enhancing self-worth, and this is the important element in the story. The king resigns himself to the fact that he cannot gain affection. The mutual storytelling technique can be quite useful for introducing salutary options, options not considered by the patient. The story I told in response attempts to do this.

Gardner: Once upon a time there was a king and he thought that it would be very nice to be famous, that is, it would be very nice if everybody thought he was great. And, in addition, he thought it would be nice if everybody liked him. So he decided that he would conquer many lands and conquer many people.

Well, he had a large army and he was successful in doing this. He was able to conquer a lot of people. But when he would visit the lands that he had conquered, instead of everybody cheering for him, they either didn't show up at all or, when they did show up, they would hiss and boo. They wouldn't clap and they would call him bad names. And this made him very sad. So he said, "Maybe I haven't conquered enough lands. Maybe if I get more lands and I conquer more people, maybe then I'll be liked and everybody will think I am great." So he conquered more lands and more people and he was very sad to find that the same thing happened—that people still didn't like him.

So then he went to a very famous man and he said, "That's the way I'll be famous. I'll kill this famous man. This is a great man. He's liked by everybody. If I kill him then I'll be famous." So he went to this famous man.

Patient: (mumbles)

Gardner: Pardon me. Were you going to say something?

Patient: Oh, nothing.

Gardner: "Yes. I'll kill him and then I'll be the famous one instead of him." So he went to this famous man, and he went into his house, and he went over to him and he said, "I'm going to kill you."

And the famous man said, "Well, why do you want to kill me?"

He said, "Because you're so famous. If I kill you, then I'll be famous in your place."

And the man said, "I can't stop you from killing me. You have an army and I certainly couldn't protect myself. However, I think you're making a mistake."

And the king said, "Why is that?"

The man said, "Because if you kill me you still won't be famous. You won't be liked by everybody and you won't be great."

The king said, "Why not? Then there would be nobody else. You're the most famous and well-liked person in the world."

And the man said, "Yes, I am one of the most famous and well-liked people, not in the world, but certainly among all the people around here in all these lands. One reason for that is because I'm nice to people. I do things that are good, and the people like the things that I do. You have the idea that the way to be liked by people is to conquer them, to suppress them. Do you know what *suppress* means?

Patient: No.

Gardner: To get the better of them, to push them down, to be their boss, or to be able to threaten them, or to be able to rule them. He said, "You think that's the way to get people to like you or to admire you, or to think you're great or to be famous." He said, "That's not the way. If you kill me you won't be famous; you won't be great; people won't like you. They'll still hate you. They'll hate you because you're cruel to them. One of the reasons that people like me is because I'm nice to them—it's as simple as that—and if you kill me they're not going to think you're great."

Well, the king was quite surprised when he heard that, and he realized that he had been trying to get people to like him by putting them down all the time, and threatening them, and conquering them. Do you know what *conquer* means?

Patient: Yeah, like . . . um . . . having more by taking the country and ruling them.

Gardner: Right.

Patient: So he could rule over it.

Gardner: Right. He thought that that was the way to get people to like him. And he said to the wise man—he said to this famous man—"You know, you're wise. You've got the right idea and I never realized that before. I'm going to spare your life. I'm not going to kill you because you have given me information that can be very helpful to me, and if it works I'm going to reward you."

Anyway, the king went out and he went down to the people and he said to them, "I've been making a terrible mistake. I've been trying to get you to like me by trying to be more powerful than you, by trying to conquer you, and I realize now that that has been a terrible mistake. And I'm going to try to get you to like me by doing good things. I'm going to try to help you people. I have a mighty army. I have a lot of money and I'm going to try to help you people because so many of you are poor."

So the king started to do very good things with the people and he tried to make them happier and healthier. He tried to do good things so their lives were better. And then the people started to like him because he did nice things for them.

And one day he went to that famous man and he said, "You have given me some very helpful advice and as a reward I'm going to make you my chief adviser." Do you know what an adviser is?

Patient: A person who tells the king. He gives advice and he suggests things to him.

Gardner: Right. Right! He said, "Whenever I have any troubles or problems I'm going to ask you to help me because I have great respect for what you have to say." And he invited the man to live with him on the palace grounds as one of his closest associates, as one of his chief advisers. And it was truly then that the king became well liked. People admired him. They respected him and they considered him to be a great king. And that's the end of the story.

Do you know what the lesson of that story is?

Patient: Hmm. What?

Gardner: Try to figure it out. What's the lesson of that story?

Patient (after a long pause): That you can't make yourself famous by ruling – by being boss of people, and ruling over a lot of things and places.

Gardner: Right. And how can you make yourself liked and famous?

Patient: If you do things that people like and if you help the people?

Gardner: Hhmm. Now do you think this story has anything to do with you?

Patient: I don't really know. I don't think so.

Gardner: Think a minute more. Do you think there's anything about this story that is in any way like you.

Patient (after a short pause): I can't think of anything.

Gardner: Do you think that you are in any way like the king in your story?

Patient: I don't know.

Gardner: Let's see what your mother has to say. (Therapist directs attention to mother.) Do you think she is any way like the king in her story?

Patient's mother: A little bit. Yes, because she doesn't try to be nice to the people around her. She gets angry at them.

Patient: Which people?

Patient's Mother: Your mommy, your daddy, your brothers.

Patient: Well, they're always bothering me.

Patient's Mother: You do, but you should, you know, there's always going to . . .

Patient (interrupting): But the people didn't bother the king.

Patient's Mother: Oh, I see. That's how it's different. But if somebody bothers you a little bit, you shouldn't really turn around and hit them hard. Of course, if somebody is joking. If you are teased a little, especially if it's your younger brother, you shouldn't get angry at him and turn around and hit him.

Gardner: Well, I say that you're like the king in that you try to get the best of people by correcting them a lot. That's one way that you do it. When you say "not exactly" so often, you know, or "Well, that's not exactly right," I think that's one way of putting people down and trying to get the best of them. Do you think you do that?

Patient: I don't know.

Gardner: Well, that's one of the things that I see you do, that you try to get the better of people and you put them down and correct them a lot, and tell them that they're wrong in the little things that they say. And I think you have the idea that people are going to think you're kind of smart or something and that they'll like you more. Is that possible?

Patient: What? No.

Gardner: Well, that's how it looks to me. And what happens is that people just like you less. Anyway, the point I am making is that some people do things in which they think that people are going to like them more—like this king in your story was trying to get people to like him more by conquering more lands, and it ended up with their liking him less. And in my story he learned from the wise man that what he was doing to get people to like him more, that is, by conquering them, was only getting him to be liked less, and that the way to be liked more is to do likable things—to do things that people will really like you for—not to try to conquer them or get the better of them. Now do you understand the moral, the lesson?

Patient: I understand the lesson, yes.

Gardner: What is it? Just repeat it so I'm sure you understand it.

Patient: That if you conquer a lot of lands and you rule over a lot of things you won't be famous.

Gardner: Uhmm. And what is the way to be famous in life?

Patient: To help other people.

Gardner: Uhmm. Right. That's one way. Correct. Okay, that's the end of our program today. Anything else you want to say?

Patient: No.

Gardner: Okay. Good-bye everybody. Do you want to say good-bye?

Patient: Good-bye.

In my story I introduce an alternative way of gaining affection from people, mainly by acting benevolently; I suggest that if one does this, there is a greater likelihood that one will be admired and loved. It could be argued that all I am doing here is encouraging the patient to suppress her resentment and to act benevolently, and in this way gain affection. There is a certain validity to this argument. However, I was encouraging the patient at other times to express the resentments that she felt more directly rather than split hairs and criticize. The argument that conscious control, repression, and suppression of symptoms are antitherapeutic and solve nothing is not valid. As discussed, they may play an important role in therapeutic change.

I believe that one of Linda's fundamental problems was that of low self-esteem. She was angry and frustrated over the fact that she wasn't getting affection from others, and this only brought about a further lowering of her feelings of self-worth. If she were to utilize maneuvers that would gain her genuine affection, it could result in her being less angry. In addition, more attention from friends could enhance her self-image. Accordingly, such suppression could lessen the underlying problems that originally brought about the symptom. In other words, even though she might begin acting benevolently in a somewhat artificial way, she might learn that this method might gain more benevolence and affection from others than by subduing them. This could make her feel better about herself, that is, raise her self-esteem. More friends could also result in her becoming less angry. Because anger lowers self-esteem (when one feels angry one doesn't feel good about oneself), its reduction can be ego-enhancing. Suppression therefore might result in the interruption of Linda's vicious cycle. Even though the interruption started with conscious control and suppression, it can result in permanently healthy adaptations.

The story certainly lends itself to additional interpretations, which are not necessarily contradictory in that more than one theme can be woven into the same story. The king might represent the patient's father, whom she views as a subjugator. As mentioned, the father used his intelligence and knowledge as a weapon for degrading others, and this was where the patient probably learned this technique. The first half of the story then is basically saying to the father that his subjugation of her would only result in hatred of him. It was difficult to say how much of the father's pedantic hair-splitting was directed at the patient. It is probable that some was, but that most was directed toward adults (more ego-enhancing foes to conquer). It is safer to say, however, that the patient was observer to her father's use of knowledge as a weapon and could not but believe that some of his hostility would be directed toward her. In the service of focusing on one theme, and thereby increasing the likelihood that my responding story would be received, I did not focus specifically on this aspect of the patient's story.

The transferential element is also to be seen in the story. The wise man might very well represent me. She is ambivalent toward me. Part of her would like to destroy me, possibly because she views me as a potential subjugator, like her father. But this would be a speculation. The story merely describes the wise man as someone who is famous and whose fame can somehow be acquired if he is replaced by another. However, "the people" prevent the king from killing the famous man. I suspect here that there is a part of her that would like to preserve me. I dealt with the transferential issue by having the king in my story show great respect for the famous man—so much so that he ultimately engages his services as a residential trusted adviser.

At the end it was clear that the patient appreciated (at least intellectually) what I was saying and on two occasions, both at the time of the completion of my story and at the time of the post-story inquiry, was able to state accurately what the moral of my story was. However, she did not appear to be consciously aware that the story related to her, and when this was suggested by me and by the mother very directly, she again denied that it had any relevance to her. It is possible that she did appreciate its relevance, but was not going to admit this to us (which was consistent with her passive-aggressivity) or that she really did not consciously appreciate at all that the story related to her. I cannot be certain which alternative is the more likely.

The interchange described above took place during the last session prior to Linda's summer vacation. When she returned in September she had eight more sessions. At the end of that time the parents reported that Linda was now going to school without any resistance, that she was doing better, and that she had more friends. Linda and her parents stated that they wanted to discontinue treatment and I agreed. Although Linda still retained some of her aloof qualities, she had certainly become less passive-aggressive, and her hair-splitting had also significantly reduced. I believe that interchanges such as those described above contributed to Linda's improvement, even though she rarely admitted that the stories we told pertained to her.

☐ TEN
SIBLING RIVALRY

INTRODUCTION

A discussion of children's competition leads us naturally to the subject of sibling rivalry. We hear much about sibling rivalry in child psychiatry, but less about siblings and their effects on self-esteem. The very appearance of a second sibling is generally a blow to the self-esteem of the first. Prior to the appearance of the secondborn, the firstborn child is generally "king (or queen) of the universe." Prior to the appearance of the secondborn, the firstborn commands the full attention of the parents. When the sibling appears, the new child is not simply a diversion that results in loss of half of the attention, but much more because the newborn infant requires significantly more attention than the older child. In accordance with the previously discussed concept of "reflected appraisals," the child tends to assess his (her) own self-worth on the basis of parental affection and involvement. Accordingly, the older child cannot but feel a loss of love and, by extension, a loss of self-worth. The situation is well compared to the one in which a husband comes home with a new woman and tells his wife that she'll be living there in the home, that the newcomer's a great person (both in and out of bed), and that he's sure that because they are all loving people they are all going to love one another and live in harmony.

Sibling rivalry is normally fierce. To devote much time to its vicissitudes in the evaluative or therapeutic process is usually wasteful because such inquiry typically adds little meaningful information. If the mother, for example, says that the child fights often with his brother, I will ask her how often. If the frequency is less than 10-15 fights a day and if there is no history of dangerous trauma being inflicted, then I usually say something like: "That sounds like par for the course. What other problems are there?" Of course, if a sibling is having nightmares in which he (she) screams out: "No, no, Jerry. Don't beat me!" then the rivalry is probably pathological. Also, the absence of overt manifestations of sibling rivalry suggests a family in which aggression is significantly inhibited.

SIBLING RIVALRY AND THE EDUCATIONAL PROCESS

The generalization that firstborns are usually more serious and striving in school is valid. Firstborn children usually have only their parents to identify with. The secondborn, however, not only identifies with parents but with the older sibling as well. And the older sibling, the aforementioned seriousness notwithstanding, is still a child and exhibits many childlike qualities. Accordingly, the secondborn child is more likely to be less serious, compulsive, and self-demanding than the first. And all subsequent children, as well, having more older siblings to identify with, are even more likely to be less compulsive types. In a society that places high priorities on academic performance, the more successful student is more likely to be a source of pain and humiliation to a less successful younger sibling. The problem may be accentuated by insensitive teachers who frequently compare the less academically successful younger sibling with the older. The problem is further intensified by the fact that the older sibling, by virtue of his (her) age, is likely (in the majority of families) to be far more competent than the younger sibling. It is rare for the younger child to take into account the fact that when the older sibling was his (her) age, he (she) was no more successful. All the younger one seems to appreciate is that the older sibling always seems to be able to do things better and knows more things as well.

There are times, however, when the younger sibling is the more competent, and this doesn't relate to any severe problems in the older's physical or emotional development. The younger may have been born more intellectually gifted or have more talents or skills than the older. Under these circumstances the older child never seems to be able to catch up to the younger one, at least in certain areas. In such cases the older child's self-worth suffers significantly because of the continual negative comparison with a sibling. And such feelings of low self-esteem may interfere significantly with the child's academic motivation. It is as if the child reasons: "Why should I try? I'll never catch up to him (her)." A self-esteem problem engendered by the sibling situation may impair school performance in other ways. The child may become excessively competitive and yet fail, as the competitor always seems to win out. In larger families children may displace the anger they feel toward the more successful sibling onto younger siblings or peers. Some may develop psychological symptoms designed to deal with such anger in ways more socially acceptable than acting out.

PSYCHOTHERAPEUTIC APPROACHES

The treatment of children whose academic difficulties relate to their continual exposure to a more successful sibling may be extremely difficult. From the outset, one may have the feeling that the child never would have been brought to treatment had the sibling not been born. Removing one of the children from the family is clearly an inappropriate solution in the majority of such cases, especially when the children are younger than 12 or 13. I generally do not recommend boarding schools for children under that age range because I am a firm believer in the importance of an intact family in ensuring a child's healthy psychological development. When treating children in this situation, it is important for the therapist to try to correct any distortions the child may have—

distortions that are contributing to the feelings of low self-worth associated with the negative comparison with the more successful sibling. For example, younger children who are constantly comparing themselves unfavorably to older siblings must be helped to appreciate that most often the older sibling was no further along and exhibited no greater degree of competence when he (she) was at the age of the patient. It can often be useful to help the younger child develop areas of competence that the older child does not possess or does not show an interest in. If one is successful in helping the younger child achieve a sense of competence in areas that the older child is either uninterested in or deficient in, this can be quite therapeutic.

Sometimes the parents can make changes in the home that may be useful. For example, there are parents who subscribe to the rule that the youngest should go to sleep first and the oldest last. Sometimes the differences may be as small as five or ten minutes, but they believe it is important for the self-esteem of the oldest to put the younger child to sleep earlier. I have, at times, suggested to parents that they are using the child's age as their criterion for sleep-time rather than physiological need. The amount of time one should sleep should be determined by physiological needs. Children a year or two apart may not need different amounts of sleep, especially as they get older. My general experience is that parents tend to put children to sleep too early and that often their own need for relief from child-rearing obligations is a more important determinant of their children's bedtime than their empirical observations regarding how much sleep their children require. If the younger child can do quite well by going to sleep at the same time as the older, I generally suggest it. Under such circumstances, I advise the parents to tell the children that the determinant of sleep-time is not age but physical need. Any loss of self-esteem the older may suffer because of this arrangement is, I believe, minimal, and the service to the younger child more than outweighs any potential disservice to the older.

Sometimes parents will strictly refrain from praising an older child in order not to further lower the self-esteem of the less competent younger one. This is truly a disservice to the older.

The parents might make reasonable attempts to praise the older child in situations in which the younger is not likely to be directly involved. But I would not recommend a total moratorium on praising the older child in the presence of the younger. We all need some "audience" when we are complimented, and the older child deserves one as well. If a parent can, with conviction, comfortably talk about an area of competence in which the older child enjoys superiority—even over the parent himself (herself)—this can be reassuring to the younger child. It gets across the message that the younger child is not alone regarding the unfavorable comparison, and this can lessen the child's sense of ego-debasement. Furthermore, by speaking comfortably about their own "impairment," the parents serve as a model for healthy recognition of human differences and healthy acceptance of the fact that there will always be others who will be superior to oneself in certain areas. And some of these *others* can even be one's children.

Clinical Example

Gary demonstrates well the impact of an older brother's academic successes on a youngster's self-esteem and academic performance. The situation is one in which I had a clue about a central problem when I first saw Gary in the waiting room—even prior to my first words. He was 12 years old and in the sixth grade at the time of the initial interview. When I entered the waiting room, he was sitting between his parents, absorbed in a book. The book was so propped on his knees that its title, ALGEBRA, was prominently displayed—so much so that it was hard to avoid seeing it. As I approached, I introduced myself and extended my hand to the patient first. He was seemingly so absorbed in the book that he made no response to my overture. His mother tapped him on the shoulder and both parents interrupted his reading with comments about the fact that I was standing there waiting to greet him. He then looked up and apologetically said, "I'm sorry. I was busy studying my algebra."

We then went into my consultation room. Again, as soon as he sat down, Gary's nose was once again in the book. When I began asking basic-data questions, his parents again had to chide him about his absorption in the book and encouraged him to attend to the session. Because of his deep involvement in the book, I was far less interested in getting basic data at that point than in finding out what the significance of the book was for Gary. This is an important therapeutic principle. When the therapist is involved in an interchange with a patient and another event is taking place simultaneously that is serving as a distraction, the therapist does well to direct attention to the distraction in that it may be a much more important issue to focus on than the original material. The therapist who pursues the original route, while making mental notes of the distraction for future reference, may be depriving the patient of an important therapeutic experience. Furthermore, focusing on two issues simultaneously is likely to compromise one's involvement with and appreciation of both. I knew here that I could certainly get the basic-data questions answered subsequently, but I might not soon have another opportunity to focus on the algebra book at the very time of Gary's absorption with it. I was certain that it had psychological significance for Gary, but I did not know what it was. I suspected also that it was probably related to some central problem. The therapist who would have gone along with the parents at that point and required Gary to put down the algebra book and answer questions would have made a technical error and possibly deprived himself (herself) of important information at the most propitious time for its revelation.

Accordingly, I said to Gary, "I see you're really interested in algebra." This comment, of course, is one of many that one could use to open up the issue. I decided to use it because it begins at the point of a reality, namely, Gary's deep absorption in the book, and it was not an observation that could be easily refuted. There was nothing specific about the comment. Even if a specific speculation I threw out at that point proved to be valid, it would be a contaminant in that it might direct the patient into a particular channel that was not the most significant or relevant. Also, even if it were correct, I do not like to get across the idea that I am a mind reader, and a correct guess can often promulgate this delusion about the therapist. I much prefer the approach in which both the patient and I view me as the ignorant interrogator, someone who lacks knowledge and is ever questing for it. Furthermore, the speculation might be incorrect or irrelevant. If the patient then has the opinion that, as the psychiatrist, I must be "right," then it might lead him (her) into an area of inquiry that might be therapeutically useless and even detrimental.

I did not ask a *why* question either, e.g., "Why are you so absorbed in that algebra book?" I am very conservative with regard to my use of *why* questions. Although a psychoanalyst, and although deeply committed to the theory that underlying psychodynamic factors contribute significantly to the development of psychogenic pathology, I am very wary of the *why* question. I much prefer an approach in which the patient explores *when, where, how,* and *which.* The concrete information that such inquiry provides will often lead one into a more convincing explanation about *why* than a question that directly jumps over this data-collection process into the *why* area. When *why* is asked *after* such exploration, one is more likely to get a more meaningful explanation. I believe that my comment, "I see you're really interested in algebra," was more likely to provide the kind of preliminary factual data that would help me understand why Gary was so engrossed in his book. Last, *why* questions are likely to be more anxiety provoking than the aforementioned concrete types, are more likely to produce resistances, and are therefore more likely to remain unanswered.

As is well known, the Rogerians make extensive use of comments such as the one I made to Gary. They typically and repeatedly will begin their comments with "I see you're. . ." and "So you're. . . ." My criticism of those who use this technique is that they do too much of this—to the point where it cannot but be a simplistic therapeutic technique and a source of irritation to the patient. In addition, they use the same approach to speculate about feelings, with the claim that they are labeling them: "You must be feeling very bad about. . ." and "That must make you very angry when. . ." Elsewhere (Gardner, 1986a) I have detailed my extensive criticisms of this approach.

In response to my comment Gary stated, "Yeah, it's my favorite subject. I even like it more than the subjects I'm taking. They don't start algebra until the eighth grade, but I can learn it even though I'm in the sixth grade." At this point Gary's mother interrupted to tell me that this was one of the reasons why he was getting such low grades. His teachers were complaining that instead of attending to what they were trying to teach him in class, Gary frequently was reading his algebra book. They suspected, as well, that he really was not learning very much algebra because he showed little evidence for having mastered the prerequisite mathematical material. Gary then continued, "My brother thinks he's such a bigshot because he was made president of the Computer Club even though he's only in the tenth grade. I'm just as smart as he is." There is no necessity for me to quote further Gary's comments. I am sure it is obvious to the reader what was going on here. Gary was fiercely competitive with his older brother, who had distinguished himself in the computer area. Gary's burning desire to compete successfully with his brother was so great that he was blinding himself to the fact that he was compromising his education, even in the mathematics area. Unfortunately, Gary was unable to appreciate the relationship between his algebra obsession and his brother's successes. Although I did not press the point (I generally consider it antitherapeutic to press any point), there was no route of inquiry or discussion that was able to get Gary to appreciate how his fierce rivalry with his brother was contributing to his academic problems.

Gary's therapy was not too successful. This was simply related to the fact that his brother's very existence in the home was a continual source of his feelings of low self-worth. There were other problems in the home that were contributing to Gary's low self-esteem. These were formidable and had been generations in the making. His treatment was discontinued after two years, with only minimal improvement.

Clinical Example

Certain cards in *The Talking, Feeling, and Doing Game* can be useful in evoking discussion in this area.

Question: What's the best number of children to have in a family? Why?

Response: I think the best number of children to have in a family is between two and five. I think it's a very bad idea for parents to have only one child. Although that child may get a lot of attention, that child is also a very lonely child. No matter how many friends such a child has, he or she still doesn't have *any* brothers or sisters. He goes to sleep alone every night and he doesn't have the fun of having a brother or sister in the house in the evening and often even during the day or weekends. I feel sorry for such a child. However, if a child has more than four or five brothers or sisters, it's hard for the parents to give each one of the children the proper amount of attention. Often, in such large families, children tend to get neglected. Therefore, I say that the best number to have is between two and five.

There are some children, however, who wish they didn't have any older brothers or sisters. They may be very jealous of an older brother or sister because the older one does things better. There are some children who stop trying to do anything because an older brother or sister always seems to be better at most things. This is a very bad idea. Such children should realize that when they reach the age of the older brother or sister, they'll probably do just as well. They should try to spend more time with children their own age and compare themselves with children their own age. If they'd stop comparing themselves with their older brothers and sisters, and just compared themselves more with children their own age, they would feel better about themselves. They might then start doing things again. What do you think about what I've said?

* * *

Clinical Example

In this example I will provide more extensive clinical data from the treatment of a boy whose problem was directly related to unfavorable comparison with a sibling. Stan entered treatment at the age of 10-1/2, when he was in the fifth grade. He presented with a variety of complaints. Although considered to be very bright (he was in the 95th-99th percentile on national standardized tests), he was doing very poorly academically. His academic motivation was at a very low level and his work was poorly organized. He frequently forgot his assignments and was continually procrastinating. His parents described him as ever taking the path of least resistance and always trying to avoid responsibility. There was very little follow-through on any activity that he initiated or that was initiated for him.

Stan exhibited the same difficulties in extracurricular areas. Although he exhibited definite musical talent, he would only sporadically practice the piano and so achieved very little competence. He was well coordinated and had intermittently demonstrated competence in a variety of sports. However, he absolutely refused to practice and so was never sought after as a desirable teammate. He would not initiate contact with friends, but did respond when invited by others. Because of his lack of reciprocity, he had few friends. When he did initiate contact with friends, it was always at the mother's prodding. Stan most preferred to spend time listening to rock music. He also read voraciously. Because of his high intelligence, he did learn significantly from his reading, and the knowledge he so accumulated contributed to his high scores on national standardized tests. Because the material he chose to read was often irrelevant to his academic pursuits, what he learned did not reflect itself in his school performance.

Stan had been referred by his teacher in the gifted and talented class he attended one afternoon a week. Because of his high intelligence, he had been placed in that class and had remained there for three years. However, the teacher described his motivation as very poor and his disorganization as a central problem. She also described significant procrastination—so much so that she frequently had to remind Stan about his assignments and he was always asking her for extensions. Because of his high intelligence and his creativity, she had recommended that he remain in the class even though he was the poorest performer in the group.

Stan was the younger of two children. His 12-year-old brother, Larry, excelled in practically every area in which he involved himself. He was a straight A student whose teachers invariably described him as "a pleasure to have in the class." "It's because of kids like him that I enjoy teaching." Larry was well mannered in school and *never* gave his teachers any trouble. He excelled in many sports, played the clarinet, was in the school band, and was often chosen for leading parts in school plays. He both sought and was sought by friends and was well liked. Over 95 percent of all telephone calls that came into the home for one of the children were for the older brother.

To make matters worse for Stan, Larry's home behavior was "exemplary." In the morning he invariably made his bed. He got dressed with clothes that he laid out for himself the night before. He happily took baths or showers. He never had to be reminded to brush his teeth. He ate every food that was offered him, and every bit as well. He always remembered to take off muddy shoes before entering the house. He never forgot to walk the dog on those days that were assigned to him. He turned off the television when he was told to. And he went to sleep without a fuss. (Poor Stan!)

Another problem related to the patient's after-school schedule. Piano lessons have already been mentioned. Stan took one lesson a week and was supposed to practice every day. He attended Hebrew school two afternoons a week and every Sunday morning. Throughout the school year he was at various times involved in tennis, soccer, and Little League baseball. This situation created a conflict for me as well. The child was clearly in need of treatment and I believed that twice-weekly sessions were warranted. However, I knew well that his therapy might then become another onerous after-school activity, squeezed into an already heavy schedule. Accordingly, I decided to schedule one full-hour session per week, rather than two 45-minute sessions. I would guess that it comes as no surprise to the reader to learn that Larry had absolutely no trouble with the same schedule of after-school activities.

Stan had another problem with his brother and other children as well. He was a somewhat timid child and was fearful of asserting himself, both with Larry and peers. In spite of Larry's perfect manners and exemplary behavior, there were times when he would pick on his younger brother. (In a sense, this was a healthy manifestation on Larry's part, considering how "perfect" he was in so many areas.) In response to such teasing and taunting, Stan would often say nothing and just "clam up." His hesitancy to defend himself against peers was, I believe, playing a role in his difficulty in maintaining friendships. I suspected that the pent-up hostility engendered by such teasing was also playing a role in his difficulties. I could not be more specific at the time other than to speculate that pent-up hostility is invariably associated with feelings of frustration, dissatisfaction with oneself, and low self-esteem. With such an attitude about himself, it was likely that his motivation, curiosity, and enjoyment of learning would be impaired.

The parents felt themselves to be in a terrible bind. They recognized that one of Stan's problems related to his unfavorable comparison with his brother. However, they were convinced (and I agreed with them) that if Stan were only to apply himself, there was little doubt that he would equal his brother's accomplishments. Although I could not agree with them that the goal of Stan's treatment should be that he be as exemplary in every area as his brother, I did believe that he was capable of enjoying the same successes. The parents knew that their placing pressure on Stan to work harder only increased his resistance. However, when they would "pull back," he would do practically nothing. They tried to find some middle road, but this didn't seem to help either.

The transcript presented here provides excerpts from a session during his second month in treatment, when we played *The Talking, Feeling, and Doing Game.*

> *Patient:* "Make believe you're having a bad dream. What's the dream about?" It shouldn't be a real dream? Just made up?
>
> *Gardner:* Just make believe. No, no, not a real dream, just a make-believe dream.
>
> *Patient:* Okay. Um. I'm in the desert and I'm being chased by a tiger. And he's chasing me all over. Then more tigers keep coming and then a lot more animals are chasing me around. The end.
>
> *Gardner:* The end?
>
> *Patient:* Yeah.

Gardner: Then you wake up.
Patient: Then I wake up.
Gardner: Okay. Did you say before that you had a real dream that you wanted to say, that you wanted to tell?
Patient: I was just wondering.
Gardner: Do you recall a real dream that you can tell?
Patient: Well, I had one that I kept having over some time.
Gardner: What's that one?

I believed that there were two possible explanations to the self-created dream. On the one hand, I considered the possibility that it was within the normal range of nightmares that children frequently have. I view the ominous figures in such dreams to represent the pent-up hostilities that all children inevitably harbor in response to the restrictions and frustrations that all must tolerate in life. I also considered the possibility that the tigers and other animals who were pursuing the patient represented his parents, specifically their pressures on him to fulfill his academic, extra-curricular, and social involvements. In order to ascertain which of the two speculations might be more valid, I decided to get information about actual dreams the patient might have recalled.

Patient: It was that I went to the circus with my dad. We went into this tent and there was this huge bee, a queen bee, and she locked one of us up in the cage. I had this dream a few times and sometimes it was my dad and sometimes it was me in the cage.
Gardner: Uh huh. And it was this queen bee that did that?
Patient: Yeah.
Gardner: When did you have this dream?
Patient: All the time at night, about when I was four or five.
Gardner: Four or five, uh huh.
Patient: I had it many times.
Gardner: You never told me that. You know, in dreams things stand for other things. Do you know that?
Patient: No.
Gardner: Yeah, it's true. Like let's say in a dream—let's say a boy is angry at his father and he's afraid to tell his father how angry he is. So he might have a dream in which he's hitting the father of a friend with a baseball bat, or something like that. And in this way he gets out the anger that he feels toward his father. Do you understand that?

Patient: Hmm.

Gardner: That people stand for other things. Who could the queen bee stand for in your dream? Who do you think?

Patient: I don't know.

Gardner: Who is the queen of your house?

Patient: My mom.

Gardner: Think it might stand for your mother?

Patient: Well, I don't think so, because I wasn't angry at my mom.

Gardner: You're not angry at your mom?

Patient: No.

Gardner: Well, does your mother ever do anything that gets you angry?

Patient: Sometimes.

Gardner: What kinds of things does she do that gets you angry?

Patient: Well, like, for example, today I came home and I just slipped on the snow on the walk and got all wet, so I told her and she said to me go out and sweep the walk so it's not wet any more. And I didn't want to because I have other things to do. I have to practice the piano and do a school project, but she says everybody has responsibilities and so I went and did it.

Gardner: All right. Now let me ask you this. You see in the dream it said that the queen bee has you locked in the cage sometimes or your father locked in the cage sometimes. What can the cage stand for?

Patient: Forced into doing things?

Gardner: Yeah, forced into doing something like what?

Patient: Like cleaning the walk and shoveling snow.

Gardner: Yeah, like shoveling snow. But I'm wondering whether it gives you the feeling that you're caged in by her, that you have to do too many things. Remember when we spoke before about all the different things you have to do: piano lessons, Hebrew school?

Patient: I think that's all. It's just that I have Hebrew school twice during the week.

Gardner: Twice. . .I remember there were other things that you had to do too, as I recall. Aren't there other activities?

Patient: I have to go to Sunday school.

Gardner: Sunday school. And didn't you have some other things like Little League, or soccer, or tennis?

Patient: Oh, yeah. Tennis I have and that's on the same day as piano. I don't have much time to do work.

Gardner: Okay. And then do you have anything else? Do you have any soccer? Do I recall correctly?

Patient: I had, but it's over now. And then I have baseball coming up.

Gardner: Baseball is coming up. Hmmmm. I see. So do you ever feel caged in with all those things, like you're in a cage. You don't have much movement.

Patient: Sometimes.

Gardner: Does that get you mad?

Patient: Sort of.

Gardner: Hmm. Do you ever say anything?

Patient: Yes. I say I'm too busy sometimes and I say, "Do I have to go today? I have so much work."

Gardner: Uh hmm. I see. And what happens then?

Patient: Well, I usually just go and do it anyway.

Gardner: Uh hmm. Does that get you upset?

Patient: Sometimes.

Gardner: Well, you don't tell people you want to quit these things, like piano. You say you don't want to quit it.

Patient: I don't want to quit it.

Gardner: Uh huh. You don't.

Patient: No.

Gardner: So what are you going to do?

Patient: I'm going to keep doing it.

Gardner: You're going to keep doing it, but keep doing it poorly. You're there, you hang in there, but you do it poorly. What do you think you can do about that?

Patient: I'm going to try and practice.

Gardner: Well, I hope so—or else quit some of these after-school activities. Do one or the other. Doing them all in a half-assed way can't make you feel very good, and it also gets your parents on your back a lot and this must make you feel like you're in a cage. What do you think about what I've said?

Patient: You're right. I think I'll try to practice more.

Gardner: Well, if you've decided to stick with all these activities, I hope you'll try harder. But if you cut down on a few, that wouldn't be so bad either, in my opinion. I think, however, that you can do them all if you try very hard, because you're smart enough. I just think it would be a bad idea to continue along in the way you are now.

The patient's repetitious dream lent support to my second speculation about his response to the card that instructed him to make up a dream, namely, that the tiger dream related to Stan's feelings that he was being persecuted by his parents in relation to their pressuring him to involve himself more assiduously in his curricular and extracurricular activities. In the ensuing discussion I tried to help Stan see what he was doing to himself and to support the option of his reducing somewhat his extracurricular involvements and obligations.

> *Gardner:* My card says, "A girl was listening through the keyhole of the closed door of her parents' bedroom. Her parents were talking and didn't know she was there. What did she hear them say?" The parents were talking about the fact that the girl was doing very poorly in school and her parents were wondering whether they should send her to a private school.
>
> And the mother was saying, "I think she should go to a private school and then she'll do better."
>
> And the father said, "No, I don't think that's going to make any difference. It's all in her head. It's her attitude. And if we spend all that money on a private school, she's still going to have the same attitude and I think that's a waste of money." So who do you think won the argument?
>
> *Patient:* The father.
>
> *Gardner:* Why?
>
> *Patient:* Because he had the best idea. It was in her head.
>
> *Gardner:* Yeah. That's right. It was in the little girl's head and it wasn't changing the school that was going to make things different. Right?
>
> *Patient:* Right.

The parents had brought up the question of transferring Stan to a private school from the excellent public school he was attending. They hoped that more individual attention in the private school might be useful for Stan. I expressed my opinion that I did not believe that such a transfer was likely to prove useful for Stan. The parents knew quite well that the public school he was attending was one of the best in the state. They knew, also, that even when given one-to-one tutoring, Stan tended to be lax and not fulfill his obligations. Accordingly, I did not think that the transfer was a reasonable course of action and that the extra expense involved would prove to be a worthwhile expenditure. Furthermore, the family's financial situation was such that the transfer would create hardship. However, even if the family were affluent, I would not have made a different recommendation. My response to the card, of course, makes reference to this issue and my position on it.

* * *

Gardner: What does your card say?

Patient: It says, "Make believe you're doing a sneaky thing." I'd be playing a trick on my brother.

Gardner: What would the trick be?

Patient: I don't know, mix up some things in his room, or if he had done something to me, then I would get him back.

Gardner: Okay, what kind of thing would make you want to do a sneaky trick on him?

Patient: If he had bothered me, or if I was doing that 'cause he played a trick on me.

Gardner: Does your brother bother you very much?

Patient: Yes.

Gardner: Anything changed since we talked about that?

Patient: Well, he's been doing it a little less.

Gardner: A little less.

Patient: And I've been fighting back more.

Gardner: You've been fighting back more. Good! Give me an example of something that you've fought back on.

Patient: Well, like when I was helping him with some work he had—a poster. He asked me, you know, to help with his poster. And he started teasing me and calling me names and so I called him names back. And I quit helping him with the poster. And then he started hitting me and sitting on me. Then he pulled my hair and that hurt. So I started yelling and I yelled at him about it and asked him how would he like it if someone did that to him.

Gardner: What did he say to that?

Patient: He didn't say anything. He stopped and looked sorry.

Gardner: Good. Good. Okay, you get a chip for that.

The patient's anger inhibition problem has already been mentioned. I had encouraged him to assert himself more with those who taunted him, both his brother and peers. Apparently, my advice was heeded and the patient had the salutary experience of asserting himself.

* * *

Patient: "What's the best story you ever heard or read? Why?" I have a lot of different stories because I read a lot, but one of them that's one of my most favorite stories is *Charlie and the Chocolate Factory.*

Gardner: Okay. Why is that your favorite?

Patient: It has a lot of funny things in it. It's a funny book and it's sort of like a nice book. It's about this poor kid who was to be — what do you call someone who got to inherit a lot of money or things.

Gardner: He was an heir.

Patient: Yeah, an heir of the person who owns the largest chocolate factory in the world. They were very poor but he found a dollar on the street and he bought a few candy bars and he got a gold ticket, which means that he gets to go to the chocolate factory and get a tour from the owner. All the rest of the kids got into wild and crazy things and they all got in trouble. And they all go, you know, one kid got squeezed into a tube in the Chocolate River and one girl got thrown down a garbage hatch. And all sorts of weird things.

Gardner: Okay. What's the main thing about that story you like so much?

Patient: Well, its a good book. It's pretty easy to read and I like the things that go on.

Gardner: Uh huh. You mean the funny exciting things?

Patient: Yeah.

Gardner: Well, I'd like to say something about that story. Although I am sure it's a lot of fun to read, there's something about that story that I don't like, that rubs me the wrong way.

Patient: What's that?

Gardner: Stories like that make children think that it's easy to get rich very quickly, that with just some luck a poor person can become very rich. It just doesn't happen that way in real life. That story is very much like a fairy tale. It doesn't tell about *real life*. It gives people the idea that without doing anything, one can become very rich. It gives people the idea that you can often find a dollar in the street, and that's not so. Of course, once in a while, you do find some money in the street. However, no one ever got to own a big chocolate factor by luck. The people who own the Hershey Factory in Hershey, Pennsylvania, didn't get it by luck. The people who started that business many years ago had to work very hard for a long time in order to build up a big business. Even now the people who run it still have to work very hard. Many of them are the descendants of the original owners. From what I understand, it's still a family business.

Anyway, that's why I don't like that story too much. It gives people the idea that you can accomplish a lot by doing very little and that's not so in the real world. What do you think about what I've said?

Patient: I guess it's true.

I used the get-rich-quick message in the *Charlie and the Chocolate Factory* story as a point of departure for comments on the absurdity of that common fantasy. I wish to emphasize here that at no point in this interchange did I make direct reference to Stan's problems in this realm. Stan was operating with the delusion that somehow everything would work out well for him in spite of the fact that he did not accomplish very much in any particular area. As mentioned previously, unpalatable messages are best communicated when talking about third parties, and this is what I was doing here. I believe that the most efficacious way of communicating unpleasant messages is via the utilization of symbols and the experiences of others. Helping the patient gain insight is a fringe benefit and may also provide additional therapeutic clout, but I do not consider it a crucial part of the psychotherapeutic process. I did, however, attempt to see whether he could relate what I was saying to himself. I do not have the strong need to have patients see such linkages, but if they do, I will certainly participate in the discussion. If they do not, I do not feel that they have been deprived of the most important part of the psychotherapeutic process.

Gardner: Does what I've said have anything to do with you?
Patient: I guess so.
Gardner: How?
Patient: I guess I don't do as much work as I should.

Gardner: That's right. Okay. My card says, "Make up a dream that has feelings in it." Well, I'm dreaming that I'm a kid and I'm in school, and the teacher announces a very big test. And I say, "Ah, that's no problem, I know it all." So I don't study. And the next day I walk into the classroom and I'm scared stiff as she hands out the papers. I'm afraid I'm going to fail. And my knees are knocking, and my teeth are chattering, and I'm very, very frightened. And I'm then very sorry that I didn't study. And I wake up like I was in a nightmare. I'm really very upset and I wake up and I'm glad it was only a dream. And I have great feelings of fear there and I'm sorry for not having studied. Anything you want to say about that?

Patient: Nothing much.

Gardner: Okay, now it's time to stop. You get three extra chips because you're ahead. So how many do you have?

Patient: Eight.

Gardner: You have more than I have. I only have one. Okay. You're the winner of the game.

This is one of my common answers for children who are oblivious to the self-destructive effects of their lack of school commitment. I try to convey the idea that there are people who take their work very seriously and who suffer from significant lapses of commitment to their academic obligations. Generally, this response is of greater interest to those children who do experience some remorse over their academic performance. Although Stan was not in deep grief over his low grades, he was not oblivious to them either. Although he did not wish to discuss further my response to the card, he did listen with interest and involvement.

The following excerpts are from a session that took place exactly one month later, a session in which we again played *The Talking, Feeling, and Doing Game.*

Gardner: Okay, what does your card say?

Patient: "You're standing in line to buy something and a child pushes himself in front of you. Show what you would do?" Okay, well, first of all, I would probably say, "Excuse me, I think I was in front of you," and if he either didn't pay attention or said something back to me, I would try saying that again and try to be as hard as possible.

Gardner: Okay. Suppose he still didn't do anything. Suppose he ignored you and still stayed in front of you.

Patient: Well, then I would try doing it back to him and see how he liked it.

Gardner: Uh huh. Suppose he was bigger than you.

Patient: Well. . .it depends on what his reaction was if I pushed in front of him. I'm pretty sure he wouldn't try to do anything in front of a crowd. . .so I would just say, "I was in front of you and would appreciate it if you would stop pushing and shoving."

Gardner: Uh huh. So you'd try to get him to stay where he's supposed to be.

Patient: Yeah.

Gardner: Right. But suppose he was much bigger than you. What would you do?

Patient: Well, I don't think it really matters how big . . .

Gardner: Well, a kid your own age or smaller might listen to you more than a kid who's bigger.

Patient: Well, if he really didn't listen to me, if I was with someone older, I would tell him, or I would tell someone who works there.

Gardner: Very good. Okay, you get a chip.

The question, of course, relates directly to the patient's self-assertion problem. In the interchange I supported his solutions to the problem, solutions that appeared to be appropriate to me and reflected steps forward in Stan's asserting himself. I am not speaking from the merely theoretical level here. His response did reflect actual changes in his behavioral pattern.

* * *

Gardner: My card says, "If people could come back to life after they die, what would you like to be like? Why?" Well, I would like to be very much the way I am with one exception. Sometimes I work too hard. I push myself too hard and that's not a good idea. It's a bad idea to push yourself too hard. . . . It's also a bad thing not to push yourself hard enough. The best thing is something in the middle. What do you say about that?

Patient: I think that's true.

Gardner: You agree?

Patient: Yeah.
Gardner: Okay, I'll give you a chip for that. Okay.

My response reflects an impairment that I see in myself, an impairment that has had certain fringe benefits, however. As I have mentioned so many times previously, such revelations of a therapist's deficiency can be therapeutic in that they lessen the likelihood that the patient will view the therapist as perfect. Such unfavorable comparisons can contribute to the intensification of a patient's feelings of low self-worth, and this is the last thing that most patients need. In Stan's case, having an older brother who many viewed as "perfect" would have made it particularly difficult for him if he viewed his therapist as "perfect" as well. Furthermore, I used the response to contrast my problem with his own, which was clearly the opposite problem of too little work. Both are problems and both warrant rectification.

* * *

Patient: "What do you like learning about most? Why?" Well, I'm interested in geometry because I want to be an architect and to me an architect would have to know about geometry.
Gardner: Okay. Tell me, is it easy to become an architect? What would you say?
Patient: It's not too easy . . . you have to go to a good . . . a pretty good school . . . some people think you have to be a whiz at math to be an architect, but it's not really true. You just have to know the basics.
Gardner: Would you say you have to work hard to be an architect?
Patient: Yes, I would say.
Gardner: I would say. Would you say you have to work *very* hard to get into a good architecture school?
Patient: Yes.
Gardner: Yes, I would say so too. Let's say you have to be fairly good at math . . . you don't have to be a genius or anything . . . but you have to be competent or, more important, you have to add on to the competence if you want to get into a good architecture school. If you don't, you may not get into any architecture school at all. Okay, you take a chip.

I used the patient's response to put in a good word for the work ethic. I also reminded him that failure to adhere to the work ethic might result in career disappointment.

> *Gardner:* My card says, "What part of your body do you like the least? Why?" I would say the part I like the least are my toenails. When I was in college, a long time ago, I got some kind of infection in my toenails . . . some kind of fungus infection that gets into the toenail and it never went away and that's something I live with all my life. So that's the part of my body I like the least. Can you say anything about that?
>
> *Patient:* No.
>
> *Gardner:* Everybody has parts of themselves that they don't like and parts of themselves they like, you know? Everybody's a mixture of things they like about themselves and things they don't. What would you say are the part or parts of your body that you don't like?
>
> *Patient:* Well . . . it's hard . . . one part of my body that I don't like is my skin because it's very sensitive and it's very light and I get sunburned, which is very painful, especially the skin on my back. When I was in camp in the summer, I got an infection on my back from mosquito bites and I couldn't go swimming and it was very painful.
>
> *Gardner:* So that's your weak point . . . your skin . . . the part you don't like too much. Mine is my toenails. Let's see, I get a chip for my answer and you get a chip.

My response again related to Stan's self-esteem problem. I described a deficiency in myself in a matter-of-fact way. In addition, I asked him to discuss a deficiency of his that might parallel mine. Viewing his therapist as having deficiencies can make the patient more comfortable with his (her) own and this can be useful for patients such as Stan who suffer with a self-esteem problem.

> *Patient:* My card says, "What part of your body do you like the most? Why?" Probably I have two parts. My head, because without my head I would be nowhere.
>
> *Gardner:* And where would you be?
>
> *Patient:* Well, you know the head is probably one of the most important parts and my legs because I'm a very fast runner and I like to run and I hope to join the track team in high school.

Gardner: You know the part of my body that I like the most is my brain. You know why? Because the brain helps me think, helps me figure out problems. It makes my life easier. When I see there's a problem, I think about it and I think in advance of consequences. Do you know what consequences mean?

Patient: Yeah.

Gardner: I think in advance of consequences . . . what does consequences mean?

Patient: It's something . . . like if you do something . . . what will happen as a result.

Gardner: Right, right! When you think in advance of consequences, it saves me a lot of trouble. That's why my brain is the part of my body I like the most.

Patient: That's probably true for most people.

Gardner: Okay, you get a chip for saying what you said and I get a chip for saying what I said.

My main message here was that the patient would do well to think about the consequences of his behavior, especially in the academic and social realms. Although I made no direct reference to these areas of deficit (there are times when it is judicious not to do so), my hope was that the message would at some level be considered relevant and useful.

Gardner: My card says, "What is your favorite color? Why?" My favorite color . . . I have two favorite colors . . . green and blue. They remind me of nature. Blue reminds me of the sky and green of trees, grass, and beautiful places. I like to travel to places where it's beautiful to look at and I love scenery. Those are my favorite colors. It makes me feel good when I see these beautiful things.

Patient: That's funny because those are my favorite colors.

Gardner: Same favorite colors? What are *your* reasons for having those favorite colors?

Patient: Well, I like the look. Well, first of all I used to not like green as much. One reason now that I realize is when I was playing soccer and I was on the *All Star Team* for the first time, my shirt was green, and I liked that shirt . . . I liked the color of it . . . I wore it a lot because I was proud of it. And blue I like because it goes with green.

Gardner: Okay, your chip and mine.

Enhancing one's ability to enjoy aesthetic pleasure can be ego-enhancing and is well viewed as a general antidote for feelings of low self-worth. My response here attempted to contribute to this goal.

> *Patient:* It says, "Do something funny." Hmmm . . .
>
> *Gardner:* Well, if you want to say something funny, say something funny or do something funny.
>
> *Patient:* It's kind of hard to do something funny.
>
> *Gardner:* What about saying something funny if you can't do something funny. (Pause) Can't think of anything?
>
> *Patient:* No . . . not really.
>
> *Gardner:* Do you want to pass this one up?
>
> *Patient:* Yeah.
>
> *Gardner:* Do you want me to say something funny? Do you want to hear a funny riddle?
>
> *Patient:* Okay.
>
> *Gardner:* Tell me, what's invisible and smells like worms?
>
> *Patient:* I don't know.
>
> *Gardner:* Try to figure it out. What's invisible and smells like worms?
>
> *Patient:* I can't think of the answer.
>
> *Gardner:* Okay, I'll tell you. A bird's fart.
>
> *Patient* (laughing): That's pretty disgusting!
>
> *Gardner:* Well, I said something and you laughed, so I must have said something funny.
>
> *Patient:* Okay.

The introduction of humor adds a certain levity to the therapeutic session and is part of the seductive process described earlier in this book. In addition, healthy laughing is ego-enhancing. And any kind of ego-enhancement the therapist can provide serves to alleviate feelings of low self-esteem.

> *Gardner:* My card says, "A girl was crying. What was she crying about?" Well, what happened was that she was in the gifted and talented class and it was the end of the school year, and she learned that she was not going to be in the class again. She was crying and she went to the teacher and she cried to the teacher, "Why aren't I going to be in that class again?" (Therapist imitates crying.) "Why am I not going to be in that class?" What did the teacher say?

Patient: The teacher said, "Because you weren't doing your work. . . . If you want to be in the gifted and talented, show it!

Gardner: She was gifted and talented in that she had . . .

Patient: But she didn't show it.

Gardner: The thing is that half of being gifted and talented is to be lucky enough to be born smart or talented. And the other half is that you have to work at it. The teacher said, "Listen, you're gifted and you're talented, but you're not working at it."

Patient: I wouldn't cry though.

Gardner: What would you do?

Patient: It's not much of a big thing. You've been in a special class that a lot of other people don't get to be in, and they're not crying because they're not in it.

Gardner: But she was in it *already.*

Patient: Right.

Gardner: But you wouldn't cry.

Patient: No.

Gardner: If you were next year not to get into the gifted and talented class, would that bother you?

Patient: It would bother me, but I wouldn't go crying about it. I would try and get in the next year, the year after that.

Gardner: Well, some kids would be very upset. Some kids— this particular girl that I was talking about—was *very* upset because it meant a lot to her. Why do you think it meant a lot to her. What's your guess?

Patient: Well, she probably liked it a lot . . .

Gardner: And she learned some interesting things and . . . there's things that I don't like because I miss math. But she was smart enough to miss a little math.

Patient: Yeah.

Gardner: Going in the G and T [Gifted and Talented].

Patient: Right.

Gardner: Well, this particular girl . . . she was willing to miss math once in a while and she was smart, and she could make it up, but for her it was an interesting class. She enjoyed learning the extra things, but the teacher was right. She had been kind of lazy, hadn't handed in projects, things like that, so they decided not to put her in the next year. But they said to her, "There still may be an opening the *following* year if you prove yourself capable of working very hard, and we'll consider you for the following year." So what do you think happened to her?

Patient: She probably tried and then the following year . . .

Gardner: Tell me, what other thing about the G and T don't you like?

Patient: I don't think there is much that I don't like about it . . .

Gardner: Okay, so anyway, this is what happened to this girl. She was really crying, and she was really sad, but it helped her learn a lesson—a lesson to remember that at times you have to do things you don't like. If you want to get the pleasures of the G and T, you have to do sometimes the things you don't like. And that's what she learned.

My comments here focused on the untoward consequences of not fulfilling one's obligations. There was active discussion between the patient and myself regarding his involvement in his own gifted and talented class. He admitted there would be some remorse if he were not allowed to continue. I tried to get across the notion that there are others who would be much more upset. My hope was that this might engender in him a little more motivation to take the class more seriously.

Patient: "A boy heard his mother and father fighting. What were they fighting about? What was he thinking while he was listening to them?" The boy was passing the closed door of his mother and father's room and he heard them arguing and he heard them say, "That boy really needs some help. He's not doing his work the teachers are saying. And he's not doing his responsibilities and even at home he doesn't want to do his homework. He'll goof off and watch TV."

And the father said, "I think we should have a special tutor that comes on the weekends."

And the mother said, "That would be a waste of time and money, and he wouldn't like it just as much on the weekends." She said, "I think that it's just that he doesn't think he can do the work. He doesn't believe . . . he thinks he's not able to do it."

And the boy was listening to all this, and he was thinking, "Maybe they're right . . . maybe I do think that I'm not too smart. I'm going to try and do all this work and then I'll show them that I can do it.

Gardner: What do you think? Is that what happened?

Patient: Yeah.

Gardner: What gave him the idea that he wasn't smart?

Patient: Well, he just wasn't trying as hard, so when he didn't get the A's, he felt that he was not capable of getting A's, but he really was.

Gardner: When he got the A's, he felt he was capable, is that it?

Patient: Then he found out that he really was smart.

Gardner: Did anything else happen to him that made him feel that he wasn't particularly smart?

Patient: Well, his friends would tease him when they got A's, A+'s and he got B's.

Gardner: Was there anything else that made him feel that he wasn't smart?

Patient: Well, when he didn't concentrate on his homework and watched TV and then as far as his homework went, the teacher said, "This is sloppy." He then thought, "It will be just as bad if I do the work."

Gardner: He didn't have much confidence that he'd do well, is that it?

Patient: No.

Gardner: Anything else that made him feel he wasn't smart?

Patient: No.

Gardner: Sometimes a kid feels he's not smart because somebody in the family is doing something very well. Did this happen to him? Were there any family members who might have made him feel he wasn't smart?

Patient: No.

Gardner: Sometimes a kid feels he isn't smart because he has a brother or a sister who's a very good student.

Patient: He was an only child.

Gardner: Oh, he was an only child. That wasn't his case.

Patient: Yeah.

Gardner: Because there are some kids who have a brother or a sister who is really a hot-shot student. And it makes them feel like they're stupid, and they kind of lose interest in school because they feel they can't do it. Have you ever heard of such kids?

Patient: I've met a few.

Gardner: You've met a few.

Patient: You see, we had this health quiz and it was around Valentine's Day, so the teacher had a heart on the board that said, "Teachers love hard workers," and if you got a 100 on the quiz, you would sign your name. So, some of the people (I was one of them) who got a 100 went into the other room—a room we saw where nobody was—and we drew a heart on the board and we wrote, "Hard workers love teachers." And we signed our names, and when the teacher came in, she said something, she said, "It tends to be true that people who work hard tend to like their teachers and like school. But the people who don't, tend to say, 'It's all the teacher's fault. The teacher doesn't like me.'"

Gardner: How are you? Where would you put yourself?

Patient: I think I'm one of the . . . I like my teachers, and I think I work hard.

Gardner: Do you think you work hard enough?

Patient: Yes.

Gardner: Well, what about the fact that the teacher complains that you don't get your projects in on time and things like that.

Patient: Well, that was *before* . . . now I'm trying to work hard.

Gardner: Why is that? Why are you trying to work hard?

Patient: Because I realize that laziness isn't going to get me anywhere.

Gardner: Isn't going to get you anywhere?

Patient: Working hard is . . . (mumble) . . .

Gardner: I'm not clear about what you're saying. Say it again.

Patient: If I just laze off, I won't get into a good school, and I won't get the things I want.

Gardner: Like what?

Patient: Like if I want to be an architect.

Gardner: Now what about . . . I mentioned before . . . there are certain kids who lose their confidence and lose their interest because they have brothers or sisters who are very good in school. I was wondering if that was your situation.

Patient: No, not really. My brother is good in school, but there are some things, even though he's two years older, that I'm just as good at and better than him. For instance, spelling. He was never a good speller. And he's a good student, but I'm just as good.

Gardner: So you don't think that you get squelched or . . .

Patient: He helps me sometimes . . .

Gardner: Or you lose your ambition because of him?

Patient: No.

Gardner: As I understand it, he's a pretty hot-shot character in terms of he gets up in the morning, he makes his own bed, he makes his own breakfast, he does his chores, and he's really always doing the right thing at the right time.

Patient: We have this requirement . . . (mumble) . . .

Gardner: This requirement that what?

Patient: That when we wake up in the morning, we make our beds.

Gardner: And does he fulfill that requirement? Does he do what's required?

Patient: Yeah.
Gardner: What about you?
Patient: I do my work . . .
Gardner: As much as he does?
Patient: Yeah. Sometimes I'll forget if I'm in a rush or don't get up early enough.
Gardner: Does he forget?
Patient: Yeah.
Gardner: Who forgets more, him or you?
Patient: I think probably you do.
Gardner: That means you forget more?
Patient: But we all usually make our own breakfast, unless there's something like . . . my mom's cooking. I don't usually do . . .
Gardner: What about his doing his assignments? Is he pretty good about that?
Patient: Yeah. He sometimes doesn't get his assignments in on time.
Gardner: Who doesn't get his assignments in on time more— you or he?
Patient: I don't know. He gets C's a lot more. And he has stuff that he doesn't get and like the teacher called up and reminded him . . .
Gardner: Okay, so you don't think your problem with not doing your assignments on time has anything to do with your brother.
Patient: No.
Gardner: But there are some kids who are that way, right?
Patient: Yes.
Gardner: How does it affect them—these other kids? They don't do their assignments if they have a hot-shot brother or sister. What happens then?
Patient: Most of them don't have a hot-shot . . .
Gardner: But those who come from a family where there is a hot-shot . . .
Patient: There are no . . . I don't think it affects them . . .

As can be seen here, I made attempts to link the patient's difficulties in school with his brother's outstanding performance there. He repeatedly denied that there was any relationship. He claimed that the boy in his story was an only child. At another time he claimed that the situation in my story had no relationship to that in his story. Later he described his brother as being lax and getting C's. This was definitely not the case. Last, he denied that even the siblings he knows are affected by older siblings' successes. Although there was no actual agreement on the patient's part that there could be any relationship between an older sibling's success and a younger sibling's failure, either in his case or anyone else's, he did admit that he had met a few such individuals. I believe that I did get across the concept here, a concept that ultimately did prove useful.

> *Gardner:* Okay, let's do one more turn and then we're going to stop, okay? My card says, "If you only had one month to live, how would you spend it?" Well, I would try to do as much as possible the things that I like to do, like working in my office and treating patients, you know, working with you now and playing these games, writing my books, and stuff like that, traveling around, being with my family. I would try to do just the things I had been doing—work and play. I like play—I think it's fun; but I like work things, too. It makes me feel good when I accomplish something. You know what I mean?
>
> *Patient:* Yeah. All work and no play makes Jack a dull boy.
>
> *Gardner:* What about all play and no work. What happens then?
>
> *Patient:* You're still pretty dull.
>
> *Gardner:* Yeah. All play and no work makes you pretty dull, too. Huh?
>
> *Patient:* Although sometimes if you're an athlete, it pays.
>
> *Gardner:* Yeah, right, that's a different story. But somebody who never learns anything, who only plays, is pretty dull.
>
> *Patient:* Yeah.
>
> *Gardner:* So both are bad—something in the middle is better—so I would get the joys of work and the joys of play. And I would hope that my last month to live would not be too painful. Of course, I'd be very sad because life has so many rich things, you know, there's so many wonderful things in the world.
>
> *Patient:* If I only had one month to live, it would depend on my age, because I think that kids, when they're younger, tend to go through different stages of life, and I would probably do what I like most at the time.
>
> *Gardner:* Which is what?
>
> *Patient:* Well, it depends on the condition. If I was in pretty

good condition, I could do anything, but I would probably do my normal stuff. If I was kept in bed, I would write and read a lot.

Gardner: Write and read. Yeah, I know you like reading a lot.

Patient: I also like to write, too.

Gardner: Okay, those are most of the things that you like to do. Reading is good. What would you say is the main reason why reading is good?

Patient: You get information and you get pleasure, too.

Gardner: Right! That's a very good thing to have. You get pleasure out of getting information.

Patient: What's great about books is that you can take them anywhere—in bed, in school, everywhere. A book is like a portable encyclopedia.

Gardner: Right! Right! There's only one thing that you do sometimes with reading that has a negative side to it. What's that?

Patient: I don't know.

Gardner: Well, I say that sometimes you read, which is very good—but sometimes you read *instead* of doing your work. Is that right? Instead of doing things for school.

Patient: When I'm in school or when I'm at home?

Gardner: At home. Instead of doing homework or projects, sometimes you read.

Patient: No, I don't do that. Sometimes reading *is* my work. The teacher says read a lot.

Gardner: Right. I understand that sometimes you read instead of doing your work. You read other things that you're not supposed to read—stuff that isn't assigned for school—that you get so involved in *that* reading you don't do your schoolwork.

Patient: I don't think . . . maybe one or two times.

Gardner: Yeah, this is what I understood from your parents.

Patient: I try not to do that.

Gardner: Because that's a bad idea.

Patient: I used to do that because I used to have books cluttered all over and comics, but I keep all this stuff away from my desk.

Gardner: Good. It avoids temptation.

Patient: Yeah.

Gardner: That's a good idea. Well, I'm glad to hear that you're not doing that as much, because it's always a *great* thing to read and as you say, you get a lot of information and you become very learned. But at times it's not wise to read certain books when you're supposed to be reading other books for school. Do you know what I mean.

Patient: Uh huh.

Gardner: Okay, listen, we have to stop here. Let's count up. You get three extra chips because you are ahead. Now, how many do you have? I have five. How many do you have?

Patient: Ten.

Gardner: So, you're the winner. Congratulations!

Although there was some denial exhibited here, the interchange does reflect some progress on the patient's part. He was indeed spending less time reading material that was irrelevant to his school assignments. In addition, he was spending more time on his homework. Stan did well in treatment. His therapy lasted about six months. The closer his achievements approached those of his brother, the more confidence he acquired and the more he committed himself to his work. Because I did not consider his brother's "goodness" to be completely healthy, I did not attempt to help Stan reach his brother's level of perfection. That would have resulted in the substitution of one disorder (perfectionism and excessive compliance with authority) for another (disorganization and impaired commitment to obligations and other activities). I believe that the patient left therapy with a healthy commitment to a middle path.

⬜ ELEVEN
PERFECTIONISM

Perfectionistic children are likely to suffer with feelings of low self-esteem. The perfectionism may be compensatory in that it is a mechanism designed to compensate for feelings of low self-worth. However, it may result in producing even further feelings of low self-worth as the child predictably fails to live up to the high standards that have been set. We see here a typical example of the psychopathological symptom, namely, that it is designed to enhance self-worth and ends up doing just the opposite. In this section I will focus on the way in which problems in the realm of perfectionism can affect both self-esteem and a child's school performance.

PARENTAL FACTORS IN CHILDREN'S PERFECTIONISM

There are parents who are so insecure that they cannot admit occasional deficiencies to their children. They believe that any such revelations will cause the child to "lose respect." They do not appreciate that true respect involves the recognition of both assets and liabilities. They fail to realize that respect will still be there if the assets genuinely outweigh the liabilities. If the children of such parents do not come to appreciate the parental deficiencies themselves, then they may come to view their parents as people who are either perfect or very close to it. Even when a parent does reveal deficiencies, most children still tend to view their parents as more powerful, wise, effective, and efficient than they really are. From the child's vantage point, parents are giants. The child's inferiority to the parents in practically all areas is painfully apparent to them and contributes to feelings of inadequacy. (As mentioned, Alfred Adler, especially, emphasized this factor as a central element of the etiology of many forms of psychopathology.) Under the best of circumstances, therefore, the child is likely to develop mechanisms to compensate for these feelings of comparative inadequacy. Parents who need to present themselves as flawless to their children increase the painful disparity between themselves and their children and will add thereby to this source of their children's feelings of inadequacy. The healthy child will use genuinely adaptive compensatory mechanisms (such as the development of talent, skills, and traits that provide real ego enhancement); the disturbed child may use specious maneuvers (boasting, stealing, and grandiose thinking) to make up for this relative inadequacy.

Most often, parents are unsuccessful in promulgating the myth of their infallibility. As the child grows older, he (she) comes to appreciate the parental deficits in that they will inevitably reveal themselves in the course of the child's development. However, there are children who grow up still believing that their parents are perfect, or close to it. Such youngsters cannot but be disappointed with other individuals. They all inevitably reveal their deficits and become thereby compared unfavorably with the "perfect" parents. Such children cannot but be disappointed with all who reveal flaws. Such youngsters thereby suffer continual disillusionment in their relationships with others. They may continually be in search of those who, like their parents, will be "flawless." Relationships with "perfect" people, maintained as they must be by denial of deficiencies and delusions of faultlessness, are at best unstable and generally short-lived. These children are likely to have difficulties in their relationships with peers and with dating in adolescence. Later on, they may become intolerant of the inevitable deficits their co-workers reveal, and they may have particular difficulty with supervisors and bosses. Even more, they may have difficulty if they themselves are placed in administrative or supervisory positions, because they become intolerant of the inevitable deficiencies and weaknesses their employees will reveal. In marriage, as well, they are prone to become dissatisfied in marital relationships, and this may contribute to their becoming divorced one or more times.

Psychotherapeutic Approaches

Perfectionistic parents must be helped to appreciate that presenting themselves as infallible is a terrible disservice to the child. They have to be helped to gain the ego-strength to reveal their deficits. It is important that such parents be encouraged to take opportunities to confront their children with their own frailties. They need not resort to artificial or contrived examples, because life inevitably provides enough natural, ordinary, and predictable failures. For example, if mother leaves the cake in the oven too long, she could tell her daughter, "You see, it's just what I've been telling you: everyone makes mistakes at times." If father dents the car, he can say to his son, "This is an example of what I've been telling you. No one is perfect."

The therapist, as well, does well to point out areas of parental perfection. There are some parents who may find this intolerable. They may say, "I won't sit here and let you criticize me in front of my son." However, the same parent might be quite comfortable criticizing the son in front of the therapist. Such parents have to be helped to gain the ego-strength to tolerate such criticisms, to appreciate that they are benevolently given, and to be helped to recognize that this position is a disservice to the youngster. Most often the therapist's criticism of parents relates to child-rearing practices and other encounters with the child. However, there are times when the therapist may have occasion to criticize a parent because of encounters with the therapist. This is especially common in private practice with regard to payment of fees. Some parents will then invoke the criticism moratorium as a mechanism to protect themselves from being confronted with their failure to fulfill their financial obligations. They may say, "I don't discuss money in front of my children." To comply with this request is a disservice to the child. It protects the parent from exposure of a criticism—a criticism that is appropriate to divulge to the child. In addition, compliance with such a demand deprives the child of the opportunity to observe the therapist asserting himself (herself), something that most children in therapy have to be encouraged to do.

Very successful parents may, by the very nature of their success, produce very high standards in their children. However, my experience has been that when the children of such parents become unduly perfect—when they strive not merely for good performance but for perfect performance—and when they become exaggeratedly frustrated at failing to achieve perfection, other factors are usually operative. For example, in the pursuit of his (her) success, the parent may have neglected the child. Or the parent may have been actively competing with the child or instilling unrealistic standards of excellence. In all these situations, it was not the parental success alone that caused the child to be unduly perfectionistic, but additional contributing factors were operative. Parental success need not produce difficulties for children; in fact, it can serve as a stimulus for the child to achieve equal or even greater competence.

PERFECTIONISM IN THE CHILD

The primary manifestation of perfectionism in the child is intolerance for error. Perfectionistic children may subscribe to the dictum that a grade of 99 is equivalent to a grade of zero. Only 100 is a passing grade. They may psychologically flagellate themselves for even the most minor errors and this may produce a chronic state of unhappiness. They may be excessively neat and have to repeat an assignment over and over until it has reached the point that they consider perfect. They may write papers over and over again, ever dissatisfied with their handwriting and the appearance of the assignment. They may excessively doubt the quality of their work.

Older children tend to be more perfectionistic than their younger siblings. In the early years of their development, the older children have only adults to identify with and therefore, primarily take their standards as their own. All subsequent siblings have partial identification with children—their older siblings—and so are likely to be more relaxed regarding what they expect of themselves. In addition, younger children who attend the same schools as their older siblings may be frequently compared to the older siblings. In cases where the older sibling has been significantly successful, insensitive teachers may unfavorably compare the younger ones to the older. ("Why can't you be like your older sister? She was such a wonderful student.") This not only intensifies sibling rivalry (which is normally fierce), but contributes to feelings of low self-worth in the younger siblings.

Perfectionistic children may be afraid to commit themselves to a particular answer that may be wrong. They may present all options in the hope that one will be right, and thereby protect themselves from the criticism of having selected the wrong answer. They may even believe that all answers have equal weight and credibility in the service of protecting themselves from being incorrect. When given a particular assignment, they may refer to every book they can get their hands on to be sure they do not miss a point. However, they may be so overwhelmed by the immensity of the task that they may accomplish practically nothing. They often fail to differentiate important from unimportant information, and such lack of discrimination may result in their getting very low grades in spite of their formidable efforts.

Some children are highly perfectionistic and are too insecure to tolerate doing average or even good work. Either they must be the best or they will do nothing. When they choose the latter course, they justify their withdrawal with the specious argument: "I'd do extremely well if I wanted to try. I've just decided not to." The flaw in their reasoning, of course, is that they probably wouldn't do as well as they would like to think. They would rather say "I quit" than suffer the humiliation of having "flunked out." By not trying, they avoid confrontation with their inadequacies and their grandiose expectations of themselves. Some perfectionistic children will not risk taking an examination because they prefer to fail as a result of their not having tried than risk the humiliation of failing after strong effort. They can then maintain the delusion that they would have done well if they had tried. Taking the test may confront them with proof of their inadequacy. Not taking it allows them to maintain their delusion of perfection.

An element in the perfectionism of some children is the inordinate need to be admired by others. Certainly, successful students enjoy the esteem of their teachers and many of their fellow students – jealous resentment notwithstanding. Their inordinate need for such adoration may drive them to slave for academic perfection.

Adequate learning involves the capacity to admit that one is ignorant (not stupid). The child must have the ego-strength to accept the fact that there are many areas in which he (she) has little knowledge. However, there must be enough areas of competence to give the individual the feeling that he (she) is a worthwhile person in spite of areas of intellectual deficit. The child must also recognize that there is nothing to be ashamed about if one is ignorant in certain areas. The healthy person appreciates that one can only know an infinitesimal fraction of all there is to be learned. He (she) is generally comfortable with the knowledge that there is at least one (or a few) areas in which some degree of mastery has been obtained. Individuals with feelings of low self-worth may believe that it behooves them to go beyond this, and perfectionism may be he result. However, the symptom is a lost cause from the outset because of the impossibility of the goal.

There are some perfectionistic children who fear that if they do well, they will be expected to operate continually at an extremely high level of excellence. They believe that one *should* be capable of such performance, but that they themselves are not. They do not seem to appreciate how unrealistic and completely unattainable such a goal is. In response to this false notion about human potential, they attempt to gain for themselves the reputation of being intellectually limited. In this way no one, neither they nor anyone else, will have very high expectations of them. In this way they can avoid the humiliations they anticipate they will suffer by not maintaining a perfect record. In the school situation, where one's capacities are most readily "objectified" (with grades, reports, and evaluations), they can accomplish this most effectively. Sadly, such children may not only convince those around them that they are intellectually inferior, but may come to believe it themselves.

Psychotherapeutic Approaches

The psychotherapeutic approach to these children's perfectionism should include their acquiring a more accurate view of their parents. All patients, regardless of age, have to be helped in treatment to gain a clearer view of their parents. As children, we tend to operate on the principle: "If what my parents do and say is good enough for them, it's good enough for me." We tend to incorporate most if not all of our parents' traits—healthy and unhealthy. We swallow the whole bag, without separating the good from the bad. Therapy, in part, involves making (often very belatedly) these vital discriminations. The child and adolescent therapist has the opportunity to provide these corrections at a time in life when they can do the most good, at a time before the detrimental effects of such indiscriminating incorporation and acceptance have had a chance to become deeply entrenched. Children and adolescents have to be helped to appreciate that their parents, like all other human beings (including the therapist), are not perfect. We all have our deficits. Helping youngsters become clear regarding which personality traits of their parents are assets and which are liabilities can be very useful. And the therapist is in a unique position to provide such information. This process, of course, may require some advance work with the parents. But if the relationship with them is a good one, their cooperation can often be relied upon.

The child of a phobic mother can be told, "You know that

your mother has many fears that she herself realizes are not real. She knows that there's nothing to be afraid of in elevators or crowded places, but she just can't help herself. She'd prefer not to have these fears and that's why she's seeing a psychiatrist." Ideally, it can be helpful to get the mother herself to verbalize comments such as these to the child.

Some children, however, seem to be "naturally" perfectionistic and do not appear to have been exposed to any of the influences I have described; perhaps there is a genetic factor operative here. This potential factor notwithstanding, in all but the most severe cases, altered parental attitudes toward performance can help such perfectionistic children. Children tend to see their parents as omniscient and omnipotent; they generally try to emulate them; and this may contribute to their perfectionism. Appreciation by the child that the parent is fallible can be helpful, and it is important that parents take frequent opportunity to confront their children with their own frailties. One need not resort to artificial or contrived situations; life inevitably provides enough natural, ordinary failures. A father does well to say, "Sports were never my thing. I was always somewhat of a klutz on the ballfield. So I got involved in board games and other things that protected me from making a public fool of myself." A mother might say, "I was never very good in math; English was my subject. When I went to high school I took the minimal amount of math necessary to graduate. And in college I was able to avoid math courses entirely." Other comments that may be helpful to these children include: "As long as you think that any grade below A is unacceptable, you'll feel lousy about yourself" and "As long as you keep thinking that the only way to be happy is to win every class election, you'll be miserable." Although many factors contribute to perfectionistic attitudes, the aforementioned approaches—if utilized over time by parents who themselves are not unduly perfectionistic—can be helpful to many children in reducing their perfectionism and thereby enhancing their sense of self-worth.

When working with perfectionistic children psychotherapeutically, therapists do well to take opportunities to reveal deficiencies of their own. Such revelations should not be contrived; rather, they should be divulged in situations in which they are natural to the situation. The better the relationship the patient has with the therapist, the greater the likelihood the child will be affected by such revelations. In the context of the good therapist-patient relationship, a certain degree of identification with the therapist takes place. If the child can identify with the therapist being comfortable revealing both assets and liabilities (note that I did not say that the child should *identify with* the therapist's liabilities), then such revelations will have achieved one of their important goals, namely, helping the child become more comfortable with his (her) own deficiencies.

The Talking, Feeling, and Doing Game provides the therapist with many opportunities to reveal deficits. A classical psychoanalytic approach is not likely to provide the therapist with any opportunities for such conscious and deliberate revelations, although the therapist's behavior might result in such exposure in spite of his (her) attempt to strictly refrain from such divulgences. The following vignettes from *The Talking, Feeling, and Doing Game* are examples of this aspect of the therapy of perfectionistic children.

* * *

Question: Tell about the worst mistake you ever made in your whole life.

Response: Like everyone else, I have made my share of mistakes in life. No one is perfect and everyone makes some mistakes. In fact, I would say there's hardly a week in which I don't make one or two mistakes and some of them might be big ones. However, I believe that I've learned to make fewer and fewer mistakes as time has gone on. I've tried to learn from my mistakes, and I think I have.

I think one of the biggest mistakes I ever made in my whole life was to become partners with a person who once owned this building with me. I didn't know him very well, and I signed a contract in which we were partners in constructing and owning this building. I should have gotten to know him better before I became his partner. Unfortunately, I learned very early that he was very unreliable and dishonest. He caused me a lot of trouble. For many years I had to remain his partner and could never rely on him to be of any help in taking care of the building. In addition, I could not trust most of the things he said. He was also dishonest with money. Finally, I had to give him a lot of money in order to buy his share of the building, and then he left.

The whole thing was a big mistake and it lasted about seven years. I should have thought more in advance before I signed that contract. I should have gotten to know him better. If I had known him better, I never would have become his partner. I learned some important lessons from that painful experience. I learned that you should not make important decisions quickly. I learned that you have to get more information about a situation before making important decisions.

Besides using the question as an opportunity for the revelation of a deficiency, other therapeutic messages are woven in. I emphasize the importance of forethought and planning, and this may prove useful for the impulsive child. My speaking about this error without humiliation or shame can contribute to the child becoming more comfortable with deficiencies within himself (herself).

* * *

Question: What sport are you worst at?
Response: I never really was *very* good at sports. So there are a lot of sports I am pretty bad at. Of the sports that were commonly played in my neighborhood when I was a kid, I would say that the one that I was worst at was basketball. I guess that I didn't try hard enough. It's not that I was born a klutz; I just think that I didn't work at it enough. I used to feel pretty bad when kids would choose up sides and I was the last one to be chosen. Had I worked harder at it, it probably wouldn't have happened to me.

The card "What sport are you worst at?" essentially forces the therapist to reveal an area of weakness. Even if the therapist were an Olympic decathalon champion, he (she) would still be provided with the opportunity to talk about a sport in which he (she) is weak. Besides providing the aforementioned benefits of such a revelation, I use the response to put in a plug for the work ethic. The response also provides the child with the knowledge that I too had my rejections and that I too was not chosen for involvement in various activities when I was a child. This is a universal phenomenon and it is helpful for the child to know that the therapist also suffered such rejections. It contributes to a sense of communion with the therapist and this cannot but be therapeutic.

* * *

Question: Make believe that any three wishes you made would come true. What would you wish for?

Response: My *first* wish would be that the ringing in my ears would stop. Years ago I got a sickness in my ears that causes them to ring. There is no cure for it and I will have to live with it for the rest of my life. I don't hear the ringing when I'm involved in something, like when I'm talking with patients or when I'm doing something that I'm interested in. I hear it most when I'm sitting alone silently. There are certainly worse things that can happen to a person, but there are also many illnesses that cause much less trouble. I have to be very careful to avoid loud noises, because that would make the problem worse. So I stay away from places where bands are playing very loudly.

Although I am describing here a physical defect rather than a psychological one, the response still reveals an area of imperfection. In addition, I describe the precautions I take to prevent a deterioration of the condition. My hope is that the child will be similarly judicious when it comes to protecting himself (herself) from voluntarily contributing to the worsening of an illness from which he (she) may suffer.

My *second* wish would be that my hearing would get better. As you can see, I have a mild hearing problem and have to wear hearing aids. I'm nowhere close to deaf by any means and don't have to wear my hearing aids most of the time. However, I do have to wear my hearing aids at certain times when it's important that I hear *everything* people say. This is especially true in the office when I'm seeing patients.

Some people are ashamed to wear hearing aids. I'm not ashamed of it and never have been. To me it's something like glasses. If you have poor eyesight you wear glasses; if you have poor hearing you wear hearing aids. I have poor hearing and poor eyesight, so I wear both. I've never been ashamed. If anyone were to laugh at me, I would think there's something wrong with that person.

The response again reveals my comfort about revealing imperfection and it may help the child become more comfortable with his (hers). In addition, it is directed to children who are slavishly dependent on the opinions of others. People with low self-esteem tend to assume that any criticism made of them must be valid. My response introduces the notion that a malevolent criticizer is the one that deserves criticism and not the person being criticized. Considering this option can be useful in the alleviation of self-esteem problems. In the context of a discussion on this point I might refer to my story "The Pussycat and the Owl" in my book *Fables for our Times* (Gardner, 1981a). This fable focuses on the issue of criticism in great detail and is designed to help those who are excessively sensitive to criticism to look more closely at the criticizer with regard to benevolence, motivation, qualifications, and appropriateness.

My *third* wish would be that all the members of my family would enjoy good health. Good health is very important. If you don't have good health, it could ruin your pleasure and many other things in life. There are many people who are very rich who would give every penny they have if they could have good health. It's important in life to enjoy one's good health and appreciate the great gift it provides.

Of course, younger children are not likely to appreciate this advice and I generally reserve it for older children. It can also serve to enhance self-esteem if one appreciates how lucky one is with regard to good health. And it can serve as a partial antidote to the lowered feelings of self-worth that come from preoccupation with one's problems.

* * *

Question: Tell about a time when your feelings were hurt.

Response: Everyone has the experience of not getting something that's very important to him (her). My feelings were very hurt when I didn't get into the medical school of my first choice. In order to become a doctor, you have to go to college for four years after high school. Then, after you graduate college, you go to medical school for four years. I went to Columbia College and wanted very much to go on to the medical school at Columbia as well. Unfortunately, I was rejected. Many students with lower grades were accepted. They couldn't take everybody who wanted to go. In fact, they took very few. It was very difficult to get into that school, and it still is. I didn't have the feeling that I had been treated fairly and believed that I was better prepared for medical school than many of those who were accepted. It's not that they were poorly prepared. I think that most of them turned out to be good doctors anyway. It's just that I thought that I was more deserving than they. Anyway, my feelings were terribly hurt.

However, the end of the story is a good one. It has a happy ending. A number of years later I became a professor at the very medical school where I had been previously rejected. Life is like that. Everybody has disappointments. Nobody gets all the things he or she wants. Sometimes people who are less deserving get something, while the more deserving people do not. This doesn't mean that the person who is rejected isn't worthy, or is stupid, or dumb, or anything like that. It sometimes just means that that person isn't appreciated, even though he (she) may be worthy of such appreciation.

I recognize that the message here is not one that younger children are likely to understand very well. Older children, however, may very well comprehend the message. However, even then it is wise to ask the child to repeat what he (she) understands my response to have been. Most children will not find this condescending if the examiner presents it in a benevolent way. Under such circumstances I might say, "What I have said is very important; therefore, I want to be sure you understand it. I'd like to hear what you understand to be the meaning of what I just said." Or I might say, "You know that what I have just said is very complicated. Many children would not understand it. I'd like you to tell me what you understand to be the meaning of the things I've said." Any confusion or misinterpretation is then clarified.

I chose to select my own academic disappointment to help the child appreciate that, on occasion, we all suffer disappointments in school. Perfectionistic children may become devastated by such failures—to the serious detriment of their academic performance. Their egos are often too weak to tolerate such disappointments. If they appreciate that rejections are inevitable and that all (including psychiatrists) suffer them, these children may be less devastated by these failures. Last, the story had a happy ending, which I hoped would provide the patient with some optimism in the face of disappointment.

* * *

The aforementioned examples from *The Talking, Feeling, and Doing Game* attempt to help perfectionistic children deal with their problems by appreciating that the therapist himself (herself) has imperfections as well and can speak of them without significant shame or humiliation. They are designed to help the patient become more tolerant of deficit—a crucial attitude to have if one is to reduce perfectionistic tendencies. The examples below attempt to reduce perfectionism in another way. Specifically, they provide the patient with specific advice pertinent to one's attitude toward one's own imperfections. They are independent of the therapist and relate to the child's view of himself (herself). The better the child's relationship with the therapist, the greater will be the likelihood that these messages will be incorporated into the psychic structure.

Question: What is the worst thing a parent can do to a child?

Response: One of the worst things a parent can do to a child is to make the child think that he (she) must be perfect. There are parents who are very unhappy with a child whose grades are below A. Unless the child gets a 100 on an examination, they're unhappy. When a child comes home with a 99 on a test, such a parent might say, "How come you only got a 99?" Children of such parents feel miserable about themselves. Because they can never be perfect, they always feel unhappy. It would be much better if the children realized that nobody is perfect, that everybody makes mistakes. Even parents who are always bugging their children to get 100's and A's are not perfect themselves. They make mistakes themselves. Such children would feel better about themselves if they came to realize that it is all right to make mistakes—not only once in a while, but even often.

My intent in the above vignette is self-explanatory. I attempt to alter a stringent dictum under which the child is operating. To the degree that the therapist can be influential in altering this dictum, he (she) will be successful in reducing this factor in the child's perfectionism.

TWELVE
DENIAL AND RATIONALIZATION OF DEFICIENCIES

Ignoring, denying, and rationalizing one's defects is obviously not a way to directly deal with them. Rather, the utilization of such defense mechanisms serves merely to entrench weaknesses, with the result that they continue to contribute to the lowering of feelings of self-worth. The principle is well demonstrated by the old anecdote about the stuttering man who enters an elevator in a New York City skyscraper.

> *Man* (to the elevator operator): S-S-S-Seventy-t-t-two, p-p-please.
> *Operator:* Going up to CBS?
> *Man:* Y-Y-Yes. I'm ap-p-p-plying f-f-for a j-j-job as a t-t-tele-vis-vision a-a-a-n-n-nouncer.

Fifteen minutes later, the man reenters the same elevator.

> *Operator:* Well, did you get the job?
> *Man:* N-N-No. Th-Th-They f-f-f-ffound ou-ou-out I w-w-was J-J-Jewish.

The story demonstrates its point quite well. To explain failures and rejections as resulting from prejudice or other irrational animosities may certainly be the case in certain situations—and it is the therapist's job to define these clearly when they occur. There is a tendency by those who are the object of prejudice to believe that all rejections result from discrimination rather than from their own personality defects. In this way they avoid painful confrontations with their personal deficiencies. The preservation of self-esteem by such avoidance is specious. Blinding children to their deficiencies may protect them temporarily from the esteem-lowering effects of such confrontations, but a heavy price is paid for this benefit. These children are deprived of the opportunity to take those steps that might rectify their defects and truly enhance their sense of self-worth.

COMMON DENIAL AND RATIONALIZATION MECHANISMS OF CHILDHOOD

Many children (especially between the ages of six and eight) have a tendency to blame others for their disappointments and misfortunes. In fights it's always the other kid who starts; they are the innocent bystanders. When they are disliked, it's the other children who are unfriendly, snobbish, and cliquish. They have great difficulty accepting their own participation in bringing about their difficulties. They may be too insecure to tolerate any defect. They many not believe they have any counterbalancing assets, and this makes it most difficult for them to allow for deficiencies. At this point, I have been practicing psychiatry about 35 years. It is extremely rare for a child below the age of nine or ten to come to treatment with the insight that he (she) has psychological problems and the motivation to alleviate them via the nebulous and unknown route of psychotherapy. Rather, the typical child I see presents with the following story: He was standing in the schoolyard minding his own business, deeply absorbed in reading his Bible. All of a sudden—without any provocation or warning—someone comes over and kicks him in the balls. At the very moment that he suffered this indignity, he happened to be reading the part that talks about turning the other cheek. Accordingly, he decides to implement this method of dealing with his enemy. In Christ-like fashion, he does not submit to animal instincts that compel him to respond in kind. Rather, he follows the biblical teachings and finds himself smashed in the head. This same patient generally considers himself to be the victim of a conspiracy among his teachers and school administrators. Although his behavior has always been exemplary, for some unknown reason they have singled him out and subjected him to a wide variety of totally unwarranted disciplinary measures. Ultimately, his parents were brought to school and threatened with a wide variety of dire consequences if their son's allegedly antisocial behavior continued.

It may be of interest for the reader to learn that during this same 35-year span, it is I who always seems to be referred these innocent victims. Other therapists get the bullies. Somehow, all the victims get referred to me, and all the scapegoaters, tantalizers, and bullies are allowed to float freely in the school and are allowed to subject *my* patients to their persecutions!

With such children the following interchange is typical:

> *Gardner:* Do I understand correctly that you have *never once* started a fight in school?
> *Patient:* That's right.
> *Gardner* (with incredulous tone): In your whole eight years of life you never *once* started a fight in school?
> *Patient* (somewhat sheepishly): Well, maybe once.
> *Gardner:* Well, tell me about that time.
> *Patient:* I can't remember it now. I'll tell you next time.
> *Gardner:* Well, we've got plenty of time. Try to think about it now.
> *Patient:* I forgot.

Children have weak egos. They have thin skins. They are very fragile. They cannot allow themselves to deal directly with confrontations in which their weaknesses and frailties are exposed. Accordingly, therapists do well not to try to get children to provide testimonies about their psychological problems and professions of their wish to alleviate them. Rather, they do well to accept the need on the part of the child to deny deficiencies and rationalize away their existence. Many of the techniques described in this book (especially the mutual storytelling technique and its derivative games) enable the therapist to deal with children in such ways that they need not consciously accept the fact that they have deficiencies.

Parents, however, should not join in with their children in the utilization of such rationalizations and denial mechanisms. Parents who blame the teacher at school when their children get into difficulty only entrench and perpetuate this problem. Some parents deny that their children could be anything but perfect; they consider the child's school difficulty to be the result of teacher inadequacy or school system deficiency. They further cripple their children by fostering in them delusions of competence and encouraging their tendency to blame others for their own deficits, thus depriving them of the opportunity and incentive to rectify their deficiencies. And this contributes to feelings of low self-worth.

This kind of displacement mechanism need not be confined to prejudice. The adolescent girl who attributes her lack of popularity to her large nose is generally disappointed after plastic surgery when the telephone doesn't start ringing. Other youngsters may attribute their interpersonal difficulties to acne, tallness, shortness, father's income, location of their home, birthmarks, or minor blemishes. Although it may be true that the particular "defect" alienates a small fraction of those they encounter, it is rarely as loathsome a quality as the youngsters believe. They have exaggerated its importance to avoid coming to terms with what may be more significantly estranging qualities. If they believe their unpopularity results from minor skin blemishes, this is no reflection on their qualities as people; they were unlucky enough to have been born that way and are being discriminated against through no fault of their own. The irrationality of others is the cause of their failure to have friends, and because they take none of the blame themselves, they can preserve their self-respect. However, to come to terms with the fact that they may be selfish, egotistical, or disrespectful of the rights of others would make them think less of themselves. In addition, it would involve them in the possibly long and arduous process of trying to rectify these deficiencies. The former attitude provides only ostensible self-respect; the latter promises genuine feelings of self-worth if the patient can pursue the course through to the rectification of the deficiencies. And it is the therapist's job to help their patients have the courage to do so.

A related maneuver is to utilize the "bad luck" rationalization. The disappointments, rejections, and calamities of life are attributed to the fact that the person has always had "bad luck." This is considered to have been a lifelong problem that dates back to childhood and may extend throughout the individual's life. The rationalization is justified by pointing to the various calamities that have befallen the individual throughout the course of his (her) life. Often, these are no more than the usual grief-causing episodes that all of us are subjected to in the course of our existence. I do not deny that there are many people who do indeed have bad luck in that they may be afflicted with crippling diseases or subjected to terrible catastrophes that were in no way related to faults of their own. I am referring here to individuals who, from the point of view of objective observers, have really had no more or less of their share of bad luck and subscribe to the "bad luck" rationalization as a way of avoiding focus on their defects, both rectifiable and nonrectifiable.

COMMON DENIAL AND RATIONALIZATION MECHANISMS OF ADOLESCENCE

Although adolescents generally have "thicker skins" than younger children with regard to their ability to tolerate confrontation with their deficits, they are generally not famous for their receptivity to such confrontations, especially in the psychotherapist's office. The stigma of having to see a psychiatrist is a formidable one, possibly greater for the adolescent than for younger children and adults. Accordingly, although they may recognize that they have problems, they often have great difficulty admitting this to themselves, and certainly not to others. These defenses against the lowering of their self-worth that would result from awareness of difficulties compromises significantly their capacity to gain conscious insight into the fact that they have problems and, by extension, lessens the likelihood that they will be motivated for treatment. Those who ultimately do get to us represent a small fraction of all those who have difficulties. And even those who are willing to come to our office are not generally committed to the principles of insight and motivation. Rather, most who come to us must often find a rationalization to justify their being in treatment. The most common rationalization is that the youngster is being coerced into therapy and is submitting to irrational and punitive parents who are forcing him (her) to see the therapist. Most adolescents subscribe to the following position with regard to their involvement in treatment: "I am a perfectly normal, healthy person. I have the misfortune of having been given by God two parents who have screws loose in their heads. In some misguided way they harbor the delusion that I have psychiatric problems and force me to see a shrink against my will. My coming to this therapist is a judicious form of submission in that the pain I suffer attending sessions is less than the punishments I would be subjected to at home if I were to refuse."

Holmes (1964) is well aware of this phenomenon and speaks of it frequently in his superb book, *The Adolescent in Psychotherapy:* "The adolescent . . . is so desperately aware of his need for help that he dare not call it by that name. He must represent it to himself and to others as an abominable infringement upon his personal rights by a meddling adult" (p. 209). The adolescent often needs what Holmes refers to as "a face-saving show of resistance" (p. 186). In fact, Holmes goes further and states that when the adolescent professes motivation for psychotherapy it is generally wise to be somewhat incredulous: "A youngster's direct request for psychiatric treatment, his sincerely expressed wish to cooperate in psychotherapy even before he has the least idea what it is, or his sober appraising of the therapist's abilities, are all representative of the kind of resistance which sends shivers of apprehension through the therapist who is experienced in treating adolescents" (p. 117).

With regard to adolescents' claims that their parents are forcing them into therapy, the realities are that no parent can actually force an adolescent to come to treatment. In fact, a parent cannot even force a younger child to attend treatment on an ongoing basis. Younger children may be physically carried into the consultation room, but even then, if the child is adamant enough in his (her) refusal, the likelihood is that the therapist will ultimately give up. And the adolescent cannot even be physically brought into the consultation against his (her) will. Even if the parent is injudicious enough to physically overwhelm the adolescent and bodily coerce the patient into the therapist's office, the therapist is not likely to go along with this method of bringing the youngster to treatment. The therapist does well to accept the patient's excuse and not attempt to help the youngster gain insight into the fact that it is a rationalization. To do so may result in losing the patient. Rather, the therapist does well to sidestep such discussions, change the subject, and try to draw the youngster into discussing other topics that may be of interest to him (her), e.g., "Yeah, I agree with you. Lots of kids are forced here by parents against their will. But as long as you're already here, and as long as they're paying for the session, we might as well talk about something, anything at all. I see you have a written dream there in your hand. Why don't we talk about that?" (The fact that the youngster has brought in a dream is confirmation that he really wants to be there, professions of resistance and hatred of the therapist notwithstanding.)

CONCLUDING COMMENTS

The main point in this section is that children, and to a lesser extent adolescents, have deep feelings of low self-worth and need to provide themselves with a host of rationalizations that are designed to protect them from conscious awareness of their deficits. Therapists should appreciate that direct confrontations and psychotherapeutic approaches that attempt to help the youngster gain insight are not likely to be effective. Rather, the kinds of circuitous routes described throughout this book are more likely to be effective. These techniques are utilized with respect for the ancient Greek wisdom, "Give a man a mask and he'll tell you the truth."

☐ THIRTEEN
TRUE PRIDE VS. FALSE PRIDE

A sense of pride, if it is to be genuinely ego-enhancing, must be based on an attribute acquired through some effort. The fewer such sources of pride one has, the more likely one will attempt to gain such feelings from qualities that have been inherited and/or effortlessly acquired. But it requires a certain degree of self-delusion to consider the easily acquired attributes to provide the same degree of esteem-enhancement as real accomplishments. Children who do poorly in school are likely to utilize these compensatory mechanisms. But I am not restricting myself to the academic realm. A child who is not a strong student may still gain genuinely healthy pride in other school-related activities such as sports, music, or drama. It is when the child doesn't have any sense of genuine pride in any of these areas that he (she) may resort to the utilization of maneuvers that appear to enhance self-worth, but basically do not.

TRUE AND FALSE PRIDE IN CHILDHOOD

Some children may attempt to compensate for their feelings of inadequacy by exaggerating their competence or boasting about exploits that never took place. Recognizing that the child who excels enjoys the admiration of others, the unpopular child may try to gain similar prestige. These are the children who describe themselves to their classmates as having been champions in various activities at summer camp. They are the ones who boast that they "never crack a book" or they "never have to do homework" when, in fact, they may be studying quite hard to get good or even passing grades. Such children, through their descriptions of interesting and unusual exploits, may enjoy some ego-enhancing attention at first. However, they live with the fear that their prevarications will be disclosed—and such feelings invariably lower their feelings of self-worth. In addition, if they have a conscience at all, they cannot but have less inner respect for themselves because of their lying. And when others discover that they have been taken in (and they inevitably do), such children may suffer even more rejection than when they had been unpopular but truthful. This increased alienation from others produces even further feelings of worthlessness. Here again, the principle is well demonstrated: The psychopathological symptom, which is in part derived to enhance self-worth, usually ends up by lowering it—its other "benefits" notwithstanding. Although other factors may contribute to this kind of lying, the attempt to enhance self-esteem is central.

Therapists of such prevaricators do well to impress upon them that they will invariably end up being less liked rather than better liked when others realize they are being lied to and that they can be liked for themselves without being "the champ." In addition, they should help such children develop traits and abilities that will genuinely attract others so that duplicity as a way of gaining affection will be unnecessary.

The Class Clown

Most classes seem to have at least one clown. These are the children who basically feel unloved and dupe themselves into believing that the laughter of their classmates is a sign of their affection for them. They seem to be blind to the fact that the other children are more often laughing *at* them rather than *with* them, and they delude themselves into thinking that the other children's enjoyment of their antics reflects respect. However, they are still not the ones who get elected to class offices, who are invited most frequently to birthday parties, or who are selected early when teams are being formed. In response to this further rejection (and loss of respect), they may resort to even more hare-brained escapades in the futile attempt for acceptance. What results, of course, is even further alienation—and the vicious cycle may continue.

Therapists do well to try to impress upon such children that their antics are losing them friends, rather than gaining them, and that the other children are still not seeking them, in spite of the fact that they laugh at their jokes. If they are successful in demonstrating this to the child, they may be able to reduce the likelihood that the patient will resort to this ego-debasing maneuver. Again, therapists must help such youngsters develop genuinely attractive traits that will draw people to them if they are to give up the clowning pattern and not substitute equally self-defeating forms of relating to their peers. Demonstrated here is another well-known therapeutic principle: If you're going to try to take something (a symptom) away from somebody, you're not likely to be successful if you don't, at the same time, try to give them some compensatory substitute in return.

The Briber

Children whose behavior is such that their peers do not voluntarily seek them may find that "philanthropy" can gain them an amazing degree of popularity. Doling out candy, money, small toys, and other gifts may make the difference between standing on the sidelines and being one of the team, if only as a pinch hitter. The "gifts" may make the difference between spending a lonely afternoon in the house and being one of the gang, if only as a follower. The child may resort to stealing money from parents and siblings to support such charitable enterprises. Although purchasing friends in this way may temporarily relieve such children's loneliness and its associated feelings of worthlessness, inwardly the children know that the friendships so gained are specious, that they depend upon continual bribery, and that they are being exploited. Such awareness inevitably lowers feelings of self-worth.

Again, therapists of such children must try to impress upon them that they are being taken advantage of and that those who play with them only for a price are not true friends. More important, they must help these children rectify those patterns that are alienating their peers in the first place and replace them with modes of relating that will enhance rather than detract from feelings of self-worth.

The Cheater

Cheaters do not have, or do not believe they have, the competence to be successful in the activity in which they cheat. They do not seem to appreciate that reaching a goal dishonestly cannot provide the same degree of satisfaction and enhanced self-worth, or the same sense of accomplishment, as coming by it honestly. They do not seem to appreciate that the gratifications they may derive from the dishonestly attained goal are generally more than counterbalanced by the inner feeling of shame associated with the knowledge that the accomplishment was not genuinely earned. Children who cheat on school examinations can be told: "You really can't feel good about having gotten that high mark by copying." In addition, they can be reminded that it is likely that their classmates have observed what they did and that this certainly is not going to enhance popularity.

Generally, when a child cheats when playing a game with me, I tell him (her) that it is no fun for me to play games with someone who is cheating and I will only continue to play as long as the rules are followed. Having the *living experience* that cheating may threaten the continuation of an enjoyable experience, as well as lessen the affection the youngster enjoys from someone who is held in esteem, may serve as an effective deterrent. In addition, I generally ask such youngsters whether they play the same way with their friends and if so, to consider the possibility that that may be one of the reasons why they are having trouble keeping friends.

The reader should note that in such situations I do not appeal to higher ethical and moral principles when attempting to modify such a child's behavior, but rather to the child's sense of expediency and to other considerations relevant to everyday experiences. In my philosophy of things, the cheater is not being watched by someone up there who is keeping a careful record and will see to it that someday the miscreant will be punished for this transgression (either in this life or after death). I therefore cannot use such appeals to help cheaters see the errors of their ways. Those who do subscribe to this theory have a very powerful method of deterring those who subscribe to it as well. I can, however, appeal to more immediate and mundane considerations that are not only more effective in helping the child with the problem, but also avoid the additional difficulties introduced when appealing to the Almighty for help in solving the day-to-day problems of life. To be reminded that cheating makes you feel lousy about yourself and may lose you friends is honest, direct, and relevant to the child's life in the present. To invoke the wrath of God, hell's fires, and other forms of eternal damnation may scare the child out of cheating, but it may scare him into other things far worse.

The Bully

Children with a healthy level of self-worth do not need to bully others in order to enhance their self-esteem. In contrast, children who have low self-esteem and who, in addition, have significant anger that they act out are likely to become bullies. Obviously, the therapist must investigate the causes of the anger (usually in the family) and attempt to rectify those situations that are engendering the child's hostility. One must also address oneself to the factors that were operative in the choice of acting out to deal with the anger. All this does not preclude, however, my saying to the bully something along these lines: "I know you think you're quite a big shot when you beat up those little kids.

But deep down inside, you know that there's nothing so great about it and that must make you feel kind of bad about yourself. You think the kids think you're hot stuff when you go around beating up lots of kids. Some of them may; but others, I am sure, don't like you at all. They feel sorry for the children you're hitting and I'm sure you've noticed how they stay away from you." Although these comments can be very bitter medicine to swallow, they are accepted if the patient has a good relationship with the therapist. In addition, as mentioned, the therapist's attitude is more important than the content in determining whether his (her) comments will alienate a patient. When benevolently communicated in the context of a firm relationship, the most painful confrontations may be accepted.

TRUE AND FALSE PRIDE IN ADOLESCENCE

Adolescents have much to feel inadequate about. In our modern technological society they generally have not yet acquired the skills necessary for them to function independently, yet they would like to believe that they can. The disparity between their actual level of competence and that which they fantasize they have can contribute to feelings of inadequacy. Some of the methods of compensation for these feelings of low self-worth involve the utilization of false-pride maneuvers. And these operate both within and outside of the school system and affect the youngster's involvement with learning and peers.

Adolescent Omniscience

No one knows more about the world than the adolescent. There are adolescents who consider themselves the epitomization of all the knowledge that has ever been accumulated in the history of the world. Although they may not be honest enough to profess openly such an immodest opinion of themselves, every cell in their bodies communicates this view. Obviously, such grandiosity is compensatory. A common way by which adolescents deal with the feelings of inadequacy derived from this obvious disparity is scorning their elders and viewing them as "idiots." This mechanism of compensation is especially seen among the intellectual types who will use their newfound knowledge to lord their superiority over their elders. They may try to flaunt their knowledge to their parents and thereby show them up as imbeciles. Some do this with teachers and relish the opportunity to point out the inevitable errors that any teacher will occasionally make. They generally fail to appreciate how limited is their knowledge and that by virtue of their youth they cannot possibly have accumulated the depth and breadth of information that serves as a solid foundation for the expertise of their elders. I am not claiming that their elders are *necessarily* more knowledgeable and wiser, only that there is a greater likelihood that this will be the case. One of the problems attendant to the utilization of this mechanism is that the individual will learn very little from teachers, parents, and even from peers.

Delusions of Invulnerability

Elsewhere (Gardner, 1988a) I have discussed much about adolescents' delusions of invulnerability. I consider this an important adolescent manifestation that, in part, serves to compensate for feelings of low self-worth. Military leaders are well aware of the phenomenon. Adolescents make wonderful soldiers. They are old enough to have the physical stamina and strength to function admirably on the battlefield, yet they are simple-minded enough to believe that they are not likely to be killed. They can thereby be encouraged to walk into the cannon's mouth and believe that those around them may fall, but they, somehow, will be spared. Visit any military graveyard; look at the ages of those who are buried there; the average in 20th-century cemeteries is the late teens. In earlier centuries it was the early to mid-teens. In short, wars have been fought primarily by children. Adults are smart enough to stay far behind the lines and spare themselves.

The Beautiful People and Exhibitionism

Mechanisms to compensate for feelings of inadequacy pervade the adolescent's life. Adolescent girls will spend many hours a day attempting to improve their appearance. The multi-billion dollar cosmetics industry is not geared simply for adult women, but for adolescents as well. The industry knows that the best time to get women "hooked" on these products is during the adolescent years, when people are most vulnerable to believing the advertising and most likely to be obsessed with their appearance. These preoccupations are not simply for the purpose of attracting the opposite sex; they also serve to enhance feelings of self-worth. (The two go together.) Concern with the details of one's appearance also serves to ensure admission to the peer group—admission often being dependent on scrupulous imitation of the prevailing style. Acceptance into the group also serves to compensate for feelings of low self-worth, because such acceptance essentially communicates the message that the youngster is indeed a worthwhile individual if he (she) can gain admission into a particular "exclusive" club.

The half-naked muscle men that we so frequently see in public may be spending hours each day subjecting themselves to the most grueling exercises in order to enjoy the fantasy that others are impressed with their power, strength, enormous muscles, etc. Competition over who can consume the most alcohol can also serve to compensate for feelings of low self-worth. The youngster may actually hate beer, but will guzzle down as many cans as possible in order to impress his peers and thereby enhance his feelings of self-worth. Or, he may brag about how fast he has driven his car, or how flashy or expensive it is. Advertising companies, of course, are very happy to capitalize on this inanity of thinking, which extends into adult years for many (if not most) people. Of significance here is that the attribute selected for self-aggrandizement is *easily* acquired. What many adolescents fail to appreciate is that easily acquired attributes do not enhance self-worth as well as those that require long hours of dedicated labor. It is no particular feat to drink formidable amounts of beer; it is a feat to play the violin well, to be a champion chess player, to be an extremely competent basketball player, or to get very high grades on one's college entrance examinations. Youngsters who do not believe they can achieve healthy self-confidence in the latter areas are likely to resort to the former.

Materialism and Conspicuous Consumption

There is an anecdote that demonstrates this point quite well. Actually, it is best told by first asking the listener if he (she) can figure out the moral or the lesson of this story:

One day a mouse was walking through the jungle and suddenly heard the deep voice of another animal crying out, "Help, help, help!! I'm sinking in quicksand!" The mouse quickly ran to the source of the cries and there saw a huge elephant, sinking rapidly into the quicksand.

The mouse ran over to the edge of the quicksand and yelled to the elephant, "Don't worry. I'll save you. I have a Cadillac and I'll use it to pull you out of the quicksand." At this point, the mouse went over to his Cadillac and backed it up so that the rear bumper was at the edge of the pool of quicksand. He then yelled to the elephant: "Put your trunk around my rear bumper and I'll pull you out. Hurry, Hurry!" And so the elephant wrapped his trunk around the rear bumper of the Cadillac and the mouse, after great effort, with grinding of his Cadillac's motors, was finally successful in pulling the elephant out of the quicksand.

After wiping himself off the elephant said to the mouse, "I want you to know that I will never forget what you've done for me here today. As everybody knows, we elephants have wonderful memories and never forget anything. I want you to know, then, that if you're ever in trouble, just send word through the jungle and I'll do everything in my power to help you, even at the risk of my own life."

About a year later, the same elephant was walking through the jungle and he suddenly heard a squeaky voice yelling, "Help, help, help! I'm sinking in the quicksand. Please come and help me. Please! Please!"

The elephant ran toward the source of the noise and there he saw this little mouse sinking rapidly into the quicksand. He then said, "Why you're the very same mouse who saved my life last year. As I told you then, I'll never forget the good deed you did for me. And so now I'm going to return the favor and I'm going to save your life." The elephant then went over to the edge of the quicksand and, while lowering his huge penis into it, said to the mouse, "Hurry, grab onto the end of my penis and I'll pull you out of the quicksand." And so the mouse reached up, grabbed on to the end of the elephant's penis, and the elephant pulled his penis in, hand over hand, finally pulling the mouse out of the quicksand! The end.

The listener is then asked for the moral or lesson of this story. For those who haven't figured it out: "If you've got a big penis, you don't need a Cadillac." And this principle very much applies to adolescents who aspire to own fancy cars, which they believe will attract the most desirable girls (sometimes the case) and enhance their feelings of self-worth (not as likely the case). Some may neglect their studies in order to work to earn the money to buy such a car (obviously not of the latest model). Considering the rampant materialism in our society and the ubiquity of conspicuous consumption, therapists will generally have a difficult time trying to help youngsters gain insight into the futility of subscribing to such values. Although therapists may not be successful against such formidable influences, it still behooves them to try to plant the seed in which the virtues of an alternative value system are proposed.

Sexual Prowess

Sexual activities, as well, may serve to compensate for feelings of inadequacy. Adolescents are typically concerned with whether or not they are sexually attractive to members of the opposite sex. The best way to prove such attractiveness, of course, is to actually have sexual experiences. Normally, an adolescent boy will not feel that he is "a man" until he has had sexual relations. I do not consider this belief necessarily to be pathological, as long as it is put in proper perspective and the boy does not become obsessed with losing his virginity or walk around feeling worthless if he has not yet achieved the exalted status of nonvirgin. It is even within the normal range to relate the details of his sexual experiences to his peers, even with some exaggeration. Although there is some insensitivity here to the "reputation" of the girl involved, I consider such sharing and even boasting to be so common that I cannot necessarily label it pathological. It is really asking too much of a teenage boy to tell absolutely no one about his first sexual experience.

In recent years, however, there has been less stigma for the girls who have been used more for the purposes of the boys' self-aggrandizement than for sexual gratification. The boy who is obsessively preoccupied with the number of his "conquests" and who is frequently bragging about them is likely to have psychiatric difficulties, especially in the realm of low self-esteem. The more secure boy does not generally need to brag so extensively. And girls who feel inadequate may use sexual receptivity to attract boys and thereby prove to themselves that they are worthwhile. An element in girls' sexual promiscuity is the need to compensate for feelings of low self-worth. They are even willing to suffer the reputation of being a "slut" or a "whore" for the benefits they believe they are deriving in the realm of enhancing their self-worth.

Denial of Mortality

Becker (1973, 1975) has proposed that a central element in the development of psychopathological symptoms is the denial of the painful feelings associated with our realization that someday we will die. One of the ways in which human beings differ significantly from lower animals is in our ability to appreciate that we are mortal. It may be the greatest price we pay for our superior intelligence. Many psychological phenomena, both normal and abnormal, include the element of denial of our fallibility and mortality. Some people involve themselves in activities in which they flirt with death in order to prove that they, in contrast to other more fragile humans, need not be grasped by death's claws. They place themselves in extremely precarious positions and then pride themselves on their ability to come out unscathed. Skydivers, tightrope walkers, mountain climbers, speed racers, and bull fighters are just a few examples of people with a strong need to prove to themselves that they, unlike others, are invulnerable to death. The general populace admires those who demonstrate such fearlessness and will make them heroes. Moreover, the admirers need to maintain the delusion that their heroes are invulnerable. If events destroy the delusion, then the hero no longer serves his (her) purpose and is dispensed with. Once Achilles is wounded in his heel, he is no longer revered. But it is a two-way arrangement. Achilles needs to feel invulnerable to compensate for the feelings of vulnerability he has over his appreciation of his mortality. And his worshipers need to maintain the image that Achilles is invulnerable in order to give them hope that they are invulnerable as well.

This phenomenon is related to the aforementioned adolescent's delusion of invulnerability. The adolescent smokes and believes that he is immune to lung cancer and the other diseases caused by smoking. He drives at high speeds, while inebriated, and believes that he will neither be injured nor killed. He even plays "chicken" on the open road. For those not familiar with this "game," two cars – driving head on in the same lane – approach each other at high speeds. The first one to veer off the collision path is viewed as a "chicken" and the "loser" of the game. It is not just simplemindedness that is required to be willing to involve oneself in this idiocy. Also involved is the need to compensate for feelings of inadequacy by attempting to prove that one is indeed courageous. Another element, however, is its value in dealing with death fears. Once the youngsters have survived, they can flaunt their invulnerability to death.

FALSE PRIDE IN ONE'S HERITAGE

The false-pride mechanisms described here for adolescents are not necessarily confined to that age bracket. There are many individuals who continue to use such compensatory maneuvers throughout their lives. There are even some who retain in adulthood the false-pride mechanisms described for children. There are many forms of false pride that adults utilize, most of which are derived from childhood and adolescent practices. Here I focus on one, false pride in one's heritage, especially as it relates to mechanisms designed to enhance self-worth. To say "I'm proud to be an American" is not a very effective way of enhancing one's feelings of self-worth, because the person born in the United States did absolutely nothing to become an American. Because discussion of one's heritage can be a "touchy subject," one is always safer to start with one's own heritage. Accordingly, I will use this example first: The person who says "I'm proud I'm Jewish because Einstein, Freud, etc., were Jewish" has made an inane comment. The speaker is obviously trying to gain some prestige for himself by association with great Jewish men. He is trying to delude himself into thinking that he is somehow a better person because he is of the same religious background as these great contributors. Einstein and Freud have justification for feeling proud of their accomplishments (and possibly their parents and teachers for the roles they played in their growth and development), but not everyone else in their synagogue. Similarly, there is nothing to be either proud or ashamed of for being black, Irish, Italian, Afghanistanian, Timbuktuian, or anything-else-ian.

We are what we are (regarding national and ethnic origin) because of how, where, and when the genetic dice fell for us. In the 1960s many black people realized that they had done themselves a terrible disservice by agreeing with those who were prejudiced against them that being black was intrinsically inferior. No longer, said they, would they be ashamed that they are black. This was certainly an important insight. However, the usual antidote to this problem was to profess instead: "I'm *proud* I'm black." To me this is to substitute one inappropriate adaptation for another. It is as absurd to say "I'm ashamed I'm black" as to say "I'm proud I'm black." The black person did not have to pass a test in heaven before being permitted to come down to earth with black skin. There was never any contest in which the winners were allowed to be black. There was never any skill that had to be demonstrated in order to acquire this particular skin color. Accordingly, it is nothing to be proud of. But it is nothing to be ashamed of either. Pride has absolutely nothing to do with it. Therefore, it will not work to enhance self-esteem.

I believe it is important to differentiate between *knowledge* of one's heritage and *pride* in one's heritage. I believe that it is useful for an individual to have knowledge about one's heritage, to be able to place oneself at some point in the migrations of humanity. One does well to look at a globe and try to trace, as far back as possible, the paths that were taken by one's forebears prior to their arrival at the place where the individual was born. Each person has such a history, although we often know very little about the details. Such considerations contribute to one's sense of identity. But this must be differentiated from self-worth. To be on migration path A rather than on migration path B makes one different; it does not make one better or worse. To learn about ancestors who have made significant contributions for the benefit of humanity is interesting to know, but their accomplishments cannot really enhance us. Only what *we* do ourselves can enhance us. Every group can point out illustrious individuals who made important contributions to the group's growth and development. However, the same group has its own collection of scoundrels, psychopaths, megalomaniacs, etc., who are generally not mentioned when one is talking about one's heritage. It is as reasonable to feel self-enhanced because of one's famous forbears as it is to feel less enhanced because of the low-life characters who are also part of everyone's heritage. The issue here has nothing to do with pride and self-esteem; it has to do with history.

The issues I have just discussed have generally been a point of great controversy when I mentioned them in public lectures. Invariably, there are a few who become quite incensed. Some even accuse me of being a Jewish anti-Semite. Yet, in the ensuing discussion I have not heard a point of refutation that has been convincing. The rebuttals usually involve exhortations that people *should* be proud of their heritage and that those who are not should be ashamed of themselves. My guess is that those who have a strong need to subscribe to this principle do so because they have few qualities they can point to that can provide them with a strong sense of self-worth, or they may believe that they have no such qualities when they really do.

These inappropriate and maladaptive ways of interpreting one's heritage are usually communicated to children in the earliest stages of life. They teach children to utilize specious maneuvers to enhance self-esteem and they may divert their efforts from endeavors that can genuinely enhance self-worth. They teach empty boasting and false pride—qualities that are intrinsically ego-debasing.

PSYCHOTHERAPEUTIC APPROACHES

The way in which the mutual storytelling technique can be useful for helping children who use specious ego-enhancing maneuvers (in the realm of false pride) is demonstrated by Gail, who entered treatment at the age of eight-and-a-half. Her parents were divorced, but were both genuinely committed to her. Their main difficulty was in motivating Gail to study. She would daydream in school and exhibit little commitment to her classwork, both in school and afterward. She would lose her books, assignments, and notes from the teacher. Although she was getting C and D grades, she scored quite high on national tests measuring academic achievement.

At home she procrastinated whenever she was asked to assume household responsibilities. She would not listen when her parents were speaking, and often the same request had to be repeated many times over. At times she was negativistic. She complained frequently and wanted her own way. She was intermittently depressed, but not to the degree that she lost her appetite or interest in friends and recreation. Last, she tended to deny and avoid the unpleasant.

This interchange took place while playing the mutual storytelling game:

> *Gardner:* Good afternoon, boys and girls, ladies and gentlemen. Today is September 5, 1980, and I'm happy to welcome you all once again to Dr. Gardner's *Make-Up-a-Story* Television Program. It is my pleasure to tell you that our guest today has been on the show before and is now going to tell her own original, made-up story, completely made up from her own imagination, right?
> *Patient:* Yeah.

Gardner: Nothing that really happened to you or anyone you know, right?

Patient: Right.

Gardner: Okay, you're on the air!

Patient: This is sort of a weird fairy tale. Now there was this nice lion. He wasn't too nice and something about him, he had very short-cut manes. All the other lions had big, long manes. And somebody said, "I don't think that looks pretty on you."

Gardner: When they said, "That doesn't look pretty on you," what were they referring to?

Patient: That his mane was cut short?

Gardner: Okay, that his mane didn't look pretty.

Patient: It was cut short, like an inch long and all the other manes were nice and long and beautiful, and a lion comes up to him and says, "Ugh, your mane is real weird looking, I don't like you too much. I like you, but you're so weird looking and this lion had such a high, strong mane that he was proud of and he just says, "I'm not your friend any more." And then the lion with the nice long mane left.

The lion with the short mane didn't want to be anyone's friend. And so all the lions got together in little circles and the other lion, the one with the short mane, would take all their stuff and everything. If the lions were playing with something, the other lion would take all their stuff and everything.

Gardner: This is the lion with the short mane—the one who was taking stuff away from the lions with the long manes?

Patient: Yeah. All the long, beautiful-haired lions had something really nice that all lions would like—let's see, maybe a ball that lions would like to play with. Well, the lions with the long manes were standing around and talking and saying, "Oh, look at that pretty ball."

Then the short lion came and said, "What do you have in that circle?"

And they said, "Oh, nothing that you would want." And he tried to get in, but he couldn't get in. Then all the lions said, "It's working, it's working . . ."

Gardner: What was working?

Patient: I'm going to tell you that . . .

Gardner: Go ahead.

Patient: See they had a plan. They thought maybe if he didn't get what he wanted, that he would know how it felt when he said that he wasn't going to be their friend. So, then the long-haired lions said they wouldn't play with the lion with the short hair and they wouldn't let him play with them or get food with them. They had long manes but not very long manes.

Gardner: Excuse me a minute. At the beginning of the story, there was a lion with a short mane and the other lions had long manes or very long manes.

Patient: Just long manes.

Gardner: But they didn't want to have *very* long manes.

Patient: They didn't want to look ugly. They thought *very* long manes were ugly. So when their manes got very long, they cut them.

Gardner: Okay, go ahead.

Patient: Then, everybody was coming to the lion barber to cut their manes, not too short like the other lion, just the way they used to have it. When the lion that used to have the short mane could have come to town—they wouldn't let him. He had to pick his own berries and eat them all by himself until one day it was such a long time that his mane grew long and when he looked in the mirror, it was so beautiful—it was a nice, long, brown mane. Then he went up to the town and walked proudly and said, "Look at my mane, it's not short any more. It's longer than yours. I don't like your mane."

And then all the other lions came up to him and said, and they all said at the same time, "I'm sorry. You're right. The very long ones are very nice." And they all grew nice, very long manes.

Gardner: Did they then all have the same *very* long manes? Did they then think that the longest kinds of manes were the prettiest after the lion with the very short mane grew a very long mane?

Patient: Yeah, and it was very beautiful. All the other lions didn't know that very long manes would look this beautiful, but they never tried it. When they found out how beautiful it looked on this lion, they all got long, long, nice beautiful manes just like the other lion, and they all said they were sorry at the same time. Until they all got together.

Gardner: They all got together and did what?

Patient: They all got together and fixed up the city and they lived happily ever after.

Gardner: What's the lesson of that story?

Patient: The lesson is . . . let's see how I can explain this . . . You can't judge a friendship by how people look or something, you have to judge a friendship by how you like the person.

A central theme of the patient's story is the notion that individuals are judged by external and even frivolous criteria. The length of the mane is the primary criterion for assessing how worthwhile a person is. In addition, there is boasting and rejection of those who are different. Personality qualities are essentially ignored. It was with this understanding of the patient's story that I related mine. It is of interest that the patient's moral, which has little to do with the story, possibly makes some reference to judging a person by intrinsic qualities. One cannot be sure. At any rate, the game continued:

Gardner: Now it's time for my story. Once upon a time there was this lion. And if the other lions grew short manes, he would grow a long one. He always wanted to be different, but he always thought he was better than the others by being different. And he was kind of proud of that and he would walk around and boast about how different he was and how he didn't have the same kind of mane as others. If they had a middle-sized mane, then he would curl his mane or something like that. He always tried to be different and he always tried to think that he was better than they were. One day, they were all talking together in a meeting, when one of the older ones said about this lion, "He chooses something very simple to make himself feel better: how he cuts his hair. He thinks that by the way he cuts his hair that's going to make him better. It's easy to cut his hair."

Patient: But he's such a proud lion.

Gardner: But he uses something that doesn't really make him better than the others. For instance, if he worked very hard to be stronger, or if he worked very hard in school to be smarter, or if he worked very hard to become a good dancer or musician or learn an instrument or something like that, then he could be proud of that. Then he wouldn't want to say to the others, "You're stupid" or something like that. He would have something important because he had worked hard at it, but to say that you're better than someone just because you wear your hair differently or make it longer . . .

Patient: Yeah, because they could do the same thing you do . . .

Gardner: Yes, it's no stunt . . . it's no feat. So what do you think the lesson in that story is?

Patient: I can't exactly say . . .

Gardner: Well, what do you think it is?

Patient: Like, don't be different from all the others and be so proud. Everybody has differences . . . like some people have a low voice and some people have a high voice and some people just have a medium voice like me . . . but everybody has a different voice . . .

Gardner: What was the lion in my story trying to do?

Patient: He was trying to be better than all the other lions.

Gardner: And how was he trying to be better?

Patient: By fixing his hair a different way.

Gardner: And what about that way of being better?

Patient: Well, I don't know.

Gardner: Is that a good way of being better than others? If you try to be better than others, is that a good way to be better?

Patient: No. Really you shouldn't even try to be better than others.

Gardner: Well, let's just say you should try to do your best. There is a little bit of fun in being better than others. For example, if there's a race and you win the race, you feel better that you won the race, right?

Patient: You shouldn't go and say, "I won this . . ."

Gardner: You shouldn't boast about it. But, if there's a spelling contest in school and you win it, don't you feel good about yourself?

Patient: I feel good about myself, but I don't really . . . I feel sad for the others . . .

Gardner: But don't you feel proud if you've won a race, if you've won a spelling contest, something like that?

Patient: Oh, yes.

Gardner: I think it's important to know you can feel good if you win out over the others, but that's no reason to boast, to laugh at the others, or to make yourself feel you're king of the world, or something like that . . . you're better than everybody in every way. You're just better than the kids in that group, in that thing, in that contest, on that day, and that can make you feel good.

Patient: Or somebody could just come over and get a contest with you and win them all . . .

Gardner: What was that again?

Patient: Somebody could just come to a contest with you, let's say it's a spelling contest, and he could just . . . or she could just win the contest without trying.

Gardner: I never met anyone personally who won an important contest without working and trying.

The main point I wished to make in my story was that frivolous and superficial criteria for assessing self-worth do not work. It is only when the accomplishment comes about through effort that it is likely to enhance self-esteem. As is often the case, I tried to get the patient to see if she could figure out the lesson of my story. Instead of providing a lesson, she got sidetracked onto the issue of the appropriateness of trying to win out over others. Apparently, there was some guilt here over doing this and I tried to assuage it. I emphasized how good one feels about oneself after a well-fought contest and how proud one can feel about oneself after such competition. However, I was careful to point out that this does not justify flaunting one's accomplishments or denigrating those who are unsuccessful. The patient then spoke about winning a contest without trying, and I pointed out that I had never seen such a thing, again emphasizing the importance of the work ethic.

> *Gardner:* Now, the point I want to make is this, that in my story the lion thought that he was better than everybody else by doing something very simple and easy, by cutting his hair a different way, and that is *not* a good way to make yourself feel good about yourself, because it's no feat. Do you know what I mean by feat?
> *Patient:* Yeah.
> *Gardner:* What do I mean by feat?
> *Patient:* It's no big deal.
> *Gardner:* Right! It's no big deal, right. Because everybody can cut his or her hair, right?
> *Patient:* Like, some kids have their hair in the same style, but everybody is different no matter what they do.
> *Gardner:* Everybody's different, right, but what's that got to do with what we're talking about?
> *Patient:* You shouldn't try to be different from the others or boasting or anything . . .
> *Gardner:* You shouldn't boast. I think that in some things you should try to be the same and in some things you should try to be different, depending on what you want to do. If you like a certain style and you want to be like others, fine. If you don't like a certain style and you want to be different, fine, but it doesn't make you better than the others, you know?
> *Patient:* True.
> *Gardner:* Because it's no great feat, it's no big deal to wear your hair differently, wear a different dress or the same dress. You

didn't work toward it. It's no accomplishment. Do you remember that word, accomplishment?

Patient: I guess I do.

Gardner: What's an accomplishment?

Patient: I can't explain it.

Gardner: Try.

Patient: I can't.

Gardner: Try.

Patient: I'm trying . . . will you tell me?

Gardner: Yeah. It's no big feat. Accomplishment is a feat. It's no big feat to wear your hair differently. What is a big feat? Name a kind of thing that would be a big deal, something that you would be proud of?

Patient: I can name something that you could be proud of.

Gardner: Like what?

Patient: Like being a president or a governor.

Gardner: If you became president or governor, why should a person be proud?

Patient: Let's say someone real, real important is in this election, and you beat them. You'd feel proud, because let's say nobody ever beat this person before.

Gardner: That's something to be proud of . . .

Patient: Yes . . .

Gardner: And is it something easy to do?

Patient: No, it's very hard.

Gardner: That's the point! It's something that's hard. See, if you do better than another person and after you've worked at it and it's hard. then you really can feel good about yourself. You then really feel much better about yourself than if you just do something like wear your hair differently. It's no big deal. Now we have to close. What's the main lesson in my story?

Patient: The main lesson in your story is don't boast.

Gardner: Number one. Go ahead.

Patient: Don't always be different in a certain subject.

Gardner: Sometimes it's okay to be different, sometimes it's not. It depends on how you feel.

Patient: That's about all.

Gardner: What about big feats?

Patient: Big deals?

Gardner: Big deals.

Patient: Ummm.

Gardner: That it's no big deal if you do something that's easy. If you want to feel better than others, if you do something like cutting your hair, that's no big deal. If you do something like becoming a president or governor of if you've worked hard, that's a big deal.

Patient: You have to work hard to be proud.

Gardner: That's the thing! You have to work hard to be proud! That's the main point of my story. You have to work hard to be proud.

Patient: Yeah. Can I ask you a question?

Gardner: Sure.

Patient: How come every time I make a story, your story is almost alike?

Gardner: Well, it's because. . .what do you think?

Patient: Because you want things to be about the same subject?

Gardner: Right. If I see something in the child's story that's a bad idea, I will change it to something I think is a better idea. Okay?

Patient: Yeah.

Gardner: What was the bad idea in your story that I wanted to change?

Patient: What do you think?

Gardner: You try to remember. What about in the lion's story? What do you think would be a good idea to change?

Patient: I don't know, you tell me.

Gardner: In your story, what did the lion do?

Patient: He was proud.

Gardner: And did he really have something to be proud of?

Patient: No.

Gardner: Why didn't he have something to be proud of?

Patient: Because you shouldn't really be proud of a mane.

Gardner: And in my story what did we say that you should be proud of?

Patient: Something to be proud of is that you have to work hard.

Gardner: That's the most important thing. In your story your lion was proud of cutting his hair. That's nothing to be proud of.

Patient: I know, but that's part of the lesson. You shouldn't be proud just of your hair. Like if I say he wasn't proud or anything, he liked his hair but . . .

Gardner: It's nothing to boast about.

Patient: But there wouldn't be any lesson there. . .

Gardner: There's a lesson that you shouldn't be proud of something that you didn't work hard at.

Patient: But I wanted to put everything in my story.
Gardner: You wanted to put everything in your story?
Patient: Not everything . . . but most of the things I thought.
Gardner: Okay, that's a fine idea.

In the post-story discussion, it was clear that the patient got my message: "You have to work hard to be proud." I responded with strong positive reinforcement and reiterated the point. I believe that my message here "sank in" and became incorporated into the patient's psychic structure.

FOURTEEN
ROMANTIC LOVE

It probably comes as a surprise to most readers to see romantic love listed here as one of the categories of problems that relate to self-esteem and the psychogenic learning disabilities. However, romantic love is very much related to both of these areas, especially during adolescence. Romantic love may be one of the most powerful mechanisms for generating feelings of high self-worth, not only for the person who is the object of the lover's adoration, but for the person who has the romantic feelings as well. However, youngsters who are "in love" are not likely to attend to their studies. They enjoy their euphoric-romantic state much more than subjecting themselves to the tedium of academic drill, memorization, and listening to boring teachers. Accordingly, I believe some attention to the romantic-love phenomenon is warranted in this book.

COMMON CONCEPTS OF ROMANTIC LOVE

In the United States (and throughout most of the western world), the socially acceptable reason for getting married is *love*, and more specifically *romantic love*. Individuals who marry for other reasons, or who fail to include love in their list of reasons for marrying, are likely to be considered injudicious, misguided, or possibly suffering with a psychopathological disturbance. When "in love," individuals find that they experience certain ecstatic feelings when thinking about or being in the presence of a specific person (usually of the opposite sex). In its full-blown form, this blissful state appears to be all-pervasive. It enhances the pleasure that the individual may derive from even the simplest everyday activities and makes many of life's inevitable pains more tolerable. The person in love comes to the conclusion that the particular party who is the object of his (her) affection is the only one in the whole world capable of inducing this special state of elation. Lovers soon develop the deep conviction that these blissful feelings will last throughout their lives, even though they have never personally observed anyone—except on the movie or television screen—-who has sustained this state very long. Yet, this does not deter people in love from making vows about how they will feel and behave toward one another many years hence (even for the rest of their lives). Here again, the fact that the vast majority of people have not proven themselves capable of or inclined to keeping these vows does not deter lovers from making them.

A type of romantic love that is particularly attractive to adolescents is the kind that I refer to as the *Some-Enchanted-Evening-Across-a-Crowded-Room* type of romantic love. In this variety, two complete strangers, merely on viewing one another (from across a crowded room is desirable but not crucial to the phenomenon), are suddenly struck, as if by a lightning bolt from out of the blue, with intense feelings of affection and sexual attraction for one another. I also refer to this type of romantic love as the *bifurcated lightning bolt* kind of love. Here, God in heaven decides that it is now the time for these two particular individuals to fall in love. He therefore thrusts a lightning bolt down toward earth which, just before it reaches the ground, splits into two parts, each one of which invests the lovers. So magnetized, they make a beeline for one another, stomping over people in between, and "read life's meaning in one another's eyes."

I also refer to this as the *acute infectious disease* type of romantic love. Here the individuals are suddenly afflicted with cravings for one another, as if stricken with an illness. This is one of the reasons why individuals with this kind of love may refer to themselves in popular song as having been "bitten by the lovebug." In medicine we have a term, *pathognomonic sign*, which refers to the particular sign that clinches the diagnosis of a disease. The lovebug disease has a pathognomonic sign—a sign that differentiates it immediately from all other diseases known to medicine. Patients who are suffering with any other disease known to medicine would be quite upset if a doctor, when admitting them to the hospital, informed them that they would have to share a bed with another patient suffering with the same disorder. People with the "lovebug disease" have no such objections; in fact, they welcome being in the same bed together. This is the one pathognomonic sign that differentiates it from all other diseases known to medicine.

In all these cases the individuals view their attraction as coming from mysterious, almost magical, forces that instantaneously and irresistibly drew them together. Although some view the cause of the overwhelming attraction to be external (as planned for by God, for example), others attribute it to internal factors (such as "body chemistry"). I, personally, suspect that internal psychological and biological factors are the most important elements in producing this phenomenon. The individuals enter the room predisposed to the experience, and even hoping for it, because of a lack of meaningful involvement with anyone else at the time. And loneliness may intensify the craving for such an involvement. The need for an esteem-enhancing experience as an antidote to one's pains and frustrations may also be present. Perhaps the object of the intense attraction bears some physical resemblance to a once loved person, such as an opposite-sex parent or a former lover. Sexual frustration is in all probability present as well. These cravings may be particularly great at the time—explaining thereby the suddenness with which the individuals are drawn to one another. All these factors together result in a copious outpouring of hormones into the bloodstream that enhances formidably the desire of the two individuals to spend as much time as possible with one another, both physically and psychologically. In fact, they may give such high priority to being with one another that they may ignore obligations vital to their well-being. School and work especially may come to be considered far less important than the relationship. And when the two people become more involved with each other, the attraction becomes solidified by a dovetailing of both healthy and neurotic needs. (Both of these factors will be elaborated below.)

The risks that one takes by falling in love with a stranger are no different from those one takes when, for example, buying a used car from a stranger or lending money to a stranger. One does better to get a little more information before entering into such transactions, and yet it is both amazing and pathetic how individuals who would never be injudicious enough to buy cars from or lend money to unknown individuals would be willing to sign a contract in which they take an oath to live together for the rest of their lives with a "stranger from across a crowded room."

THE PSYCHODYNAMICS OF ROMANTIC LOVE

The obvious question here is why are these people doing this? What are the psychological factors operative in bringing about this state that satisfies many of the criteria for a psychopathological process: impaired reality testing, compromised judgment, impulsivity, neglect of important obligations, and (in many cases) sex without considering precautions against pregnancy and the acquisition of a sexually transmitted disease. Before discussing what I consider to be the important psychodynamic factors operative in bringing about the state of romantic euphoria, I wish to emphasize that I do not necessarily equate psychodynamics with psychopathology. Most, if not all, forms of psychological behavior have psychodynamic elements, but not all psychologically determined behavior should necessarily be considered psychopathological. Each of the psychodynamic factors I describe here runs the gamut from the normal to the pathological. Each person who is "in love" utilizes one or more of these mechanisms. And each person may utilize them to either normal or pathological degrees and in any combination between these extremes.

Compliance with Social Convention

One factor operative in the romantic-love phenomenon is compliance with social convention. In our society we consider "love" to be the most important reason for marrying another person. Of course, in other societies other criteria have been used. In some, money and power have been unashamedly utilized as criteria for matchmaking. The ancient Pharaohs routinely married brothers and sisters in order to keep power and wealth within the family. Unfortunately for the Pharaohs, genes for intellectual retardation were quite common in their families— resulting in an unusually high percentage of retarded monarchs. Marrying cousins and near relatives was a routine practice among European royalty, even up to this century. Unfortunately for the European aristocracy, genes for hemophilia were quite prevalent. The presence of these defective genes, however, did not seem to deter marriages between close relatives because of the great desire to keep wealth and power in the family. And even among commoners, marriages planned by parents is an ancient tradition, the parents considering themselves to be more judicious than their children for making such an important decision. Here again, considerations other than romantic love were generally operative in the parents' decision-making process. Although I would not recommend that we resume the practice of parents deciding whom their children should marry, I cannot say that the practice is not without its merits.

Social convention, then, deems it normal for people, especially when young, to have the experience of falling in love. In fact, people who claim that they have never had the experience are often viewed as being somewhat deficient and even unfortunate. We are much more like sheep than we would like to admit, and there are many for whom the social-compliance factor in generating romantic feelings is an important one. When one's friends start falling in love, then one starts falling in love as well. It is similar to the phenomenon by which anorexia/bulimia and even adolescent suicide have come into vogue in recent years. When it becomes the "thing to do" in the adolescent set, many adolescents are likely to go along with the crowd, even if it means acquiring some dreaded disease and even if it means killing oneself.

Romantic Love as Narcotic and Anxiolytic

I believe that an important contributing factor to the development of feelings of romantic love is the need to provide oneself with a narcotic. Like the narcotic, it quickly produces intense pleasurable sensations and thereby provides enjoyment—practically on demand. One need not apply oneself diligently over time to gain pleasure; one merely need spontaneously induce the state within oneself and revel. (One need not even have encouragement or reciprocity from the object of one's affection; "unrequited love" can produce the same euphoric state.) In addition, like the narcotic, it makes one insensitive to pain. There are many painful feelings associated with the prospect of marriage—if one is to allow oneself to think about them. One is committing oneself to a lifelong arrangement—a decision that cannot but be extremely anxiety provoking. The prospect of living—for the rest of one's life—with the same person cannot but make an intelligent and sensitive person shudder. And the awesome responsibility of rearing children is certain to produce further anxieties. Romantic love is an extremely potent tranquilizer for the treatment of such anxieties. Narcotics also dull one's senses and make one less discriminating about what is happening in the world. And romantic love assists the lover in denying deficiencies possessed by the partner, deficiencies that may be obvious to almost everyone else; deficiencies that might cause most judicious individuals to pause before making such an important commitment. As with the narcotic, the ecstatic feelings are experienced only early in its use. As time passes the drug becomes less and less capable of producing the blissful state. Alas, such is also the case with romantic love.

Romantic love, then, may be viewed as "nature's trick," a mechanism by which nature enhances the likelihood of procreation by dulling one's judgment. Lower animals just copulate and fornicate. They don't have the kind of complex cerebral cortical structure to provide them with meaningful appreciation of future events, judgment, the ability to plan for the future, and other mental mechanisms that might interfere with the procreative act. The dulling of the senses provided by romantic love, then, serves the purposes of species survival. Lower animals don't need it; we might not survive as well without it.

Self-esteem Enhancer

One of the important attractions of the romantic-love experience is that it is an esteem enhancer. We generally admire most those who have the good sense to like us (and conversely, we are quickest to dislike intensely those who are stupid or blind enough to hold us in low regard). We cannot but find attractive a person who has selected us—from all the billions of other people on earth—and provides us with respect, admiration, and sexual gratification as well. What more could one ask from another human being? Typically, the individuals bestow praises on one another to a degree not generally seen in any other situation. All stops are pulled out in the service of this goal. Even one's own mother does not hold one in as high regard as one's lover. The process may start, for example, with person A bestowing on B some compliment. Person B, thereby flattered, returns the favor. Person A then considers B to be quite judicious for having such high regard for him (her) and thinks even more highly of B. Person B, receiving even greater positive feedback, esteems A even more highly and communicates this. A mutual admiration society thereby develops, with an upward spiraling of compliments. The society is founded on the agreement: "If you'll admire, praise, respect, confide in, and find me sexually attractive, I'll do the same for you." This is indeed one of the most important attractions of the phenomenon.

Unfortunately, there are only about 400,000 words in most unabridged dictionaries of the English language, only a small fraction of which are useful in the service of complimenting one's beloved. It is even more unfortunate that the majority of individuals have only a few of these in their repertoire. As a result, the praises tend to become somewhat repetitious and they thereby lose some of their efficacy. In addition, the individuals may believe that it behooves them to maintain the high frequency of compliments, and this can be somewhat taxing and draining. Healthy people can allow the romantic-love experience to simmer down somewhat and substitute other experiences that enable them to supply fresh compliments. Those who do not may then become frustrated with this aspect of the romantic-love experience. Last, individuals with profound feelings of low self-worth are more likely to gravitate toward this aspect of the romantic-love phenomenon because the praises provide compensation for low self-esteem.

There is yet another element in the romantic love phenomenon that enhances even further the feelings of self-worth of the individuals involved. If the object of one's affections is perfect, and if one is in turn loved by that perfect person, then one must indeed be a most admirable person. It is as if the young man in love were saying: "She is perfect. Among her perfections is wisdom. She loves me. If she is wise enough to love me, I must be unique, adorable, lovable, wise, and maybe even perfect like her. Why, she even tells me that we're a perfect match."

Vicarious Gratification

In romantic love one (and even both) of the individuals may use one another for the purpose of satisfying vicariously unfulfilled desires of one's own. Probably the most common manifestation of this phenomenon is the woman who is attracted to a man of high accomplishments and "walks in his shadow" throughout the course of their relationship. She "lives through him" and gratifies her own desires for fame, fortune, success, etc., through him. Simon (1982) states it well: "We expect our loved ones to live out an unrecognized or undeveloped aspect of ourselves . . . we live vicariously through their accomplishments in an area in which we would like to develop ourselves." This factor is often operative for women who refer to their lovers as "my hero." Of course, dependency gratifications may be operative here as the "damsel in distress" is rescued by the "knight in shining armor." However, when not saving her, the knight in shining armor can involve himself in acts of daring-do that provide the woman with vicarious gratification of her own desires for such adventures. And enhanced self-esteem is operative here for both parties at many different levels. She enhances her self-worth by vicarious identification with his heroic deeds. He, of course, gains the ego-enhancement of being the hero. The damsel in distress gains the ego-enhancement of having been selected for rescue (from all the other maidens in distress), and he gains the ego-enhancement of the rescuer.

Reaction Formation to Anger

Another factor operative in the romantic-love experience is reaction formation to underlying anger. All human relationships are ambivalent, and those who are in love are no exception to this principle. However, there are individuals who believe that it behooves them to have a relationship in which there is no anger expressed—lest the relationship be viewed by themselves and others as not "the real thing." In most (if not all) human relationships, angry feelings are inevitably going to arise at some point, often very early. We cannot satisfy one another's desires all the time; the frustrations that ultimately result in all close human encounters must at times produce resentments. In healthy relationships, the individuals express these at the earliest possible times, in a civilized manner, in the hope that the problems may be resolved. If a problem cannot be resolved, and if there are many such problems, then the individuals may part ways. If, however, they are successful in resolving the inevitable conflicts that arise, they may then be in a position to maintain a relationship that may ultimately mature. Individuals who are too guilty to express their resentments, or who need to feel that there are none, are likely to use the romantic, loving feelings in the service of reaction formation. The obsessive love is then used to suppress deep-seated hatred. Most applicable to such people is the old saying:

"Love and hate are merely the opposite sides of the same coin." Also relevant here is the ancient wisdom: "The opposite of love is not hate, but indifference." The young man who writes his ex-girlfriend a 32-page letter describing all the reasons why he never wants to see her again is still very much in love and is not simply trying to convince her, but himself as well, that they should part ways. The man who is completely uninvolved not only does not write such letters, but does not even think about doing so. In fact, he does not think of the girl at all. Accordingly, romantic love not only provides a cover-up of angry feelings—for those who believe that they should not be present in good relationships—but lessens the likelihood that the individuals will work out the problems that are producing the anger in the first place. In this way it may contribute to the perpetuation of difficulties in the relationship and even to its deterioration.

Satisfaction of Pathological Dependency Cravings

Romantic love can also be used to satisfy pathological dependency cravings. It is much more socially acceptable to gratify pathological dependency with a spouse than with a parent. This would be an extension of the shift in which the adolescent transfers dependency on parents to dependency on peers. In romantic love, the dependency gratifications may be formidable and a marriage based on such cravings is not likely to be stable, because in any parasitic relationship the host and the parasite ultimately hate one another. The host resents the parasite because his (her) blood is being sucked; and the parasite resents the host because of his (her) vulnerability. At any point the host may flick off the parasite, leaving him (her) with no sustenance. And such resentments may, over time, develop into hatred when the two individuals become "locked in" with one another.

Successful Conquests

Women have been traditionally taught by their mothers (and other well-meaning advisers) not to make themselves too "easy."

Although this may sound like a somewhat passé thing to say in this age of egalitarianism, I am in agreement with this advice. Forbidden fruit *is* much sweeter. A goal attained after great effort is generally appreciated more than the one more easily acquired. Breaking down barriers, overcoming resistances, and anxieties associated with wondering whether the goal will be obtained are all part of the "mating game" and contribute to the romantic love phenomenon for both sexes. Joy comes not only in the attainment of a goal but in its pursuit.

The novelty element is also operative here. Sisters (and brothers) are rarely as much a sexual "turn-on" as the girl (or boy) next door or across the street. Although women in our society are generally more passive in this "pursuit," their seductive maneuvers, flirting, and other less obvious mechanisms for attracting men do serve the purpose of "conquest." The man may say that he has "won" the woman (with its implication of having competed with others for this prize); and she may say that she has "caught" the man (with the implication that her trap was more successful than those of the other women who were also out there in the forest or jungle with their traps). The ego-enhancement that comes from success in this game contributes to romantic love.

Competitive Gratifications

Another factor that may be operative in the romantic love phenomenon is the desire to outdo one's friends and even evoke their jealousy. One can boast to friends that one is loved, adored, admired, and even worshiped by another party. When one's friends are not having that fortunate experience at that time, it places the beloved in a superior position in the competition for success in the dating/mate-acquisition arena. One can then boast of the "good catch" and flaunt the beloved to one's friends. Again, individuals with low feelings of self-worth are more likely to utilize this maneuver.

Concluding Comments

I wish to emphasize again my point that psychodynamics should not necessarily be equated with psychopathology. Each of the above contributing factors, when present in mild degree, may very well be considered normal. To the degree that romantic love becomes obsessive and prolonged, to the degree that it becomes delusional, to the degree that it interferes with important functions (school, work, etc.), to that degree should it be considered psychopathological. The healthiest situation for the adolescent, I believe, is to have a few such experiences, but not to make any commitments under the influence of the romantic-love feeling. Adolescents are generally too young to marry and have children, and the romantic experience may result in their taking these steps. My final advice, whether it be to the adolescent or to the adult who is "in love," is this: Romantic love is a wonderful experience. Enjoy it while it lasts, but don't make important decisions under its influence—like marriage, for example!

Romantic love also entails a dovetailing of psychopathological needs, e.g., masochism in her/sadism in him; ungratified maternal needs in her/passive dependency in him; alcoholism in him/"enabling" tendencies in her, etc. I have discussed these (and others) elsewhere (Gardner, 1991); a detailed discussion of them here goes beyond the purposes of this book. Of relevance here is the fact that gratifications of these pathological interactions may also contribute to the sense of well-being that feeds into the romantic euphoria.

It would be unfortunate if the reader concluded from this somewhat cynical description that I am totally condemning the phenomenon. I believe that in moderation it can be an enriching, uplifting experience that makes life more meaningful. It has served to inspire some of the world's greatest artistic and scientific creations. The person who has not tasted its sweet fruits has missed out on one of life's most rewarding experiences. But when it is indulged in to excess, when people are so blinded by it that they enter into self-destructive involvements, I consider it a type of psychological disturbance. One can compare romantic love to the occasional alcoholic beverage. Used in moderation it can ennoble our spirits; when we are addicted to it, it can destroy us. I think that it is possible that in recent years there may have been some decrease in the tendency of people to become so addicted.

The "tell it like it is" philosophy that has become so popular in recent years may very well have lessened the tendency of people to enter into this self-induced delusional state to such an extreme degree.

PSYCHOTHERAPEUTIC APPROACHES

The psychodynamic factors operative in romantic love satisfy many of the criteria one utilizes for designating a phenomenon as psychopathological. And I am not referring here to the obviously pathological mechanisms, such as sadomasochism. Rather, I am referring to those that we consider "normal." As mentioned, there is a continuum from the normal to the abnormal, from the healthy to the sick. One criterion that can be utilized to ascertain whether the love has reached such a point that it warrants designation as pathology is whether or not it is interfering with functioning in important areas of life. If it reaches the point where the youngster is neglecting schoolwork, then it must be considered a form of psychogenic learning disability. The girl who does nothing but wait for the telephone call from her boyfriend, who lives for him entirely, is clearly exhibiting pathological behavior, and it should be designated as such. The boy who is so obsessed with his girlfriend that he does nothing but think about her—to the neglect of his studies—is also involved in a pathological exaggeration of romantic love. In such cases the therapist does well to designate the love as such and to make an attempt to understand the psychodynamic factors that are operative in this particular "case." Fortunately for the therapist—and the parties themselves—the disease has within it the elements of its own cure. The best antidote is increasing familiarity with and knowledge about the other party. The more removed and mysterious the other party is, the greater the likelihood the delusions survive. Knowledge and experience are to romantic love what sunshine is to the werewolf or vampire: in both cases there is destruction and evaporation of the process by illumination. Groucho Marx put it less poetically: "Romantic love is a disease, the cure of which is instant marriage." For the adolescent (the focus of this section), marriage is obviously not an appropriate cure and most adolescents in love are not thinking immediately of this route. The principle, however, is still applicable with regard to the therapist's appreciation that time and experience may very well be the best cures for this disorder. With time, alienating personality qualities will most often be revealed, qualities that can serve as a point of departure for discussions that will help the youngster put the personality qualities of the beloved into perspective and proper balance.

Accordingly, the therapist does well to discourage adolescents from acting impulsively and doing such things as eloping, getting married secretly, or buying an expensive ring. The usual practice of congratulating people and wishing them well after the announcement that they are "in love" may very well serve social purposes (especially that of species survival). In the therapist's office, however, although an initial compliment may be in order, the therapist does well to look more deeply into the process. Although the therapist may be viewed as a sourpuss or someone who can't share in the joy of a happy person, it is a therapeutic error to move on to other subjects and not to at least explore for the presence of psychopatholgical processes, which may not be hard to find. The therapeutic goal, however, would not to be dispel the feeling entirely. As mentioned, it can be put to constructive utilization. Rather, the therapist does well to try to ferret out the significant pathological elements and treat them.

If the relationship reaches a point of deterioration and impending dissolution (most often the case), the therapist does well to attempt to find out whether there were any qualities within the patient (often the case) that played a role in alienating the partner. These can often serve as a point of departure for useful therapeutic interchanges, interchanges focusing on deficiencies of the patient. In the context of such discussions, the patient may reveal subscription to the theory that one should be loved for what one is, without any focus on particular personality qualities. The idea that love is blind to alienating qualities that may be apparent to others is not particularly useful in terms of adapting to the real world. It is based on the other person's utilization of massive denial and even delusional thinking, not a very stable basis for a relationship. For those who subscribe to this principle, the therapist does well to try to introduce the idea that, this theory notwithstanding, we are basically loved for what we are, for the composite of all our qualities and the balance among them. If our attractive qualities outweigh the alienating ones, then we are more likely to be loved (at least by a certain fraction of the population). In contrast, if our alienating qualities outweigh our attractive qualities, then the population of potential individuals who will love us shrinks considerably. There will always be, however, a certain fraction of the population who are attracted to qualities that most find abhorrent, but one does well to help the patient recognize the pitfalls of relationships with such people.

☐ FIFTEEN
SEXUAL THOUGHTS, FEELINGS, AND ACTIONS

INTRODUCTION

Although sexual thoughts, feelings, and actions contribute significantly to romantic love, they do not necessarily coexist. There
can be love without sex, and sex without love. Because most
healthy children are not significantly involved in sexuality at the
prepubertal level, I will have less to say here about younger
children than about adolescents. The linkage between adolescent
sexuality and self-esteem is quite strong, and the youngster with
problems in the sexual/self-esteem realm may very well have
difficulties in school also, especially because preoccupations and
problems in the sexual/self-esteem realm can interfere with learning. Probably one of the best examples of this is the phenomenon—well known to educators—that girls are generally the more
serious students at the grade-school level, but boys take academics more seriously in high school. And it is in junior high
school, around the time of puberty, that these shifts occur. Many
girls, who were quite serious with regard to their studies in
elementary school, suddenly become obsessed with boys, much
to the neglect of their studies. Although the boys are obsessed
with the girls as well, they are less likely to neglect their studies
at this time (although many certainly do).

PATIENTS' SEXUALITY AND THE THERAPIST'S VALUES

It is just about impossible to separate a statement on sexuality from the values of the presenter. And this principle is still operative in the therapist-patient relationship, even for therapists who actually believe that they are not imposing their values on their patients. As mentioned elsewhere (Gardner, 1986a, 1988a), therapists are continually imposing their values on their patients. Accordingly, I believe there are two types of therapists: (1) those who do this and *are aware* of the fact that they are doing this and (2) those who do this and are *not aware* that they are doing this. Even the neutral position does not alter this phenomenon. Neutrality is still a statement; it is no less a position than being for something or against something. Sitting on the fence is no less a position than being on either side of it.

Accordingly, I will begin by presenting my own values regarding childhood and adolescent sexuality. I recognize that my values in this area are likely to be different from those of some readers and are certainly different than those of many of the patients I see. However, parents are entitled to this information regarding the therapist's values before involving their youngsters in treatment. And readers are entitled to this information because it will place them in a better position to understand my psychotherapeutic approaches.

I believe that the newborn infant is capable of sexual arousal, even to the point of orgasm. (I'm not recommending that anyone test out this hypothesis. I only consider it a reasonable extrapolation backward from my knowledge of this subject and my clinical experiences.) This potential, however, does not necessarily mean that a child will engage in sexual activities. The greater the environmental psychological and physical stimulation, the greater the likelihood the prepubertal child will become aroused and crave sexual gratification. The normal, healthy child, however, will generally not need a significant amount of sexual gratification; rather, attention will be directed to numerous other areas involved in healthy growth and development. I would consider occasional masturbation, even to the point of orgasm, to still be within the normal range, especially in our world today in which children are exposed to a significant amount of sexual stimulation, parental attempts to monitor such exposure notwithstanding.

I believe that, in the early adolescent period, it is psychologically healthy (a term that is a substitute for what *my* values are) for a youngster to engage occasionally in heterosexual caressing, kissing, and petting. In the mid-adolescent period, I believe it is healthier for things to "steam up" to the point where the youngster enjoys orgasm. And by 17 or 18 I believe it is healthy for the youngster to have sexual intercourse. However, I believe that adults do well to impress upon youngsters that the sexual experience is likely to be more gratifying if there is an ongoing intimate relationship with the sexual partner. Transient sex should be discouraged with the appreciation, however, that a certain amount of sex might still be engaged in. It is hoped that the youngster will have the *living experience* that sex in the context of an ongoing relationship is ultimately more gratifying. My values here are not that stringent to preclude entirely transient sexual experiences. At the same time, I believe that it is *crucial* that parents impress upon their youngsters the risks of pregnancy and the terrible drawbacks of out-of-wedlock teen pregnancies. In addition, they are grievously negligent if they do not warn their youngsters about the dangers of sexually transmitted diseases (STD), especially autoimmune deficiency syndrome (AIDS). The parents, however, should have some familiarity with other STD that are prevalent, especially genital warts (also called venereal warts, which is the most common STD), clamydia, and herpes. At the time of this writing (late 1991), the AIDS epidemic is becoming ever more frightening and the warnings for sexual selectivity and the use of condoms ever more compelling. Unfortunately, the adolescent's delusions of invulnerability (Gardner, 1988a) may work against the youngster heeding this warning.

Furthermore, parents and therapists do well to encourage masturbation as an acceptable release for sexual cravings. They should promulgate the notion that no human being need suffer sexual frustration and that when heterosexual opportunities are not available, masturbation is a perfectly acceptable and even desirable outlet. I have often said that the ideal birthday present for a 13-year-old boy would be a five-year subscription to a pin-up magazine and a lock on his bedroom door. And the ideal gift for a 13-year-old girl would be a vibrator and a five-year subscription to a teenage romance magazine. (Males are more likely to be "turned on" by stark visual-sexual representations, whereas females are more likely to be excited by loving and romantic fantasies.)

In my value system I do not consider abortion to be a sin or an inappropriate way of dealing with an unwanted pregnancy. I recognize, however, that there are others who believe strongly that abortion is merely another form of murder and that there is absolutely no situation under which it is justifiable. From the psychological point of view, I believe that the earlier the abortion is done, the less the psychological trauma to the mother. Abortions during the first trimester can generally be accomplished through dilatation and curettage (D and C) and are less likely to be traumatic than a second-trimester abortion in which labor is induced and an actual fetus comes forth.

In the initial interview the parents have every right to question the therapist about his (her) position on these subjects. This does not preclude inquiries into the possible psychological implications of their questions, but they are still entitled to the therapist's direct answers on these controversial issues. Classical analysts would be unreceptive to such a conversation and would use each of these parental questions as a point of departure for psychoanalytic inquiry. I am in sharp disagreement with this approach to such questions. First, the parents are not analytic patients; they are the parents of the adolescent patient. Second, before placing their youngster in the therapist's care, they are entitled to answers to these questions, and the therapist should be willing to provide them. Again, this does not preclude additional discussions regarding the analytic implications of the questions.

I recall a situation in which parents, very religious Catholics, brought their 15-year-old daughter to me. In the first two-hour consultation, they very firmly stated that they did not want me to talk about sex with their daughter. I told them that I would make no such promise and that if I am to conduct the therapy properly,

I must have the right to discuss any issue at all that I consider relevant to a youngster's problems. I told them, as well, that I would not force their daughter to talk about sex if she didn't want to, but that I cannot imagine my conducting a therapeutic program with a 15-year-old girl without the subject coming up at some time or other. I told them that if they considered this answer unacceptable, it would probably be better for them to seek treatment elsewhere. I informed them as well that I did not believe that any competent therapist would agree to such a restriction on the treatment and that if a therapist did agree to such a restriction they would do well to think about the qualifications of such a person. Although obviously unhappy with my response, they agreed to proceed with the treatment.

In the next session, the first with the patient alone, she told me that her parents had told her that they would let her proceed with the treatment (for which she argued strongly), but (unbeknownst to me) made her promise them that she would not talk about sex under any circumstances. In the course of her next two sessions, I told her that she was free to talk about anything and everything she wanted to and if there was a subject that she did not want to talk about, I was not going to coerce her. However, I informed her as well that my experience has been that the most important subjects to talk about in treatment are generally the very topics that patients don't want to talk about. However, my bottom-line statement was that it was *her* treatment and she was free to talk about anything she wanted to and free not to talk about things she didn't want to. During the next four or five sessions, she carefully avoided talking about sex. She did get some definite therapeutic mileage from our discussions of other issues, some of which were not related to sex at all and others only remotely so.

It was then that the patient came in with a dream that she herself easily recognized as having obvious sexual implications. She proceeded to inform me that her parents had questioned her after each session about whether or not she was discussing sex. Heretofore, she was able to honestly deny that she had and so felt comfortable with the treatment. Now she was faced with a dilemma. If she were to be honest and tell her parents that she discussed sex with me—even though it was she who brought in the dream and she who first recognized its sexual implications— they would pull her out of treatment. If she told them that she did not discuss sex she would be lying and she would feel guilty about that. In the course of the discussion I pointed out to her that since it was 99.9 percent predictable that her parents would discontinue her treatment if she mentioned the dream, she should consider the possibility that mentioning it might be a way for her to be removed from treatment and it could thereby serve as a resistance against the treatment. We discussed also the issue of the resistance not simply being over the discussion of sexual material but other anxiety-provoking issues that had been discussed in previous sessions. The session ended with her not knowing exactly what she would do. The following day I received a telephone call from the father informing me that he was withdrawing his daughter from treatment and that all future sessions were to be canceled. He told me that his daughter had informed him that we had talked about sex and that he was going to find a therapist who agreed beforehand not to discuss any sexual issues whatsoever. I wished him luck and, needless to say, I have never heard from these people again.

Since the late 1960s we have experienced what is justifiably called a "sexual revolution." The most dramatic confirmation of this is the ever-increasing rate of teenage pregnancies. Prior to the late 1960s, teenage girls generally were quite ashamed to admit that they had sexual intercourse or even sexual experiences. The pendulum has so shifted that many girls are ashamed to admit that they are virgins, especially after a year or two of college. Another reflection of this change is the greater freedom women have to use profanity. When I was a teenager in the 1940s, girls who used profanity were generally viewed as crude and even sexually loose. This is no longer the case.

An excellent example of this change was demonstrated by a 13-year-old girl who was recently brought by her mother at her own request. The girl sought consultation to determine whether or not she had psychological problems because most of her girlfriends had already started to masturbate and she had no urge to engage in the practice at that point. Both the patient and her mother considered this a justifiable reason for seeking a consultation. The girl freely spoke about the subject without any embarrassment. I informed her that I did not consider her to be abnormal and that some people do have strong sexual urges by her age and some do not. From everything else I learned about her, I considered it safe to predict that she would be starting to have stronger urges within the next couple of years and that at that time, if she felt the desire, I would consider it perfectly acceptable and normal for her to masturbate. However, I impressed upon her that she should not do it in order to keep up with her friends, but only because she herself felt the desire and the need.

Such a consultation would have been unimaginable 25 years ago. And I say this for two reasons. First, the youngster would not have brought it up as a reason for consultation and, even if she did, I can't imagine a mother agreeing that her failure to masturbate at 13 might very well be a manifestation of psychiatric problems. Second, even if she did get to my office for this reason, it would be hard to imagine her speaking in such a relaxed fashion about the subject. In general, my experience has been that pubertal and post-pubertal girls are far less inhibited talking to me about their sexual feelings than they were in the past, and therefore I am seeing more females in this age bracket now than I did in past years. I consider this a good trend because many of these girls come from divorced homes in which they have little if any contact with their fathers and so discussion of intimate subjects with a male can be especially useful.

DATING AND SELF-ESTEEM

Introduction

There is a very close relationship between dating fears and self-esteem. Recent changes in dating patterns notwithstanding, especially regarding the traditional passivity of girls compared to boys, the boys are still most often the initiators, and the girls are still the ones who hope to be invited out. Although they may take a more active role through flirting and more overt forms of seductivity, it is the boy who most often is required to take the initial step and extend the invitation. The situation engenders a significant amount of fear in both sexes. The girls feel vulnerable and beholden to the boys' invitations. And the boys fear rejection. What they both share in common is the emotion of fear and the threat to their self-esteem that the situation inevitably causes. Such feelings of low self-worth may affect confidence in other areas, both academic and nonacademic.

Helping Boys Make Their Initial Dating Overtures

Boys are generally quite fearful of "making the first move," lest they be rejected. The recent sexual revolution and the modern-day notions of sexual egalitarianism notwithstanding, boys are still the ones who are expected to make the first overtures. (I am not saying that this is either good or bad; I am only stating what is the prevailing practice in our society.) Many boys are filled with various rationalizations for not making the first move. My general therapeutic approach here is to utilize what I call the *door-to-door salesman principle*. I tell the boy about the experience of the door-to-door salesman who must have the guts (or "balls") to tolerate the frustrations and lowered feelings of self-worth that come with each rejection. However, they are willing to suffer these discomforts because of their awareness that a certain percentage (often predictable) will ultimately buy their wares. And this happy thought enables them to tolerate their inevitable rejections. Therapists do well to help the adolescent boy compare himself to such a salesman. They do well to reassure the boy that even if he is rejected by girl number one, and even if he is rejected by girl number two, there is certainly girl number three or four who will be more receptive. This does not preclude my looking into personality qualities of his that might be contributing to his rejection.

Some boys will rationalize their reticence to make overtures with comments such as "All the girls in my school are 'dogs' or 'ugly.'" To this I may respond, "From what you describe, it appears that sometime around 16 years ago someone put some poison in the town drinking water that brought about severe facial deformities in all the girls that were born at that time." The youngster usually gets my message. I also try to impress upon such boys that I am "100 percent convinced" that there are girls in his very high school who would be overjoyed at the prospect of having a date with him. I also try to impress upon such youngsters the fact that the girls are as "horny" as the boys and that they too are extremely desirous of forming relationships with them.

Next, we reach the point of the initial telephone conversation. Once again, I impress upon such youngsters that anxiety under these circumstances is normal, and that even overwhelming anxiety is normal. However, I inform them that the difference between the brave man and the coward is simply this: whereas both the brave man and the coward are basically afraid, the brave man swallows the lump in his throat and does the thing he's frightened of; the coward flees. I also impress upon the youngster the *nothing-ventured-nothing-gained principle*. Right now he is lonely. If he doesn't make the call he'll remain lonely. If he makes the call there are two possibilities: (1) the girl will be receptive and he is likely to have an enjoyable experience or (2) the girl will reject him and he will once again be lonely. Although such advice may seem obvious, it is not so obvious to the adolescent youngster, and he may need repeated proddings of this kind to get him to make the telephone call.

I also try to impress upon the youngster the fact that we cannot be uniformly loved by all people on earth. In fact, only an infinitesimal fraction of people are going to be strongly attracted to any one of us. Accordingly, we should not automatically take it personally when we are rejected. Although there may have been alienating personality qualities operative (which we certainly must look at in treatment), the rejection may have nothing to do with characteristics of the rejected individual but simply are related to the fact that the boy is not the girl's "type." I also impress upon the youngster that our discussion is actually the *lecture* part of the course and that more important is the *lab* part of the course in which he goes out, makes the call, and then comes back and tells me about what happened. If he doesn't have the gumption to make the call, then his treatment is likely to be sterile and intellectualized, and it won't go very far. In some cases I will even sternly tell the youngster that his making the call is a "homework assignment" and that I will be very disappointed in him if he comes back next time without having done his assignment.

I have found it useful to engage the youngster in a "practice" telephone call in which I play the role of the girl he is calling and he plays himself. We then enact various scenarios that involve both acceptance and rejection. Usually, I get significant input from him regarding what I should be saying and inform the youngster that because he knows the girl far better than I, he is more likely to provide valid speculations regarding the responses she might make. In the course of such a scenario, I educate the youngster regarding the significance of the girl's responses. For example, I help him differentiate between the response "Sorry I'm busy" with nothing stated thereafter from "Sorry I'm busy" and an invitation to discuss alternative arrangements. If the youngster is placing himself in a humiliating position, I will often point this out to him as a step toward helping him protect himself from such future embarrassment. For example, if the youngster reports to me that he had offered six different alternatives after the first telephone rejection, and was rejected on each, I will inform him that that was far too many. Two, or at most three, should be the upper limit—unless the girl provides convincing reasons why she cannot accept the invitation and suggests on her own an alternative time and place. I help the patient appreciate that such a response indicates that she is quite receptive to going out with him and that her refusal to accept the first invitation is not a manifestation of disinterest. As will be discussed in the section on group therapy, such conversations may be particularly useful when the girls in the group provide their input. And the role-playing of such conversations may also be useful.

Sometimes a boy will complain to me that the girl's situation is the preferable one in dating encounters because she doesn't have to suffer the fear of being rejected. She knows that once an overture is made, the boy has singled her out from others and is demonstrating interest and attraction. I try to point out to such boys that they are taking a narrow view of the situation and that each sex has its advantages and disadvantages in the dating situation. Furthermore, it is difficult to say which one's position is the preferable one at that stage of life. Although the boy is correct that, with regard to this aspect of dating, the girl does not have to suffer the fear of being rejected, she suffers the anxiety of not being chosen. Present mores strongly dictate that the boy be the assertive one and make the initial approach. The girls thereby experience a certain sense of impotence in that they may have little if any control over whether they will be selected. Of course, a certain amount of flirting and expression of interest in the boys may result in the boys' "coming on," but such maneuvers may very well fail.

I try to engender in each sex a sense of sensitivity to the feelings of the other. For example, a girl who is pretty, vivacious, and sought after by many boys may become insensitive in the way she rejects them and may even taunt and tantalize them in a sadistic way. She has to be helped to appreciate how hostile her mechanisms for self- aggrandizement are and has to be encouraged to place herself in the position of the boys and appreciate how she would feel in their situation. Similarly, there are attractive boys who will be cruel in their rejection of girls who have demonstrated their interest.

Clinical Example I present here a clinical vignette that demonstrates well the approach to initiate dating I used with a sexually inhibited 14-year- old boy. Harry entered treatment because of profound shyness and poor school performance, in spite of extremely high intelligence. Both of his parents were professional scientists and highly unemotional and intellectualized. Their pressures on Harry to perform well in the academic realm were formidable. Harry's poor school performance was, in part, a rebellion against his parents' coercions. In addition, they had a condescending attitude toward practically everyone and little meaningful involvement with anyone outside their family. Harry's shyness and uninvolvement with others was a reflection of his parents' attitudes about people. The family was Catholic, very religious, and puritanical in their condemnation of profanity, sex, and pleasurable activities.

After about a year of therapy, Harry joined his parochial school's computer club, where he immediately became recognized as the most knowledgeable and enthusiastic member. The activity suited him well because of his very high intelligence and his interest in activities that did not involve emotional expression. A few months after joining, he began to report in session his club's new project: computerized matching of boys in his school with the girls of a nearby Catholic school. All students in both schools were to fill out a questionnaire describing various basic physical characteristics, interests, personality preferences in members of the opposite sex, etc. All this data were to be fed into a computer, and every boy and girl would be matched to three others. A large dance was to be held, everyone was to be assigned a number, and at prescribed times each student would dance with the partners assigned by the computer.

For weeks Harry spoke excitedly of the details of this project. I was most pleased about it, not only because of his enthusiasm (a rare quality for Harry to exhibit), but because it would provide Harry with the opportunity to involve himself with girls in a way that would produce less anxiety than some of the more traditional methods of boy-girl meetings. When the week came for the students to fill out their questionnaires, Harry spoke animatedly about the large numbers of questionnaires being received and how happy he was that everything pointed to the program's being a success. In the context of this discussion I casually asked Harry what answers he had written on his questionnaire. Harry replied, "Oh, I'm not putting in any questionnaire. My job is to organize the whole thing and make sure that everything works well with the computer." I was astonished! For weeks we had spoken about this activity, and not once did I ever consider the possibility that Harry would not submit a questionnaire for himself. The session took place the day before the deadline for the submission of the questionnaires. There was little time to work things out, to help Harry assuage his anxieties, and to help him appreciate what he was doing.

Speaking more as a frustrated father than as a therapist, I told Harry that I was astonished that he wasn't submitting his own questionnaire. I told him he was making a grave error, that everybody gets nervous in such situations, and that he had to push through his fears if he was to enjoy the potential rewards of a new situation. I spoke quickly and somewhat heatedly—ending with the warning that if he came back to the next session without having submitted his questionnaire, I would not only be very disappointed in him, but very irritated with him as well.

One could argue that my approach was extremely antitherapeutic: I was coercing this boy; I was pushing him into an anxiety- provoking situation; I would be producing unnecessary guilt and self-loathing if he did not comply with my request; and I was jeapordizing the therapeutic relationship by such coercive and antitherapeutic tactics. I agree with these criticisms and I was aware of these dangers as I spoke to Harry. My hope was that this risk would be more than counterbalanced by Harry's appreciation, at some level, that my frustration, anger, and coercion came from a deep sense of concern and that only an uninvolved therapist could sit calmly by and allow him to pass up this wonderful opportunity. (I am reminded at this point of a psychiatric ward nurse who once reported overhearing a conversation among three children. The first said, "My mother's a bitch." The second, "My father's always hitting me." And the third, "My father never even hits me!" Obviously the third's situation was the worst. Having a father who never even bothers to discipline and even punish is a severe deprivation indeed.) I hoped also that the general strength of our relationship was such that he not only would comply, but that he would appreciate that I was being basically benevolent.

Harry did submit his questionnaire. On the night of the dance he "could not find" one of the girls with whom he was matched, and the second "didn't show up." However, he did spend some time with the third. But because he didn't know how to dance (and forgot my suggestion that he ask her to teach him a few steps), they talked awhile and then went their separate ways. I was not surprised that no hot romance developed from this first encounter with a female. One cannot expect a patient to overcome lifelong inhibitions in one evening. However, the ice was broken. Had I not reacted as I had, I believe that Harry would not have taken this step and I would have therefore been somewhat remiss in my obligation to him. I saw no evidence that Harry's relationship with me had in any way suffered because of my coercion; in fact, I believe that it was strengthened. However, this improvement could not have taken place if the coercion had not occurred at a time after a good relationship had already formed. To have used such an approach very early in treatment might very well have destroyed, or seriously compromised, our relationship.

Helping Girls Who Feel Unattractive

A girl in therapy feels unattractive. In the course of her treatment I try to help her appreciate that there are a wide range of facial and body types and that no one can be uniformly attractive to everyone. Although her particular appearance may not be attractive to some boys, there is no question that her appearance is attractive to others. And I point out that this is the case for everyone, including myself, and that I too have suffered similar rejections. The fact that her therapist has had his share of rejections makes it easier for her to accept hers. However, I don't stop there. I try to ascertain whether there is anything she is doing that might detract from good grooming and an attractive appearance. If this is the case, I *benevolently* point out these oversights to her and do what I can to help her rectify the situation. Sometimes, as a man, I recognize that my ability to provide such information may be compromised, and I advise her to speak with her mother, other adolescent girls, a beautician, and those who are more knowledgeable than me in this area. This does not preclude my going into the question of *why* she has not done what other girls her age are routinely doing. The adolescent girl may be more receptive to a discussion of *what* she can do for herself to improve her appearance than the issue of *why* she is not concerned with her grooming. Both areas are important, even though the youngster may be more receptive to acquiring information about grooming than delving into psychoanalytic inquiry.

If the youngster then shows efforts to improve her appearance, I make it a point to mention my awareness of the changes. But I do not do this simply at the intellectual level. When the changes are made, I don't wait (as many classical analysts would) until the youngster makes some reference to her appearance. And, when I do speak up, it's not simply at the intellectual level. For example, I am *not* likely to say, "I see you've changed your hairstyle" or "I see you're more careful now with the clothes you're choosing to wear." Rather, I will say, "I want you to know that I noticed the change as soon as you came into the room. It's striking how pretty you look now. I'm sure the boys' heads turn when you walk into the room." My hope here is to get across the message that I find the girl attractive and *somewhat* titillating. Some classical analysts would say that my comments here are seductive and therefore a terrible therapeutic contaminant. I am in disagreement. I am not communicating to the youngster specific sexual fantasies that she might now be engendering. Rather, I am merely communicating a mild level of titillation that most men would have in her presence. Holmes (1964) discusses this point in his vignette about an adolescent girl who was making efforts to make herself more attractive. With regard to the issue of what comments, if any, the therapist should make, Holmes states: "If she has put much honest labor into restyling her hair or making an attractive dress for herself, it would probably be more damaging to withhold comment. She might secretly wonder if her therapist has gone blind, but would be even more likely to marvel at the magnitude of his inhibitedness. . . . This open expression of appreciation on the part of the doctor naturally carries a hint of sexual interest. As such feelings are inevitable anyway, any effort to write them off entirely as 'countertransference' will be correctly interpreted by the patient as an act of emotional cowardice—an uneasy withdrawal from the very kinds of feelings which she finds so difficult to tolerate in herself" (p. 277).

Group Therapy

Group therapy can be especially useful for adolescent boys and girls who are having difficulty in the dating process. The group, which is a protected environment, can provide them with the opportunity for learning exactly what is going on in the minds of members of the opposite sex in a very supportive environment. The atmosphere of openness and honesty reassures them that they are not being "buttered up" and that they are really getting true facts about what the opposite sex thinks. They can also learn about the honest reaction of their same-sexed peers regarding what they do and say. Professions of independent thinking notwithstanding, adolescents are significantly dependent on peer opinion, and the group therapy experience can capitalize on this phenomenon.

One situation in which group role-playing can be useful is the one in which a boy is hesitant to call up a girl for a date. He feels awkward regarding his knowledge of what to do and say and is quite fearful of rejection because of his feelings of ineptitude. A make-believe telephone call to one of the girls in the group can be particularly useful here. The boy is invited to make his initial statement. One girl is asked to respond. This interchange then serves as a point of departure for group discussion. In the course of such discussions the youngster learns various ways to initiate the conversation and various responses that the girl may make. These are roughly divided into those that indicate receptivity and those that indicate the opposite. Although such information can generally be provided in individual sessions, it is much more effective if the provider is an adolescent girl. She is generally viewed as a far greater expert on such matters than an adult therapist, even a female therapist.

Many youngsters in group therapy are shy about entering the dating scene. Advice, pressure, and urging desensitization can be useful for such youngsters. I recall one group focusing on a forthcoming senior prom. At that time three boys in the group were quite inhibited regarding asking girls to the prom. Reassurances to them that there were certainly girls in their schools who would be most desirous of attending the prom did not help them overcome their reluctance and fears. During the same meeting there was a discussion of SAT scores. This group was particularly bright and many were applying to excellent schools. They were well versed with the format of examinations such as the SAT. In the ensuing discussion I told the group members that I was going to give them a multiple-choice question, such as the kind one sees on the SATs. It was presented as a question to see how smart they were. The question:

Which of the following courses of action would be the preferable one for a senior-high-school boy regarding attendance at his forthcoming prom?

a) Push through his fears. Ask a girl to go with him. Take her to the prom and have a good time dancing, feeling the closeness of her warm body against his, and possibly having a great time—both in and out of bed.

b) Sitting at home alone, depressed, envying all the others at the prom because of the good time they're having and then ending up the evening by jerking off and going to sleep.

c) Spending the evening with some other lonely, horny guys, all making believe that they're having a good time and trying to forget the fact that the others at the prom are probably enjoying themselves immensely

d) Going to the dance with another guy, one of you dressed as a girl.

e) If you do not consider any of the above to be an appropriate answer, then state what you would consider to be a preferable way to spend the night—when all the others in your class are enjoying themselves enormously at the prom.

Last, as the group evolves into a cohesive unit (its openendedness notwithstanding—there are still some ongoing members at any given point), they develop a sense of camaraderie that can also be ego-enhancing. One develops an attachment to the group and a sense of loyalty to it, and this makes one feel better about oneself for being a member of such a unit.

Dating, Depression, and Self-Esteem

Most of my colleagues in the field of psychiatry are deeply committed to the biological theory regarding the etiology of depression. Although I do not deny a possible neurologic predisposition for depression (especially in bipolar disorders), I still consider most depressions to be psychogenic. (Again, this does not preclude a genetic "loading.") A common source of depression in adolescence is rejection by a boyfriend or girlfriend. In fact, this is even a common reason for adolescent suicide. The most potent antidepressant will be far less effective than rapprochement with a recent girlfriend or boyfriend by whom one has been rejected. The therapist should try to ascertain whether the patient himself (herself) played a role in bringing about the rejection. Sometimes this has been the case and other times not. If so, one must help the youngster correct those deficiencies that might have been alienating in order to protect him (her) from such future rejections. Also, such youngsters need the traditional reassurance that "there are other fish in the sea." In fact, one should emphasize that there are literally a sea of boys and girls out there who are quite eager to form relationships. Of course, if factors beyond the fear of rejection are contributing to the depression, one must explore them. Elsewhere (Gardner, 1988a) I discuss in detail the therapeutic approaches to adolescent depression.

Dating, Shoplifting, and Self-Esteem

A common crime engaged in by early adolescent girls is that of shoplifting. Most often, these youngsters will steal such things as perfume, scarves, and cheap jewelry. Department store owners know this well. Some parents, when they learn about such behavior, are amazed. A common response: "I can't understand why she steals these things. Our family is quite well off. We could buy these things for her and have offered to do so. She could easily buy these things from her allowance." I believe that many of these thefts relate to the girl's belief that she is stealing something that enhances her sexual attractiveness. At some level, the girl believes that perfume purchased by her mother (an old, sexless object) is not as likely to have the same sexual allure as the same perfume that is stolen. After all, forbidden fruit is much sweeter than that which is acquired honestly. When department store owners catch such girls, they generally come down hard on them and make various threats. The usual first response is to call in the parents, enter the youngster's name on the store's record, and inform all concerned that the next time this happens, the police will be brought in. Parents do well to respond with horror and indignation over the act of stealing. One of the worst things they can do is to react with calmness or to excuse the act as normal. They do well to add to the storekeeper's measures those of their own. Just about the worst thing they can do is to bring a honcho lawyer who is going to "protect" the youngster from the consequences of her act. My experience has been that the storekeeper's warnings plus a parental fit are usually adequate to "cure" this problem. Of course, there are many other reasons for shoplifting, and it is certainly done by people who are not adolescent girls. This is especially the case in this increasingly psychopathic world in which we live. I am only referring here to this small segment of the shoplifting population and to the special motivation that is applicable to this age group.

Concluding Comments

Although one does well to try to get the adolescent to subscribe to certain principles regarding the superiority of sex within ongoing relationships as opposed to transient sex, one is not likely to be significantly successful in promulgating this lofty ideal with most adolescents. Boys, especially, need to prove themselves as "men" by having sexual relations. And girls, too, are increasingly viewing themselves as somehow inadequate if they are still virgins in their late teens. None of this may be particularly pathological in my opinion. What is pathological is the youngster who is so obsessed with sex—much more than the usual degree of preoccupation—that other functions (such as academic pursuits) are interfered with. If a girl believes that the greater the number of lovers she has, the more attractive she is, then she is likely to have problems. If she feels that no one will want her unless she provides sex, then her sexual behavior is likely to be pathological. Her feelings of inadequacy are likely to reveal themselves in other areas, and this lends confirmation to the view that her promiscuity has less to do with sex and more to do with the misguided attempt to compensate for such feelings of inadequacy. If a boy is merely using girls as objects, has little sensitivity to their feelings, and is compulsively trying to "lay" as many as he can in order to compensate for feelings of inadequacy, then this behavior too is pathological. Here, as well, feelings of low self-worth are likely to manifest themselves in other areas. This provides confirmation of the view that his compulsive sexuality is a form of pathological compensation.

SEXUAL GUILT AND SELF-ESTEEM

The Therapist's Values and Sexual Guilt

As mentioned, I believe (my values) it is normal and healthy for youngsters to begin having mild heterosexual experiences ("petting" and caressing) in the early to mid-adolescent period and to begin having sexual relations in mid- to late adolescence. Whether or not I think this is healthy is almost irrelevant, in that the vast majority of youngsters have had sexual relations by the late-adolescent period anyway—regardless of what I or anyone else thinks about it. The therapist does well, however, to help adolescent patients differentiate sharply between sexual activity in which the sole purpose is some release and sexual activity in the context of a relationship. The youngster should be helped to appreciate that the latter is generally the more gratifying and rewarding experience. Some experience with the former, however, may still be useful in that one learns more effectively about this contrast from actual experience than from some statement made by the therapist.

It is worth repeating that it is crucial that the therapist impress upon youngsters the risks of sexually transmitted diseases, especially AIDS. The therapist should attempt to differentiate between sexual behavior that is normal and that which is abnormal. Abnormal sexual behavior generally involves compulsivity. In boys it can often serve to compensate for feelings of inadequacy. For such youngsters the therapist has to attempt to differentiate the boy's normal need to flaunt sexual "conquests" from the pathological degree of such boasting. This may be quite difficult because the normal boy is likely to brag significantly anyway. For girls, the most common reasons for promiscuity are feelings of low self- worth and the belief that the only way they can get a boy's attention is to provide sex. One must deal here with the underlying factors that have contributed to the feelings of low self-worth.

When discussing the sexual activities of adolescents, the subject of confidentiality often comes up. Elsewhere (Gardner, 1988a) I discuss in detail my views on confidentiality in adolescent treatment. As elaborated there, I do not respect the adolescent's confidentiality when the youngster engages in behaviors that may be significantly dangerous to himself (herself) and others. I do not consider sexual intercourse necessarily to be a "reportable" event to the parents of the adolescent in therapy. I will, however, *consider* reporting an adolescent's sexual behavior to parents if there are definite risks associated with it. Let us take, for example, the situation in which a girl is clearly trying to get pregnant. If, after discussion of the problem in individual and group therapy, she is still trying to do so, I believe that some communication with the parents is warranted. Or if promiscuity is exposing the youngster to sexually transmitted diseases, I would consider also this to be a reportable issue. It is not that the parents can do much about such a girl's sexual activities, but they may be able to take some precautions that may lessen the likelihood of the youngster's being exposed to these dangers. For example, they may be more circumspect with regard to leaving the girl at home alone when they go off at night and on weekends. And they might check more on where their daughter "actually" is when she is supposedly visiting the homes of friends.

Many years ago I had an experience during one of my presentations that elucidates an important point with regard to the relationship between a therapist's values, confidentiality, and an adolescent's sexual activities. I was speaking to a group of pastoral counselors in Tennessee. They were mainly ministers, deeply committed to their religious beliefs. Following a presentation on the treatment of adolescents, I invited questions from the audience. One minister raised his hand and the following interchange took place:

> *Minister*: I'm having a problem in the treatment of a 16-year-old girl and I want your opinion on it.
>
> *Gardner*: Yes, what's the problem?
>
> *Minister* (somewhat dramatically): She's having sexual intercourse!
>
> *Gardner*: Yes? (This was said with an intonation implying that I was waiting for more information.)
>
> *Minister*: That's it. She's *having sexual intercourse!*
>
> *Gardner* (in a somewhat incredulous tone): I heard that. But what I want to know is *what* is the problem?
>
> *Minister* (somewhat angrily): That's the problem! She's having sex!
>
> *Gardner* (inquisitively): Why is that a problem?
>
> *Minister*: It's a problem because it's a *sin,* and I have an obligation to do everything possible to stop her from sinning.
>
> *Gardner*: How do you plan to do that?
>
> *Minister*: Well, the first thing I'm going to do is to tell her parents.
>
> *Gardner*: Let me say this to you. I suspect that what I am going to say now may never have been considered before by many of you. I suspect that many of you have never considered the possibility that sex before marriage may *not* be a sin. Now I do not claim to know *with certainty* whether or not it is. I know that some of you here believe deeply, with 100 percent certainty, that pre-marital sex is a sin. And you may be right. I just don't know. My guess is that it isn't.
>
> All therapy involves the imposition of one's own values on one's patients. Clearly, the values of most of the people here in this

room are different from many of mine. You (now turning to the questioner) may be correct that you must do everything to protect her from what you consider to be the consequences of her sins, both in this life and in the hereafter. I do *not* know whether you are or are not correct on this issue. However, there is one thing I can say to you with *100 percent certainty*. And that is this: If you do tell her parents against her will, you will no longer have a patient. The disclosure may very well protect her from eternal damnation, but it will have destroyed the therapy. This is a choice you must make.

Needless to say, I was never invited to return to speak again at that facility. In fact, I would suspect that they probably tried to find out who the person was who had so many screws loose in his head that he invited me to speak there in the first place. The vignette is presented because it demonstrates well my point regarding the importance of therapists' appreciating that they cannot avoid imposing their values on their patients, and the sexual situation is only one example of this phenomenon. To try to follow the dictum that one should never impose one's values on one's patients is impossible. Therapists must appreciate that they are continually doing so; one has to accept the consequences of so doing, whether these consequences be here on earth or potentially in the hereafter.

Sometimes a sexually inhibited boy can be made to feel less guilty about his sexual desires by my demonstrating sexual interest of my own. For example, when a boy tells me that he feels somewhat guilty about the fact that he is interested in and turned on by centerfolds of girlie magazines, I might say, somewhat sarcastically, "I think the best way I can help you with those feelings is to take a look at that magazine myself, especially the centerfold. It's only when we discuss this with an actual picture in hand that we will be in a good position to talk about your feelings. Of course, I'm doing this purely from a *clinical* point of view. (I may then start smiling.) It's not that I have any *personal* interest in seeing those pictures. It's purely for *your* therapy. If you think for one minute that I myself would be titillated by such pictures, you would be entirely wrong." Almost invariably the patient gets my message, which, I believe, helps assuage his guilt. Basically I am saying that I too find those pictures titillating, and this helps the patient feel less loathsome for having an interest. I believe that this is one of the situations in treatment where sarcasm is warranted in that it enhances the efficacy of the therapeutic message. If a boy feels inhibited about masturbating over such pictures, I try to assuage his guilt and impress upon him that this is an extremely widespread phenomenon and that most boys, if they were to be honest, would admit that they engage in the practice. If he claims that most of his friends deny that they do so, I try to convince him of the fact that they are most likely lying. I may tell him, "The vast majority of heterosexual boys fall into one of two categories: those who jerk off over these pictures and *admit* that they do, and those who jerk off over such pictures and *deny* that they do." If the youngster has any misguided or erroneous notions about the dangers of masturbation, I will try to correct these distortions. He may believe that masturbation causes sexually transmitted diseases, sterility, rings under the eyes, or other telltale signs. All these distortions must be corrected.

A 16-year-old boy once told me that he had read in the newspapers that some women in Washington, D.C., were going to protest the city's law that women are not permitted to appear in public with their chests bare, whereas men can. They were going to protest en masse by appearing publicly, completely bare from the waist up. This was told to me by a boy who was quite inhibited in telling me about his own interests in girls. In response to his comments about the Washington demonstration, I took my pen and pad and said, "That's very interesting! *Where* did you say that demonstration was going to be held? What city did you say? *When* did you say it was going to take place? I'm *very* interested in the exact day and the exact time. And I'd like to know *exactly* where they're going to be demonstrating. These are the kinds of demonstrations that *really* interest me." The patient quickly got my message. I too was telling him that I thought it was a turn-on. Of course, the patient appreciated that I was not actually going to make a trip to Washington, but my intense interest (exaggerated somewhat) transmitted to him the message that I found the prospect titillating. I then continued: "I'm fully sympathetic with what these women are doing. The law is inegalitarian and I'm 100 percent against it. I'm convinced the world would be a better place if women were free to walk around topless. These women have a definite *point* to make, or should I say *points.*" By this time the patient was chuckling along with me. I was not only providing here a guilt-assuaging message in an enjoyable vehicle but, possibly more important, I was adding a note of levity to the therapy—counterbalancing thereby what can often be a morbid and grim experience. This is likely to entrench our relationship and strengthen thereby the foundation of the therapeutic process.

General Comments on Sexual Guilt Alleviation

As mentioned previously, I use the word *guilt* to refer to the feelings of low self-worth an individual experiences after entertaining thoughts, experiencing feelings, or engaging in activities that one has learned are bad, sinful, or wrong. Generally, the "teachers" are the parents and other significant figures in the individual's life, especially people with whom one was involved in early childhood. However, throughout the course of our lives we are ever exposed to individuals who provide us with dicta that can play a role in producing guilt. Proscriptions against sex are ubiquitous and these are traditionally inculcated during the earliest years of life. It is important for the reader to appreciate that I do not belong to the school of therapists who believe that all guilt necessarily produces psychopathology. Rather, I believe that it is the therapist's role to decide whether the patient needs more or less guilt. I would go further and say that more people in this world need more guilt because they do not have enough. Therapists who automatically consider guilt a feeling to be alleviated and/or reduced will be contributing to the general pool of psychopaths of which we have far too many at this time.

Simply saying to patients that their sexual thoughts and feelings are normal and healthy may be useful, but I would consider it only a small part of a therapeutic process designed to reduce guilt. One must look into the *sources* of the guilt, especially the people who engendered it by their guilt-evoking dicta. The patient must be helped to put in proper perspective the reasons why these authorities made their statement and to ask questions regarding how judicious these dicta really are. In such discussions the therapist is ever walking the fine line between promiscuity on the one side and pathological sexual inhibition on the other. I have found this comment to be particularly useful: "The only difference between you and other boys (girls) your age I have seen is that you believe your sexual thoughts and feelings are bad. You share in common with the vast majority sexual thoughts and feelings."

Discussions in which the therapist provides advice and information can also be guilt-evoking, without direct attention to the guilt issue. Merely talking about the subject provides the youngster with the living experience that the words themselves do not have the magic power to cause any harm, and they give the youngster "practice" with talking about sexual topics and even experiencing some sexual feelings. The woman who says, "I can't understand why I'm so guilty about sex; it was never even mentioned in my home when I was a child," is providing significant information regarding the source of her guilt. If a child has a choice between a mother who gives her a lecture every day about the evils and sins of sex, and one who never talks about the subject, the youngster will probably be better off with the first mother. The former is at least mentioning the subject, whereas the latter considers it too terrible even to talk about. And the latter situation is far more guilt-evoking than the former. Accordingly, the therapist merely talking about sex may be guilt-alleviating.

For adolescent boys who are sexually inhibited, I have found certain cards in the *The Talking, Feeling, and Doing Game* to be useful as points of departure for discussion on the subject of sexuality and dating. For example, to the card "You're looking through a telescope, what do you see?" I might respond:

> When I was a teenager a friend of mine got a telescope for Christmas. I think his parents thought he'd be looking at the

moon, stars, and other celestial bodies. Although this was of some interest to us, we were much more interested in using it to look into the windows of the apartment houses in my neighborhood in the Bronx. We all thought it would really be a great thing if we could see a woman getting undressed in front of a window. Well, I want you to know that we spent a lot of time in the hope that we would enjoy such a spectacle. Unfortunately, there weren't too many girls and women in my neighborhood who were getting undressed in front of windows. But it was still a lot of fun. And it was also exciting just thinking about it.

We see here how a personal revelation about the therapist can be therapeutically useful. I am basically saying to the patient that I myself had strong sexual urges and involved myself in activities that provided me with some gratification for these impulses. My hope here was that via identification with me the patient would become more relaxed regarding the satisfaction of his own sexual desires.

GUILT OVER MASTURBATION AND SELF-ESTEEM

Introduction

Guilt over masturbation is one of the most common forms of guilt. Although less so in recent years, residua of proscriptions from the past are very much with us. It may be of interest to the reader to learn that from the 18th to the late 19th century, in both the United States and Europe, there was a massive antimasturbation movement, which reached its climax (pardon my pun) approximately 100 years ago. At that time, we experienced what can only be called a wave of hysteria in association with masturbation (Stone, 1985). Physicians (who should have known better) were at the forefront of this movement. Medical books described a wide variety of physical illnesses that derived from this practice, e.g., tics, weakness, anemia, and mental derangement. Physicians then commonly used the word *self-abuse* as a synonym for masturbation. Millions were earned by companies selling a wide variety of devices that were designed to prevent children from touching themselves. Interestingly, a physician named J. Kellogg (founder of the breakfast cereal company) was at the forefront of the antimasturbation movement. Legrand et al. (1989) have written a fascinating article in which they describe this hysteria. Therapists who subscribe to the notion that masturbation is somehow detrimental may be doing their patients (regardless of age) a serious disservice.

As a psychoanalyst I have wondered about the reasons for this inhibition, which, like most sexual inhibitions, varies from society to society. I believe one of the most important factors relates to the view that it is a harbinger of potential unwanted pregnancies. A child who is highly sexualized is more likely to become promiscuous in adolescence and is therefore more likely to provide the family with the extra burden (and sometimes disgrace) of an out-of-wedlock child. To some, *all* sex is bad and sinful, whether it be auto-, hetero- or homosexual. And this opinion may be reflexively carried down from generation to generation without questioning the justification for this notion. It may be that for some parents masturbation is a threat because the practice basically communicates to the parent: "I am not getting the gratification I need from you; I must therefore turn to myself for pleasure." Prohibiting the child from masturbating, then, protects the parent from this unpleasant confrontation. Some children masturbate because it serves well as an antidote to depression and other painful affects. Like a drug, pleasurable experiences can counterbalance the psychological pain of depression and other painful affects. For some children, it serves as a tranquilizer. This is especially the case for children who are very tense and anxious. Following an orgasm there is a general sense of relaxation. With some children it may serve as a powerful mechanism for expressing hostility. Recognizing that parents are provoked and upset by the act, they make sure to engage in it—especially in situations where the parents cannot avoid observing them—as a predictably effective weapon. Freud considered masturbation to be normal (and I agree with him on this point), but he considered masturbatory imagery to be disguised oedipal fantasies (I do not agree with him on that point). The oedipal theory is an oversimplification, and it is injudicious to consider a single psychodynamic factor to underlie the wide variety of psychological processes that can contribute to any form of human behavior.

Reducing Masturbatory Guilt

Because masturbatory guilt is intrinsically associated with low self-esteem, therapists do well to make attempts to reduce masturbatory guilt whenever possible. Adolescents do well to masturbate. It is one of the best ways to deal with sexual urges in a situation in which heterosexual activities cannot be readily satisfied. They should be helped to appreciate that there is absolutely no excuse why anyone in the world should walk around "horny." I am not recommending masturbation as being preferable to heterosexual experiences throughout life, only that in the early adolescent period it may be a superior (and certainly safer) form of sexual activity. Accordingly, the therapist does well to make every attempt to reduce masturbation guilt if present. However, the alleviation of such guilt may not be necessary for the vast majority of adolescents today. Mention has been made of the 13-year-old girl who sought my opinion because she was not yet masturbating and feared that she might be different from her friends who were doing so. She wondered whether she had a psychological problem. I certainly would not have been consulted for this purpose 15 to 20 years ago.

When discussing masturbation with adolescents I generally do not try to convey the notion that this practice is simply confined to this age group. Rather, I inform them that it is a widespread practice at all ages and that it would generally be considered normal even when there is heterosexual opportunity. I inform them that the general opinion among mental health practitioners today is that it becomes pathological when a person routinely engages in it in preference to heterosexual activities or involves oneself in it to an obsessive degree. I tell them, as well, that when other opportunities for sexual gratification are not available, then it is perfectly healthy for masturbation to be the only outlet at that time. If the person routinely prefers the masturbatory outlet over seeking heterosexual experiences, then there may be a problem. In the context of such a discussion I may relate to the youngster the maxim: "If God didn't want people to masturbate, he wouldn't have made people's arms long enough to reach down there." Or I might quote the limerick:

> There once was a woman named Croft
> Who played with herself in a loft.
> Having reasoned that candles
> Rarely cause scandals,
> Besides which they never go soft.

For a girl who may have difficulty reaching orgasm, I may recommend a vibrator or suggest that the youngster try other methods that may prove successful, such as a high-speed shower head. I try to assuage any guilt a youngster might have about being turned on by sexually explicit magazines. In fact, I have often said that an excellent confirmation present for a 13-year-old boy would be a five-year subscription to one of these magazines. For the 13-year-old girl, an analogous present would be a five-year subscription to a romantic love magazine and a vibrator.

In the last few years there have been additional reasons for my encouraging masturbation, specifically the risk of herpes and more recently AIDS. Any therapist who does not warn adolescent patients about the risk of these diseases is negligent. Because of the adolescent's capacity for delusions of invulnerability, they are likely to consider themselves immune to these diseases. Therapists do well to instill a reasonable (not paralytic) amount of fear in adolescents when discussing these and other sexually transmitted diseases in order to counterbalance some of this delusion. Last, I wish to impress upon the reader that I do not routinely encourage the initiation of masturbation when working with adolescents. Rather, I encourage it among youngsters who have strong sexual urges, but do not have a reasonable outlet for them and may find themselves getting into various kinds of difficulties because they do not give the masturbation option proper respect. Such difficulties would include promiscuity, frequenting prostitutes, seeking inappropriate partners, and suffering unnecessary sexual frustration.

The Talking, Feeling, and Doing Game can be useful for helping youngsters reduce masturbatory guilt. As mentioned, this game is not only useful in the therapy of prepubertal children but early adolescence as well. Children between the ages of 12 and 15 are generally too old to provide fantasies around doll play and sometimes too young to talk directly. *The Talking, Feeling, and Doing Game* can provide a valuable catalyst for such therapeutic productions. Two examples:

> *Question*: What do you think about a boy who sometimes plays with his penis when he's alone?
>
> *Response*: I think that it's perfectly normal—as long as he does it when he's alone. Of course, there would be something wrong with him if he did that in the open, in public; but as a private thing I think it's normal. In fact most teenage boys do it a lot, and many kids play with their penises when they're younger as well. There are some kids, however, who think that playing with their penises is a terrible thing. They think it's sinful, or wrong, or dirty. I completely disagree. Those kids are the ones that have a problem, and not the ones who play with their penises once in a while in private. What's your opinion on what I've just said?
>
> *Question*: What do you think about a girl who sometimes plays with or rubs her vagina when she's alone?
>
> *Response*: I think it's perfectly normal for her to do that when she's alone. Of course, that's not the kind of thing that one would generally do in front of other people. It's a private matter. What do you think?

For the sexually inhibited youngster these responses enable the examiner to approach a forbidden subject in a noncontrived way. Discussing the subject in itself is therapeutic as it provides the child with the living experience that such discussions do not result in dire consequences. That which is unmentionable is far more anxiety- and guilt-provoking than that which is spoken about. The child whose parents never speak about sex will generally become far more inhibited than the child whose parents preach often about the sins and evils of sex. Of course, the latter approach is likely to produce guilt as well, but probably not so much as the guilt produced by the situation in which the subject is unmentionable. For the child who is excessively guilty, I might add to the aforementioned card this response:

> There are some children who think that touching themselves is a terrible sin or crime. They think it's the worst thing a person can do. This is a strange idea because touching oneself is perfectly natural and normal. It only becomes a problem if the person does it most of the time and then doesn't do other things, or if the person feels very bad or guilty about it. Feeling that it's a terrible sin or crime is then the problem, not doing it. What are your opinions on this subject?

* * *

> *Question*: Make believe you're reading a magazine showing pictures of nude ladies. What do you think about such magazines?
> *Response*: Boy, there really are some exciting looking women in some of those magazines. I think they're great to look at once in a while. They have some of the most beautiful and luscious women in those magazines. Some people are ashamed to admit that they're interested in looking at those women. I don't think it's wrong, bad, or sinful to look at those pictures. I don't agree with those people. I think it's natural and healthy. It's only a problem if the person doesn't want to have anything to do with real people and wants to spend a lot of time looking at those pictures. What is your opinion on this subject?

This response is the one I provide for boys who are uncomfortable expressing sexual interest. Obviously, I attempt here to convey some of the excitement that most boys and men have when looking at pictures of nude women. I also attempt to lessen any guilt the patient may have over such interest. My hope is that the youngster will be receptive to my opinions on the subject and will identify with my attitude.

PROMISCUITY AND LOW SELF-ESTEEM

Psychodynamics and Therapeutic Considerations

As mentioned, I consider a girl having sexual intercourse in late adolescence to be normal and healthy. The ideal that I try to promulgate is that sex is most enjoyable in the context of an ongoing relationship, but an occasional experience outside of such a relationship can also be a source of pleasure. I emphasize also that such experiences outside of the relationship are likely to be a cause of pain and grief to one's special partner and that this must be taken into consideration before embarking on such additional experiences. I point out, as well, that in a marriage they are most often so devastating that they can contribute to the breakup of the marital relationship. I want to lay the groundwork here for dealing with a future situation and/or conflict that the adolescent may ultimately have.

If a girl is promiscuous, i.e., she indiscriminately engages in sex with a large number of boys, there is generally a pathological problem operative. Often it relates to feelings of low self-worth and the feeling that she could not attract boys without providing them with sex. I try to help such girls appreciate that they are humiliating themselves and that the lack of respect the boys have for them because of their promiscuity is likely to diminish even further their feelings of low self-worth. Some of these girls are so naive and gullible that they do not see the obvious fact that they are being exploited, so deep-seated are their cravings for any manifestation of affection. I also look into other problems that may be contributing to the promiscuity. These may relate to family difficulties, deprivation of affection from mother and/or father, and various psychological traumas that may contribute to her looking for sexual gratification as an antidote to her grief, tensions, and frustrations.

The Parental Role in Youngsters' Promiscuity

Often, but certainly not always, parents are playing a contributory role in an adolescent youngster's promiscuity. Sometimes a girl's promiscuity may relate to her mother's in that she is not only identifying with her mother, but trying to surpass her. In this quest she may even attempt to seduce her mother's lovers (and may be successful in this regard). A girl with a promiscuous father may follow in this pattern as an act of retaliation. It is as if she is saying: "It seems to me that every woman in this world is a candidate to be one of his lovers, except me. I know that he gets upset by my sleeping around a lot. That's the best way to wreak vengeance on him for his rejection of me." It is no surprise, then, that children of divorce are more likely to be promiscuous than those living in an intact family. To the degree that the therapist can help such youngsters understand and work out these underlying problems, to that degree will they be helped with their promiscuity problems.

The term *promiscuity* is less frequently applied to boys. In fact, most parents have a double standard with regard to their teenagers' sexuality. They are generally significantly threatened by a girl's promiscuity, especially because of the threats of sexually transmitted diseases and pregnancy. In contrast, a boy's promiscuity may very well be viewed as his attempts to enhance his sense of masculinity and he may considered to be "sowing his wild oats." A father may strongly encourage his son's promiscuity, seeing it as a vicarious extension of his own wishes for a wide variety of sexual experiences. He may even make such comments as: "Give her one for me." But mothers are not completely immune to this phenomenon. They too may have a double standard and get some kind of inner gratification from their sons' promiscuity. They may feel that he is enhancing his masculinity as well as providing reassurance that the youngster is not going down the homosexual track. To some degree, these parental attitudes are so widespread that they must be considered to be in the normal range. They only become pathological when they exert undue influence on the youngster's behavior, and then therapeutic work with the parents may be warranted.

Two mechanisms are most often operative, either alone or in combination, in parents' sanctioning abnormal sexual behavior in adolescents. The first is vicarious gratification. Via this mechanism the adolescent is utilized to gratify unfulfilled parental sexual yearnings. The parent, by virtue of age and possibly marital restrictions, is generally not as free to engage in as wide a variety of sexual activities as the adolescent. The adolescent, therefore, lends himself (herself) well to satisfying vicariously parental sexual cravings. It is as if each time the youngster engages in a sexual activity, the parent enjoys similar satisfaction. However, in order to enjoy such gratification the parent must have information, details, and even on occasion observation of the sexual activity. Vicarious gratification may be conscious and/or unconscious.

The other mechanism is reaction formation. Here the parent is not consciously aware of the underlying desires that the adolescent involve himself (herself) in the sexual activity. Rather, it is expressed as its opposite, that is, the prohibition and denial of the adolescent's sexual activities. There is an obsessive preoccupation with the adolescent's sexual life in the form of obsessive denunciation and excessive restriction. Such a parent, however, does not realize that each time the condemnation is verbalized, a mental image of the adolescent engaging in the sexual activity appears in the parent's mind. Accordingly, the wish is gratified via the visual imagery that the preoccupation provides, and the guilt is alleviated via the denunciation process. It is as if the parent is saying: "It is not that I want my adolescent to have sex. No, it's just the opposite: I *don't* want my adolescent to have sex. In fact, I *hate* the thought and will do everything possible to prevent such a terrible thing from happening."

For example, a mother gives her daughter long lectures about the evils of sex and warns her before each date about the terrible things that can happen if a girl engages in such activities. Following each date she cross-examines the youngster—especially with regard to every single detail of any possible sexual encounters. When the youngster denies such involvement, the mother is incredulous and accuses her of lying. When, inevitably, she describes some activities the mother's facial expression changes completely. Although her words are words of condemnation, her facial expression is one of agitated excitation. She craves more and more facts and unconsciously relishes every detail. This situation is reminiscent of the name of a song that was popular when I was a teenager: "Your lips tell me no-no, but there's yes-yes in your eyes." At some level the youngster recognizes what is going on and complies with the mother's wishes, gratifying vicariously thereby the mother's desires and protecting the mother from guilt via the utilization by the mother of the mechanism of reaction formation.

While I was in residency training, during the late 1950s, I saw a 14-year-old girl, Joan, whose mother demonstrated the aforementioned phenomenon quite well. I saw the girl in the psychiatric clinic, where she was referred because she had been "gang raped" by 14 or 15 boys. The girl and her mother were not exactly sure how many boys it was, but it was in that range. This took place in the girl's bedroom while her parents were away one evening. On gaining further details, it was clear that there was absolutely no forced entry, either into the girl's home or into her vagina. In fact, the girl had invited a few boys to come over and "have some fun," and they were even asked to bring along some friends.

When getting background history I learned from the mother that she always considered it important to impress upon her daughter the dangers of sex. Accordingly, from the time Joan was five or six, she began to lecture her on how sinful sex was and the terrible things that could happen as a result of it—including pregnancy and sexually transmitted diseases. (In those days they were called venereal diseases.) However, the mother also related how she appreciated that teenage girls need "privacy." Accordingly, starting at about the age of 12, when a boy would come to the home to visit Joan, the mother would allow Joan and her friend to go into the bedroom and even close the door. But she insisted that the door not be locked. Periodically, without advance warning, the mother would charge into the room. Not surprisingly, she would often find the youngsters at various levels of disrobing, would then chide them for what they were doing, and insist they put their clothing back on and stop fooling around. She would then close the door because she knew she could then "trust" her daughter not to do it again. Of course, this trust did not extend more than 15 minutes, at which time the same scenario was repeated.

Obviously, with this programming, it was no surprise that this girl was "gang raped." This vignette is an excellent demonstration of the mother's utilization of this girl for vicarious gratification of her own frustrated sexual needs. The mother set up a situation that would ensure that she would gain the gratifications she desired, namely, observing her daughter engaged in various sexual acts. In addition, the mechanism of reaction formation was utilized; by lecturing her daughter on the evils of sex and reprimanding her when so engaged, she could assuage the guilt she felt over what she was doing.

The next example of this phenomenon is an unusual one (as the reader will soon come to see) in that it involves a personal and professional experience of mine—combined into one person. The story begins in high school when I dated briefly a girl who attended the same high school. I was 17 and Virginia (a not inappropriate pseudonym, as the reader shall soon appreciate) was 16. During our first date she informed me—in very emphatic terms— that she had every intention of being a virgin when she got married. It is important to appreciate that this took place in the late 1940s, when such was the official position of most girls whom I dated. Such professions, therefore, would not expose the individual to the kind of ridicule that they might in many circles these days. As the evening progressed I was surprised by how readily she brought up the subject of her virginity and how frequently she mentioned it. At the end of the second date, her mother called me into the bedroom for a private conference. There she told me that I seemed to be a nice young man; however, I should know that her daughter had every intention of being a virgin when she got married, and Virginia had the mother's full support on this resolution. When she was sure that I had gotten that message, she dismissed me from the room.

Throughout the third and fourth dates, it became apparent that Virginia was obsessed with this virtuous goal and it became clear that, unlike her girlfriends, she really meant it. Her peers, although they would occasionally profess such intentions, generally showed some flexibility with regard to this resolve and engaged in a variety of activities that led me to the conclusion (and hope) that they might not last long regarding their commitment to this principle. I, at that point, hoped (desperately) that I would *not* be a virgin when I got married—especially because I planned to go to college, then medical school, then internship, and then residency—training that might last until the time I was around 30. As I saw it, I was 17 and already considering myself somewhat retarded regarding "how far" I had gone—if I could believe my friends (who, of course, would never lie about such matters). As far as I was concerned, the sooner I lost my virginity the better, and so Virginia and I parted ways. Clearly, Virginia and I had "irreconcilable differences."

We then went down our separate paths in life. Every few years, when the subject of compulsive commitment to the state of virginity would come up, I thought of Virginia and wondered whether she had gotten married and, if not, whether she was still a virgin. The answer came about 30 years after graduation from high school. I received a telephone call in my office one day from a woman who asked me if I would see her 16-year-old daughter on an emergency basis. She described the situation as being an urgent one because during the previous weekend, while she and her husband were away on vacation, her daughter had a "sex orgy" in the house with some of her friends. Worse yet, the male participants in this orgy were said to have been black and Hispanic (the family was Jewish). Last, she had good reason to believe that this all took place under the influence of drugs. I informed the mother of my usual practice of seeing the youngster and both parents in a two-hour consultation, during which time I see the three in varying combinations, as warranted. And so an appointment was made.

I can still remember my astonishment when I walked into the waiting room that day and saw not one, but two Virginias. The older Virginia was still named Virginia. (I had not linked the mother's name with my former high school date, especially because her last name was now different.) Although clearly 30 years older, I immediately recognized her as the girl I had dated in high school. Her daughter, whom I will call Sally, could have been a clone of the girl I had dated. After the initial introduction I informed the parents that it was my usual procedure to see teenagers first and then bring the parents into my office. However, I thought it important that we have a little chat before my interview with their daughter. I first asked the mother if she remembered me. She looked at me, somewhat quizzically, and replied that she did not. I asked if she had any recollection of ever having seen me at any point in her life, especially during the teen period. Again, she emphatically stated that I was totally unfamiliar to her and that she was quite sure she had never seen me. I then informed her that we had dated briefly while in high school. She was incredulous. She agreed that she had indeed attended the high school I named, but insisted she had not dated me. In order to provide her with further "evidence," I mentioned the names of a number of people whom we knew in common. She remembered some of them, but still insisted that she had no recollection of me. I decided not to pursue the matter further in the waiting room and came to the initial conclusion that she had probably blotted out of her awareness "sex maniacs" such as myself.

I then went into the consultation room with Sally. After sitting down, I had the feeling that a time machine had transformed Virginia back to the way she was 30 years previously, so uncanny was the similarity between the daughter and mother. The girl was a clone of her mother. It was as if she had inherited the genes of only her mother and none from her father. Perhaps, I thought, her mother was indeed a virgin when she got married and, not only that, was a virgin when she conceived, and I was dealing here with an immaculate conception. And I even wondered whether Virginia might *still* be a virgin. Sally interrupted my musings and probably did so in part because of the strange expression I must have had on my face as I looked at her. "Doctor Gardner," she said, "my mother is a nut! As long as I can remember, she's given me this shit about being a virgin when I get married. As far back as I can remember she's been telling me about how proud she is of the fact she was a virgin when she got married, and that her grandmother was a virgin when *she* got married, and that she has every intention of me being a virgin when I get married. And my father's bought that crap. He's always told me about how proud he is of the fact that my mother was a virgin when they got married. I've often said to him, 'Maybe no one else wanted her.'" As she spoke I kept thinking:

"Incredible, I can't believe it. Maybe it's true what they say about truth being stranger than fiction."

The daughter then continued: "I assume she told you a story about a sex orgy that I supposedly had with black and Puerto Rican drug addicts. This is more of her crap. The woman's off the wall. What really happened was this: My girlfriend and I went out on a double date. Her boyfriend is black. He's a great kid. He's one of the best students in the class. In fact, I think I like him more than I like the boy I was going out with, but she doesn't know that. Anyway, after the movie we went back to the house. I know I promised my mother that I wouldn't bring anybody back, but what the hell! There was nothing illegal about what we were doing. Then the four of us shared *one joint*. That was it. One joint she turns into drug addiction! It was the second time I did it and I really didn't even enjoy it. My boyfriend and I went into the bedroom and fooled around a bit. I'm still a virgin and it's lucky that I still have sexual feelings. With a mother like her, it wouldn't be surprising if I ended up frigid or something like that. There's no way I'm going to be a virgin when I get married, but I'm not ready for it yet. It's crazy to marry someone that you haven't gone to bed with. I don't know where she's coming from. That's the whole story. I'm not lying to you."

There was nothing in the girl's story, either in the way she told it or about the facts that she had presented, that led me to believe that she was not being honest. Furthermore, I had "background information" that made her story quite credible. Inquiries into other aspects of Sally's life revealed no evidence of psychopathology. She was doing well in school, had many friends, and was not causing her parents difficulties at home in other areas. Apparently, she had grown up in a fairly healthy way in spite of her mother's obsession. I suspect that this was due to the influence of peers and society at large, a society in which more permissive attitudes toward sex served to counterbalance the puritanical indoctrination of her mother.

I then brought the parents in, and the girl confronted them directly with the disparity between what she claimed happened and that which her mother fantasized. It was clear that the mother's renditions were fantasy and a reflection of her own problems in this area. In the course of the interview Virginia–not surprisingly–told me that she had always vowed that she would be a virgin when she got married (apparently thinking that this was news to me) and that she had always encouraged her daughter to follow in her footsteps in this regard. Virginia's husband then stated: "I'm in full agreement with my wife. I was very impressed on our first date with the fact that she felt so strongly about being a virgin when she got married. That was one of my main attractions to her." Virginia continued: "Yes, I knew that my husband really respected me. He never made advances like the other boys. He never pushed for sex like the others." All I could say to myself while listening to this was: "It takes one to marry one" and "For every man there's a woman."

Near the end of the interview, I informed the parents that I did not consider their daughter to be in need of treatment. I recognized that a direct statement to the mother that it was she (and also the father) who needed therapy would not have worked at that moment. Accordingly, I recommended family counseling in the hope that the mother might ultimately become a patient herself. The mother was receptive to this idea and was quite astonished when I told her that it would not be possible for me to serve as the therapist. She was surprised by my statement and asked me why. When I told her that our past relationship precluded my having the kind of objectivity necessary for successful treatment, she replied, "What relationship?" I told her again that it was my firm belief that we did indeed have a relationship in the past, and that as long as *I* believed that (even if it were only a fantasy), my serving effectively as a therapist was not possible. Once again, she was unconvinced. I was not going to argue with her on this point. Also, I told her that even if there had been no previous relationship between us, I would have recommended another therapist anyway–because of my belief that in this situation a female therapist was warranted. I informed her that I believed she might be more receptive to comments about her daughter's sexuality if they came from a woman. She agreed that this would probably be the case, because both she and her husband were firmly convinced that all men—even psychiatrists—were obsessed with sex (with the exception of Virginia's husband, of course). Accordingly, I referred the family to a female colleague with whom they lasted about two sessions. My colleague informed me that the mother left claiming she would have no further involvement with therapy because all psychiatrists (regardless of sex) were obsessed with sex and she would have to find another way to ensure that her daughter would be a virgin when she got married.

This vignette is presented as an example of a situation in which a parent's pathological attitudes about sex could contribute to psychopathology in an adolescent. Fortunately for Sally, she somehow avoided developing psychopathological reactions to her mother's attempts to indoctrinate her. The most likely outcome for Sally would have been some identification with her mother's obsession, which she might have transmitted down yet another generation. However, as mentioned, I suspect that the sexually freer environment in which she grew up probably served to counterbalance her mother's influence and put her on a more reasonable course. Another possible outcome of such indoctrination could have been sexual promiscuity. Certainly the mother's preoccupation with sex provided her with fantasy gratifications; however, she utilized the mechanism of reaction formation to assuage the guilt she felt over her sexual cravings. Each time she told herself she would not have sex until she got married, she had to have some kind of sexual fantasy—in which she ostensibly was not going to indulge. The fantasy about Sally's being a virgin until she (Sally) got married must have involved fantasies about Sally's sexuality. Under these circumstances, it would have been reasonable that Sally might have acted out her mother's unconscious wishes. We do not know more than a fraction of those factors that determine the way in which psychopathology will develop and the factors that prevent its occurring. My hope is that Sally has finally interrupted the traditional psychopathology of her family heritage.

Now to another example of how pathological sexual attitudes in a parent can produce pathological sexual behavior in an adolescent. Many years ago, while I was serving as a psychiatrist in the military, a colonel once came to me, quite depressed, claiming that this was the most painful and humiliating day of his life. The story, he stated, began 17 years previously when his wife gave birth to their oldest, a boy: "The obstetrician came out of the delivery room and told me that my wife had just given birth to a boy and that both she and the child were doing fine. The first thought that came to my mind was, 'The thing I fear most is that this boy will grow up to be a homosexual. I hope I never live to see that day.' And so, in order to prevent that terrible thing from happening, I bought him these porno books when he was three and four years old. I bought both homosexual and heterosexual porno books. I showed him the pictures in each and explained to him how the things that the men were doing to each other were *bad*, and how the things the men and women were doing together were *good*. When he was 13 years old, and started to mature physically, I told him that he never had to worry about sexual frustration, because I was going to take him to a 'nice lady' who was going to teach him about sex. So I took him to a house of prostitution where he had his first experience with a woman. I told him that anytime he wanted money to go back I would give it to him. And last night, Doctor, the thing I was most terrified of, occurred. The military police came and informed me that they had found him in bed with a sergeant engaged in homosexual activities."

This boy was almost destined to become homosexual, so great were his father's unconscious pressures on him to go in this direction. The boy's compliance was in part related to his recognition, at some level, that a homosexual was exactly what his father wanted him to be. With such programming, with such inculcation of homosexual imagery, with so many warnings to stay away, the child could not but be tempted. This father, although he had never engaged in a homosexual act himself (in fact, he exhibited disgust and anger toward anyone who had), was a man who basically had strong homosexual inclinations that he could not admit to himself. His preoccupation with the fantasy that his son might become a homosexual was basically the wish that he do so—disguised as a fear. The image that appears in a person's mind is the most important manifestation of his (her) genuine wish. The words that one conjures up in association with the image can serve to deny the wish's true intent. The thought "I hope he doesn't grow up to become a homosexual" reflected the father's basic wish that the boy do so—to satisfy vicariously, through his son, his own unconscious wish to become one. Putting the desire in the negative form of a fear served to lessen his guilt over unconscious awareness of his basic wish. The boy was driven to comply with his father's wish, and allowing disclosure was most probably his way of communicating his compliance. I subsequently obtained some verification of this when I learned that the father wanted exact details of the nature of the boy's homosexual involvement. It was clear that he was then gaining vicarious gratification from these explanations.

ADULT-CHILD SEXUAL ENCOUNTERS
AND LOW SELF-ESTEEM

I recognize that what I am now going to state is an unpopular thing to say at this time (late 1991) but I will say it nevertheless: adult-child sexual encounters do not *necessarily* result in the child's developing psychopathological reactions, whether it be low self-esteem or any other forms of psychopathology. An important determinant regarding whether or not such encounters will indeed produce such results is the attitude of society at large. One of the surprises that met western explorers when they came to the South Pacific in the 17th and 18th centuries was the widespread practice of various kinds of adult-child sexual encounters without particular consequences for the children. This is in line with Hamlet's oft-quoted wisdom: "There is nothing either good or bad, but thinking makes it so." If a society considers such an encounter a heinous crime, then the child is likely to view the encounter as a despicable one, no matter how pleasurable and acceptable the activity may originally have appeared to the child. Engaging in a sinful act produces feelings of low self-worth.

In western society we generally view adult-child sexual encounters as a crime or a sin. Some of the most draconian punishments are meted out to pedophiles, punishments which I believe deprive them of their constitutional rights to reasonable and fair punishment. Even when there is no evidence for untoward psychological reactions (a situation that many find hard to believe), the terms *sexual molestation* and *sexual abuse* are almost invariably utilized. There are many who hold that it is *impossible* for a child to have a sexual encounter with an adult without untoward psychological effects. Yet there are some very good studies that indicate that these encounters do not necessarily cause such effects. One of the important determinants as to whether the study will result in such findings is the way in which questions are posed. If the questions are all posed in such a way that untoward psychological effects are expected, then the study will confirm that prophecy. In contrast, if the questions are more neutral, without "loading" in one direction or another, the likelihood is that a larger percentage of the interviewees will deny untoward effects. Contrast, for example, the question "What were the detrimental effects on you of your childhood experiences with sex abuse?" with "In what way, if any, did your sexual encounters with an adult in childhood affect your future life?" Kilpatrick (1986) conducted a study of adult women's reports of early childhood sexual experiences with an adult and took great care to avoid structural bias in her questions. Sixty-eight percent of her sample had positive self-report responses to their experience, and 38 percent claimed that it was mostly or entirely pleasant. Only 25 percent of her sample self-reported that their experiences were essentially unpleasant.

It would be an error if the reader were to conclude that I am a proponent of sexual encounters between adults and children. Considering the attitudes of the society in which we live (and we cannot divorce ourselves from them) and considering myself as a product of such a society, I view a sexual encounter between an adult and a child as a form of exploitation. However, I am fully aware that my attitude is a reflection of the society in which I live, and that it is not the only way to view such encounters. I believe that this attitude puts me in a better position to deal effectively with children who have such experiences. I do not automatically approach their therapy with the view that they have been subjected to a heinous crime and that they have involved themselves in a sinful act. Such a position by the therapist is likely to entrench the feelings of low self-worth that are often suffered by children when they come to learn about society's attitude toward what has transpired. Many of these children do *not* need treatment; rather, they need a period of decompression and reassurance that they will be protected from further sexual encounters. Even those whose encounters might genuinely warrant the term *molestation*, because they have indeed been abused, may not need treatment. Even those who warrant the label *post-traumatic stress disorder* may not require treatment. The post-traumatic stress disorder is the only disorder in the *DSM-III-R* in which the symptoms serve the ends of treatment. Each time the individual re-experiences the trauma, he (she) becomes desensitized to it. It is a natural form of systematic desensitization. Conducting therapy under these circumstances may serve to only muckrake what might be left alone. Such unnecessary therapy can only lower self-esteem.

Some therapists who work with these children consider one of the important purposes of therapy to be to help the child vent rage toward the perpetrator. Dolls are set up and the child is encouraged to vent hostility against the dolls, both physically and verbally. Profanities may be used, and various kinds of hostile acting-out toward the doll are encouraged. Although there are some family perpetrators who indeed are so compulsive with regard to sex abuse that the child must be removed from them entirely, there are many for whom this action is unjustified. Especially when the perpetrator is the father, such therapeutic practices may cause lifelong alienation from a person who might still have provided important input to the child, the molestation notwithstanding. Such input involves factors that could contribute to the child's enhancement of self-worth. A child deprived of a parent is less likely to develop feelings of high self-esteem. The child who has been genuinely molested may indeed suffer with feelings of low self-worth. The child may have been coerced and subjugated, experiences that inevitably lower self-esteem. The child may have been threatened with dire consequences if the abuse was divulged. The sexual abuse may have been only one example of many forms of subjugation. The feelings of low self-worth associated with such encounters may be lifelong, and the therapist, then, must have limited goals. If the child was an initiator (sometimes the case, especially if the child had previous sexual encounters), then the child must be helped to reduce the guilt (and its associated feelings of low self-worth) that the child is likely to suffer.

It would be far beyond the purposes of this book to discuss in detail the treatment of children who have had sexual encounters with adults. My purpose here has been only to focus on a few aspects relevant to considerations of feelings of self-worth.

CLINICAL EXAMPLE

Ralph's situation provides an excellent example of the relationship between a sexual inhibition problem, low self-esteem, and academic difficulty.

Ralph entered treatment at the age of 16-1/2 with the chief complaint that on two occasions he had failed to maintain an erection when he had the opportunity for sexual intercourse. Two different girls were involved, and he was terribly humiliated over his failure to perform sexually. Not surprisingly, Ralph was highly motivated for therapy. Background inquiry revealed that his parents were divorced when he was three years old and he grew up primarily with his mother. He had no siblings. His father was a man with a schizoid personality, and following the separation his father had practically no desire for involvement with other women. This was the situation at the time Ralph came to treatment. He would see his father on the average of once every other week, usually on a weekend day. From the outset, his father had practically nothing to say to him, and Ralph most often found visitations "boring." For many years their primary activity was looking for bottles in garbage dumps, in the hope that they might find one that was of such value that it would be considered a collector's item. This activity characterized their relationship. As the years passed Ralph became increasingly frustrated with the visitations, especially because both of his parents insisted that he go.

Another problem related to poor school performance. For many years Ralph lived in a dream world regarding his academic performance, with absolutely no appreciation of how deeply he was sinking. When Ralph entered treatment he was beginning the eleventh grade and he began to appreciate that his chances for acceptance to a good college were very small. The best that he could hope for was acceptance into a mediocre college – and only if he were to work very diligently from then on. Actually, it was not until he started therapy that he became fully appreciative of how grave his academic situation was. He still maintained the delusion that somehow he would get into a good college. This delusion was fostered by his father, who continually told him not to worry about his grades and that no matter how poorly he did he would still get into a good college via a "WASP outreach program." It came as quite a surprise to Ralph when I informed him early in treatment that, to the best of my knowledge, there was no such thing as a WASP outreach program and that his father's belief in such was a manifestation of his own lack of contact with reality.

It was obvious that Ralph suffered with significant feelings of low self-esteem, in part related to the poor model that he had with his father. Furthermore, not having very much concrete to point to in the accomplishment realm, he could not use competence as a source of enhanced self-worth. Because he had nocturnal erections and because he was physically healthy, I concluded that his sexual performance problem was entirely psychogenic and that it related, at least in part, to his feelings of inadequacy. Accordingly, I informed him that the best thing I could do for him would be to help him gain confidence in any area that we could in the hope that enhanced self-worth in other areas would give him increased confidence in the sexual realm and thereby help his impotency problem. I also told him that it was likely that in the course of the treatment other factors would probably be found—in both the sexual and nonsexual realms—that could be linked to this problem.

Early in the therapy Ralph decided that he wanted to discontinue entirely his relationship with his father. He spoke bitterly about how he was becoming increasingly frustrated with the forced visits and that he had absolutely nothing to say to his father. His father had a job as a bureaucrat, hated his work, and spent most of his time in bars (although he was not an alcoholic). I discussed the pros and cons of this decision with Ralph and, in spite of my detailed inquiry, he was not able to think of any good reason to support the argument that he should continue seeing him. Accordingly, he informed his father that he was taking a "leave of absence" from the visitations and that he might resume visits in four to six months, but perhaps not. The interview transcribed below took place about one month after this decision had been made, during which time he had not visited with his father—although his father had called him on a couple of occasions to get him to change his mind.

During the fifth month of treatment, at the end of December (relevant to this discussion), Ralph came to the session and related two dreams, neither of which I will focus on at this point. Following our discussion of these, Ralph "ran out of steam" and so I asked his mother to join us. This is typical of what I do in such situations. I keep one of the parents of my adolescent patients in the waiting room. I invite the parent into the consultation room when I have gotten as much mileage as possible from my work with the adolescent alone, or if something comes up that warrants the parent's immediate involvement. The transcript begins, halfway through the session, when the mother was invited to join us.

> *Gardner (to mother):* So, he doesn't have that much to talk about? He had a couple of dreams which we did what we could with, but I don't think that they were crucial to understand for his main problems. One of the issues touched upon—(to patient) you

don't mind if I'm talking about the dream do you?—(to mother) a dream situation which probably was derived from a movie in which a woman in her twenties, whose husband was unfaithful to her or something like that, came on sexually to a teenage boy. That was the theme of the movie and he kind of locked into that in the dream.

Patient: Uh huh.

Gardner: In the dream he had some kind of involvement with the woman, but you don't see him as gravitating toward women ten years older than himself or something like that? I don't think it's a problem for him. A pattern to be turned on by that.

Mother: No.

Gardner: I think it's kind of normal. But I don't see it as a question of a pattern of any kind. Then it might be a problem.

Mother: Yeah.

Gardner: Then you know it would certainly deserve more attention. So what have you been seeing at home?

Most classical psychoanalysts would, I suspect, consider me to have made a serious error here. They would be certain that this is a "classical oedipal dream" and that this "older woman" represents the patient's mother and that Ralph's oedipal problems have been intensified by the fact that he had been living alone with his mother during the previous 13 years. I cannot deny this possibility. However, other possibilities must be considered and then the likelihood of each of the various explanations ascertained. In Ralph's case, there was no ongoing pattern of such oedipal manifestations, either clinically or in his fantasy life. Not only was this the *only* dream that he had had of this type, but it had followed his viewing a television program in which a teenage boy did indeed have an affair with a woman in her late twenties. I inquired of Ralph as to whether he was routinely turned on by women in that age bracket. He stated that he certainly was by movie actresses and women in pin-up magazines. However, his major attention in the real world was directed to girls in his school and neighborhood whom he found enormously attractive. My final conclusion was that although this dream might have had a minor oedipal contributory factor, this boy did not suffer with an Oedipus complex. Nor did I believe that his impotency problem related to oedipal problems: specifically, that he could not function with girlfriends because they reminded him of his mother. Rather, I considered the more likely explanation to be related to his massive feelings of inadequacy, some causes of which have been described. Had there been in the clinical picture maternal seduction, a "mommy's boy syndrome," or other clinical symptoms suggesting an unresolved Oedipus complex, I certainly would have considered this possibility. My final conclusion was that this was an erotic dream stimulated in a teenage boy by a movie in which the protagonist had an affair with a woman in her late twenties and he was providing himself with a similar gratification in his dream.

Mother: I mean this week it's been quiet with the holidays. We've spent a lot of time at home.

Gardner: Uh huh.

Mother: He's been excited about driving, so we've been going all over driving. So, if anything, I see him being peaceful at home.

Gardner: Uh huh.

Mother: I don't see any activity. I don't know of any activities with girls. He slept over his friend's house last night. Ken and he must have hung out today, but it's been pretty quiet at home with the holidays.

Gardner: Uh huh.

Mother: At home the only issues we have are just a normal kind of back and forth. For instance, saving money for a car. Other than that, there's been no other issues at home.

Gardner: Uh huh.

Mother: He keeps on forcing himself to save hard, I think for a car. My feeling was he had received over $300 for Christmas presents or was it $400? I think it was about $400 and at first Ralph was only going to put about $150 in the bank. He wanted to spend the rest on clothes and that was the only issue. The other issue I think, I don't know if you discussed with Dr. Gardner, that you received money from your dad?

Gardner: Oh, you did get money from your father?

Mother: He received $200.

Gardner: Oh yeah? This is *very* important to discuss. Okay, *this* you didn't mention to me. Was there any special reason why you didn't mention it to me?

Patient: I forgot.

> *Gardner:* Okay, let's talk about it. When exactly did you get the money?

As soon as I learned from the mother that the patient had taken $200 from his father, all the red lights began flashing in my brain. This boy had only recently told his father that he didn't want to see him anymore, and yet he had now accepted $200 from him. There was no question that this decision warranted detailed inquiry. Accordingly, I immediately informed both the patient and his mother that I considered this important to discuss and first asked whether there was any special reason why he hadn't mentioned it to me. This question was asked because of my belief that his failure to do so represented guilt, shame, or other feelings that could contribute to psychological resistance to explore a conflictual issue. When the patient responded, "I forgot," I did not embark upon an inquiry regarding the psychological significance of forgetting. Rather, I decided to move right ahead and get the details of the transaction. This is where the therapist's judgment comes in. I certainly could have taken the route of his gaining insight into the psychological importance of forgetting and I might ultimately have hit "pay dirt" anyway. Rather, I chose to get directly to the money issue because half the session was already over and I had a strong feeling that I wanted to focus on this issue while it was still "hot." The principles of psychological forgetting could wait for another session; this could not. Generally, my first step in such explorations is to get the mechanical details of the event. In this way I am in the best position to decide how to explore. Accordingly, I asked him, "When exactly did you get the money?"

> *Patient:* Christmas.
> *Gardner:* Okay. Christmas and today's the 28th of December. Was it before Christmas?
> *Patient:* On Christmas, uhm Christmas eve.
> *Gardner:* Christmas eve on the 24th. Through the mail?
> *Patient:* He gave it to my grandmother 'cause we go to my grandmother's and he gave it to her and she . . .
> *Gardner:* Grandmother meaning *his* mother?

Patient: No, her (pointing to his mother) ma.

Mother: He dropped it off at my parents' house.

Gardner: Okay. And was there a note inside?

Patient: Just a card.

Gardner: Was it a check? A check. Was it a standard printed card? Did it have any personal message on it?

Patient: Standard.

Gardner: There was no personal message added. And what did you think when you saw it?

Patient: First I wasn't going to accept it, but figured I really do need the money and he is my father, so I decided to keep the money.

Gardner: You're going to use it toward a car?

Patient: Yeah, I guess so.

Gardner: Okay. It sounds like there's a little bit of a question in your mind. There seems to be a kind of doubt, positive and negative. What are the arguments against it and what are the arguments for taking the money?

Patient: Against is I *really* don't want to take anything from him. I don't want him to think that there's still a connection, because I took the money and then . . .

Gardner: By the way. A question! Last year, what did he give you?

Patient: The other year $150. But this year he gave, he added my allowance that he owed me.

Gardner: Oh, so he broke it down.

Mother: Uh huh.

Patient: He gave me Christmas money and he gave me allowance money.

Gardner: Uh huh. Okay. Go ahead. Arguments against?

Patient: Against are I don't want any connections with him and he might think that there is and I don't really want anything from him. That was one of the negatives. Positive was that he is my father. I do need the money really bad and that taking it, well not taking it wouldn't really get me anywhere.

Gardner: And taking it, what does that get you?

Patient: That would get me money towards my car, which I *really need.*

Here I advised the patient to explore the advantages and disadvantages, the positives and negatives, of his taking the money from his father. Not only was I trying to get him to do this for this particular dilemma, but my hope was that he would use this approach in the future when dealing with other conflicts. As can be seen, he was receptive to this suggestion. The approach helps patients make decisions in conflictual situations and it is a principle that can be useful throughout life. It is one of the important benefits patients can derive from therapy. I then decided to get the mother's input.

> *Gardner (to mother):* What are your thoughts about his taking the money?
>
> *Mother:* The check is still sitting at home. I have mixed emotions with it. I kind of feel with Ralph.
>
> *Gardner:* The same positives and negatives?
>
> *Mother:* Yeah. I have very many mixed feelings.
>
> *Gardner:* But the balance is tipped in the direction of his taking it?
>
> *Mother:* Yeah, he kind of leans towards taking it.
>
> *Gardner (to mother):* If *you* were in his position what would you do?
>
> *Patient:* You also have to think that the money is for allowance *and* for Christmas, so it's not like he just gave me all this money for Christmas.
>
> *Mother:* The allowance I never understood.
>
> *Patient:* He owed me allowance money.
>
> *Mother:* I mean support. Support I can see. I mean he only gives us through probation. It's a normal check that comes once a month for $35 a week. I've been getting that since Ralph's five. But he's never supported us any other way financially and I don't think he'll support us with his college degree except that fund he did start that could be about $8,000.
>
> If I was Ralph (clearing her throat), I mean I agree with Ralph there is one part of you that doesn't want anything to do with him, and he did have that conversation with him three weeks ago in the car on Sunday. [Mother is referring here to the conversation in which Ralph told his father that he didn't want to see him again, for a few months at least.] Then the other part says that if he still forces Ralph every six months to see him. . .
>
> *Patient (interrupting):* If I didn't have the conversation with him and he gave me the money . . . if I didn't talk to him and then he gave me the money, then I wouldn't take it.
>
> *Gardner:* Uh huh.

Patient: Since I had the conversation with him, then he decided to give me the money anyway.

Gardner: Okay. But the conversation, as I recall, ended with your saying, "I may get in touch with you at some point in the future, but my wishes are to cool it at this point for the indefinite future." Correct?

Patient: Uh huh.

Gardner: And do you have any idea how long that will be?

Patient: 'Til I call him.

Gardner: Uh huh.

Patient: Not for a while.

Gardner: Try to be more specific. I know it's hard to be specific on something like this but try.

Patient: Six months.

Gardner: Okay and then *after* that? Again projecting yourself into the future?

Patient: Seven months.

Gardner: So you might see him once mid-year and then once around Christmas time next year or something like that?

Patient: Maybe.

Gardner: Now let's say next year. Let's say you see him mid-year, June or July. Do you think that he should still be giving you an allowance?

Patient: No. He stopped the allowance.

Gardner: He stopped the allowance? When did the allowance stop?

Patient: Oh it stopped at Christmas pretty much.

Gardner: You mean when you said bye-bye?

Patient: Uh huh.

Mother: The allowance was $120.

Gardner: $120?

Mother: What does he usually pay you a week?

Patient: Ten dollars. I don't know he owed me for a while.

Mother: I think on the check it said $120 for allowance the rest was Christmas.

Mother: So $10 a week. Now that I am talking about it, it probably would be best to rip up the check and just say we do not want anything from you.

Patient (angrily): And then my car is not going to happen!

Mother: Uh huh.

Patient: That $250 is a *lot* of money!

Mother: But that's not going to get you the car. You know that.

Patient: It's going to get me a lot. I can't make $250 at my job so quickly. I *need* that money. I would love to rip it up if I had money, but I can't!

Gardner: Excuse me, I thought it was $200.

Patient: $250.

Gardner: $250. It was a $150 present and $100 back allowance. The back allowance is what was owed?

Patient: Back allowance, $120. Christmas, $130.

Gardner: Okay so let's talk about dividing it up into two. The $120 is back allowance. That part you have no problem with? That was promised.

Patient: No, I do have a problem with that.

Gardner: Because . . .

Patient: Well I didn't really want to take it, but I mean I don't really want it, but I mean I *need* the money.

Gardner: Is that a reason to take it?

Patient: Yes, he *is* my father and he does owe me the money so . . .

Gardner: He owes you the allowance. Okay, let's separate the allowance and the Christmas present. Okay, the allowance is owed you. But why is the allowance being discontinued now?

Patient: Because he said, I mean he said when I'm seventeen the allowance stops anyway.

Gardner: Uh huh.

Patient: So you know it stops anyway now.

Gardner: When are you going to be seventeen?

Patient: February. But I mean I'm not expecting any allowance anymore 'cause I said I don't want to see you anymore so it kind . . .

Gardner: Okay, so the allowance was understood. Let me get back to you (to mother). Let's talk about both of those as separate issues. If you were in his position, would you take both, or one, or neither?

Mother: As you kept talking about it, I would take neither. At first I thought I'd take it. And I think I had that reaction just because his father has done so little. Sometimes you wish you could take the money for some of the hell he's put us through and I think that's what we both feel sometimes.

Gardner: That he's doing so little that . . .

Mother: He's done so little. Sometimes, I mean, even when he goes to college and we just feel financially we wish he could help us more.

Gardner: Because he has no intention of contributing toward college, so you feel this?

Mother: He's cried poverty for too long. He's cried poverty and he doesn't have much money, obviously with his salary.

Gardner: Uh huh.

Mother: I think it's not right on my part even to say we'll take it sometimes because it's money that we could use towards, say, his car. But if you get down to the conversation Ralph had three weeks ago, I guess we have a double standard answer. If Ralph said he wanted nothing else to do with him . . . I think if Ralph had wanted to stay on a relationship with every three or four months, and just talk to him, and see how he was doing, and his dad wanted to support him, I think it would be a different situation. So I guess, as we talk about it, the best thing to do would be to mail it back.

Patient (angrily): What's the sense in mailing it back?

Mother: Or ripping it up.

Patient (exasperated): Ohhh. Nooo.

Mother: I think if you mail it back and just . . .

Patient: Well, I don't have any money. I *need money*. He is my father. I *can* accept money from him!

Gardner: You know, we will probably end this meeting *without* my telling you what to do, because it's like telling someone to get married . . .

Mother: I know.

Gardner: You know, and not to get divorced. It's in the category of making important decisions for people.

Mother: Uh huh.

Gardner: But it *is* my job to help clarify the weights on the balance, the positives and negatives. What I see missing here in you, Ralph, is a sense of honor and dignity. Let me use an extreme example. Let's say a guy stole your wallet and you said to him, "What kind of a terrible thing to do?" and he'd say, "Well, I *need* the money" as his justification. What would you think?

Patient: Well, if you're trying to use that as an example, it's not, I mean, yes I understand I don't want to take the money, I don't want anything to do with him, but I *need* the money!

Gardner: Okay, but your need for the money . . .

Patient: . . . is greater.

Gardner: . . . is greater than your sense of embarrassment over your compromising your dignity. Right? When you say "I wish I could not take it," it's because you want to preserve dignity. Is that correct?

Patient: Yeah.

Gardner: The dignified thing to do would be to not take the money.

Patient: Well, I wasn't going to at first, I wasn't.

Gardner: Okay, was that out of a sense of dignity and pride?

Patient: But out of a sense that I didn't want anything from him.

Gardner: But what?

Patient: I had like a week to decide.

Gardner: Okay, if you didn't want anything from him, you don't take his money, so it's related to the dignity-pride issue.

Patient: I really don't want to take it, but I need it.

Gardner: Why? Why don't you want to take it?

Patient: 'Cause I need it.

Gardner: Pretend you didn't need the money. What would you do then?

Patient: Okay fine! If I didn't need the money, I'd rather give it back in a second.

Gardner: Why would you give it back? Why would you not take it?

Patient: Because I don't want to have anything to do with him.

Gardner: Okay, I'll elaborate on that point. You don't want to have anything to do with him but . . .

Patient (interrupting): So he'll know that I don't want to have anything to do with him and it will make me feel better.

Gardner: Okay.

Patient: . . . that I didn't take it, that I turned down that much money.

Gardner: Okay, it would make you feel better to be able to stick to your principles, right?

Patient: It's not going to make me feel better in two months when I don't have a car.

Gardner: Okay, so you're saying that the bad feeling of lack of dignity is less than the bad feeling of a lack of a car.

Patient: $250 is a *lot of money.*

We see here the patient dealing with his dilemma. We see also my helping him focus on the minor evidences of guilt that he first exhibited when he spoke about the money his father had sent him. I believed that his failure to tell me about the money related to his appreciation that I might bring him to the point of recognizing that there was an exploitive aspect to his acceptance of the gift. My hope was that he would come to the point where he would make a decision in which he would give up the money from the recognition that his embarrassment, guilt, and loss of pride was a heavy price to pay for the money. In the discussion I brought the mother in to get her input on this issue. At first, both the patient and the mother were willing to take the money from the father. However, as a result of my inquiry they both came to see that they were compromising their dignity by doing so.

Gardner: I think that you have to divide the money into the allowance, which he owes you, and the Christmas present, which is a kind of, you know, is a Christmas present for the past or the future. You know what I mean. Is it for someone that you feel good about around Christmas time and you want to make a statement about their relationship?

Patient: I just don't see it as money that he gave me. I just see it as a check that he wrote off just to give me. That's all I see it as.

Gardner: Just money to give you. Well, what do you think was going on in his head as to why he gave it to you?

Patient: Maybe it'll make him feel better that I accept it.

Gardner: Okay. You think maybe it reduces his guilt?

Patient: Yeah.

Gardner (to mother): Do you think it's a pay-off or do you think it's a bribe? You know the man. What do you think is his reason for giving him the money?

Mother: The guilt. I think it's the guilt.

Gardner: The guilt over his what?

Patient: The guilt. I don't think so 'cause I don't feel no guilt and I . . .

Mother: Your dad's guilt makes him feel like giving you the money.

Patient: Aah! Yeah I'm sure it's that!

Mother: 'Cause I think your dad still thinks you're still going through this adolescent period. And that is why you won't see him.

Patient: Nah, he doesn't! I made that clear to him. I don't really care. The whole thing is I *need* money! That's the whole thing I need the money.

Mother: See, I don't think that's the strongest statement.

Patient: Yeah, it is the strongest statement, Mom. I would love to rip it up. If it was less money, I would rip it up.

Mother: But Ralph, if a car you're saving for is a $1,000, $250 less is not that much of a difference. $250 short of a car.

Patient: It's short enough. It's a lot more than I have.

Mother: I would let you borrow $250 from me as a loan.

Patient: No!

Mother: We're not talking about $2,000 here. I mean it's hard to get the money, but $250 for you is not the biggest issue of a minus for this car.

Patient: It's $250 more than I have.

Mother: Two-hundred-fifty dollars is not going to buy you a car.

Patient: Who cares. That's not the point.

Mother: Yeah, but I think that's . . .

Gardner: Okay, let me say this to you, Ralph. One of your problems that brought you here is self-confidence, right?

Patient: Uh huh.

Gardner: You came to me because of not performing in the sexual situation. We are all in agreement it's related to fears and psychological factors and that there's nothing wrong with you physically at this age and with your health.

Patient: Uh huh.

Gardner: We also agreed that a *factor* involved in that problem is low self-esteem. Right?

Patient: (Nods affirmatively)

Gardner: One of the goals of your therapy has been to help you deal with things in general, to make you a more secure person, so that when the inevitable time comes that you're in the bed scene, you'll feel like a more secure person. Okay. Do you see what I'm driving at?

Patient: No. I understand that you're analyzing my problem.

Gardner: Yeah, but why am I bringing this up now at this point in what's seemingly a digression from . . .

Patient: Because a stronger person would rip up the paper.

Gardner: A stronger person would say, "I don't want the money." It's a loss of my dignity to take this . . .

Patient: I know it is.

Gardner: Money.

Patient: But I *hate* giving up all that money.

Gardner: I understand that, but you have to think of your pride, and dignity, and self-confidence.

Patient: I don't see it as that.

Gardner: And that makes it even more a test of your . . .

Patient: I see the check as money, not my dad . . .

Gardner: It's almost like a Bible story or something (chuckling) (mother laughs also). You know what I mean, a test of your dignity.

Patient: When I look at the check, I don't think of my dad and I don't think he's giving it to me. I just think of it as money in my hand, money that I need. I don't think of him.

Gardner: What I'm saying is that you should give thought to . . .

Patient: I know, but I'll rip it up! I know I'm going to rip it up. I'm just saying why I should keep it.

Gardner: Oh, you *are* going to rip it up now?

Patient: I already know I am. It's just the point.

Gardner: Why? Why are you going to do that?

Patient: 'Cause I've explained the pros before.

Mother: He hasn't deposited the check and it could have been deposited.

Gardner: Yeah, but something happened here in the last half-hour that has made you change.

Patient: No, I totally didn't want to take it before.

Gardner: Had you not had the misfortune of having this session with me, you might have deposited it (chuckling).

Patient: Exactly!

We see here how the patient suddenly changed his mind and stated that he was going to return the money. He also stated that he had *previously* made the decision, but then agreed that our conversation in this session played a role in his decision. I believe that I addressed myself to his original ambivalence and that my comments and inquiry served to mobilize those forces within him that recognized that taking the money would result in a loss of dignity and pride. However, when I merely addressed myself to the untoward effects of his taking the money, he was adamant that he was still going to do so. It was only after I pointed out to him that such loss of pride and dignity might contribute to a perpetuation of his low self-esteem, and that this might then contribute to a perpetuation of his sexual problem, that he suddenly changed his mind. It is not often that a therapist has the opportunity to provide such a persuasive argument.

Gardner: So this has been a very costly session.

Mother (laughing): Yeah!

Gardner (laughing): It's like $100 (for this session) plus $250 (loss of money from father,) whatever it is.

Mother (laughing): You may owe us on this one!

Gardner: But the question is this, the question is what happened *here* that made you change? I don't want you to be saying, "Dr. Gardner, I'll do whatever you say. I'll do it! Yes sir, Yes sir!"

Patient: No. I mainly want to rip it up 'cause I want my dad to eat the check that I'm going to rip up. I want him to notice I didn't take the money out. I want him to know that and that will make a big statement towards him that he'll know that I don't want anything to do with him.

Gardner: Okay, alright, well that's certainly a way.

Here the patient states his recognition that rejecting the money is a strong statement to his father that he wants to cut off the relationship. In contrast, taking it might give his father hope that he wants to maintain the relationship.

Patient: And if I took the check, that'll show I'm weaker towards him.

Gardner: That you didn't mention before, but that's a factor because if he is doing it as a bribe, taking the money gives him hope. If the bribe element is in there, among the others, then it gives him hope that you'll be tempted when you take the money. Ripping it up is a real slap in his face of a very powerful form.

Patient: That's what I want. There's also another reason now that I feel better that I was able to rip up the check.

Gardner: And why do you feel better?

Patient: That I resisted money over . . .

Gardner: What?

Patient: Myself.

Gardner: What did I say here that made you switch your statement? Made you change your mind?

Patient: Well it just made me think more that my dad will get more happy than I will if I deposit the check.

Gardner: Because he will . . .

Patient: Lose dignity over that and he'll gain hope.

Gardner: Uh huh. Okay.

Patient: And if I don't take the money, I'll gain dignity and lose money, but also he'll lose hope.

Gardner: Uh huh. Okay. So it will serve other purposes. It's a very important point, the dignity thing, especially in our world today when there are so many people who are exploitive and take what they can, and they're not taking into consideration their own sense of dignity.

Patient: I did that when I went out with him last time. He kept forcing me to take an allowance, but I wouldn't take it, I wouldn't take it. When I saw the check, it just didn't seem like he was giving it to me. That's why one of the reasons I was more into taking it, but now it sucks and now I don't have $250 anymore.

Gardner: What are your feelings toward me in all this?

Patient: It's not your fault.

Gardner: Yeah, but I opened my big mouth, right?

Patient: Yeah, so? Well I mean, your mouth was mainly what I was thinking anyway.

Gardner: Was it really? Did you have in your *own* mind, the dignity issue?

Patient: Yeah, I did.

Gardner: The sense of honor. How come you didn't mention it prior to my saying it?

Patient: I was just like putting the check aside. I wasn't going to bank it. I wasn't going to do anything with it right away.

Mother: It came with a card. I didn't see the card but . . .

Patient: It didn't say anything.

Mother: He crumbled it up and threw it in the garbage immediately. Yeah, I mean he kept the check.

Gardner (to patient): I'm a little unclear about whether you *really* were going to rip it up prior to our meeting today. I mean even if we hadn't met, would you really have ripped it up?

Patient: I don't know.

Mother: (frowning incredulously)

Gardner: Your mother's a little dubious.

Patient: Uh . . . Uhm . . . Uh . . . I really don't know. I mean, if I actually gave it thought I would've, but I think I was more to just cash it in and that was it.

Gardner: That's the feeling I have. That's what your mother figured.

Patient: Yeah. But if I thought about it I would've.

Gardner: Uh.

Patient: But I just didn't want to think about it 'cause I just wanted to cash it.

As can be seen, the patient was wavering back and forth regarding whether he would or would not have cashed the check had we not had the session. I would have liked to have been able to give Ralph credit for thinking of returning the check himself, but this did not appear to be the case. He had not mentioned the gift to me in the early part of the session and, until I mentioned the relationship between the return of the check and his sexual problem, he adamantly refused to consider returning it. However, I wanted to give him the benefit of the doubt and so pursued the question regarding whether he really had previously thought about the option of not cashing the check. My final conclusion was that my comments in the session were the crucial factors in tipping the balance in the direction of his not cashing the check. I then switched, as I often do near the end of the session, and asked the patient to state clearly the main points covered during the session and the main things that had been learned.

> *Gardner:* Okay. What's the main point here, the main principle for yourself in terms of future incidents of this kind?
> *Patient:* Dignity.
> *Gardner:* Very important! Very important dignity; at times it costs you money.
> *Patient:* $250.
> *Gardner:* At times you have to eat your heart out to preserve it.
> *Patient:* It's a lot of money, 'cause now when my birthday comes I could have had money too, but . . .
> *Gardner:* Let's divide it up between the $130 and the $120 in your view of things and whether the dignity is . . .
> *Patient:* Well I don't, I don't want to take either amount. I don't want to take either, because my allowance I didn't really deserve. It's like I never did anything for him.
> *Gardner:* Uh huh.
> *Patient:* So, I'm not going to take either! The allowance wasn't really . . . I really didn't do any chores for him.
> *Gardner:* Uh huh.
> *Mother:* He's got a job right now, one night a week. It's not getting him all the money for the car, but he has to realize he has to get out there and work a little bit more.

Gardner: What you're doing is a true test of your psychological strength. Let me tell you something here. When I was in college, one of the books I read was Plato's *Republic*. Have you ever heard of that?

Patient: I've heard of Plato.

Gardner: Yeah, the *Republic* is one of his most famous books and, uh as I recall, one of the things that he said in there was, "Virtue is its own reward." The word *virtue* refers to many different things. In modern language, it translates into doing your own thing, like a farmer is being virtuous when he farms, an engineer is being virtuous when he's building whatever things he engineers. Plato expands this idea into a knife as being virtuous when it cuts.

But another derivative meaning of the word *virtue* is that when you do the good thing, you feel good about yourself and it makes you a bigger, stronger person, and even though you may suffer the pain of the loss of the money, you have the compensation of being able to throw out your chest and say, "I did the right thing" and "I did the good thing" and "It took a sacrifice to do it." When you do the virtuous thing, it builds manhood and it builds strength. And it's what may result in great admiration by others who see you. I myself feel that what you're doing is an admirable thing, and it's a hard thing for you to do, and I'm appreciative of that; but I respect your strength of character for doing this! I don't know what your mother thinks about that, but I would like her to say something on it too (turning to mother). What are your thoughts on it?

I decided at this point to use a classical reference to hammer home the point about the ego-enhancement that comes from being virtuous. My purpose here was threefold. First, I wanted to emphasize my message. Second, I wanted to give this patient, who had a long way to go with regard to intellectual curiosity, a taste of the classics. My hope was that he would have the living experience that the information contained therein could be useful to him today in his everyday life. Mention was made of the patient's poor academic performance, and my comments here addressed this issue. Last, I wanted to compliment the patient on his decision. I am very judicious when I compliment patients. However, when I do compliment a patient, it generally has great impact because it is a rare occasion. Furthermore, my patients get the message that I reserve compliments for situations in which they exhibit qualities that genuinely deserve my praise. The compliments then become significantly ego-enhancing. I then turned to the mother with the full knowledge that she too would provide further support and reinforcement for my ego-enhancing praises.

> *Mother:* My thoughts are the same. I think if he doesn't take the money he'll feel good about himself. And I think it would take a lot of strength. Because I think the day he even went out with his dad and his dad tried to hand him the $120, I think Ralph felt good that he refused it.
>
> *Gardner:* Uh huh.
>
> *Mother:* I mean that day he came home saying that he just wouldn't take the money and I think he was proud of himself.
>
> *Gardner:* You see your father, and I said this before, is more to be pitied than scorned. He has a serious personality defect in his ability to involve himself as a human being, as a father to his son. Giving the money is not going to work for him. Taking the money may give him the idea that he does have a relationship. It's another factor operative here. It may give him the idea that it's created some kind of a bond with you. It would be a delusion, a false belief, to compensate for the lack of a relationship, but it doesn't work.
>
> *Mother:* And he's never been there for the love or the emotional parts, so when you think about his taking money it's really . . .
>
> *Gardner:* It's the only thing he can provide.
>
> *Mother:* Uh huh.
>
> *Gardner:* Your taking it might foster or perpetuate that particular distortion on his part, that there's a link, that there's a bond there and it's really a money bond. It's a money trap. It's a money tube, but if it were in the context of a loving, ongoing relationship and was part of his love and part of his obligation, you know, that would be a different story. Kids need that in part, you know, because they don't have the ability to earn on their own. Well look, before we close I'd just like to hear what your final thoughts and feelings are about what I said.
>
> *Patient:* All right. I believe in them.
>
> *Gardner:* Be more specific. I'd like to have a *specific* answer.

One of my favorite words in the therapeutic situation—as well as in life in general—is the word *specific*. Generalizations and abstractions provide very little information. A specific example nails things down and enables individuals to be much clearer about what is being discussed. Without specifics, communication can be meaningless; it is almost as if the participants are going through the motions of having a conversation. It is only with concrete examples that true communication is possible.

> *Patient:* Well, if I did think about it, I would, I know, tear up the check.
> *Gardner:* Okay. Well, you know my hopes are that you would think about it automatically without any kind of reminding.
> *Patient:* Yeah.
> *Gardner:* Reminding you, or intervention on my part, and that it would become part of you because we all face these things in life.
> *Patient:* Yeah, I know it.
> *Gardner:* It's good if it can become an automatic part of you. Okay, so let's close here.

My final comments here are most important. They focus on one of the important elements in the therapeutic process, namely, helping patients reach the point where they are no longer dependent on the therapist, where the healthy modes of dealing with life's problems become incorporated into the patient's psychic structure and are utilized automatically. And this is one of the ultimate goals of treatment.

My primary purpose in presenting this detailed therapeutic vignette was to demonstrate the relationships between subscribing to healthy values and self-esteem. In Ralph's case it was my hope that the enhancement in self-worth that therapy was designed to bring about would contribute to the alleviation of Ralph's sexual performance problems as well as his academic learning problems. And this is what ultimately came about.

☐ SIXTEEN
IMPOTENCE, SELF-ASSERTION, AND POWER

A feeling of impotence is often central to feelings of low self-worth. To the degree that one feels powerless to deal with life's situations, to that degree will one's self-esteem suffer. Feelings of impotence can be dealt with, in part, by self-assertion, which, if successfully utilized, enhances self-esteem and, when completely successful, produces feelings of power. It is important, however, for therapists to make a clear distinction between healthy and pathological types of self-assertion and power. Healthy use of self-assertion and power enhances self-worth; in contrast, unhealthy utilization, initial ego-enhancement notwithstanding, ultimately lowers self-worth.

IMPOTENCE

As mentioned earlier in this book, Alfred Adler considered derivatives of the child's sense of impotence to be the basis of most forms of psychogenic psychopathology. Mullahy (1955) states:

> For Adler, inferiority feelings are inherent in the human situation. To *"be a human being means the possession of a feeling of inferiority that is constantly pressing on towards its own conquest"*

(Adler, 1938). The struggle for self-preservation and for bodily and mental equipoise, bodily and mental growth, the striving for perfection, support the view that the fundamental law of life is that of overcoming deficiencies and inadequacies. The life process is to be regarded as a struggle aiming always at a goal of adaptation to the demands of the world. Since there is a discrepancy between the demands and problems raised by the external world and man's equipment and powers, mistakes and at least partial defeats are inevitable. . . .

Yet Adler's attitude is, in general, optimistic in regard to the human situation. "Who can seriously doubt," he says, "that the human individual treated by nature in such a stepmotherly fashion has been provided with the blessing of a strong feeling of inferiority that urges him towards a plus situation, towards security and conquest? And this tremendous enforced rebellion against a tenacious feeling of inferiority is awakened afresh and repeated in every infant and little child as the fundamental fact of human development" (Adler, 1938). . . .

He [Adler] puts enormous stress on the difficulties of the infant and child situation. Every child's instincts, he says, "are baffled in their fulfillment by obstacles whose conquest gives him pain. He realizes at an early age that there are other human beings who are able to satisfy their urges more completely, and are better prepared to live. . . .

He [the child] learns to over-value the size and stature which enables one to open a door, or the ability to move heavy objects, or the right of others to give commands and claim obedience to them. A desire to grow, to become as strong or even stronger than all others, arises in his soul. To dominate those who are gathered about him, becomes his chief purpose in life, since his elders, though they act as if he were inferior, are obligated to him because of his very weakness. Two possibilities of action lie open to him. On the one hand, to continue activities and methods which he realizes the adults use, and on the other hand to demonstrate his weakness, which is felt by these same adults as an inexorable demand for their help. We shall continually find this branching of psychic tendencies in children " (Adler, 1927).

Human relations will be understood in terms of struggle, not in terms of cooperation with one's fellow men or in genuine love. Such an "inferiority complex" drives the individual to overcompensate for his weakness by creating for himself an exaggerated and unrealizable ideal of personal importance, embodying all the powers and natural gifts of which the child believes himself deprived.

As mentioned, it is unfortunate that Freud did not give appropriate attention to Adler's ideas. We need power over the forces of the world if we are to survive, and the infant, having so little power, cannot but feel somewhat helpless and even impotent with regard to his (her) ability to deal with these formidable forces. Considering the profound impact that early life experiences have on our subsequent psychological development, it is no surprise that residua of our childhood feelings of impotence remain with us, to varying degrees, throughout the course of our lives. We all have these feelings. We differ only in the degree to which we will admit them, both to ourselves and others. Those who have enough ego-strength to accept such feelings of impotence, putting them in their proper place, and compensating for them with healthy forms of real compensation are likely to do well for themselves in this world. Those who do not, those who cannot tolerate awareness of their weaknesses, are likely to develop one or more of a wide variety of forms of psychopathology that are designed to suppress, repress, and compensate for this sense of impotence.

In the educational realm, one source of such feelings of impotence results from the use of coercive techniques by a parent. The child who is manipulated and molded into a pattern that the parent believes is best for that child is likely to suffer with feelings of impotence as the child is required to comply with the parental coercions. The parent who, for example, decides early in the child's life (sometimes even before the child is born) what particular goal in life the child is going to be required to pursue is showing little, if any, respect for the child's natural inclinations. This programming begins long before the child has any conscious awareness of it. All the youngster knows is that, as far back as he (she) can remember, attempts were made to require the child to become involved in a particular career path. Most often there are elements of compensation and vicarious gratification in the parental coercion.

A good example of this phenomenon is the woman who aspires to be an actress. However, in her late teens her career is suddenly interrupted by a pregnancy. Not surprisingly, the mother may decide that this child will be a great actress someday, and that there is no age at which she is too young to start on her career. Accordingly, the child is dragged around for auditions for any part that is offered, no matter how young the aspiring actress is. As the child grows older, aspirations in any other realm become squelched by the mother, and may even become suppressed and repressed by the child. However, if these career tendencies in another direction are strong, the child is likely to suffer with deep-seated feelings of impotence. The boy whose parents decide (again, before he is born) that he will be a great doctor someday may suffer with similar feelings of impotence if he does not have the strength to pursue his own path in spite of the parental coercion.

Children who are so treated may develop a psychogenic learning disability as they consciously or unconsciously attempt to thwart their parents. The unconscious route is safer because the child can thereby absolve himself (herself) of any conscious responsibility for the school failure. The youngster knows, at some level, that school failure is the most potent form of vengeful gratification against such coercive parents. Watching their parents writhe, scream, squirm, and pull their hair out provides these youngsters with a sense of power that compensates for the feelings of impotence they previously felt. For such parents I suggest the following comments to the youngster who is destroying his (her) education for these reasons:

> We know that what you've been doing the last couple of years relates to anger at us, more than anyone else. And this is especially the case with your education. Sure we've made mistakes; but we certainly don't deserve this. We've come to appreciate, through our work with Dr. Gardner, that we've been too coercive regarding your education and that we should have shown greater flexibility. Okay, we've made a big mistake. Let's say that you get the extreme vengeance you want. You'll have your father and me rolling around on the floor, tearing our hair out, crying our eyes out, and beating ourselves. So what, then, will you have accomplished? Yes, you will have gotten vengeance, but what you are *not* considering is what you have to do to yourself in order to hurt us. All you see is the vengeful gratification, and don't see the *self-*

destructive aspect of what you're doing. You're going down the tubes in school. Someday we won't be around to give you food, clothing, and shelter. Then where will you be? Yes, you will have gotten the gratification of wreaking vengeance on us, but maybe then you'll see that you've destroyed yourself as well.

The messages contained in this recommended "speech" for parents are also implied—somewhat less dramatically—in the course of the youngster's treatment. These messages can be incorporated into the mutual storytelling technique and its derivative games, as well as while playing *The Talking, Feeling, and Doing Game.* It can also be directly stated for those youngsters who are receptive to receiving therapeutic communications at the conscious level.

Relevant here is the ancient "knowledge-is-power" wisdom. This not only relates to what can be learned in the educational realm, but what can be learned, in general, in life. Psychotherapy, more than anything else, teaches people how to deal effectively with the problems of the world (Strupp, 1975). It thereby lessens the sense of impotence that contributes to feelings of low self-esteem.

IMPOTENCE AND ENVY

The Random House Dictionary of the English Language (1987) defines envy as "a feeling of discontent or covetousness with regard to another's advantages, success, possessions, etc." *The American Heritage Dictionary* (1971) defines envy as "a feeling of discontent and resentment aroused by contemplation of another's desirable possessions or qualities, with a strong desire to have them for oneself." The definition of envy, then, involves feelings of discontent about oneself, feelings that produce low self-esteem. "Covetousness," the desire to acquire for oneself the other person's possessions, is involved. The goal here, of course, is to compensate for the feelings of inadequacy by the acquisition of the other person's possessions. Typically, the possessor enjoys certain social benefits, especially power. The woman, for example, who considers her looks plain (whether this is true in reality or a delusion is irrelevant here) may be envious of the more attractive woman whom she views as having the power to lure men and thereby gain the gratifications attendant to their "capture." The poor man who envies the rich man similarly envisions himself benefiting from the powers that the rich man enjoys.

Webster's New World Dictionary (1966) has a more elaborate definition: "Uneasiness, mortification, or discontent at the sight of another's superiority or success, accompanied by some degree of hatred or malignity, and often or usually with a desire or an effort to depreciate the person envied." I believe the Webster definition is more honest in that it admits to the malicious feelings that the envious person has toward the person envied. There is a sense of frustration regarding the disparity between the envied person and the one who envies. Frustration produces anger, and anger is associated with "hatred or malignity." Depreciation of the envied person is a predictable result, whether or not it is overtly expressed. Bly (1990) states that when a friend of Carl Jung would report to him, "I have just been promoted!" Jung would respond, "I'm very sorry to hear that; but if we all stick together, I think we will get through it." Clearly, Jung is being more honest than most would be in this situation.

Differentiation should be made between envy and jealousy. Although there is much overlap, the differentiation between the two that is most meaningful to me is that jealousy is the same as envy with one additional component, namely, that the jealous individual feels that he deserves to possess what the envied person has. It is almost as if the envied person has taken away these particular qualities, characteristics, possessions, etc., from the envious individual. Probably the best example of this would be the delusion of a spouse's infidelity.

I believe that envy is part of the human condition. People who assert themselves and try to provide themselves with reasonable degrees of success, competence, and the acquisition of possessions will feel less envious of those who have them. Those who do not assert themselves are destined not only to be deprived, but also to feel envious. In extreme cases the envy is an ongoing feeling that contributes to a chronic state of low self-worth. Barth (1988) provides a good summary of some of the analytic views on envy.

Envy is not given the attention it deserves in the educational system and in the psychotherapy of children with psychogenic learning disabilities. There was a time, especially in the 1970s, when schools tried to dispense with grades entirely. The purpose here was to reduce competition (which was considered intrinsically bad) and to protect the feelings of low self-worth that less successful students would have when they compared themselves to the more successful. This was doomed to failure. Even if no tests are ever given and no grades are ever provided, the students themselves inevitably size one another up and know very early in the game who is more or less successful. I recall one second grader who appreciated this phenomenon quite well. He began his session one day quite upset, was on the verge of tears, and said, "The teacher told us that she's going to have three reading groups: the hamsters, the chipmunks, and the bunny rabbits. She put me in the bunny rabbit group, where all the stupid kids are." It took this child only a few seconds to see through the teacher's deception.

As mentioned earlier, competition is an inevitable part of the human condition (I believe it is neurophysiologically programmed) and envy is an inevitable derivative of the competitive process. Unsuccessful students are inevitably going to suffer with envy and the feelings of low self-worth that are its concomitants. It matters not how skilled and trained the therapist is; it matters not how many times per week the patient is seen; as long as the youngster is doing poorly in school, and as long as the youngster is going to be surrounded by others who are more successful, that youngster is going to feel envy. Whether or not it is admitted (by the patient and/or the therapist) is irrelevant here. What is relevant is that the feelings will be experienced. If such feelings are experienced overtly, then the psychological pain is obvious. Often, however, the feelings are covered up in a variety of ways, each of which is designed to provide some compensation for the feelings of low self-worth that the envious youngster experiences.

For example, deprecation of the more successful is a common mechanism. Successful students may be viewed as "nerds," "grinds," or labelled in some other pejorative way—depending upon the term that is in vogue at the time. Younger children may scapegoat the more successful students. Bullies are famous for picking on the more academically successful.

It is important for the reader to appreciate that my comments here refer to schools that can justifiably be referred to as educational institutions, places where true learning is going on and where the teachers and most of the students have a reasonable degree of commitment to the educational process. Unfortunately, we are experiencing an ever-growing number of schools that do not satisfy this basic educational criterion. Accordingly, in such places (I will not call them schools) there is little if any learning, little if any prestige enjoyed by those who do learn, and so there is little envy.

Denial of academic goals is another mode of adaptation that aims to reduce envy. Such youngsters talk themselves into believing that they aren't interested in academic success anyway; they remove themselves to varying degrees from the academic track. These youngsters, of course, become drop-outs. Such "dropping out" does not necessarily take place on the final day when these youngsters remove themselves from school. Psychologically, they can start on the first day, and every classroom has some of these students.

Children who are subjected to the taunts and other pathological reactions of the envious, that is, those who are envied, may also need help in therapy. They have to be helped to recognize that those who are successful will inevitably be envied by the unsuccessful, and that envy includes within it hostility. They have to be helped to appreciate that those who are pathologically envious have problems, but that a certain amount of envy is predictable and one of the prices that they must pay for their success. Those who are excessively dependent upon the opinions of others have to be helped to "thicken their skins." They have to be helped to appreciate that they are not necessarily what others consider them to be. The stories "The Parrot and the

People" and "The Pussycat and the Owl" in my book, *Fables For Our Times* (Gardner, 1981a), may be helpful in this regard. There are some successful children who are so sensitive to and pained by envy-derived hostility that they compromise their educational efforts. Obviously, this is a serious mistake and therapists do well to do everything possible to help these children avoid such methods for dealing with envy.

SELF-ASSERTION

An early step toward reducing feelings of impotence is to mobilize oneself in the direction of compensating for the deficiency(ies) that are contributing to the sense of impotence and its associated low self-esteem. Failure to assert oneself results in a situation of ongoing frustration and this cannot but lower self-worth. Frustration produces hostility, and people who are smoldering with pent-up hostility, because they have not stood up for their rights, have little respect for themselves. They denograte themselves because of their passivity. Their pent-up anger in itself precludes a feeling of self-satisfaction. Accordingly, therapists do well to help such patients assert themselves by not allowing themselves to be taken advantage of, and appropriately expressing their resentments.

My experience has been that helping people assert themselves is one of the more easily accomplished goals in treatment. The situations in which individuals fail to do this are more readily circumscribed, and the specific actions that one must take to demand one's rights are often easily identified. Patients, then, must desensitize themselves to the anticipated negative effects of such assertion and have living experiences that confirm that all the anticipated consequences are not forthcoming. The reader will note the word *all* in the previous sentence. Generally, there is negative feedback to which people who assert themselves will inevitably be subjected. However, people with inhibitions in this realm often exaggerate the extent of this feedback and consider there to be more than what actually exists.

Beginning in the 1970s, and continuing up to the present, we

have seen the growth of a wide variety of self-assertion therapeutic programs. Often, the people who conduct such programs
are quite naive with regard to the complexities of the therapeutic
process and consider inhibition of self-assertion to be a central
factor in most forms of psychopathology as well as the myriad
other problems that beset all of us in life. They would give their
followers the impression that once they start asserting themselves
properly, all will be well with them and there is no goal in this
world that cannot be achieved. Those simple-minded enough to
be taken in by all of this are often provided with self-assertion
exercises, the purpose of which is to provide individuals with
practice in asserting themselves.

An example of such an exercise: A man is advised to go into
a haberdashery and tell the salesperson that he wishes to buy a
shirt. From the outset, he makes it clear that he will not simply be
satisfied by measurements of his neck, chest, and arm length and
then purchase the shirt simply on the basis of the size indicated
on the collar. Rather, he insists upon trying on the shirt, a
procedure that involves the salesperson's painstakingly removing
all the pins, tissue, cardboards, and other items that may be
packaged within the shirt. After going through this procedure 10
to 15 times (or as many times as the individual can get away with
before being asked to leave the store), the individual decides not
to buy anything (which, of course, was the original intention).
People with self-assertion problems are instructed to steel themselves against any embarrassment they may feel over acting out
such "exercises in self-assertion" and learn to deal with impunity
the negative reactions they anticipate the salesperson will have.
In the guise of helping people assert themselves, these group
leaders are perpetuating sadism and teaching insensitivity to the
feelings of the victims of these exercises. Accordingly, therapists
do well to put self-assertion into the broader picture of therapeutic recommendations. Furthermore, they must be exceedingly
sensitive to the feelings of those with whom the patient is
asserting himself (herself). They must be sure that the goal is a
healthy one and that the self-assertion is indeed useful for all
parties concerned.

Children who do not assert themselves may have trouble in school, both in the behavioral and academic realms. They may be afraid to raise their hand and ask questions, lest they be considered stupid. They have to be helped to appreciate that "there is no such thing as a stupid question" and that the best students are often those who are the freest to continually ask questions. I suspect that in most classrooms more than half the children do not know what the teacher is talking about, yet do not raise their hands to get clarification, even when the teacher invites them to do so. If one multiplies this time spent sitting in a state of ignorance by weeks, months, and even years, it is easy to appreciate how this inhibition in itself can contribute significantly to a psychogenic learning disability. Children who are fearful of fighting back and thereby discouraging the inevitable taunts and teasing of their classmates may come to fear school. Their high state of tension may contribute to their finding excuses for not going to school at all, contributes to the development of psychosomatic complaints, or may impair their concentration when attending. A child who dreads school is not likely to learn very much.

Teachers commonly say to children: "Raise your hand if you'd like to. . . ." The child who fears being singled out as different under such circumstances is not likely to gain the gratifications derived from the particular assignment or appointment. In class discussions the children who fear giving the atypical or unacceptable response are likely to squelch their educational creativity and constrict their knowledge base. Children have to be helped to appreciate that the person who "bucks the tide" may ultimately provide great contributions to human knowledge. In contrast, those who blend in with the woodwork are likely to lead very boring lives and are not likely to contribute to the advancement of humanity. Children do well to be taught, in school and in therapy, the old Chinese proverb: "He who sticks his head above the crowd is bound to get hit with rotten eggs." This should not be interpreted as a warning to duck one's head down to the crowd's level; rather it should be interpreted as an impetus to thrust oneself above the crowd in order to gain the benefits to be derived from such self-assertion and develop a thick enough skin to tolerate the inevitable negative feedback that comes the way of the person who does so.

Children should be taught, again by both their therapists and teachers, that the best students are those who accept with receptivity, but not with gullibility, what their teachers have to say. If they agree, they should incorporate that information into their general fund of knowledge. If they disagree, they should not merely reject the information, but try to find a better answer. They should become comfortable disagreeing with their teachers and not feel that such disagreement is improper. Of course, this attitude becomes much more meaningful in the higher grades, but it is applicable at lower grade levels as well. I am not suggesting an atmosphere in which anyone's opinion is as good as anyone else's or that all opinions are equally worthy of expression. Comments and judgments have to be made on the opinions and conflicting information provided. What I am saying is that a good educational atmosphere provides freedom of expression and encourages the self-assertion of all students.

In many situations self-assertion may be frightening. This is especially the case when the youngster anticipates negative feedback far above and beyond what is likely to take place in reality. In addition to clarifying the situation and correcting the distortions, the therapist must encourage the youngster to act in spite of the tension and anxiety. Such youngsters must be helped to "swallow the lump in their throats" and to do the frightening thing in spite of their fears. Such desensitization is as much a part of the treatment as the correction of the cognitive distortions. In fact, attempts to simply correct the distortions without the child's having the living experiences that they are not valid is not likely to prove therapeutically effective. Some of the stories in my *Dr. Gardner's Stories About the Real World (Vol.I)* (Gardner, 1972a), *Dr. Gardner's Stories About the Real World (Vol. II)* (Gardner, 1983a), and *Dr. Gardner's Fables for Our Times* (Gardner, 1981a) deal with this issue and may be useful to read with the child in the therapeutic situation as well for assigned therapeutic "homework."

The Talking, Feeling, and Doing Game

The game includes cards that allow the therapist to provide the responses relevant to the issue of self-assertion.

> *Question:* You're standing in line to buy something and a child pushes in front of you. Show what you would do.
>
> *Response:* Let's say I'm a kid and I'm standing here in line and some kid pushes himself in front of me. A part of me might want to push him away and even hit him. But another part of me knows that that wouldn't be such a good idea. I might get into trouble or he might hit me back and I might get hurt.
>
> So the first thing I would do would be to say something to him like, "Hey, I was here first. Why don't you go back to the end of the line and wait your turn like everybody else." If that didn't work I might threaten to call some person like a parent, teacher, or someone else around who is in charge. But sometimes there are no other people around to call, so I might just say that it's not worth all the trouble and that all it's causing me is the loss of another minute or two.
>
> If, however, the person starts to push me, then I might fight back. But that would be the *last* thing I would try. Some people might think that I'm "chicken" for not hitting him in the first place. I don't agree with them. I think that hitting should be the *last* thing you should do, not the first. I don't think that people who hit first are particularly wise or brave; rather, I think they're kind of stupid. So in this situation I'd talk first and try to solve the problem. If that didn't work, I'd drop the whole thing. It's not worth fighting about.

Here I provide the child with some guidelines for self-assertion. What a child does when someone pushes in front of him (her) provides an excellent opportunity for the therapist to provide this information. The reader will note here that I am not a proponent of the "macho" reaction in which the individual is advised to reflexively stick up for his rights and use attack as the first line of defense. Nonaction and flight are not given the respect they deserve in our society. Elsewhere (Gardner, 1988a) I have elaborated further on this point.

* * *

Question: Make believe someone grabbed something of yours. Show what you would do.

Response: I would first try to use talk before using action. I'd tell the child to give it back and threaten to grab it back if he or she didn't return it. If the child was my size or a little taller, I'd try to grab it back, providing it wasn't something that could break. If it was something that could break and/or the person was bigger, I would threaten to call the teacher or my parent(s) if it wasn't given back immediately. I might ask a friend or two to help me get it back. But I wouldn't just stand there, say nothing, and let the person get away with it.

This response is designed for youngsters with self-assertion problems. My response provides advice regarding the sequence of steps one does well to follow when one's rights are being infringed upon. Once again, I attempt to engender the notion that physical action should not be the first line of defense in most situations.

* * *

Question: If a fly followed you around for a day and could then talk about you, what would it say?

Response: "I followed Dr. Gardner around all day and I noticed that the people he's with hardly ever have any doubt in their minds about what he thinks. He's not afraid to tell people what's on his mind and to express his thoughts and feelings. He avoids a lot of trouble this way. If people had to wonder what he thought, there would be a lot of confusion and trouble. He also gets many things accomplished that he wouldn't have if he didn't speak up.

"For example, during his lunch break one day, he went to a restaurant with a friend. He asked to be seated in the *No Smoking* section. After they were there awhile, a man sat down at the next table and started to smoke. Dr. Gardner immediately complained to the waiter and the man was asked to either put out the cigarette or sit in the *Smoking* section. The man quickly apologized and put out the cigarette. Some people probably would have sat there and said nothing. However, Dr. Gardner didn't. By speaking up, he stopped a person from doing something that was making him uncomfortable.

"During the evening he went to the movies with his wife. The sound was on much too loud and lots of people were bothered. However, no one was doing anything about it. They just sat there uncomfortable. Dr. Gardner got up, went out to the lobby, and asked for the manager. He asked the manager to lower the volume of the sound. At first, the manager didn't believe him, so he asked the manager to go into the theater and hear for himself. The manager did so and realized that Dr. Gardner was right. He then lowered the volume and everyone was more comfortable. Again, he saved himself and other people a lot of trouble by politely and firmly expressing his thoughts and feelings. Of course, every once in a while, he may not express his thoughts and feelings and this usually causes some trouble. Such silence helps him remember that the best thing, most often, is to tell people about things that bother you—but to do so in a polite way."

This is another example of my view that it is useful for therapists to help patients learn important principles to live by that can be applied to specific situations as they arise. Clearly, my hope here is that this description will impress upon the patient the value of self-assertion. My hope also is that my own ways of dealing with these problems will serve as a model for the youngster.

POWER

Power basically refers to the ability to do or act, that is, the capability of doing or accomplishing something. It is the opposite of impotence. Without power, we are helpless. Powerlessness lowers feelings of self-worth; power is a useful antidote for such uncomfortable and even devastating feelings. Power often has a pejorative connotation. This is unfortunate, because it is not necessarily the case. Such "bad press" stems from the failure to differentiate properly between healthy and unhealthy use of power. Healthy use of power is ego-enhancing; unhealthy use of power is ultimately ego-debasing, the immediate gratifications notwithstanding. Healthy power is associated with a sense of competence in dealing with life's problems. Unhealthy use of power results in exploitation, control, and even destruction of others. These are the people whose ultimate aim appears to be to dominate the whole world, although necessity may satisfy them temporarily with lesser positions. Every age has its examples, the most recent ones in this century are Adolf Hitler and Joseph Stalin. John Dalberg-Acton (Lord Acton, 1887) said, "Power tends to corrupt, and absolute power corrupts absolutely. Great men are almost always bad." The generalization holds, but Acton admits to exceptions (". . .*almost* always bad"). He is right, however, that the temptation to overuse power and thereby become corrupted is formidable.

Accordingly, in our work with patients we do well to help them enhance their self-esteem by gaining power; yet we also do well to make sure that they differentiate well between healthy and unhealthy uses of power. There is a type of guilt that is basically a delusion of control in situations in which the individual does not indeed possess such power. The notion, "It's my fault," can be a delusion that provides the believer with a feeling of control over situations in which there is basically none. Elsewhere, I have described this phenomenon in parents with physical disease (Gardner, 1969b), as a central mechanism in religious belief (Gardner, 1969a, 1970a), and as an important contributing factor to the development of certain psychiatric symptoms, e.g., depression, catatonia, and prejudice (Gardner, 1970a).

Becker (1973, 1975) has proposed that a central element in the development of psychopathological symptoms is the denial of the painful feelings associated with our realization that someday we will die. One of the ways in which human beings differ significantly from lower animals is our ability to appreciate that we are mortal. It may be the greatest price we pay for our superior intelligence. Many psychological phenomena, both normal and abnormal, include the element of denial of our fallibility and mortality. Such phenomena (examples to be described below) essentially represent an attempt to gain power over situations in which we are basically impotent. We involve ourselves in activities in which we flirt with death in order to prove to ourselves that we, in contrast to other humans, need not be grasped by death's claws. We place ourselves in extremely precarious positions and then pride ourselves on our ability to come out unscathed. Sky-divers, tightrope walkers, mountain climbers, speed racers, and bullfighters are just a few examples of people with a strong need to prove to themselves that they, unlike others, are invulnerable to death. The general populace admires those who demonstrate such fearlessness and will make them heroes. However, the admirers need to maintain the delusion that their heroes are invulnerable. If events destroy the delusion, then the hero no longer serves his (her) purpose and is dispensed with. Once Achilles is wounded in his heel, he is no longer revered. But it is a two-way arrangement. Achilles needs to feel invulnerable to compensate for the feelings of vulnerability he feels over his appreciation of his mortality. And his worshipers need to maintain the image that Achilles is invulnerable in order to give them hope that they are so as well.

This phenomenon is related to what I term the adolescent's delusion of invulnerability (Gardner, 1988a). Adolescents smoke and believe that they are immune to lung cancer, emphysema, cardiovascular disorders, and the host of other diseases caused by smoking. They drive at high speeds, while inebriated, and believe that they will neither be injured nor killed. They even play "chicken" on the open road. For those not familiar with this "game," two cars—driving head on in the same lane—approach each other at high speeds. The first one who veers off the collision path is viewed as "chicken" and the "loser" of the game. It is not just simplemindedness that is required for willingness to involve oneself in this idiocy. Also involved is the need to compensate for feelings of inadequacy by attempting to prove that one is indeed courageous. Another element, however, is its value in dealing with death fears. Once the youngsters have survived, they can flaunt their invulnerability to death.

There are some who rationalize their helplessness, consider themselves impotent to control what happens to them, and subscribe to such dicta as "Whatever will be will be" and "I leave it in God's hands." These people subscribe to the view that there are higher powers that predetermine all the details of their lives, even to the point where there is "a book" in which such directives are written, inevitably controlling every element of their existence. Full commitment to this philosophy works against the individual's striving to empower himself (herself) to control the events of one's life. A therapist who subscribes to this view of the world is seriously compromised, especially with regard to helping people take efforts to have some control over their destinies. Therapists do better to subscribe to the ancient wisdom well stated by the theologian Rheinhold Niebuhr:

> Give me the serenity
> to accept the things I cannot change,
> the courage to change the things I can;
> and the wisdom to know the difference.

Some children with psychogenic learning disabilities do indeed subscribe to the "Whatever will be will be" philosophy and take the attitude that somehow things will work out academically without the necessity of their applying themselves. The therapist does well to investigate such a patient's family background and ascertain whether either of the parents subscribe to this life philosophy. It is hoped that the pattern will not be a deep-seated one, because if it is, the chances of the therapist helping may be very small. There are entire societies and religions in which this tenet is a central element. Such religions are most attractive to people whose total life may be one of hopelessness. The religion, then, helps these people resign themselves to their plight. Children with such a philosophy have to be helped to appreciate that things are not just going to work out, that they themselves will be responsible for their failures, and they themselves have the power to do better. Some children are continually exposed to parental messages that they will not succeed, e.g., "You'll never amount to anything" and "You're a born loser." Implicit in this statement is the notion that the child is intrinsically and even genetically powerless and probably would do well just to submit to this reality. Obviously, therapists must do everything possible to bring about a discontinuation of such statements and to rectify the problems that may be contributing to the parents' statements. The child also must be helped to appreciate the inappropriateness and even cruelty of such denigrating predictions.

Children have to be helped to appreciate that self-assertion and the power that one acquires as a result of it is not accomplished without discomfort and even pain. The achievement of a goal is not generally obtained easily, and the more ego-enhancing the goal, the greater the likelihood great efforts will be necessary in its attainment. There are some children who subscribe to the dictum: "If it feels good I will do it; if it doesn't feel good, I don't want any part of it." Homework, drill, and the self-abnegation that is inevitably involved in dedication to one's studies are placed in the category of those things that do not "feel good." Such youngsters feel quite comfortable not doing their schoolwork with the explanation, "I don't like doing it." For them, that in itself is enough of an excuse. Considerations like homework's importance and the future consequences of not doing it are not taken into consideration, so powerful is their commitment to this principle of living. Schools with too much "respect" for children's wishes, schools in which they do not believe in telling children to do things they do not wish to do, may entrench this basically self-destructive pattern in the child. Schools should prepare children for life. Life involves frustration tolerance and the willingness to subject oneself to present discomforts in order to enjoy future goals and to protect oneself from the untoward consequences of entirely avoiding current self-abnegation. Such children continue to suffer with the feelings of low self-worth attendant to their failure to work and deprive themselves of the sense of ego-enhancement that comes from having power over one's school grades and teacher's comments.

There are some children who strictly avoid exposure to tension and anxiety, two forms of unpleasant emotion. Their basic life philosophy is this: "If it makes me anxious, I'll have no part of it." Their fear of these feelings is so great that they deprive themselves of the benefits they would acquire if they were to push through their tensions. They avoid such activities as auditioning for a school play or recital, trying out for a school team, or presenting to a class. Children may view with respect and even awe those who are successful in these endeavors, but they may not be able to tolerate the tensions associated with obtaining such goals. Such patients have to be helped to appreciate that they have within their own hands the power to strive toward and even obtain such distinctions, but they will have to "thicken their skins" and tolerate the discomforts attendant to their acquisition. Success does not come easily, nor does it come without discomfort and even psychological pain. Of bibliotherapeutic value in this regard is my story "The Girl Who Wouldn't Try" in my *Dr. Gardner's Stories About the Real World, Vol. I* (Gardner, 1972a).

Children who are scapegoated, who feel powerless at the hands of their persecutors, also have to be helped to overcome the tensions and anxieties associated with self-assertion. Flight is ego-debasing and humiliating. Self-protection and retaliation are options that are inevitably associated with tension, anxiety, and even pain. Children who are willing to tolerate these unpleasant and even painful feelings may ultimately gain the respect and even fear of their taunters and thereby protect themselves from their persecution. A good analogy for the youngster is one's response to a barking dog. Most often, if one stands one's ground, if one does not let the dog know that one is afraid, the dog will not continue barking or pursuing. If one flees, the dog is likely to chase. However, standing one's ground may be frightening, and one may have to tolerate the knee knocking and the teeth chattering associated with such a stance. The child has to be helped, as well, to appreciate that the brave person and the coward are not as far apart from one another as one might initially believe. Both share in common their fear of the danger. The brave person "stands his (her) ground" and tolerates the discomforts attendant to standing up to the danger; the coward submits to the forces within themselves that dictate flight, a course that might not be the most judicious. I have found "The Adventures of the Cowardly Lion" in my *Dorothy and the Lizard of Oz* (Gardner, 1980a) and "Jerry and the Bullies" in my *Stories About the Real*

World, Vol. I (Gardner, 1972a) to be useful bibliotherapeutic techniques for children with this problem. Children who are scapegoated may be so fearful about going to school that their learning will be compromised. In extreme cases they may be so fearful that they will refuse to attend school entirely. They will thereby be deprived of the accumulation of knowledge so necessary for the acquisition of healthy power.

Adolescents who suffer from deep feelings of impotence may gravitate toward groups, especially antisocial groups, in order to provide themselves with compensation. The group has a power that the individual does not possess. In fact, the combined power of a group is greater than the sum of the individual powers of each of its members. The group is truly an example of a situation in which the power of the group is greater than the sum of the powers of each of the individuals within it. It thereby provides an individual with a feeling of enormous expansion of one's capabilities. If the group is involved in antisocial behavior, that too can provide additional feelings of power. The expression of anger can produce such feelings because anger expression per se serves to compensate for one's sense of impotence and frustration. Intrinsic to the antisocial act is the feeling that one need not submit to the rules of society, one takes matters into one's own hands, and one has the ability to thwart them. Obviously, adolescents swept up in such groups are not going to attend significantly to their studies, if they go to school at all. The end result is that they learn little if anything, their educational process becomes wasted, and they are likely to end up with deep-seated feelings of low self-worth. Subsequently, having few if any skills, they are ill equipped to enter the job market and will then suffer even further feelings of low self-worth.

Clinical Example

Ralph entered treatment at the age of nine-and-a-half because of antisocial behavior at school and at home. In both places he was referred to as "a constant terror" and as "a menace." His behavior was so bad that he learned little in the second grade, and he had to repeat it.

Ralph's father abandoned the family soon after his birth and had practically nothing to do with the boy throughout the course of Ralph's life. His mother owned a store and was not able to give her children (Ralph had an older sister, two years his senior) proper attention. The children would come to the store after school, and Ralph would often antagonize customers, with the resultant loss of business for his mother. During the first two years of Ralph's life it was clear he was not growing at the proper rate. A growth hormone deficiency was diagnosed and, at the time that I first saw him, his height and weight were that of a five-year-old, as was his general body structure. Accordingly, he was often referred to as "the midget" and scapegoated by children in his school and neighborhood. However, Ralph would commonly pick on children his own age, challenge them to fight with him, and, of course, would inevitably lose because of the size discrepancy. This did not dissuade him, however, from continuation of this "macho" method of attempting to compensate for his feelings of low self-worth. Ralph could best be described as a "little tough guy" who maintained this facade everywhere – in school, neighborhood, in his mother's store, and even in my office. Clearly it provided him with compensation for the feelings of low self-worth he felt over his short stature as well as a vehicle for the release of anger he felt over the abandonment of his father.

A few months prior to the beginning of therapy, Ralph began treatment with Protropin, a synthetic growth hormone. Ralph was one of the first children to be placed on this medication. Previously, the hormone had to be extracted from hundreds of cadavers in order to provide one child with treatment for a year. Obviously, the expense of such therapy was enormous, the supply was extremely limited, and there was much controversy over who would be selected for therapy. Protropin, which became a boon for these children, was manufactured by E. coli bacilli, whose genetic programming was altered in such a way that they produced human growth hormone.

I believe that Ralph's anger stemmed primarily from the privations he had suffered throughout the course of his life. Ralph's father had abandoned him, and his mother could not give him the compensatory attention he needed because of the necessity of her working. Furthermore, he felt insecure and even impotent because of his small stature, and this too was a source of great frustration and anger. This anger was being acted out wantonly and irresponsibly in every possible direction. But the anger expression provided him with an additional gratification, a gratification not enjoyed by children of normal height and size. Specifically, it was giving him a sense of power to compensate for the feelings of impotence he felt in relation to his growth hormone deficiency. His picking fights with children his own age was a maneuver designed to provide him with a sense of power in compensation for this sense of impotence.

These interchanges took place while playing the *The Talking, Feeling, & Doing Game* during Ralph's third session:

> *Gardner:* You get a yellow card. All right, what does the yellow card say?
>
> *Patient:* "How do you feel when you meet a new person?"
>
> *Gardner (repeating the question):* "How do you feel when you meet a new person."
>
> *Patient:* Weird.
>
> *Gardner:* Weird. Why do you feel weird?
>
> *Patient:* Because you never know what they're going to do.
>
> *Gardner:* What might they do? What might a new person do?
>
> *Patient:* They might hurt you.
>
> *Gardner:* A new person might hurt you. How might the new person hurt you?
>
> *Patient:* By him beating you up.
>
> *Gardner:* Hhmm. The new person might beat you up.
>
> *Patient:* A lot of times they just do that.
>
> *Gardner:* You mean the person will just go around beating you up, just like that? Hmm, just like that the person will beat you up—without your doing anything? Hhmm?
>
> *Patient:* Yup.
>
> *Gardner:* You know what I say about that?
>
> *Patient:* What?
>
> *Gardner:* It doesn't happen that way. Usually if a person is going to beat you up it's because you're doing something. If you start up with that person, if you hit that person, call them names or something like that, then that person might want to beat you

up, but people just don't go around beating people up for nothing. That's my opinion. What do you say about that?

Patient: Yeah.

Gardner: Do you ever start beating up people?

Patient: No, only unless they . . .

Gardner (interrupting): Only what?

Patient: Only unless they start it like then I hit back.

Gardner: Okay, but you never start it yourself. Huh?

Patient: Sometimes.

Gardner: You do, huh?

Patient: Everybody does.

Gardner: Yeah, but I understand that most of the times you're the one who does it. That's what I understand from your mother and your sister—that most of the time you're the one who starts hitting other people. What do you think about that? Is that true?

Patient: Hhmmm. Yeah.

Gardner: Why is that?

Patient: I like to.

Gardner: You like to. Hmm?

Patient: No, I don't like to beat up people.

Gardner: But you do it a lot, don't you? Don't you hit people a lot?

Patient: Only in a fight.

Gardner: Only in a fight. But I understand you start a lot of fights. Am I correct?

Patient: Yeah.

Gardner: Why is that? Why do you start so many fights? That's the important question.

Patient: I don't know.

Gardner: You know what it says to me about you? It says that you got a lot of anger in you. Hmmm?

Patient: Yup.

Gardner: What is all that anger about?

Patient: I get upset very easily.

Gardner: Why do you get upset very easily?

Patient: I don't know.

Gardner: Usually a person who gets upset very easily is someone who has got a lot of anger in him over something and then little things get him very angry very quickly. Are you that kind of person?

Patient: Sometimes, yeah.

Gardner: Well, what's the anger in you? What are you so angry about?

> *Patient:* I don't know.
> *Gardner:* Okay, I'm going to make a guess. Okay? Can I guess what you're so angry about?
> *Patient:* Yeah, you could.
> *Gardner:* I'm guessing that you're angry about your size. That's what I think.
> *Patient:* Yup, you got it!

The reader will note that I was using the card as a point of departure for a psychoanalytic inquiry in which I was attempting to help Ralph gain insight into the sources of his anger. After questioning him a few times, it was clear that Ralph was not coming up with any meaningful answers. Accordingly, I decided to present him with what I considered to be an important psychodynamic factor that was fueling his hostility, namely, his anger over his size. However, it is important for the reader to note that I do not present confrontations in an authoritarian way with the implication that I indeed do know *why* he is doing something. Rather, I present my psychodynamic speculations as a "guess" for the patient's consideration. It is common practice among many therapists to present their interpretations in a more definitive way. I think this practice is antitherapeutic. First, it is grandiose on the part of the therapist to believe that he (she) can actually know exactly what the reasons are for any patient's behavior. We only have speculations. The therapist who presents his speculations as facts cannot but bring about a situation in which the patient is going to view the therapist as omniscient and as having information about the patient that he himself (she herself) does not know of. This is definitely antitherapeutic. It lowers patients' self-esteem. Accordingly, it may work against a primary goal of treatment—which is to enhance patients' sense of self-worth. Here, my hunch proved valid and the patient had a "gut reaction" to my suggestion: "Yup, you got it!"

> *Gardner:* I've got it, huh? You think that's the number one thing?
> *Patient:* Yup.
> *Gardner:* Tell me about your thoughts and feelings about that, about your size.

Patient: It's just that I don't like being small. I can't do as much things.

Gardner: You don't like being small and what else?

Patient: I can't do as many things as other people can.

Gardner: Yeah, that's right. I understand that you're getting some medicine now that's going to help you get taller. Right?

Patient: Yup.

Gardner: Do you know what that medicine is called?

Patient: Protropin.

Gardner: Yeah and what does that do?

Patient: It helps me grow up.

Gardner: Hhmmm. When did you start getting it?

Patient: A couple of months ago.

Gardner: Are you starting to grow from it?

Patient: Oh, yeah. I grew an inch in three months!

Gardner: Wow! One inch in three months. How did you feel about that?

Patient: Good.

Gardner: That's great, huh?

Patient: Yeah.

Gardner: That's terrific. Let me congratulate you. (As the therapist grasps the patient's hand to congratulate him, the patient squeezes the therapist's hand very tightly, a manifestation of his macho approach to human relationships.) Ooooh! Ooooh! that's quite a grasp you have there. Boy, you gotta be careful with that. You know that could hurt a person. For a kid your size that's a pretty powerful grasp. (Therapist's hand is still being squeezed by the patient.) Ooooh, ooooh, that's pretty strong. That's pretty good. Let me feel that muscle. (Patient flexes his arm muscles for therapist to feel.) Hey, that's some muscle. Let's see the other muscle. (Patient flexes his other arm muscle.) Look at that! Let's show it on television here. Look at that muscle this guy has. Look at the big muscle here. That's pretty neat. So your Protropin is starting to work? I'm going to write here that you have a very strong handshake. Right! And I want to write here that you have very big muscles, powerful muscles.

Obviously, my purpose here was to provide communications that might contribute to an enhancement of Ralph's self-worth. I congratulated him on his powerful grasp, felt and admired his biceps muscles, and confirmed that the Protropin was indeed exhibiting its effects. Because Ralph began the Protropin before puberty (when the epiphyseal plates of the long bones fuse), he could hope that he might reach the full height he was destined to have had he not had a growth hormone deficiency. There was still the possibility that he might not reach such stature. (Unfortunately, children who start growth hormone after puberty cannot expect such dramatic results.) I then continued on the original subject: his anger.

> *Gardner:* Okay, now. We were getting back to all the anger that you have and we were talking about how you're very angry and that you do things like starting to hit people and things like that. Right?
>
> *Patient:* Yeah.
>
> *Gardner:* Well, why do you do that? So you're angry over the fact that you're short, although now you have this medicine that's going to help you grow tall faster. Right? Okay, now let's talk about your hitting people. Why should you hit people because you're short? (Patient lifts the microphone.) Do you want to put that down please. Why should you hit people because you're short?
>
> *Patient:* I don't know.
>
> *Gardner:* So you're angry because you're short, but why hit people?
>
> *Patient:* Oh, there are people who bug me all the time.
>
> *Gardner:* No, but sometimes you hit people who don't bug you or bother you. You said yourself that you start up a lot. Right?
>
> *Patient:* Yeah.
>
> *Gardner:* Well, why do you do that?
>
> *Patient:* I don't know.
>
> *Gardner:* Can I guess?
>
> *Patient:* Yes.
>
> *Gardner:* I guessed right before about your anger. Right?
>
> *Patient:* Yeah.
>
> *Gardner:* I thought you were angry because you're small. I may be wrong. Sometimes my guesses are right; sometimes my guesses are wrong. I guess that it makes you feel like a bigger guy.
>
> *Patient:* Why do you have those cubes over there?
>
> *Gardner:* Hey, what did I just say to you? I was just making a guess as to why you hit people a lot.
>
> *Patient:* I don't know.
>
> *Gardner:* I'll say it again. Now listen carefully. One of your problems is that you don't pay attention. It makes you feel like a

bigger guy when you hit people. It makes you feel like a big shot. What do you think about that?

Patient: (no response)

Gardner: It's wrong—wrong guess? Oh, it's just a guess. So if I'm wrong, what is the right answer?

Patient: I don't know.

Gardner: Hhmm. Well, I think it makes you feel bigger and stronger. Hhmm? Do you think I'm wrong?

Patient: Yup.

Gardner: Well, that's my guess. But you can't come up with a better answer, can you?

Patient: No.

Gardner: Hhmm. Look, when you hit people it lets out some of your anger, huh?

Patient: Yup.

Gardner: Do you know what happens when you do that?

Patient: They get angry at me.

Gardner: They get angry at you. Is that what you said?

Patient: Yup.

Gardner: And then what happens?

Patient: Then they hit me back and I get more angry.

Gardner: So what should you do? What's the best solution to that problem?

Patient: Go away.

Gardner: Hmm?

Patient: Go away.

Gardner: There's a better solution.

Patient: Hit back.

Gardner: No. Don't start hitting them in the first place.

Patient: Yeah.

Gardner: What do you think about that solution?

Patient: Yeah, do you know what I used to do?

Gardner: What?

Patient (while punching the pillow of the couch): Hit a pillow.

Gardner: That's better than hitting other people, you know, but a pillow is not the best solution either. You know why?

Patient: Why?

Gardner: Well, what does that accomplish when you hit a pillow?

Patient: It gets the anger out of me.

Gardner: Yeah, but it doesn't really solve the problem, hhmm? You're still angry about being short, right?

There are therapists who, at this point, would praise the child for his judicious displacement of anger. I personally am not a strong proponent of this commonly used therapeutic technique. Although it does have some cathartic value, it does not direct the patient's attention to the primary problem and therefore is not likely to ultimately prove effective. It has some positive value in that the patient is at least releasing emotions, but the anger is not being directed toward the source of the resentment. Rather, it is being displaced onto an inanimate object and thereby will accomplish little else beyond the initial catharsis.

> *Patient:* Well, then I forget about it and then later on I get angry again.
> *Gardner:* Hhmm. Right. But what can you do or think that can help you be less angry? Hitting pillows is okay, but there are better ways of dealing with your anger.
> *Patient (almost shouting):* I don't know.
> *Gardner:* Hhmm. Well, one thing is to accept the fact that you are shorter and you're getting the medicine that's going to help you be taller and how tall you'll get from it I don't know. The thing is that—this is the hardest part—and that is to accept the fact that maybe you're going to be shorter than other people even with the medicine, but maybe you won't be. What am I saying?
> *Patient:* Can we get on with the game?
> *Gardner:* No, you don't want to talk about that part?
> *Patient:* Yeah.
> *Gardner:* You'd rather not talk about accepting the fact—I said accept the fact that you are short. See if you stop wishing that you were very tall. The more you stop wishing you were tall, the less angry you will be.
> *Patient:* Yeah.
> *Gardner:* What did I just say?
> *Patient:* The less you wish to be tall, the less angry you will be.
> *Gardner:* Hhmm. The less that you wish you're tall, the less angry you will be. Right?
> *Patient:* Yup.
> *Gardner:* Can you do that?
> *Patient:* I'll try.
> *Gardner:* Okay, say that again just so I'm sure you understand what I am saying?
> *Patient:* Yes, I'll try.

Gardner: Go ahead try. Say it again.
Patient: The less I hope that I'll be tall, the less I will be angry.
Gardner: Do you think that's true?
Patient: Yup.

Here I have provided the patient with some direct advice I hoped would be helpful for him in reducing his anger. Anger often stems from frustration. Frustration comes when an individual wants something that he (she) cannot have. If one changes one's mind about the thing one aspires to, and decides to stop hoping for something that one cannot have, then one is less likely to be angry. This is an important therapeutic principle, so important that I asked the patient to repeat my message, just to be sure that he understood it. I will often do this in treatment, especially with children. Some adults may be offended by my request that they repeat what I have said, but most are not. I believe that the failure to be resentful relates to their appreciation that my request that they repeat my statement is benevolently motivated and does not have the implication that they are stupid.

Gardner: Hhmm. See as time goes on, even without the medicine, you will grow somewhat taller. How much taller we don't know. With the medicine you will grow even taller. How far we don't know. But if you walk around saying, "Oh, how terrible. What a terrible thing this is. I'm shorter than other people," the more you keep wishing that you will be taller, the harder it's going to be for you and the more angry you are going to be. And no matter how many pillows you hit, if you keep wishing that you were taller all the time, you will be angry. Now what am I saying just now? What did I just say?
Patient: I can't repeat all that.
Gardner: Well, try.
Patient: The more you hit the pillow, it's not going to help you. Just gonna take it out and you're just gonna get it back. But if you try to stand the anger then you'll . . . (mumbles).
Gardner: Say that again. The more what? The more you hit the pillow—go ahead. Say it again now.
Patient: How come I have to say this again?
Gardner: Because this is very complicated. I want to be sure you understand it. Say it again.
Patient: Okay, I'll say it once more.

Gardner: Go ahead.

Patient: The more you hit the pillow, it's going to just take it out and then you're going to get it [the anger] back. But if you forget all about the anger, then you'll—I mean if you forget that you're tall—I mean short—then you'll think you're tall and you'll be happier.

Gardner: Right, you won't be so angry. Very good. Okay, you did very nicely there on that one.

Patient (interrupting): Can we get on with our game?

Gardner: Yeah, we are going to, but first of all I'm not going to give you one chip for that; I'm going to give you two chips because you answered so many things.

Now it's my chance to go. Okay? I got a nine. (Counts spaces as he moves his pawn.) One, two, three, four, five, six, seven, eight, nine. (Reads from card.) Okay, mine says: "A girl was crying. What was she crying about?" What was this girl crying about?

Patient: Who has to answer that?

Gardner: I have to answer it. That's my question, although if you want to answer it, you can answer it and get a chip if you want.

Patient: I don't want to answer it.

Gardner: You don't want to answer it?

Patient: Nah.

Gardner: Okay. In my story this girl was crying because her hair was brown and she wanted to have hair that was red. And she was crying about that. And she had a sister—a teenage sister—who also had hair that was brown. And the teenage sister came over and said, "What are you crying about?"

And the girl said, "My hair isn't red and I like red hair."

And the older sister said, "But you know you were born with brown hair and that's one kind of hair. There are different kinds of hair color. Some hair color is brown, some is red, some is blond, and, you know, different people have different color hair and then when you get older your hair gets gray and there's just different kinds of hair. And that's the way your hair is and that's the way nature made your hair and it's not going to change by crying."

But the girl was still crying and said, "But what can I do to change it?"

The older sister answered, "You can't. It's always going to be brown. Now you can color it, you can dye it if you want. Maybe that will make you feel a little bit better, but it still will grow in at the roots as brown hair." Right?

Patient: Eh.

Gardner: And the older sister said, "I think the best thing you can do is to accept the fact that you have brown hair and that different people have different color hair and that no one color hair is better than any other color hair. And then you won't be so upset and then you won't be crying." So what do you think the girl did?

Patient: Stopped crying. *Gardner:* Why?

Patient: Because she . . . (mumbles) . . .

Gardner: Say it again. I'm not clear. You're mumbling a little bit.

Patient: I couldn't hear you very well because you were talking very fast.

Gardner: Okay, should I say it again?

Patient: Yes.

Gardner: Okay. What did I say? The girl was crying. Why was she crying?

Patient: Because her hair was brown.

Gardner: And what did her teenage sister say?

Patient: She asked her why she was crying.

Gardner: Go ahead. And?

Patient: She told her that when she gets older her hair will get gray and she could dye it, but she can't make it red. She'll never make it red unless she dyes it and I can't remember the rest and you got very fast.

Gardner: I said something about stopping being upset about the fact that her hair is brown and that there are different colors of hair. Right? What are some of the different colors of hair?

Patient: Blond, red, orange, green.

Gardner: Do you know anyone with green hair?

Patient: Yeah.

Gardner: Real green hair?

Patient: No, no, no.

Gardner: Real hair—just the way people are born. Real hair.

Patient: Ah, yes, orange hair.

Gardner: Orange, no.

Patient: Yes, yes, yes.

Gardner: People make their hair orange if they want.

Patient: No, I've seen them.

Gardner: Well, I believe those—maybe you're talking about someone who has red hair maybe—and you're calling it orange?

Patient: No, it's orange, orange hair.

Gardner: Okay, anyway. The thing is there are only certain numbers of different color hair. Right?

Patient: Yeah.

Gardner: And so what did the older sister advise her? What was the advice of the older sister?

Patient: She said that she'll never have her hair orange or red because it's the way it's made.

Gardner: Hh hmm. She'll never have it red because that's the way it's made. So what did the girl do?

Patient: She stopped crying.

Gardner: Because.

Patient: She stopped and thought of it.

Gardner: She stopped what?

Patient: And thought about it.

Gardner: She stopped thinking about what?

Patient: She stopped and thought about what her sister said.

Gardner: And then what did she think when she thought about it? What did she then do?

Patient: I don't know. She stopped crying.

Gardner: And how was she able to stop crying?

Patient: Because her older sister told her.

Gardner: To stop crying. Is that why she stopped?

Patient: No, no, no.

Gardner: Because her older sister told her what?

Patient: Because she'll never have her hair orange.

Gardner: Yeah and therefore what?

Patient: So she could dye it if she wants.

Gardner: Yeah and what else did she do?

Patient: Stopped crying.

Gardner: Now she could stop hoping that it would change, which it won't.

Patient: Yeah.

Gardner: And when you stop hoping for something that you can't have, then she wouldn't be crying anymore.

Patient: Yup.

Gardner: Because she wouldn't be sad.

Patient: Hh hmm.

Gardner: There are different kinds of hair and if you're hoping that your hair will change, it won't. There's little you can do. You can change it a little bit, you know, coloring it. But basically it's going to stay the same. Okay.

Patient: You get a chip.

Gardner: I get a chip and you get one too because you gave some answers, too. Now it's your chance to go. Throw the dice. Go ahead. It's your chance now. Go ahead.

Using the girl's hair as a metaphor, I was basically repeating the same message that I had previously communicated, namely, that one cannot change the body that nature has given us. One might be able to make minor changes (such as dying one's hair), but one can't change one's basic biological makeup. A person who keeps hoping for such changes is going to be angry and miserable. When one gives up hope for attainment of impossible goals, one is more likely to become less angry and, in Ralph's case, be less likely to act out antisocially. As was true for my previous messages, I was not one hundred percent certain that my communications had sunk in completely. However, when working with children, the therapist does the best he (she) can and hope that the reiterations will ultimately drive home the point.

> *Patient* (throws the dice and then moves his pawn): One, two, three, four, five, six, seven, eight, nine.
> *Gardner:* Okay. Go ahead.
> *Patient:* Good. (reads his card) "What do you do very well? Make believe you're doing that thing." *Gardner (repeating the question):* "What do you do very well? Make believe you're doing that thing."
> *Patient:* Making sharks.
> *Gardner:* Making. . . ?
> *Patient:* Sharks.
> *Gardner:* Oh, you mean by making them you mean drawing them?
> *Patient:* Yeah.
> *Gardner:* Okay, make believe you're drawing a shark.
> *Patient:* (makes believe he's drawing a shark)
> *Gardner:* Hh hmm. Hh hmm. Okay. Okay, now that's very good. Now you get a chip for that. Now I want to ask you—you told me, when I saw you a couple of days ago. . . . You told me that you love to draw sharks. Right?
> *Patient:* Yeah.
> *Gardner:* And why do you like sharks so much?
> *Patient:* I don't know.
> *Gardner:* Well, what do sharks do that you like so much?
> *Patient:* They eat people!
> *Gardner:* They eat people. What's so good about that?

Patient (laughs): Nothing.

Gardner: You think that's funny?

Patient: No.

Gardner: Yeah, what do you think the person feels like who's being eaten?

Patient: Hurtin'.

Gardner: Hurtin'. Anything more?

Patient: They're getting ready to die.

Gardner: Yeah, how does that feel?

Patient: Uh huh, no. Not so good.

Gardner: Not so good. That's terrible. Right?

Patient: Yup.

Gardner: That person really feels—I mean that's the worst possible thing you can imagine happening to somebody. Can you think of something worse than being eaten up by a shark?

Patient: Yeah, being struck by lightning.

Gardner: That's pretty bad too.

Patient: Guess what?

Gardner: What?

Patient: I have a great white shark tape that says getting struck by light . . . by getting bit by a shark is less attracting . . . that means hurting . . . as much as getting struck by lightning.

Gardner: It hurts as much?

Patient: It hurts less.

Gardner: Than being struck by lightning?

Patient: (nods affirmatively)

Gardner: Yeah, but it's pretty hard to think of things that are as bad as that. Right?

Patient: Yeah.

Gardner: You really gotta think hard to think of things that are worse than being eaten by a shark. Right?

Patient: Yeah.

Gardner: But you seem to like to think about things like that. Hmm?

Patient: Not really.

Gardner: Well, you draw a lot of sharks. You told me it's your favorite thing to draw. Right?

Patient: Yeah.

Gardner: And you told me it's one of the things you do best. Right?

Patient: Yeah.

Gardner: Okay. So that tells me that you like doing it a lot and you like thinking about things like people being eaten up by sharks. Right?

Patient: Yeah and that's the way the action is! They're not actually getting eaten by it.

Gardner: It's just stories about it. Is that what you're saying?

Patient: Yeah, yeah!

Gardner: Okay.

Patient: It's like the action.

Gardner: Would you say that those are angry stories, in your opinion?

The reader will note here that once again my interpretation is not given as a definitive statement; rather, it is presented and then followed with "in my opinion." This opens up the possibility to the patient that he could present an alternative opinion if he wished to.

Patient: No.

Gardner: I would, in my opinion.

Patient: Why?

Gardner: Well, it's a story about a person being eaten up by a shark. That's a pretty angry thing for the shark to do. Right?

Patient: No. It's because it's hungry and it's food. And it struggles just like a fish would do.

Gardner: Oh, hhhmm. So the shark is just entitled to eat up people?

Patient: Yeah, but not usual.

Gardner: Not usual, right. Well, in my opinion—and try to follow what I am saying now—the fact that you like to think about things like that tells me that this is part of the anger you have in you.

Patient: I don't think so.

Gardner: You don't think so.

Patient: But I don't know.

Gardner: See, my thought is that if you have less anger you won't be thinking so much about sharks eating people and you would think about more pleasant things. What would be more pleasant things to think about, for example?

Patient: Playing Nintendo.

Gardner: Playing Nintendo. Another thing?

Patient: Watching regular movies.

Gardner: Watching what?

Patient: Regular movies.

Gardner: Regular movies, like what kind of movies would be a regular movie?

Patient: "Star Wars."

Gardner: "Star Wars." Right. But thinking about sharks is a way of getting out anger. What do you think about that?

Patient: Oh, yeah!

Gardner: It is. You agree with that. Why do you say that?

Patient: Because you think of it and you forget all about the anger. And then you're happy and then you go and tell everybody about it.

Gardner: Is it something like pillows?

Patient: Something like it, but not quite.

Gardner: How is it like it and how is it different?

Patient: It's like it how because—sorry I don't mean to have this stuff. . .(scratching arm). . .

Gardner: What is that you're talking about?

Patient (pointing to rash on body): This.

Gardner: What is that?

Patient: Poison ivy.

Gardner: Oh, you scratched it. That's all right. That's understandable. You don't have to apologize. So, go ahead. How does thinking about sharks and drawing sharks— especially sharks eating up people—how does that let out anger?

Patient: Because you're like thinking about it and you're getting to the mood where you won't look at sharks or look at shark books and then you forget all about it.

Gardner: Are you saying it gets out the anger?

Patient: Well, it cons you into it, but it—it—it takes—then you're all happy and stuff for a long time until the next day.

Gardner: So it's like pillows. Are you saying that? Letting out the anger makes you happy for a while?

Patient: Yeah, but not like a pillow does. A pillow doesn't take out as much anger.

Gardner: Oh, the thing about sharks lets out more anger.

Patient: Yeah.

Gardner: Okay, remember what I said before about what you should do with your anger—what I said before about why pillows don't work too well with anger?

Patient: Yeah.

Gardner: What did I say?

Patient: Uh, uh, uh. What? No, I don't remember what you said about it.

Gardner: Now think about what I said before about pillows and anger. Did I say that was a good way of letting out anger?

Patient: No.

Gardner: Why did I say it wasn't?

Patient: I don't know.

Gardner: Well, do you get angry again after a while?

Patient: Yeah.

Gardner: Hh hmmm. Why did I say it doesn't work?

Patient: 'Cause you get angry again the next day.

Gardner: Right. And do sharks work to get out the anger?

Patient: Yeah, every once in a while. It's better than pillows.

Gardner: But don't you still get angry the next day?

Patient: Yeah, but not very quickly.

Gardner: Okay, so sharks work better than pillows for you. Okay.

Patient: Yeah, but pillows like take three or four hours and then you got your anger back.

Gardner: And a shark? How many hours will a shark last?

Patient: A whole day.

Gardner: You mean drawing shark pictures?

Patient: Looking at sharks, thinking about sharks, reading about them, and stuff like that.

Gardner: Okay, that will keep you in good shape for a day. See, I'm not saying it doesn't work at all. I'm just saying there's a better way. What did we say before about one of the causes of your anger?

Patient: Um, I'm afraid I can't remember.

Gardner: You don't remember what I said? It had something to do with what thing—one of your problems—something to do with . . .

Patient (interrupting): . . .causing my anger.

Gardner: What is one of the causes of your anger, the biggest cause, the number one cause of your anger?

Patient: Being small.

Gardner: Right, being small! And what did we say would be a better way of not being angry other than pillows?

Patient: . . .(mumbles). . .

Gardner: Huh?

Patient: Stop thinking about it.

Gardner: And what else? Stop thinking about it and think what? What kind of thoughts should you have instead?

Patient: Think. . .
Gardner: Huh?
Patient: Think nice and don't worry about it and think that you're gonna get bigger, but you're not really going to do it.
Gardner: Right. Then it's okay. It's not so terrible.
Patient: Yeah.
Gardner: And that you're not gonna get big and you stop hoping for something that can't happen.
Patient: Yeah.
Gardner: When you stop hoping for something that can't happen, then you don't feel so bad about it.
Patient: Yeah. Can we play again?
Gardner: Yeah, right. Okay. Let's see, whose card was that?

Once again, I cannot say that I had the full conviction that Ralph had heard fully all that I had said. He did, however, appear to understand some of my messages. Again, it is unrealistic for the therapist to hope that every communication will be completely absorbed by the patient, regardless of age. Obviously, the younger the patient, the lower the percentage of messages that will be understood and the greater the need, therefore, for their reiteration. Last, the reader will note that I had forgotten whose card had just been answered. When the game is being played optimally, this often happens. The players are so swept up in the responses and the derivative interchanges that they forget whose card was being answered.

Patient: Mine.
Gardner: That was yours. You get a chip for that. That was about the thing you liked doing most. Okay, now it's my chance. (Tosses dice.) Nine. (Moves pawn 9 spaces.) 1, 2, 3, 4, 5, 6, 7, 8, 9. (Picks card.) Mine says: "Act like a spoiled brat." You know, I'll tell you. I'm not gonna do that. I'm not gonna get the chip because I don't want to act like a spoiled brat. I don't want to do that and I'd rather not get the chip than to act like a spoiled brat because—why do you think I don't want to act like a spoiled brat? What's your opinion on that?
Patient: Nothing. If that was mine, I would say, "Forget it."
Gardner: You would say that too. Good. I'm glad to hear you say that. Do you ever act like a spoiled brat?

By not answering the card, I was communicating to the patient a message about my revulsion of antisocial behavior. So revolted am I that I will forego the opportunity to get a chip rather than even imitate an antisocial act. I then asked the patient his opinion about my response in the hope of making it a point of departure for a therapeutic discussion—especially a discussion concerning his own antisocial behavior. The patient then responded that he would have answered the card in the same way. We see here an excellent example of the modeling process that takes place in therapy. It is a good statement of the patient's relationship with me as well.

> *Patient:* Yeah.
> *Gardner:* When? When do you act like a spoiled brat?
> *Patient:* Practically every time.
> *Gardner:* Yeah, what kind of spoiled brat things do you do?
> *Patient:* Bother my sister and eat in the living room and stuff like that.
> *Gardner:* What?
> *Patient:* Bother my sister, eat in the living room . . .(mumbles). . .
> *Gardner* (repeats): Bother your sister, eat in the living room, and what else?
> *Patient:* Ignoring my ma.
> *Gardner:* And ignoring your ma. Uh huh.
> *Patient:* Okay. I'll let you have a chip for that anyway.
> *Gardner:* Uh huh. Okay.
> *Patient:* Because you're being a good sport.
> *Gardner:* No, no. I'll tell you, I'd rather not. I'd rather not get that chip because I haven't acted like a spoiled brat. And the rules of the game are that if you want to get a chip, you have to do the thing and I just don't want to act like a spoiled brat.
> *Patient:* Okay.
> *Gardner:* Now I want to ask you a question about your acting like a spoiled brat. Why do you act like a spoiled brat?
> *Patient:* I don't know.
> *Gardner:* Think about it.
> *Patient:* Because of my anger.
> *Gardner:* Okay, let's talk about that. What about because of your anger?

Patient (getting upset): Well, we went through that a million times already!

Gardner: But with most people that I see, we have to repeat things many times over so that they can remember these things and then that helps them stop doing the wrong or the bad things. Now tell me about your acting like a spoiled brat and your anger.

Patient: Well, I don't want to act like a spoiled brat and I don't try to, but it's like I get the anger out? I don't know how.

Gardner: But you like acting like a spoiled brat. Hum?

Patient: I don't know how that does . . .

Gardner: Okay, what was one of the things you said you do when you act like a spoiled brat?

Patient: Annoy my sister.

Gardner: Annoy your sister. Okay, what do you do to annoy your sister? How old is your sister?

Patient: My sister is eight.

Gardner: And what things do you do?

Patient: Take her things.

Gardner: Okay. Does that help get out anger?

Patient: It's fun. It's like you do something—like it's fun—and—but it's like she doesn't think I'm having fun. She thinks I'm like trying to annoy her. But it's . . .

Gardner (interrupting): She thinks what? She doesn't think you're having fun. She thinks what?

Patient: I'm trying to annoy her.

Gardner: Well, it sounds like to me that you are if you take her things. What kinds of things do you take, for example? Sit over here so you'll be on TV.

Here, the reader can see once again how I require specific examples. To say that he takes his sister's "things" does not provide me with a visual image of exactly what he is taking. There are thousands of his sister's possible possessions that he could be taking, and each one might provide a different point of departure for a therapeutic interchange. Accordingly, I asked him for specifics before proceeding.

Patient: Like I would take her UNO cards.
Gardner: Her UNO cards and that annoys her.
Patient: Yeah.
Gardner: You think that's fun?

Patient: Well, not to annoy her, but just—it's fun.

Gardner: Yeah, but is that letting out anger?

Patient: Yeah.

Gardner: Uh hum. And is that a good way to let out anger?

Patient: It's one of the quickest ways.

Gardner: Is it anything like pillows and sharks?

Patient: Oh, no, no, no.

Gardner: Hmmm. It's not?

Patient: No.

Gardner: Why not?

Patient: I don't know. It's just like—I don't know why it's . . .

Gardner (interrupting): Just think about it. Is there any way it could be like pillows and sharks?

Patient: Well, I don't know.

Gardner: Well, think about it. Could it be like pillows and sharks?

Patient: Yeah, it could.

Gardner: How is it like pillows and sharks?

Patient: If I did it enough.

Gardner: Yeah, how is it like pillows and sharks?

Patient: Oh, it isn't. It's just like it takes it [the anger] out for about an hour-and-a-half.

Gardner: Oh, it does take it out for an hour-and-a-half. Pillows and sharks let it out longer or better. Is that what you're saying?

Patient: Yeah.

Gardner: It is not as good as as pillows and sharks.

Patient: Yeah.

Gardner: But it's the same thing, but just not as good. Right?

Patient: Yeah.

Gardner: Sharks are the best, pillows are in the middle, and bothering your sister is the least best. Right?

Patient: Yeah.

Gardner: Is that what you are saying?

Patient: Yes.

Gardner: So what can you do about the hitting your sister thing?

Patient: I don't hit her.

Gardner: Bothering her, annoying her, taking her UNO cards. What can you do about that?

Patient: I don't know why I do it! It's something inside me.

Gardner: Yeah, but what did we just say? What are we talking about now as one of the reasons why you might be doing this?

Patient: I don't know.

Gardner: Well, we just were saying.
Patient: My anger.
Gardner: Yeah. It's another way of getting out anger, like sharks and pillows. It doesn't work as well as sharks and pillows.
Patient: Well, it does get it out for a while.
Gardner: Yeah, so what can you do about that?
Patient: Stop.
Gardner: You see it gets her angry at you. It gets your mommy angry at you, right?
Patient: Yeah.
Gardner: And then everybody is down on you. Right?

Here, rather than appeal to the patient's gaining insight into how his various maneuvers release anger (pillows, sharks, and bothering his sister), I focus on the more mundane element, namely the fact that expressing his anger in these ways alienates his mother and sister. My hope here is that this reminder might increase his motivation to reduce his angry outbursts.

Patient: Yeah.
Gardner: So what will you do about that?
Patient: Stop that and find something else.
Gardner: Like what? What can you try?
Patient: Uh.
Gardner: Why don't you put the dice down on the table. What can you do instead?
Patient: I'm cold.
Gardner: We'll be stopping soon. What can you do instead of hitting your sister?
Patient: Go ride my bike.
Gardner: That's something – ride your bike.
Patient: Just do ramps. Show off.
Gardner: Okay. What can you do about the anger so you won't be so angry?
Patient: That's exactly what I said.
Gardner: Say it again.
Patient: Go ride my bike. Do ramps, show off.
Gardner: Do ramps?
Patient: Yeah.
Gardner: What are ramps?
Patient: That's like little board that's up like that. It goes up like that.

Gardner: You're not on television now. Come over here and show here.

Patient: It goes here. It's a little board like that. It goes up a bit and you drive your bike off it.

Gardner: Oh, you drive your bike off a ramp. Okay, you do ramps and what else? I understand. You ride the bike off a ramp.

Patient: Yeah.

Gardner: And what else can you do instead of hitting your sister?

Patient: Okay, can we get on with the bike—I mean with the game?

Gardner: Just hold it. I want to ask you a question. Is that going to solve the whole problem, just going on a bike instead of hitting your sister? That will help. It's fun to have a bike. You know when you have fun you get less angry? Did you know that?

Patient: Yeah.

Gardner: If you do fun things that are good fun, healthy fun, like riding a bike, doing ramps, or things like that, as long as it's not too dangerous, you get out anger. Huh?

Patient: Yeah. One time. . . .

Gardner (interrupting): You can get out anger, but it's fun stuff and you don't feel as angry when you have fun things.

Patient: Yeah.

Gardner: But what else can you do so you won't have as much anger?

Patient: I don't know.

Gardner: What did we say before?

Patient: Stop thinking that you're big—but you're not going to get big, but stop wishing.

Gardner: Right! Stop wishing. It's not going to help.

Although I was not sure earlier that the patient had really gotten my message about giving up hope on lost causes as a way of reducing anger, it was clear here that he had remembered my message and was repeating it accurately.

Gardner: Okay. Whose chance? It's your chance. Go ahead. We're gonna stop soon, but it's your chance. Go ahead.

Patient: Hey, it was your chance.

Gardner: No, it was just mine on act like a spoiled brat. Go ahead. You go. It's your chance.

Patient: (throws dice)

Gardner: What have you got there?
Patient: Seven.
Gardner: Go ahead.
Patient (counts and moves his pawn): One, two, three, four, five, six, seven.
Gardner: Wait a minute. That says: "Go back two." One, two. Okay, what does your card say?
Patient: I don't like it.
Gardner: Read it.
Patient: I can't read all that.
Gardner: Sure you can. Go ahead.
Patient: "A girl was the only one in the class . . ."
Gardner (helps read the card): "Not . . ."
Patient: "Not . . ."
Gardner: "Invited . . ."
Patient: "Invited to a birthday party. Why do you think she wasn't invited?" Oh, boy!
Gardner: A girl was the only one in the class not invited to a birthday party. Why do you think she wasn't invited?
Patient: Because she wasn't the nicest?
Gardner: Because she wasn't what?
Patient: The nicest.
Gardner: Okay. What was she doing that wasn't nice?
Patient: Throwing paper airplanes and annoying people.
Gardner: Annoying people. Right. And so what happened?
Patient: She wasn't invited.
Gardner: What do you think of that?
Patient: What?
Gardner: Do you think it was right that they didn't invite her?
Patient: Yeah.
Gardner: Would you want someone like that at *your* party?
Patient: No.

Here I was trying to help the patient reduce his antisocial behavior by trying to get him to envision himself in the position of others, those who are the objects of his antisocial behavior.

Gardner: Throwing planes and annoying people? Hmm?
Patient: No.
Gardner: So what could she do about that?
Patient: Stop doing it.
Gardner: Do you do things like that?

Patient: Yeah, I do make paper airplanes, but I don't throw it at people.

Gardner: Okay, but you annoy people.

Patient: Yes.

Gardner: Hmm. Who do you annoy besides your sister?

Patient: I'm cold and I have to go to the bathroom.

Gardner: Okay, we're going to stop the game very soon and then you can go. Can you hold it in just a couple of more minutes?

Patient: Yeah.

Gardner: Okay. Now, who do you annoy?

Patient: My ma.

Gardner: Hh hmm. Give me an example of something you do to annoy her.

Patient: I eat in the living room.

Gardner: And what does she say about that?

Patient: She doesn't like that at all.

Gardner: Why do you that?

Patient: I watch TV while I eat.

Gardner: But why do you do that bad thing? You know it bothers her. Why do you do that—eat in the living room when she doesn't want you to?

Patient: Well, I don't want to, but I just want to watch TV.

Gardner: Yeah, but you do it. You're the boss of yourself. Hmm? You control what you're doing.

Although I am fully appreciative of the power of unconscious processes to control human behavior, I never lose sight of the mechanism of conscious control and appeal to it as much as possible. In the early part of the session I was focusing on unconscious processes, especially the anger that is being released through hitting pillows, drawing sharks, and bothering his sister. This does not preclude my focusing on conscious control to suppress the acting out of anger, unconscious motivating factors notwithstanding.

Patient: Ah, I just hit my funny bone!

Gardner: Okay, listen, we have to stop soon, so I want to ask you. Why do you do that?

Patient: I don't know. It's just like I want to watch TV. I want to watch my favorite show.

Gardner: I think it's like what you do to your sister. You annoy her.

Patient: I don't want to annoy her.

Gardner: But you do. It's the same thing. With your sister you think it in your mind: "I'm gonna to annoy her. I'm gonna take her UNO cards." With your mother, you don't do what she wants you to do and you get the same result. What am I saying here?

Patient: That if you do the same thing, but to a different person, you're gonna only get the same thing.

Gardner: Say it again. I'm not clear what you are saying.

Patient: You heard me.

Gardner: I still don't know if you understood what I said.

Patient: If you do the same thing to a different person, you're going to get the same thing back.

Gardner: Hh hmm. See what I am saying with your sister is that when you annoy her you say: "I'm going to get those UNO cards." You're thinking about it. With your mother, you just don't think about it. You just don't listen to her. You tune her out. You eat food in the living room. You watch your TV. Right?

Patient: Hh hmm.

Gardner: You're just kind of ignoring her. Right?

Patient: Sort of.

Gardner: That still gets her angry. Right?

Patient: Yeah.

Gardner: Hh hmm. Is that a way of letting out your anger?

Patient: Yeah, just . . .(mumbling). . .

Gardner: How is it a way of letting out your anger?

Patient: I don't want to annoy her. It's like something in me.

Gardner: Pardon me.

Patient: It's like something in me. I don't want to annoy her.

Gardner: But you do. That's part of your anger, too. By not doing what people want you to do, that's a way of letting out anger. Did you ever know that?

Patient: Yeah.

Gardner: What am I saying, so I am sure you understand it?

Patient: If you do bad things to somebody, it's another way of letting out your anger.

Gardner: Well, I said something like—that's like your sister. This is something different. If you don't do the things that you're supposed to do. . . .

Patient: Hh hmm.

Gardner: Now what did I say?

Patient: If you don't do the things that you're supposed to do, then . . .(mumbling). . .

Gardner: No, it helps you let out anger.

Patient: Hh hmm. It helps you let out anger.

Gardner: Do you see that?

Patient: Yup!

Gardner: Give me an example of that where not doing what you're supposed to do helps let out anger.

Patient: I can't do that.

Gardner: Hh hmm. You can't give me an example?

Patient: No. Okay, yeah. I will. I'll call. . . .

Gardner: What's that?

Patient: I'll call Helen (patient's sister).

Gardner: You want to call Helen? Why? Wait a minute, wait a minute. Why do you want to call Helen? Stay here. Come on over here.

Patient: I'll call Helen and say: "Come here. I want you to help here. Forget it." That would be letting out my anger.

Gardner: Say that again now. Come over here.

Patient: If I walk out the door and I asked Helen to come up here. . . .

Gardner: Yeah, and why would you do that?

Patient: And I said: "Nah, forget about it. Go back down."

Gardner: Oh, that would bother her. You'd be playing a little game with her. A trick?

Patient: Yeah.

Gardner: Okay, listen. We have to stop here. We're going to have to talk more about this. This last thing I think we have to talk more about. It's a way of getting out anger by *not* doing what people want you to do.

Patient: Hh hmm.

Gardner: Now what's the main thing you learned today? What did you learn today from this game?

Patient: What game?

Gardner: This game. What did you learn?

Patient: Things that you're supposed to do.

Gardner: What things are you supposed to do?

Patient: Be good.

Gardner: And what else did you learn? To be good, that's right. What else?

Patient: Not to get as angry and not think that you're gonna stop wishing that you can't be tall.

Gardner: And if you stop wishing about being tall, what would happen?

Patient (practically whispers): I have to go to the bathroom bad.

Gardner: Okay, you have to go to the bathroom bad?
Patient: (Nods affirmatively)
Gardner: Okay, let's just say good-bye. Okay?
Patient: Good-bye.
Gardner: Good-bye everybody. This is the end of the game of August 18—sorry, August 26, 1988. Good-bye. All right. Let's count up who wins. I think you win. One, two, three, four, five, six, seven, eight, nine, and I have six. You are the winner. Congratulations. (Patient grasps therapist's hand and squeezes hard.) Wow, what a muscle! Okay, go to the bathroom and come right back. Okay.

Although there was a somewhat piecemeal incorporation of my messages, some of them did indeed get through. In subsequent sessions similar themes were emphasized, and they contributed to an improvement in the patient's behavior. This session was presented in its entirety. It provides the reader with a good example of a typical session, not a fragment in which only the most dramatic moments are recorded. It was selected for placement here because it provides a good example of the relationship between power and self-esteem. Ralph was compensating for the feelings of low self-worth he suffered in association with his growth hormone deficiency by a macho stance and antisocial behavior. Although his anger, in part, related to his father's abandonment, its release also served to enhance Ralph's self-worth because antisocial acting out gives one a sense of control and power. However, like all psychopathological mechanisms, it ultimately defeats its purpose because the alienation the individual ultimately suffers results in the lowering of self-esteem.

SEVENTEEN
ANGER INHIBITION

In this chapter I focus only on a narrow aspect of anger inhibition, namely, its effect on self-worth. As mentioned, inhibition in self-assertion lowers self-worth. When such inhibition produces ongoing frustration, anger inevitably results. Children who are smoldering with pent-up hostility for not standing up for their rights have little respect for themselves. They derogate themselves because of their passivity, and their suppressed anger interferes with feelings of self-satisfaction. Associated thoughts include "Why did I let him get away with that?" "What an idiot I was for not doing something?" and "That was one of the stupidest things I did, not telling him off." Obviously, all of these self-denigratory thoughts lower feelings of self-worth.

Although depression, in the adult sense, is not too common in childhood, it certainly does exist. Children are generally happier, more optimistic, and less weighted down than adults by the responsibilities of the adult world. Children who live in deprived environments may very well become depressed. By *deprived* I am not only referring to socioeconomic deprivation, but emotional deprivation that may exist even in the most affluent homes. Such children could justifiably be considered to be suffering with reactive depressions. Those children who are depressed because of psychological problems, especially in-trapsychic problems having nothing to do with the environment, may be so, in part, because of the repression of hostility. Such children, like their adult counterparts, are inhibited in overtly expressing their resentments. They turn their anger inward against themselves (a safer target), and self-flagellation and self-disparagement result in significant lowering of self-esteem. The therapeutic goal here is to help such children direct their hostility toward the appropriate source, so that the irritations that are engendering the anger can be more effectively handled. Children who are preoccupied with self-denigrating thoughts and filled with pent-up rage, are not likely to concentrate well in school, and their performance is likely to be compromised. This, in itself, contributes to feelings of low self-esteem. In addition, the feelings of low self-worth that result from their self-flagellation may spread to compromise their optimism, their self-assertion, and curiosity—problems that will then serve to compromise their school performance even further.

There is a component of anger release that serves to com-pensate for feelings of low self-worth. When a person is angry, adrenalin is being secreted in higher concentrations into the blood stream. The physiological fight reaction is being mobilized, with its associated feeling of strength and power. I am not claiming that this is purely an ego-enhancing experience, espe-cially when the anger is a manifestation of overreaction and compensation for feelings of impotence. But even then, there is an element of ego-enhancement associated with the expression of anger, the concomitant negative effects on self-esteem notwith-standing. This ego-enhancement can sometimes enable people to provide embarrassing material about themselves that they might not otherwise reveal. It is as if the esteem enhancement that is produced by the anger compensates for the esteem lowering that results from the revelation. In his discussion of the antisocial adolescent, Holmes (1964) states: "If given the opportunity to rear up on his hind legs a little, he is able to confide much information about himself without experiencing the serious loss in self-esteem which would come from submitting helplessly to an omnipotent adult and poring out his heart like a baby." Holmes continues: "When arguing, he is able to reveal things about himself which he could not possibly speak of in a quiet, expository tone." However, Holmes also recommends that the therapist, in response, argue with the patient: "Getting into arguments with the adolescent, patient or not, is both inevitable and useful. It does not signify either a loss of dignity for the therapist or a disruptive lapse in treatment."

Although I am in agreement that adolescents may need anger to reveal themselves, I am not in agreement that therapists do well to argue with their angry adolescent patients. Although such arguments may prolong the period of the adolescent's self-revelatory anger, I believe that arguing with the adolescent does produce a "loss of dignity for the therapist." A therapist's arguing implies that the therapist has some strong need to convince the adolescent that the therapist is right and the youngster is wrong. Such responsive arguing suggests that the therapist's self-esteem will be lowered if the adolescent is not convinced of the wisdom of the therapist's position. However, a therapist's arguing would be justifiable in a situation where the therapist does indeed have something to lose if the argument is not won, such as the situation in which there is a threat to the therapist's life, property, etc. But under those circumstances meaningful therapy may no longer be possible.

EIGHTEEN
PARENTAL OVERPROTECTION AND OVERVALUATION

PARENTAL OVERPROTECTION

In this chaper I focus on parental overprotection of a child as it affects self-esteem. I emphasize the implications of such self-esteem lowering on the child's educational process. As mentioned, any influence that compromises school performance has a negative effect on self-esteem and intensifies problems in that realm.

Overprotected children inevitably suffer with feelings of low self-worth. They do not develop the talents and skills necessary to function independently. They inevitably compare themselves unfavorably with their peers, who are much more capable of doing things on their own. Others walk to school alone; they must go with their mothers. Others are allowed to swim in the deep water; they are not. Others are allowed to venture forth from their homes with much greater frequency than the overprotected child. Others are permitted sleepover dates; they are not. Others attend day camp; they do not. Later, others go to sleepaway camp; again they are deprived of this important growth experience. Low self-esteem is intrinsically associated with low self-confidence, and this cannot but compromise the child's academic performance.

There are parents who, under the guise of helping their children with their homework, actually do it for them. They point out the youngster's mistakes or screen the homework beforehand so that the child can be assured of handing in perfect papers. Such a parent is seriously undermining the child's development of a strong sense of self-worth. Such children cannot possibly enjoy a feeling of mastery if they have not indeed "mastered" the subject. Such parents would do their children a service if they were to pull back, ask the child if he (she) is sure that the homework is now correct, and recognize that the lowered feeling of self-worth that comes from a poor grade will ultimately serve the child well in the future. It is likely that the child will then become more vigilant with regard to reviewing the homework in order to protect himself (herself) from future such disappointments. Parents with a thick enough skin to do this do their children a great service. A few poor grades ultimately do far more for such children's self-esteem than all their A's in homework — high grades that were obtained by significant parental assistance. The low marks may mobilize such youngsters to learn on their own, whereas their high marks, essentially obtained by their parents, may cripple them educationally.

The preferable attitude for parents to take is to view the child's homework as primarily a matter between the child and the teacher. I am not saying here that younger children shouldn't be reminded to do their work. Nor am I saying that parents shouldn't utilize such mechanisms as "You can't watch television until you finish your homework." I am only saying that the parent should not be the one who actually does the homework or screens it to such a degree that the child is assured of perfect marks. The parent should be available to help the child, but in ways that stimulate the youngster's own efforts and encourage enthusiasm. Parents should help children figure things out for themselves rather than figure things out for them. The principle is best described in an old proverb that goes something like this: "If you give a man a fish, you have provided him with a meal. If you teach him *how* to fish, you have given him a meal for life." Similarly, the father who makes models for his son so that they "look better" is sabotaging the child's attempt to gain a feeling of self-confidence. The mother who cannot allow her daughter to cook her own rather mediocre cookies and interferes so that they "come out better" robs the child of an important growth experience. Such children may become psychologically paralyzed. They become incapable of performing up to their age level in many areas, they cannot help but compare themselves unfavorably with their peers, and they inevitably suffer from feelings of inadequacy.

PARENTAL OVERVALUATION

Some parents subscribe to the dictum: "If my child says it or does it, it must be okay, it must be right." They may believe that most forms of psychopathology are the result of society's suppression of natural thoughts and feelings; the healthy child is one who has achieved "self-actualization" and expresses his (her) "true self."

Children in these families are likely to develop a host of difficulties in a world that is not going to indulge them in the way their parents have. They are not taught internal controls and limits, which are so important to learn in order to function well with others. They become self-indulgent and are likely to be a source of irritation to others. Having been brought up to believe that whatever thoughts or feelings arise within them must be "right" and "good," they may become distrustful of others and attempt to rely on themselves in situations with which they are ill equipped to deal. This will produce feelings of inferiority as they cannot cope at an age-appropriate level with life's problems. Children with the delusion that they can say or do no wrong are not likely to win the affection of their peers. They will view them as "know-it-alls" and as individuals who cannot be relied upon to cooperate and be sensitive to the feelings and thoughts of others. The rejection and alienation they suffer lessens further their self-respect.

In the classroom, especially, these children are likely to have difficulty. At home, such a child may have come to believe that he (she) is "king (queen) of the world." In the classroom, however, the child is not going to enjoy such status. Such children, therefore, might find the egalitarianism of the classroom intolerable. They become demanding and self-indulgent and find intolerable the fact that the teacher treats them just like everyone else. The resentments and dissatisfactions so engendered distract the child from the learning process. In some cases these children do seduce the teacher into treating them with special regard. However, the enhanced sense of self-importance that they may then enjoy is more than compensated for by the negative feedback of their peers, who view them as "privileged characters" and as "teacher's pets." And such epithets cannot but contribute to the child's feeling of low self-worth.

THE MUTUAL STORYTELLING TECHNIQUE

The mutual storytelling technique can be useful in helping children deal with parental overprotection and overvaluation problems that affect their self-esteem.

Charles, an eight-and-a-half-year-old boy, was referred for treatment because of severe immaturity problems. He spoke in a whining, sing-song manner, and had no friends other than occasional contacts with children three years younger than himself. Charles had no sense of responsibility regarding his schoolwork and household chores. He cried easily, and tried to cover his deficiencies in patent falsehoods. His mother was extremely overprotective. To her, Charles could do no wrong. This attitude, in part, was a reaction to the father's attitude, which was basically that Charles could do no right. He often berated his son with comments like "You're just a baby" and "Why can't you be like the other kids?"

When I first saw Charles I was informed that his mother was dying of leukemia. (This treatment took place at a time when anti-leukemia drugs were much less effective than they are now.) During the first few months of Charles's treatment we focused on his dealing with his mother's forthcoming demise. Unfortunately, she did pass away during his fourth month of treatment. Charles told this story about six months after his mother's death.

Patient: Can you help me?

Gardner: Well, all right, I'll help you start the story and then when I point my finger at you, you say exactly what comes to your mind.

Once upon a time a long, long, time ago in a distant land far, far, far away there lived a – –

Patient: Car.

Gardner: And this car – –

Patient: Helped all the people cross the street. It was like a mechanic. Then one day the car went into a crash. Its name was Auto. So all the lights were broken and the children didn't know how to cross the street. So they all got sad. So a man fixed Auto's car and they were back to normal.

And the lesson of that story is: You should always know how to cross the street because when you go to school you're going to have to cross the street and if nobody's helping you, oh, you're in a lot of trouble.

The car named Auto represents the patient's mother who had died six months previously. She had been his "guiding light" and, as the story demonstrates, when she dies in an automobile accident in which the car's lights are broken, the children are left without guidance—"they don't know how to cross the street." Although there is a magic restoration of the car—a reflection of the boy's wish that his mother be alive again—the moral reveals his understanding—from messages imparted in previous stories—that one cannot fully depend upon others. One must develop the ability to handle many of life's situations oneself, or else "you're in a lot of trouble."

With this understanding of the patient's story, I told mine:

Once upon a time there were these kids and these kids used to depend a lot on a certain car. That car did a lot of things for them. It used to take them to different places, even to short distances where they could really walk or ride their bike, and it would often light their way across the street, even when it wasn't that dark. And this car thought it was doing these kids a favor by doing all these things for these kids, but then the kids gradually realized that this car wasn't doing them very much of a favor because they weren't learning to do things on their own. If it was going to light the streets for them all the time and take them to places when they could walk by themselves, they might not be able to walk as well on their own. And if it was going to drive them everywhere, it wouldn't help them in that they would not know the ways to get different places and wouldn't have the practice of doing it on their own. So gradually they decided only to use the car in emergency situations and they felt much better about themselves after that, because they had learned to do these things on their own.

And the lesson of that story is that when you learn to do something on your own you feel very good about yourself. But, on the other hand, if you depend on somebody else to do things for you, it may be more comfortable, but you really don't feel good about yourself.

Did you understand what the story was about? What did you understand the lesson of that story to be?

Patient: Well, it was like when somebody who always crossed you and they die, then you have to learn to do it all by yourself. You feel good if you learn to do things by yourself.

Gardner: That's right! You feel much better about yourself if you've learned to do things on your own.

In my story I referred to the mother's overprotectiveness: the car would carry children distances that were short enough for them to walk; it would light their way across the street even when it wasn't dark. The children become aware of the paralyzing dependency that the car's favors threaten. They decide to do much more on their own, and they feel "much better about themselves." I stressed the important relationship between competence and self-esteem. My moral reiterates the same message.

It is of interest that, although in my story there is no mention of the mother's death and her symbolization as the car, Charles introduced these elements in his story following mine. Although they reveal his appreciation of my communications, his general involvement in therapy was minimal after the immediate problems related to his mother's death were worked through and therapy was prematurely terminated.

THE TALKING, FEELING, AND DOING GAME

The next clinical example, an extended vignette from *The Talking, Feeling, and Doing Game*, demonstrates a number of the points that

I have made in this section. It is taken from the therapy of Frank, a ten-year-old boy who came into treatment because of erratic commitment to education and disruptive behavior at home. He was highly intelligent and could easily have been an excellent student. However, he only intermittently dedicated himself to his studies, and high grades were sporadic. At home he was excessively argumentative, and this was a frequent source of frustration to his parents.

In his early childhood his parents, especially his father, were indulgent toward Frank. This was partly related to his overvaluation of his firstborn child. It was almost as if Frank could do no wrong. In addition, the father enjoyed Frank's rebellious behavior and through it derived vicarious gratification of his own inclination for such rebellion. The father had been somewhat rebellious in his own earlier years during the late 60s and early 70s, but never to the point where he got into serious difficulty. In addition, an inordinate amount of attention was centered on Frank by his parents and extended family members. Such pampering and indulgence resulted in Frank's having very low tolerance for the usual restrictions of school and other constraints that became appropriate as he grew older.

Frank's self-esteem was very low. It was very difficult for him to tolerate even the mildest criticism, and he was ever defensive about discussing his difficulties. He always had an explanation—often quite elaborate and ingenious—to justify his behavior, no matter how inappropriate. At times he would make up stories about experiences he never had, or would exaggerate those that he did, in order to compensate for his feelings of low self-worth. Another way in which he would compensate for his feelings of inferiority was to denigrate his parents (both of whom were quite competent people).

As mentioned, Frank was quite bright. In addition, he was quite creative in his use of the English language. His capacity to formulate clever similes and metaphors was unique for a child of ten. These would sometimes have a humorous quality. The vignette presented here demonstrates these qualities, as well as a number of the points I have made regarding techniques for enhancing children's self-worth.

Gardner: Today is Wednesday, the 10th of November, 1982, and I am happy to welcome you once again to Dr. Gardner's program. Sit back, relax. Our guest and I are playing *The Talking, Feeling, and Doing Game.* Go ahead, what does your card say?

Patient: "One night, while at camp, a boy wet his bed. How did he feel when he woke up in the next morning?" He probably felt soggy and . . .

Gardner (interrupts): He felt what?

Patient: His pants probably felt soggy—whatever he was wearing and when he got up he probably felt very uncomfortable, and a little embarrassed.

Gardner: Uh huh. You know, my guess would be that that boy didn't listen to his parents and others and his doctor maybe who told him that he shouldn't drink any fluids after supper. A lot of kids . . .

Patient: Or it could be that the counselors told him to go in the bushes, but . . .

Gardner: Just before he went to sleep.

Patient: That's right.

Gardner: Yeah. And what happened was that he said, "Man, nothing's going to happen. I don't have to listen to them." So he didn't go in the bushes, and he drank a lot of water before he went to sleep, and as a result of that he wet. And he had himself to blame for his own embarrassment the next morning when all the kids knew that he had wet and there was this terrible smell over everything. So he was really sorry that he hadn't listened to the others about not drinking water before going to sleep.

Feelings of embarrassment inevitably contribute to feelings of low self-worth. In this interchange I emphasized the principle that there are things one can often do to protect oneself from suffering embarrassment and the associated feeling of low self-esteem.

Gardner: My card says, "What is one of the stupidest things a person can do. Show someone doing that thing." Well, I would say that one of the stupidest things a person can do is not to think in advance about what he or she is doing, about not thinking about consequences. Do you know what consequences are?

Patient: Yeah.

Gardner: What are consequences?

Patient: When something good happens after you do something.

Gardner: Well, sometimes, but it's often just the opposite! Consequences would be like if you don't study for a test the next day . . .

Patient: You suffer the consequences.

Gardner: You suffer the consequences. You get a poor grade. That's consequences. Or if you rush through your homework. So that would be a consequence. Now a consequence is one of the things that happens as a result of something else. If you study hard, the consequence is that you get a good grade and you feel good about yourself. That's a consequence. And I would say that one of the stupidest things a person can do is not to think about consequences, not to think ahead about what the results are going to be the next day or afterwards when you do something wrong. Then you get into all kinds of trouble. That's consequences. Some people say, "We'll worry about tomorrow when tomorrow comes." And I would say that's a pretty stupid thing to do because then you get into all kinds of trouble.

Patient: Uh hmm.

Gardner: Like, for instance, if there's a rule, you know, you don't cross against a red light. What are one of the consequences if you ignore a red light?

Patient: You die.

Gardner: You might get killed by a car. Right, right! So that's a stupid thing to do, not to think about consequences. Okay. So what does your card say?

My response does not directly relate to self-esteem issues. However, it is indirectly relevant in that appreciation of untoward consequences can motivate one to do that which is in one's best interests. Doing what is best for oneself generally enhances self-worth, and doing the opposite usually brings about a lowering of self-esteem.

Patient: "Tell about something that is very good to do. Make believe you're doing that thing." Well, a thing that is very good to do with my mother and father would be to get an honors, or a very good mark on a test or suffer the consequences. You get the consequences.

Gardner: I see, you enjoy the consequences.

Patient: Yes, my mother and father would feel good and be proud of me.

Gardner: All right, now, tell me. One of the results of that— one of the consequences of that—is that your mother and father would feel good. Okay? Could you name two other consequences of that—two other results of that?

Patient: I would . . .(mumbles) . . .

Gardner: What?

Patient: I'd probably go to a video parlor.

Gardner: Well, I wasn't thinking of that. But that would be one, too, if they got you a present for doing well. But I was thinking of something else, something about how *you'd* feel.

Patient: I'd be extremely happy.

Gardner: You'd be happy. You'd be proud! Right?

Patient: Yeah.

Gardner: Right. And any other consequences or results?

Patient: I don't know.

Gardner: I could think of *one* other.

Patient: Tell me what?

Gardner: You would learn more, which is what school is all about in the first place. Right?

Patient: Hh hmm.

Gardner: You'd have more information and more knowledge right. You'd be a smarter person. Hmm?

Patient: Yes.

Gardner: So there would be other consequences in that. Okay, you get a chip.

The patient spoke about the ego-enhancement he would enjoy if his mother and father were to be proud of an academic accomplishment. When I asked him about other benefits to be derived from doing well in school, his first response was that he would be taken to a video parlor. Although such a promise might enhance school motivation, I generally discourage it because it does not focus on the gratifications to be gained from learning in its own right. Rather, it focuses on some external reward and thereby misses an important point regarding the purposes of education.

I then asked the patient to direct himself to some internal rewards or consequences of his doing well in school. He responded that he would be happy. I agreed with that and added that he would be proud. I specifically used the word *proud* in order to focus on the esteem enhancement that he would enjoy from doing good work in school. I then went on to focus on the value of knowledge in its own right and how smart a person can feel after acquiring knowledge. This too can enhance self-esteem.

Gardner: My question is, "What is your favorite food? Why do you like that food? Make believe you're eating that food." Well, my favorite food is chocolate ice cream. So why do I like that food? I like that food because it's very sweet and I like the flavor of chocolate and it's cold and just very good. Make believe you're eating that food (imitates eating ice cream). However, with chocolate ice cream, like many other good things in life . . .

Patient (interrupts): It will melt.

Gardner: What?

Patient: Melts.

Gardner: It melts. Sure, if you eat it in the sun it will melt. If you're foolish enough to walk around with this ice cream in the hot sun, you'll have it all over your hands. But I have to—with chocolate ice cream—I've got to fight temptation. Do you know what fighting temptation means?

Patient: Yeah, it means you want it so bad that you can eat it by the gallons, but you can also get sick.

Gardner: Right!

Patient: Then you'll pay the bad consequences and they'll bring you to the hospital.

Gardner: What are the bad consequences?

Patient: Teeth fall out.

Gardner: Okay, and you get . . .

Patient: Cavities.

Gardner: Cavities, yes.

Patient: You can get a little sick.

Gardner: Well, sometimes. You'd probably get a little sick if you ate too much.

Patient: You'd get sugar diseases.

Gardner: What are the sugar diseases?

Patient: I don't know.

Gardner: All right, you get fat, and when you get fat one of the things that will happen is the arteries in your body get clogged up and get fat. And then you get things like strokes and heart attacks, and it just puts a strain on your heart to be fat. That's another consequence of eating too much. So you've got to fight temptation and not do all the things you'd like to do, because then you may have future consequences. Okay. Okay, what does your card say?

Here again, my response does not directly relate to self-esteem problems, but it does have some indirect relevance. Physical disease is extremely ego-debasing. Protecting oneself from the development of such diseases thereby protects one's feelings of self-worth. Such "preventive medicine" often involves self-discipline and fighting temptation.

> *Patient:* "If you could change your age, how old would you want to be? Why?" Well, I'd want to be about 18.
> *Gardner:* 18?
> *Patient:* Yes, 18.
> *Gardner:* Well, why 18?
> *Patient:* Well, one is because I'd get my driver's license and two, I'd go to college, which I think is a lot of fun.
> *Gardner:* Hh hmm. A lot of fun.
> *Patient:* Yeah, I hear people say, "It's great, great. You should go, go." They say, "It's great. It's great. You should go." That's what my mom says.
> *Gardner:* Oh, it's great.
> *Patient:* Yeah.
> *Gardner:* Uh huh. Well, what are the other great things about college? You say it's a lot of fun.
> *Patient:* Yeah, you get to take the subjects you want to learn.
> *Gardner:* You get to take the subjects you want. That's right. That's a good thing about college.
> *Patient:* You get to mail letters. You get some cards and packages from your parents.
> *Gardner:* Cards and packages from your parents. Right. But you could also learn a lot of interesting things there as well.
> *Patient:* Maybe I'd like to be 12. I think I'd like to be 12 because I'd be graduating from my school, not for the fact that I don't like the school, but for the fact that I'd like to graduate.
> *Gardner:* You'd like to graduate?
> *Patient:* That's right. Like you ask someone when you go to medical school, you're anxious to graduate from medical school.
> *Gardner:* Because?
> *Patient:* You can get your . . . you become a doctor.
> *Gardner:* What are your career plans at this point? Some kids at your age have some ideas. Do you have any idea on what you want to do when you grow up?

Patient: Hmmm, I might want to become a lawyer. Some people say, "You'd be a good lawyer. You'd be a good lawyer."

Gardner: Why do they say you'd be a good lawyer?

Patient: Because I like a fight. That doesn't change my mind.

Gardner: Yeah, you really hang in there, huh?

Patient: Yeah.

Gardner: If you were a lawyer, and I needed a lawyer, I would seriously consider you. I don't know how you'll turn out, but you have one quality that is good for a lawyer to have and that is you'd fight to the end, you know, and take the case to the Supreme Court if necessary. Right?

Patient: Yeah.

Gardner: Uh, huh. But there's another quality of yours that I think you have, another talent, another skill, that might serve you well if you were a lawyer or would serve you in other professions as well. Do you know what I'm talking about?

Patient: No.

Gardner: Oh, think about how I've complimented you on a number of occasions.

Patient: Brain?

Gardner: Something to do with the brain, right.

Patient: Smart?

Gardner: Smart. It's a kind of smartness.

Patient: I don't know.

Gardner: Well, you have a capacity to select word combinations that are unique and good writers have that, where they just pick the right word that gets a certain flavor across. It's not the usual word for something. It's an unusual way of saying something which adds a certain color and adds a . . .

Patient (interrupts): Picture.

Gardner: Picture, yes, in that it's better than the words one might generally use. So it would add to the attractiveness and the interest on the part of any reader if you were to choose to do any kind of writing. Do you know what I'm talking about?

Patient: Yeah.

Gardner: Could you give me an example from your own memory of that kind of talent?

Patient: Well, I can't think.

Gardner: Try to. Try to give me an example of how you use an *unusual* word which says better than the *usual* word what you want to say.

Patient: Well, I guess as you say that I have that talent, then I must have had that talent in the first grade because I've used those words now.

Gardner: Can you think of an example?

Patient: Yeah, well when I was in second grade our teacher showed us how to make a bookmark, and so I wrote a small, short book on space travel. Not fact, but you know, stories about people that go to space.

Gardner: Yeah.

Patient: I made a book about them and the teacher said it had very big words.

Gardner: Do you remember an example? I do very well with examples. I told you that. I'm the kind of person who . . .

Patient (interrupts): What's examples? Like specifics.

Gardner: Yes, specific examples do better for me. I understand something better when I have a specific example. Otherwise I sometimes get confused about what the person is talking about.

Patient: I guess an example that I found is instead of saying . . . I can't think of one.

Gardner: Let's hear from your father. See if he can give us an example.

Father: I can't think of one off-hand. There are so many.

Gardner: Uh huh. You can't think of any at this point?

Patient: It's hard to think of one.

Gardner: I've seen them on a number of occasions. I remember once you were describing your father. I remember one, when you were talking about your father, how mighty and strong he was, and you were saying something about how the seas rolled back or something when he was around. The mighty . . .

Patient (interrupts): I said that he thinks that when he tells the sea to roll back, it has to roll back. And that's an example of telling me that and telling you that he thinks he has a lot of power!

Gardner: Hh hmmm. Right.

Patient: And he has the power of making his own rules for the world, and making the sea listen to him is going to take a lot. In Greek myths when Hercules pointed with the arrow that had been dipped in the poisonous bull's throat and said, "If you don't calm your waves down, I'll shoot the arrow at you."

Gardner: Who was he talking to there?

Patient: Hercules was commanding the sea.

Gardner: Oh, and he was going to shoot this arrow at the sea.

Patient: That was because this arrow had a tip that was dipped—when Hercules killed a certain kind of animal he dipped the arrow in the animal's blood, which was still poisonous. If he shot it at the sea, the whole sea would die.

Gardner: Okay, so what happened?

Patient: So the sea rolled back.

Gardner: I see, the sea was scared.

Patient: That's right. And I guess when my Dad read that story he got carried away and thought that if he used his powerful big voice, he would make the sea roll back.

Gardner: I see. Well, that's the kind of thing that I think gets your messages across in a rich way. It's examples like that.

Father: Otherwise, he'll quote something creatively, like the examples you gave of the boy who lit 15 fires in a row and then there was a 16th fire set. And people didn't know exactly who set the 16th fire. And you asked him, "Who do you think lit the 16th fire?" You used the example when he was denying his involvement in trouble in school in a class where he's been a known troublemaker. And I think most kids would pick the obvious and say it was the same boy. But Frank said, "Better it is for 100 guilty men to go free than one innocent man be convicted." Now he's quoting somebody else, but he quoted it absolutely in context to defend an obscure and indefensible legal position.

Gardner: Frank, do you know what your father is saying?

Patient: Yeah.

Gardner: What is he saying?

Patient: He's saying that I got the message to you that you could be accusing an innocent person. If a lawyer doesn't use that saying—if one lawyer uses that saying, which I don't understand why they don't—he should really do it. I mean he'd say, "You're putting an innocent man in jail." And then he says, "No, I'm not." And then he says, "Oh, yeah. Well, someone once said, 'It's better that 100 men go to jail than to put one innocent man in jail.'" I mean that would really be terrible.

Gardner: Right, but what you see I was saying to you is that if a person lights 15 fires and then a new fire breaks out, the first person that they're going to think did it is the one who set the previous 15. That's why I was saying that if you do a certain thing—we were talking about something you were doing that caused trouble—

Patient (interrupts): It's like the boy . . . (mumbles) . . .

Gardner: What's that?

Patient: It's like the boy who howled wolf.

Gardner: Right, right. So that the person who has been convicted of that crime previously tends to be under high suspicion when the same thing happens again. And then you came up with this old saying, "May 100 guilty men go free than convict one innocent man." That's the kind of creative thinking that you have that I think you should know about. This is a talent and skill that might serve you well.

Father: This is also what we were talking about. Frank says the story is about the boy who howled wolf. It's not exactly accurate. Actually, it's about the boy who *cried* wolf, but Frank changes it creatively.

Gardner: Cried wolf, right.

Patient: I prefer howled wolf.

Gardner: Okay, that's a good way of putting it. He howled wolf. That's another example of what we're talking about.

Patient: Or the wolf howled boy!

Gardner: Or the wolf howled boy?

Patient: Yes, the wolf howled boy. That's in *my* story book.

Gardner: Oh, you changed that story?

Patient: I've changed a lot of stories.

Gardner: Did you change that one to the wolf howling boy?

Patient (nodding affirmatively): Uh huh.

Gardner: How did you change the story?

Patient: In the other way around, there was a pack of wolves and there was a boy who came around to bother them. So the wolf kept on howling, "Boy, boy," exactly the other way around.

Gardner: And what happened when the wolf howled, "boy"?

Patient: Well, the first time the boy wasn't there. The second time he wasn't there. The third time he *was* there.

Gardner (interrupts). Wait a minute. The third time the *boy* was there?

Patient: That's right. The boy was dangerous now because he had a shotgun. You get it?

Gardner: Then the wolf howls "boy," but there's not a boy there.

Patient: That's right. Then he howls, then he howls again a few days later and there's no boy there. He howls a third time and everybody didn't believe him that the boy wasn't there, but he was, and the boy killed him with a shotgun.

Gardner: I see. Okay. That's another creative variation. Okay. Very good. Why don't we stop on this question. Whose question was this anyway?

Patient: Mine.

Gardner: It was your question. Okay, you get a chip.

This segment demonstrates well the point I have made so many times previously that the therapist does best, when attempting to enhance a child's feelings of self-worth, to point out specific areas of competence. I had mentioned at the outset that Frank had creative talent with regard to writing ability as well as his capacity for utilizing simile, metaphor, and allegory. The interchange demonstrates well this capacity. When he himself was not capable of providing an example, I asked his father to do so. His father's contribution here is an excellent example of the value of a parent working as my "assistant therapist." In addition, when the patient himself was unable to come up with examples of his creativity, I did so.

Gardner: Okay, my question is, "Of all the places in the world, where would you like to live the most? Why?" You said you know what I'm going to say?

Patient: Yeah.

Gardner: Okay, what am I going to say?

Patient: Where you live right now, probably.

Gardner: Okay, and why am I going to say that? What do you recall?

Patient: Because you're happy where you live.

Gardner: Uh huh. Okay.

Patient: This is your question.

Gardner: It's my question, but you remember the answer. So I just wanted to know if you remembered the answer. I agree with you that the place I live in now is Tenafly, which I like very much. And the reasons I like it is, on the one hand, it's a kind of civilized community. It's pleasant, it's pretty, and it's relatively safe and the air is fairly clean, and yet it's close enough to places in New York where there are museums, where there are universities, and a lot of people who are interested in learning. So it gives me an opportunity to be near great centers of learning, which I like very much. Also, those places have a lot of people who are interesting. And I like that too. I like to live in a place where there are a lot of people who are interested in learning and discovering things. That's why I like to live where I am. Do you want to say anything about that?

Patient: No.

Gardner: Okay. All right, so let's count up. Wait I forgot to take a couple of chips. How many chips do you have?

Patient: Three.

Gardner: Is it a tie score? I think so.

> *Patient:* Yeah, just about.
> *Gardner:* Okay, let's say good-bye. Good-bye.
> *Patient:* Good-bye.

I used the card in this session to talk about some of the important reasons I have chosen to live where I do. I emphasized my fascination with learning and my enjoyment of people who have similar interests. I believe that the acquisition of knowledge is ego-enhancing and my hope here was that some of this attitude would filter down to Frank. I believe that he was a receptive audience in that, his problems with school performance notwithstanding, he was a boy who genuinely enjoyed learning and was proud of the talent and skills previously described.

NINETEEN
VALUES AND ETHICS

DEFINITION OF TERMS

I use the word *values* to refer to what a particular culture or society considers to be good and bad, that is, valuable and not valuable. I use the word *ethics* to refer to one subdivision of values, that is, the things we consider good and bad in our relationships with others, what we consider ethical and unethical. There are therapists who state that their treatment does not involve in any way the imposition of their own values on their patients. This is at best naive and at worst a lie. Therapy involves an attempt to change a person's behavior. If a therapist starts with the assumption that behavior A is inappropriate, unacceptable, or sick (euphemisms for "bad"), that is a value judgment. If the therapist is going to try to change behavior A to behavior B, then that therapist is making the assumption that behavior B is more acceptable, appropriate, and healthy (euphemisms for "good"). All this is inextricably loaded with values. If the therapist believes that substituting the word *sick* for *bad* and the word *healthy* for *good* removes the treatment from the realm of value imposition, then that therapist is very much out of touch with the reality of what is going on in the process.

Ethics refer to standards of conduct and practice. I will use the words *ethics* and *morals* interchangeably, although some would make a distinction between the two. Morals often have a broader implication, referring to the accepted customs of conduct and right living in a society and to the individual's practice in relation to these, for example, *the morals of a civilization.* Ethics often refers to high standards of honest and honorable dealings in a profession or business, for example, the ethics of the legal profession. Because these distinctions are often not made, I will use the terms interchangeably.

I use the word *virtue* to refer to those thoughts and deeds (values and ethics) that the individual's culture or society considers admirable. Virtues, then, are those values and ethics that are considered "good." People who have accepted these values, who have the deep conviction that they are estimable, and who incorporate these principles into their daily living will feel good about themselves when they conform with them and bad about themselves when they do not. Thus the ancient wisdom: "Virtue is it's own reward." Accordingly, values, ethics, and virtue all relate directly to self-esteem.

For example, giving to others is an activity that most children learn is a "good" thing to do. Children, however, are not famous for their spontaneous generosity. As they grow older, however, they can gradually come to incorporate this value if they see their parents genuinely get some pleasure from giving (not merely preaching it). If the parents have been successful in engendering this value in their children, generosity in itself can then provide them with feelings of satisfaction about themselves and contribute significantly to the enhancement of self-esteem. This does not mean that the children's inner gratification in performing a benevolent act cannot be heightened by the praise of others—a totally natural desire. However, if the need for praise and external appreciation is the main motivation, then the giving is done for purposes of self-aggrandizement and the enhanced self-esteem so produced may be specious. Also, people who give because they feel they must suffer to be appreciated have little chance of deriving any enduring sense of self-worth from their giving.

Living in accordance with the values of one's culture can provide an individual with deep-seated feelings of self-worth. But giving is only one of many such values in our culture, and each society has its own values. This is what I believe is being referred to by the "Virtue-is-its-own-reward" concept. Although the proverb is considered cliché and trite to many, it has great validity nevertheless. The basic tenets upon which values rest are laid down in childhood. It is then that parents, through example and word, can impart principles that may provide the child with important ego gratifications and a heightened sense of self-worth, especially if these values are adhered to as the child grows older.

THE THERAPIST'S EDUCATIONAL VALUES

One value in our Western industrialized society that is relevant to the academic situation is educational success. Although not as widespread as I would consider desirable, being a good student is given premium value in many homes. Those who subscribe to this value are more likely to do well in school. Those who subscribe to this value and do not do well in school are likely to feel bad about themselves. Those who do not subscribe to this value will generally not suffer any loss of self-worth if they gain little from their academic experience. The therapist who treats children with psychogenic learning disabilities should be someone who subscribes to the value of education. This is generally true for most people who are therapists because they would not be therapists if they hadn't committed themselves assiduously to the educational process. Unfortunately, there are some therapists who are not deeply committed to the educational experience as a value in its own right. Often this is expressed in subtle forms. They may view education primarily as a stepping stone to a higher paying job. They may be more committed to their patients gaining entrance into prestigious institutions than focusing on what is actually being learned for its own sake. Such compromises in their commitment to the value of education is likely to be filtered down to their patients and interfere with their treatment of children with psychogenic learning disabilities.

Clinical Example

There are many cards in *The Talking, Feeling, and Doing Game* that provide the therapist with the opportunity to impart values supportive of educational pursuit and thereby contribute to the development of high self-esteem.

> *Question:* Make believe you're doing something that makes you happy.
> *Response:* I'm making believe that I'm writing a book. I'm holding the pencil here and I'm writing on this paper. Some people think that writing is just a lot of hard work. There is no question that it is a lot of hard work, especially writing a book. However, it makes me happy to write a book. It's not only while I'm writing it that I feel good—most often, but not all the time—but also when it comes out. It really gives me a good feeling of accomplishment. I can look at the book, hold it in my hand, and know that *I've* written *that book.* Also, it makes me feel good when people compliment me on the book. Of course, there are some people who don't like the book. Although I feel a little bad when I learn about that, I have many more good feelings that come from those who like my books.

There are individuals whose values do not include book learning. As a writer, and as someone who has involved himself in a long educational process (to age 36), I clearly am committed to the notion that education, reading, writing, and book knowledge are "good things." This notion is imparted in my response. As a subscriber to this value, I have gained significant ego gratifications from endeavors that enable me to comply with it. When providing this response, my hope is that the child who is listening will incorporate this value into his (her) psychic structure.

* * *

> *Question:* Make believe you're doing something kind.
> *Response:* I'm making believe I'm a kid in school. I'm a very good student, and the teacher has asked me to help another boy who is not such a good student. I help him once in a while, and it makes me feel very good about myself to see his progress. I'm thinking that I'm a very good teacher or professor, or something

like that. It makes a person feel good when they're of use to others. Kind acts make people feel good.

The value being espoused here is that of helping a less fortunate companion. However, such help is being provided in the academic realm. Accordingly, there is an implicit adherence to the value of education as well. My hope here is that the patient might aspire to the academic level where he (she) might very well be asked by a teacher to tutor another child.

THE WORK ETHIC

People who are committed to the work ethic will enjoy the enhanced sense of self-worth that comes from "a job well done." Those who do not subscribe to this value are not likely to enjoy such gratifications, even though they may (in some cases) receive external recognition. Commitment to the work ethic is *crucial* if a youngster is to succeed in school and enjoy the ego-enhancement that comes from such success. The therapist does well to recognize clearly that school for the child is almost identical to work for the adult. Although there may be minor differences, the overlap is so formidable that for all practical purposes they can be viewed as identical phenomena. School, more than anything else, should prepare the child to function as an independent, self-assertive human being in the adult world. It is not simply what is learned there that serves this goal. It is the attitude toward work, the commitment to it, the curiosity, and the willingness to tolerate discomfort that must be taught in the lower grades if the child is to carry these values into adult life. In games such as *The Talking, Feeling, and Doing Game* and the mutual storytelling technique and its derivative games, the therapist can impart such values symbolically without the child really knowing that reference is being made not only to schoolwork at that point but to future job attitudes.

Clinical Example

The Talking, Feeling, and Doing Game includes many cards that provide the therapist with the opportunity to give responses related to the work ethic. It is important for the reader to appreciate, at the outset, that Harry was particularly resistant to talking directly about his feelings about his mother, her three marriages, and the indignities he suffered at the hands of the three primary men in their life.

> *Question*: What's the best story you ever heard or read? Why?
>
> *Response*: Of all the books that I ever read when I was young, the one that I remember to have been the best was the one describing the life of Thomas A. Edison. As you probably know, Thomas A. Edison was one of the greatest inventors who ever lived. Although he wasn't the only man to work on these things, his inventions were important—giving us the electric light bulb, the phonograph, and the moving picture camera. He was a poor boy who grew up in Ohio. He was a very hard worker and was an extremely curious person. He was immensely interested in how things work.
>
> He had a laboratory near his home in New Jersey, and it is said that he would sometimes work most of the night on his inventions. He loved learning about how things work, and he loved trying to figure out better ways of doing things. To this day, people all over the world use his inventions. To this day, he is remembered as having given us some of our greatest inventions. He must have really felt great about himself because of all the good he did for other people. It was mainly his curiosity and hard work that did these things both for himself and for others. It was Thomas A. Edison who said: "Genius is 1 percent inspiration and 99 percent perspiration." Do you know what that means?

Edison epitomized the gratification and fame that can come to someone who is strongly committed to the work ethic. I emphasize here the great benefit that can come to others from the efforts of a strongly motivated person. My aim is to engender some desire on the youngster's part to view Edison as an admirable figure worthy of emulation and inspiration. Obviously, one such message is not going to achieve this goal. However, the seed is planted and with reiteration over time it is quite possible that Edison will become incorporated into the youngster's psychic structure and join with other introjects to serve as a model for identification and emulation.

Clinical Example

Harry was a boy who had little commitment to the work ethic, not only in school, but with regard to his whole life in general. Harry entered treatment at the age of ten because of acting-out behavior in the classroom. Although very bright, he was doing poorly academically. He did not do his homework and would lie to his parents about his school assignments. He did not pay attention in the classroom; rather, he would whisper, hum, shout out, and disrupt the classroom in a variety of ways. He did not exhibit proper respect for his teachers and his principal. At home, as well, he was a severe behavior problem. He was openly defiant of his mother's and stepfather's authority and did not respond to punishment. In spite of this, Harry had an engaging quality to him. Adults especially found him "a pleasure to talk to." The parents of the few friends he had also found him a very likable and charming boy, and they could not believe that he involved himself in antisocial behavior.

Harry's mother was married three times. He and his sister were the products of her first marriage. His father was a sales representative for a large corporation and had been away from the home frequently during the first two years of Harry's life when his parents had still been living together. When the father was with the infant, he tended to be cool, aloof, and disinterested. Harry's mother was a secretary who began working full-time when Harry was two months of age. He was then left to the care of a series of babysitters, most of whom were unreliable and some of whom were punitive. Unfortunately, both parents tended to ignore the signs of the babysitters' maltreatment.

When Harry was two years old, his parents separated. During the next year he and his sister lived alone with their mother. Following the separation of Harry's parents, there was a custody dispute. Both parents wanted custody, and each claimed to be the superior parent. Harry's father claimed that his wife was promiscuous and, therefore, unfit to take care of the children because she had had a transient affair during the marriage. The trial took place in a rural area in the Midwest, and the judge supported the father's position. After three months with his father, the latter returned the children to the mother with whom they were still living at the time of treatment.

When Harry was three, his mother's man friend moved into the home, and they were married when Harry was four. This was a very stormy relationship, and Harry witnessed many violent battles between his mother and her second husband. In addition, her second husband used corporal punishment to discipline Harry. About two years after he moved into the house, his mother's second husband deserted, and neither the mother nor Harry heard from him subsequently.

When Harry was nine, his mother's third husband moved into the house, and he was the stepfather who was involved at the time Harry began treatment. Like his predecessor, Harry's new stepfather was extremely punitive. He used the strap primarily using the argument, "It was good enough for my father; therefore it's good enough for me." Harry's mother basically encouraged her husband to use the strap on Harry. When I expressed my opinion that, at ten, Harry was much too old for physical punishment and that I did not believe that corporal punishment was serving any purpose for Harry, both parents disagreed. I emphasized to them that it was my belief that they were making Harry worse, not better, and that there was no evidence that such beatings were reducing his antisocial behavior. In fact, I expressed to them my opinion that it was increasing the frequency and severity of his acting out. Again, they would not listen. The following interchange took place while playing *The Talking, Feeling, and Doing Game.*

> *Patient:* "What do you think about a boy who lets his dog make a mess in the house? What should his parents do?" His parents should not let him do what he wants and tell him that if he wants a dog, he's going to have to take care of his messes and everything.
> *Gardner:* And suppose he still doesn't listen?
> *Patient:* Then if he doesn't listen, he's not going to have a dog.
> *Gardner:* Right. And that would be a sad thing. Do you know any other way to do it?

Patient: No.

Gardner: I can't think of one. If he wants to have the fun of a dog, he has to have . . . what's the word?

Patient: . . . the fun of the dog, then he has to take care of the dog.

Gardner: Right!

Patient: If he does not want the fun of the dog, then he is not going to get it.

Gardner: Right! He has to have the responsibility, and he has to do things sometimes he doesn't like. That's how most things are in life. They're a mixture. If you want to get a certain amount of fun, you have to do certain things you don't like sometimes. Do you know anything that's not like that?

Patient: (nods negatively)

Gardner: Well, it's hard to think of something that isn't like that. There's always a mixture.

Okay, my card says, "Of all the things you learn in school, what do you like learning about least? Why?" Well, I don't go to school anymore, but I remember when I was in school the subject that I didn't like very much was economics. Do you know what economics is? What is economics?

Patient: Sort of like a job.

Gardner: Well, it's something like that. It didn't interest me very much, but I knew I had to take that subject if I wanted to pass in high school and in college. You know?

Patient: Yeah.

Gardner: They just required it. Because I wanted to get my diploma and finish up and because I wanted to take the other courses, I knew I had to take it. I had to take the bad with the good. Do you understand?

Patient: Yes.

Gardner: That's something like we were talking about before, that nothing is perfect and everything is a mixture. What do you think about that?

Patient: (nods negatively)

Gardner: You don't like that idea too much?

Patient (without much conviction): It's okay.

Gardner: It's okay. Is there anything like that in your life? Accepting the bad with the good? Do you know of anything in your life that's like that? I do. Do you have to accept bad things with the good things in any part of your life?

Patient: Yeah, I do.

Gardner: Can you give an example from your life of that?

Patient: No.
Gardner: I can think of one.
Patient: What?
Gardner: Your parent's divorce. There are things there where you have to accept the bad with the good. There are things with your parents' divorce that have to do with accepting the bad with the good.
Patient: No.
Gardner: Oh come on, you can think of something.
Patient: I don't want to say it.
Gardner: You don't want to say it. Well, okay. That's too bad. In this game you get chips for answering. Right? Do you feel like playing this game? Okay, because part of the game is to answer the questions. So if you want to get a chip, you have to say something about your parents.
Patient (interrupts): Well, you've got to answer your question. I don't.
Gardner: I answered already. I answered with economics. But I'm giving you a chance to get an extra chip if you can say something about your parents.
Patient: No, I don't want an extra chip.
Gardner: You don't want it. Okay.

One of Harry's problems was that he refused to accept responsibility. He did not want to suffer any discomfort or inconvenience. He fit well into the category of deprived children who live by the pleasure principle because they have never been rewarded with love and affection when they practice self-restraint. I tried to use the examples of the dog and the subject of economics to get across the point that tolerating discomfort is often necessary if one is to enjoy certain benefits. On an intellectual basis, the patient appeared to be somewhat receptive. I then tried to shift into a discussion of the advantages and disadvantages of parental divorce. However, Harry would have no part of the discussion. The lure of the chip reward did not serve as an incentive. Accordingly, I did not pressure him any further and we proceeded with the game.

This interchange with Harry raises an important technical point in the treatment of patients. Some therapists take a very passive position regarding pressuring the patient to speak about a specific subject. They consider this not only respectful of the patient's wishes, but believe that to do otherwise is to invite further resistance to the treatment. They also believe that such urging can be anxiety provoking and that it is antitherapeutic per se. I generally do not pull back so quickly when a patient exhibits manifestations of resistance and/or anxiety when discussing a "touchy subject." I believe to do so might deprive the patient of an important therapeutic experience. Some patients need a little urging and are better off afterward for having experienced the thoughts and feelings attendant to dwelling on the sensitive subject. The therapist cannot know beforehand how much anxiety and resistance will be engendered by suggesting further inquiry into a given area. The therapist should be exquisitely sensitive to whether or not his (her) pressure is producing undue anxiety and/or resistance. If such appears to be the case, it is time to "pull back." Here, I believed that Harry approached that point where he adamantly refused to pursue this subject — even after being informed that he would thereby deprive himself of another chip. He firmly stated, "No, I don't want an extra chip." I got the message, and we proceeded with the game.

> *Gardner:* Let's go on then. My question is, "What do you think your life will be like 20 years from now?" Well, 20 years from now I will . . .
> *Patient* (interrupts): You might be dead in 20 years.
> *Gardner:* Well, how old do you think I am?
> *Patient:* Forty-two.
> *Gardner:* Thank you very much. I appreciate the compliment. No, I'm going to be 50 next month. What do you think of that?
> *Patient:* I thought you were 40 something.
> *Gardner:* I am 40 something. I am 49, I am 49 and 11/12. So twenty years from now I will be 50. (Therapist laughs as he immediately recognizes the slip and its obvious significance.) I really wish I would be fifty. Twenty years from now I will be 70. Do you think I'll be dead?
> *Patient:* Yes.
> *Gardner:* You think so?
> *Patient:* Yes, because my uncle was in the hospital and he died.

Gardner: There are a lot of people who die before 70, and there are many who don't. I certainly hope that I'm still alive.

Patient (speaking with warmth and conviction): So do I.

Gardner: Anyway, if I am alive, and I think I probably will be, I can't be 100 percent sure, I will probably still be a psychiatrist and will be trying to help kids.

Patient: But you will not have me as a subject (sic) because I will be 30 years old.

Gardner: You will be 30 years old? What will you be doing then? I will be doing psychiatry.

Patient: I will be an auto mechanic.

Gardner: An auto mechanic.

Patient: Do I get a chip for that?

Gardner: Okay, you get a chip for that. I hope you will be a *good* auto mechanic, and I hope you have a very *good business.*

Patient: Yeah, so do I. Lots of money!

Gardner: But you have to work very hard at it, you know. Whatever you do, if you're going to goof off, if you're an auto mechanic and you goof off, you're not going to have any customers. People are not going to come back. But if you do a good job, then you'll have many customers. Right?

Patient: (nods affirmatively)

Gardner: Okay. Very good.

One could argue that Harry's thinking I might be dead 20 years from now was definitely a manifestation of hostility. Although I admit this is certainly a possibility (especially because it was preceded by my strongly encouraging him to talk about the touchy subject of his parents' divorce), his comment may have had nothing to do with hostility. It is important to appreciate that Harry was 10 years old and I was mid-to-late middle-aged. Children's appreciation of adults' ages is often limited. Furthermore, his appreciation of the significance of a 20-year advance in my age is also likely to be somewhat distorted. I did not automatically assume that his interjected response reflected hostility. (I do not doubt the possibility either; I only considered it unlikely.)

I did, in the true analytic spirit, ask Harry to guess my age rather than blurt it out. However, in Harry's case, I did not consider it a fruitful area of inquiry to delve into his erroneous speculation any further. His guess that I was 42 instead of 49 was not, in my opinion, conclusive evidence for some kind of psychodynamically determined error. To have done so could have been antitherapeutic in that it would have involved us in an inquiry into a subject that might or might not have had psychological significance. I was content to leave the issue alone and reveal my actual age. As mentioned, I believe there is often an important benefit to be derived in treatment from such revelations. They bring the patient and therapist closer, and this may be more important than an analytic inquiry. Even though the therapist may be depriving the patient of some important psychoanalytic insight, this may be more than compensated for by the strengthening of the therapist-patient relationship brought about by such divulgences.

I answered the question by informing Harry that I fully intended to be continuing as a psychiatrist in 20 years. I wanted to get across the notion that I find my work interesting and enjoyable, and that the prospect of retiring completely is not only distasteful to me, but would be completely out of character for me. My hope was that some of this attitude toward productive endeavors might filter down to Harry.

Harry then answered the question and offered that he would be an auto mechanic. I generally follow through with such interruptions because they often provide useful therapeutic material. Unless the interruption is obviously a resistance maneuver, I "milk it for all it's worth." It would be completely outside of the philosophy of the game for me to say to the patient, "Hey, wait a minute now. This is my question. You wait your turn." Such a response would totally defeat the purpose of the game—which is to elicit psychodynamically meaningful material from the patient.

The patient emphasized the material benefits to be derived from being an auto mechanic. I took this opportunity to introduce a comment about the work ethic and the importance of doing a good job and establishing a good reputation. I do not believe that the statement "hit him in the guts." However, it behooves the therapist to transmit his (her) therapeutically important messages and hope that they will ultimately be received. In no way did I consider Harry's switching the subject to his future life as an auto mechanic to be a resistance maneuver. Rather, I welcomed it from the realization that the school and work ethics are analogous and that anything I could say about his work as an auto mechanic would be likely to have applicability to his school work. Furthermore, because Harry was extremely unreceptive to discussing his school work directly, I viewed discussion about the principles of being an auto mechanic to be a potential vehicle for talking symbolically about Harry's school difficulties in a way receptive to him.

> *Patient:* My card says, "What would you do if you found $10,000?" If I found $10,000, first I would return it to the police station to see if it is anybody's. Then, if it is not anybody's, then I would know in 30 days that I would get to keep it. If I get to keep it, then I am going to buy my own auto mechanic shop.
> *Gardner:* That's a good purpose.
> *Patient:* So my store will be nice, and many people will come. So it will be a nice clean place to get your car fixed, and washed, and everything, and take every bit of advice to make people's cars look nice. It will be a real, nice, clean place.
> *Gardner:* To create a good impression. Right?
> *Patient:* Yeah, to create a good impression.
> *Gardner:* That's important. It's important to create a good impression. It shows you have pride in your place; but it's also important that you do good work, you know. There are some places that look flashy and nice, but the work is no good.
> *Patient:* Mine is going to look flashy and do the best work.
> *Gardner:* Okay. I think that the important thing is the work. The second important thing is how it looks.

Here, the patient again focused on external appearances and made no mention of the quality of work that his auto mechanic shop would provide. I praised him on his interest in a clean shop that made a good appearance. But, I also emphasized the importance of high-quality work. This was especially important for this boy whose commitment to the work ethic in school left much to be desired.

These interchanges on the subject of the auto mechanic shop

represent what I consider to be among the most efficacious forms of child psychotherapeutic interchange. To the casual observer, the patient and I are involved in a relaxed discussion on the somewhat neutral and even banal subject of auto mechanic shops. There is almost a "folksy" quality to the conversation. From the patient's point of view it is probably just that; simply a conversation. From my point of view, however, much more is going on. At every point I am actively concerned with two processes: (1) the ostensible conversation and (2) the underlying psychodynamic meaning of what is going on. What may appear to be a relaxed conversation is, for me, almost a facade. The wheels are constantly going around in my head. I am concerned with both of these processes simultaneously. I am ever trying to relate my comments to the patient's basic difficulties and how they are reflected in what he is saying. This is the way I transmit my most important therapeutic communications. I cannot emphasize this point strongly enough.

Freud referred to dreams as "the royal road to the unconscious." I am in full agreement. And I would consider stories and conversations of this kind to be the royal road to therapeutic change in children. Even with adults the process has merit. Quite often in the course of the session with an adult patient I will relate an anecdote or an event that has relevance to his (her) problems. It is a way of getting home a point using an extremely powerful vehicle, one that is far more powerful, I believe, than a therapeutic approach that relies on gaining insight into unconscious processes. Last, it is an approach that has history to recommend it. It is an ancient method that has survived to the present day because of the universal recognition of its efficacy.

> *Gardner:* "Of all the things you own what do you enjoy the most? Make believe you are doing something with that thing." I would say that one of the most important things I own is my typewriter. (therapist imitates typing)
> *Patient* (interrupts): Isn't that your favorite thing? What about that? (patient points to mounted video camera)
> *Gardner:* You like that too?
> *Patient:* Yeah!

Gardner: Why do you think I would choose that?

Patient: Because you could make movies.

Gardner: That is a lot of fun. I think that's a good answer too. That is also one of my favorite things. I like the TV because I can see myself on television any time I want.

Patient: You can say "hello," and you can look at the television, and see yourself say hello.

Gardner: Yes, but more important than that, it helps me be a better psychiatrist.

Patient: It does?

Gardner: Yeah, because we are playing this game here and people see themselves on television, and it helps them see themselves better, and it helps me be a better psychiatrist in this way.

Patient: Uh-oh!

Gardner: What is uh-oh?

Patient: You're supposed to have two of these chips.

Gardner: Oh, did I forget? Okay, I guess I forgot. (therapist takes chip) Okay. Let's get back to the question. You were close when you guessed the TV camera, but I was not going to say that. I was going to say *typewriter* because with the typewriter I write books, and stories, and things like that. It makes me feel very good because when I write a book—and especially when it comes out—it makes me feel good that I created something.

I began responding to the question about my favorite possession by mentioning the typewriter. I planned to use it as a point of departure for discussing the gratifications I enjoy from writing. My hope was that this would engender in Harry greater motivation in his academic pursuits. However, he interrupted me and pointed to the video camera that was recording the program that we were making. As mentioned, I generally welcome such interruptions because they usually relate to issues that may be more relevant to the child than those that I may be focusing on at that point. (Of course, when the interruption is a reflection of resistance, then I do not permit it and insist upon my right to return to my card and answer my question.)

I allowed the digression and got as much mileage as I could out of a discussion of the video camera and the closed-circuit television system. I got in the message that it was useful for helping people see themselves and this, of course, is a crucial aspect of treatment. I did not get very far with this explanation when the patient noted that I had failed to collect one of my reward chips. When the game is being played at its best, both the therapist and the patient may forget whose turn it is and may forget to collect the reward chips. Following the rectification of this error, I returned to the typewriter theme and focused on the good feeling I have when a book of mine comes out. At that point Harry interrupted me again, and the following interchange took place.

> *Patient* (interrupts): What's that over there? (Patient points to a pile of just-published books, *Dr. Gardner's Fables for Our Times* [1981a].)
> *Gardner:* That's my new book. It just came out.
> *Patient:* When?
> *Gardner:* The book came out yesterday. Would you like to borrow a copy?
> *Patient* (very enthusiastically): Yeah!

The psychological significance of this interchange concerning the new book, as well as the subsequent conversation, will be more meaningful with the following background information. I routinely give a complimentary copy of my book *Dr. Gardner's Stories About the Real World Vol. I* (Gardner, 1972a) to every new patient. These stories cover a wide variety of conflict situations of childhood, and it is a rare patient who does not relate to at least one of the stories. I use the child's reactions as a point of departure for therapeutic interchanges. Accordingly, Harry had been given a copy of this book during my initial consultation. Subsequently, I lent him a copy of my *Dorothy and the Lizard of Oz* (Gardner, 1980a). Unfortunately, he lost the book. When he told me of the loss, it was with a complete absence of embarrassment, guilt, remorse, or a desire to make restitution. Because of this I told him that I would only lend him another book with the understanding that if he lost this one, he would have to pay for it. I imposed this requirement in order to provide Harry with a useful therapeutic experience. Not to have made some attempt to require responsibility on his part would have been antitherapeutic. This is just the kind of *living experience* that I consider important in therapy. Therapists should seize every opportunity they can in order to provide patients with such experiences. The interchange over the lost books is an excellent example. Harry absolutely refused to accept the book with that proviso. We discussed it for a few minutes and I tried to impress upon him that I felt bad that the book was lost and that I wanted to protect myself from further losses. I also tried to help him appreciate his own lack of remorse over the loss, but this fell on deaf ears. From the conversation I knew that he wished to borrow the book, but I knew also that he did not wish to assume responsibility for its loss. I believed that my refusal to lend him the book without "protecting myself" might have been a more valuable therapeutic experience than any discussions we had or might have had on the subject.

This is what I was thinking when Harry pointed to the new book. It was not placed there to attract his attention. (I do not set up artificial situations like this in therapy. No matter what items are present in the therapist's office, the pressure of the unconscious is going to invest them with special meaning in accordance with the psychological processes of the patient.) Harry immediately expressed interest in the book, and I thought this would be a wonderful opportunity to offer to lend him a copy. He responded with enthusiasm.

> *Gardner:* I'll let you borrow a copy, but let me ask you something. If you were in my place, would you be hesitant to lend the book? Should I be hesitant to lend you a book?
> *Patient:* I think you should *give* me the book just like you gave the *The Real World Stories.*
> *Gardner:* Okay, but what about *lending* you a book? You don't think I should lend you the book?
> *Patient:* No.
> *Gardner:* Why not?
> *Patient:* I don't know.
> *Gardner:* I had an experience with you that made me hesitate to lend you a book. Do you remember that experience? What was the experience?
> *Patient:* The last . . . book you lent me I lost.
> *Gardner:* Yeah, I lent you a book and you lost it.
> *Patient* (angrily): So don't give me the book. I don't really care.

Gardner: But if I just give it to you, that won't help you remember not to lose things.

Patient: Ah, I don't want your book . . . just forget it!

Gardner: It's a new book of fables called *Dr. Gardner's Fables for Our Times.*

Patient: I don't really care about it. You can keep it for yourself.

Gardner: I just want to say something. If I lend it to you now . . . I would like to lend it to you and give you a second chance. I never condemn a person for one mistake. Do you know what I mean? You're entitled to a mistake; everybody makes mistakes. But it makes me hesitant; it makes me a little concerned. How about this? I'll lend you the book?

Patient (interrupts): No, I don't want it!

Gardner: Let me tell you what I'm suggesting.

Patient: I don't want it!

Gardner: I'll tell you what. I'll lend you the book, but if you lose it, you have to pay for it.

Patient: No, I'm not going to do it.

Gardner: Why not?

Patient: Because I don't *need* the book.

Gardner: Okay, that's up to you, but I would have liked you to have borrowed it, but I'm not going to lend it to you just like that, because I'm afraid you might lose it or not take good care of it. But maybe you'll change your mind. If you change your mind, let me know.

Patient: Okay. Did you answer your question?

Gardner: I think I did.

Patient: Wait . . . what was that question?

Gardner: "What are my favorite things?" I said my typewriter because it makes me feel good when I write books and the books help other people. Books help other people with their problems. They teach them things and lots of people say they learn a lot from them, and that makes me feel good too. You feel good when you do something that helps other people. Do you do things that make you feel good? What do you do that makes you feel good?

Patient: I'm nice to people.

Gardner: That's right, it makes you feel good when you're nice to people, right?

Patient: Yeah.

Gardner: Right. You get a chip for that answer, because it was a very good answer. And I get a chip for my answer.

It was quite clear that Harry really wanted to borrow the book, his repeated denials of interest notwithstanding. However, he absolutely refused to assume any responsibility for the book he lost. I tried to seduce him into making a commitment by continuing the conversation in the hope that it would intensify his craving for the book. Although I was unsuccessful in getting him to make the commitment to provide restitution if he lost the book, I do believe that he had a therapeutic experience. I provided repercussions for his casual attitude over the loss of the book I had previously lent him, and he had the living experience that book owners, under such circumstances, are likely to be reluctant to lend him additional volumes. He suffered the frustration of not being able to borrow the book. This, I hoped, would be a useful therapeutic experience. There was no analytic inquiry here; there was little, if any, insight gained by Harry. However, something therapeutic was accomplished—the lack of insight on Harry's part notwithstanding.

Many therapists are far less enthusiastic than me about interchanges such as these. They are deeply committed to the notion that without insight there cannot be therapeutic change. They subscribe deeply to Freud's dictum: "Where there was unconscious, there let conscious be." I am not as enthusiastic as Freud was over the therapeutic benefit of insight. I am much more impressed with the therapeutic changes that occur from experience as well as from messages that are imparted at the symbolic level. For therapists who are deeply committed to the insight route to change, I often provide the analogy of my scuba-diving experience. My instructor repeatedly advised the class that it was vital for all of us to learn ways of dealing with emergency situations while under water. The worst thing that one can do in such situations is to hold one's breath and swim to the top as rapidly as possible. It is one of the quickest ways to kill oneself. Accordingly, we were repeatedly advised to fight the impulse to rise to the top when we were in trouble. We were meticulously taught the various ways of dealing with underwater emergencies. I can tell the reader from personal experience that the urge to hold one's breath and rise to the top under such circumstances is enormously compelling. It seemed that every force and reflex in my body was dictating such a course of action. It was only with formidable self-control that I fought these urges on two occasions when I had difficulty. Of course, my knowledge of the consequences of submitting to them was of help in my suppressing these impulses.

I mention the scuba experience because it relates directly to those therapists who are deeply committed to insight as the primary mode for helping their patients. Just as my scuba instructor urged me to fight my impulse to hold my breath and rise to the top, I suggest that therapists fight their impulses to pursue the insight route. I suggest that they consider the alternatives discussed in this book. I do not view insight as totally meaningless in the therapeutic process, but I generally view it as less significant for children than it is for adults, and even for adults it is a low-priority therapeutic modality. It is frosting on the cake. I am in agreement with Frieda Fromm-Reichmann who said, "The patient needs an experience far more than an insight." The reader interested in providing patients with bibliotherapeutic material related to the work ethic might wish to refer to my stories "The Wise-Guy Seal," "The Squirrel and the Nuts," and the "Beaver and the Owl" in my *Fables for Our Times* (Gardner, 1981a).

PUNCTUALITY AND RELIABILITY

For over 30 years now I have trained medical students, residents, and psychology interns at the Columbia-Presbyterian Medical Center in New York City. The hospital is situated just north of Harlem in an area that has seen significant poverty in the last 25-30 years. In mid-century the population was primarily white: Irish, Italian, Jewish, and others of European heritage. Since the 1950's it has become progressively more Hispanic and black. For many years now I have been giving my medical and nursing students, residents, psychologists, and social workers the following important message during my first meeting with them at the onset of a one-year process in which I supervise them in the treatment of patients:

If the good fairy came down from heaven and told me that she would put in the drinking water a magic pill that would cure one symptom—and one psychiatric symptom only—for all the people who live in the neighborhood of the Columbia-Presbyterian Medical Center, I would have no problem giving her an immediate answer. I would ask her to put in the drinking water a pill that would create a sense of urgency for punctuality for all the people in this neighborhood. There are many factors operative in the problems with which these people suffer. I am fully aware of the prejudicial attitudes that are playing a significant role in their plight. However, if you view them simply as the innocent victims of prejudice, you will be doing both society and them a terrible disservice.

One of the factors operative in their difficulties is their failure to have this sense of urgency and tension regarding the keeping of appointments. Most do not carry watches (even the most inexpensive ones), and most do not have a sense of tension that most of us here have regarding being late to an appointment. They need to have the feeling that others are being inconvenienced and even getting angry when they are late. The Hispanics refer to this as the "manyana philosophy" and speak of it with a slight sense of pride and even arrogance. The implication here is that we compulsive Caucasians are somehow getting fewer gratifications from life because of our slavish commitment to our appointment books. This sense of superiority is a thin rationalization for some deep-seated recognition that it is a serious liability. It is one of the important reasons (but certainly not the only one) for the poverty to be seen in Central and South America and other parts of the Spanish-speaking world.

The blacks, too, pride themselves on their subscribing to "black man's time." Being two or three hours late for an appointment is perfectly acceptable and Caucasians are told that they just don't understand this cultural difference. In New York City, during the 1960s, many of the stores in Harlem were owned by white people (especially Jews). The blacks considered themselves to have been exploited by these entrepreneurs and sometimes literally burned down their stores and drove them out. Thereafter, the U.S. government provided generous and ample small-business loans to encourage blacks to enter into their own businesses. Yet, more than 20 years later, in these same areas, one finds that most of the stores are not owned by blacks. Rather they are owned by Vietnamese, Indians, Koreans, Chinese, some Jews, and people from an assortment of other ethnic groups. I believe that the main reason for this relates to the absence of a father figure to provide a model for the children for the kinds of qualities necessary to run a small business, namely, reasonable education, commitment, punctuality (not "black man's time" but "white man's time"), and adherence to the work ethic. Blacks are not oblivious to this problem. One black comedian gave the following advice to his people (words are not accurate, the message is): "Do you want to know how to get ahead in this world? I'll tell you how. My advice to you is that you get up in the morning, take a pencil and a piece of paper, follow around an Oriental, and make notes of exactly what he does every single minute throughout the course of the day. Then you start doing the same thing."

If you consider this statement of mine to be prejudice on my part, then you must consider it prejudice on the part of that black comedian as well. Rather, you would do well to look clearly at the reality of this problem and do everything possible to help these patients overcome it. One thing that could help would be strict adherence to your therapeutic schedule. If a session is scheduled to begin at 2:00 p.m. and end at 2:50 p.m., you should spell this out very clearly to the patient. If patients arrive at 2:45, they should be given a five-minute session. And if they arrive at 2:51, there should be no session at all. (Of course, I am not talking here about life-threatening emergencies.) Providing these patients with the *living experience* that lack of punctuality will have negative feedback may be the most important benefit they derive from your treatment. One of the most important reasons why you are in this medical center, serving as a therapist, and they are out there living in poverty is related to this very important difference between the two of you.

Unfortunately, for over the third of a century during which I have been supervising therapists, it is very rare for the patients to learn this important lesson. By the end of the year they are still missing many appointments and, when they arrive, they still have the same frequency of latenesses as when they started. Not surprisingly, this coincides with the maintenance of their level of poverty. Relevant to this chapter is the low level of self-esteem that is attendant to such poverty; low self-esteem that is in part a result of the failure to be committed to the value of punctuality. Obviously, schoolwork suffers as the child's parents do not feel the strong need to get the child to school, or if they do feel that need, they do not feel it is important to be on time. Of course, there are exceptions. Of course, there are some patients who are committed to session punctuality at the outset or who do indeed learn about it in the course of the treatment. But these, unfortunately, represent a very small fraction of the population served by the Columbia-Presbyterian Medical Center in New York City.

HONESTY

"Honesty is the best policy" is an old cliché. Unfortunately, it is not often taken very seriously, especially in these days of increasing psychopathy in our society. Quite often, in my work with patients—especially adolescents and adults—when dealing with the various solutions to a problem, I will say to a patient, "You know you thought of three or four ways of dealing with this, but you haven't mentioned even once what I consider the simplest and most obvious course of action to take at this point. Do you know what I'm talking about?"

Often, the patient doesn't have the faintest idea what I am referring to. At that point I will say, "How about considering old-fashioned honesty?" When we consider in detail the drawbacks of that approach when compared to its advantages—both present and future—the patient may come to see the judiciousness of this ancient wisdom. Its utilization increases the likelihood of a successful solution to a problem. The failure to use it is likely to result in complications that not only compound difficulties, but contribute to feelings of low self-worth. And this principle holds in the educational process as well. If one subscribes to the value of intellectual honesty, it gives one a good feeling about oneself. Intellectual dishonesty not only deprives an individual of this important psychological benefit, but may result in derivative and spin-off consequences that may be even more ego-debasing. Children who get a high score on examinations feel genuinely good about themselves. In contrast, those who cheat may very well get some pleasure from their high grades, but inwardly they know that their marks have not been obtained honestly and so they do not enjoy the same sense of ego-enhancement.

Clinical Example

The Talking, Feeling, and Doing Game includes many cards that provide the therapist with the opportunity to give messages related to this issue.

> *Question*: Suppose two people you knew were talking about you and they didn't know you were listening. What do you think you would hear them saying?
>
> *Response*: I might hear the people saying that I'm the kind of a person who is direct and honest. Although people might disagree at times with what I've said, they would agree that I am direct about what my opinions are and don't pussyfoot about them. They know that when they ask me a question, they'll get an honest and direct answer with no hedging, beating-around-the-bush, or saying things that I don't believe to be true. I am not saying that they would say that I never lied in my whole life and that I never will, only that they are pretty confident that I'll be honest with them.
>
> You see, I believe that there is truth and wisdom to the old saying that "honesty is the best policy." If you tell a lie, you have to go around worrying that people will find out that you've lied. Also, lots of people feel bad about themselves when they lie. They feel guilty about it. And when people find out that you've lied, then they don't trust you even when you've told the truth. So these are the main reasons why I find it better to tell the truth rather than to lie. What's your opinion on this subject?

Identification with the therapist and modeling oneself after him (her) is an important part of the therapeutic process. This is very similar to the educational model in which the child learns, in part, because of identification with the teacher and the desire to gain the same gratifications that the teacher enjoys from learning. The therapist not only serves as a model for learning, but should be serving as a model for other desirable attributes as well, e.g., healthy self-assertion, sensitivity to the feelings of others, feelings of benevolence toward those who are in pain, and the handling of oneself with dignity and honesty. This card enables the therapist to provide examples of such traits. However, the therapist should select traits that are particularly relevant to the patient's problems. Furthermore, the therapist must avoid presenting these with a flaunting or holier-than-thou attitude.

The reader who is interested in utilizing bibliotherapeutic techniques related to the honesty issue might wish to refer child patients to my story "The Hundred Dollar Lie" in my *Stories About the Real World, Vol. I* (Gardner, 1972a) and "Leo the Liar" in *Stories About the Real World, Vol. II* (Gardner, 1983a).

PHILANTHROPY AND THE GOLDEN RULE

It is not by pure chance that the "Golden Rule" is often singled out as one of the most important values to which humans should subscribe. Central to the survival and progress of a civilization is the willingness of the individuals within it to give consideration to the thoughts and feelings of others and to treat others as well as they would treat themselves. Although most people have a long way to go when it comes to subscribing to this dictum, we do well to teach it to our children and promulgate it whenever we can. Those who do subscribe to it will feel an enhanced sense of self-worth. In contrast, many who do not (unfortunately, I am not saying all) will deprive themselves of this important source of ego-gratification.

Therapists do well to take every reasonable opportunity to impart to their patients the importance of sympathy (an emotional resonance with another person) and empathy (an intellectual appreciation of what is going on within another individual). Children are not famous for their ability to understand these cognitive ideals, and the younger the child, the less capable he (she) is to utilize them. My book *The Girls and Boys Book About Good and Bad Behavior* (Gardner, 1990) provides in bibliotherapeutic fashion information in these areas, which are generally understood by children aged seven and older. The didactic text is complemented by anecdotes and vignettes. Children are not famous, either, for their sense of philanthropy and their willingness to make sacrifices on behalf of others. In a sense, they are very much psychopathic and the therapist does well to appreciate this. However, these little psychopaths need to be acculturated and the therapeutic process should serve to contribute to the development of a sense of philanthropy.

Subscribing to the golden-rule dictum in school will certainly help the child's grades and conduct. Although it does not have a direct effect on academic performance, it has an indirect one nonetheless. Specifically, the better one feels about oneself, the more secure and stable a human being the individual will be, and the greater the likelihood that one will do well in the academic realm. Such stability enhances one's ability to tolerate the discomforts and frustrations that a good education inevitably entails. Such stability enhances the likelihood that one will have the relaxed attitude and the curiosity that serve as important enhancements to education. Furthermore, exhibiting such qualities to the teacher will enhance her regard for the child and improve their relationship. And this too, because of the modeling and identification processes, will enhance the child's education. I am not suggesting here for one moment that the child should be artificial with regard to showing sympathy and empathy for the teacher; I am only suggesting a normal, healthy degree of such involvement.

Clinical Example

The Talking, Feeling, and Doing Game provides many cards that provide the examiner with many opportunities to give responses related to this issue.

Question: Tell about an act of kindness.
Response: A good example of an act of kindness would be visiting someone who is sick in the hospital and giving up a fun thing that you'd prefer to do. Let's say that a boy was in an automobile accident, injured his leg, and had to be in the hospital for six weeks. Even though his mother and father visited him often, he was still very lonely. His really good friends were those who were willing to give up fun things like playing baseball, watching their favorite television programs, or just hanging around and relaxing. Instead they went to visit him in the hospital. He was very grateful when they came to see him. And they felt

good about themselves for their sacrifices. Visiting the friend was an act of kindness. Do you know what the word *sacrifice* means?

This is the type of response I provide to self-centered patients, those who have difficulty putting themselves in the positions of others. In the ensuing discussion, I try to help the egocentric patient appreciate the feelings of loneliness suffered by the hospitalized child. I also try to engender in the patient the feelings of self-satisfaction and enhanced self-worth that come from benevolent acts.

Clinical Example

Andy entered treatment at the age of nine, when he was in the fourth grade. The presenting problems were temper outbursts in school, low frustration tolerance, and a significant degree of self-denigration. Andy was an extremely bright boy who was so advanced in mathematics that he was receiving special tutoring at the ninth- and tenth-grade levels. In spite of his advanced mathematical competence, he was getting B and C grades because of his temper outbursts in the classroom.

Andy was born with hypospadias, a congenital abnormality in which the urethral opening is found at some point along the ventral aspect of the penis, rather than at the tip of the glans. During the first five years of his life he was hospitalized on five occasions for operative repair of this congenital defect. During these hospitalizations it was necessary to tie his hands to the bed rails in order to prevent him from tampering with the dressings. Accordingly, Andy not only suffered with the physical pain associated with his operations but with the psychological stress related to his lack of understanding as to why he was suffering.

Andy had an identical twin brother who was completely normal physically. Furthermore, the brother was also extremely bright, and the two of them took their math tutoring together. The brother, however, did not exhibit any psychological problems and was getting extremely high grades. Nor did he exhibit the self-denigration problem and feelings of low self-worth. The boys had a younger sister who did not manifest any difficulties either. The parents had an excellent relationship between themselves and among the members of the family. I believed that Andy's symptoms were related to the traumas he had experienced in the first four years of his life and that had he been born physically normal he would not have needed psychiatric attention.

Andy's therapy went quite well. From the outset we had an excellent relationship. I was immediately attracted to him, mainly because of his warmth of personality and his strong desire to be helped. His high intelligence, I believe, also contributed to his therapeutic progress. There are some who hold that brighter people do not necessarily do better in treatment. Although it is certainly true that there are many highly intelligent people who are also so sick that they cannot profit significantly from therapy, I believe it is also true that the more intelligent a person is, the greater the likelihood he (she) will be successful in whatever endeavor the person chooses to be involved in—and therapy is one such endeavor. In the course of his treatment Andy learned to handle his anger more effectively and to deal with issues very early, before he suffered significant frustrations and pent-up anger that would ultimately result in temper outbursts. He learned to respect himself more, and this was associated with a reduction in his tendency to berate himself for the most minor errors. The vignettes from *The Talking, Feeling, and Doing Game* that are presented here are from a session that occurred in his sixth month of treatment, about a month before it terminated.

> *Gardner:* Good afternoon, boys and girls, ladies and gentlemen. Today is Tuesday, December 2nd, 1980, and I'm happy to welcome you once again to Dr. Gardner's program. Our guest and I are playing *The Talking, Feeling, and Doing Game* and we'll be back with you when it's time for someone to answer a question. Okay, you go.
>
> *Patient:* My card says, "A girl was listening through the keyhole of the closed door of her parents' bedroom. They didn't know she was listening. What did she hear them saying?" Now

she heard them saying that she, she had a temper tantrum, and they were talking about how to punish her.
Gardner: What were they saying exactly?

The reader will note that from the universe of possible responses the patient could have provided here, he selected the one that related directly to his presenting symptoms, namely, temper tantrums. His response is a strong statement of the power of the unconscious to select those responses that are most relevant to psychological processes operative within the patient, processes that are pressing for release.

Patient: The father said to cut off her allowance for a week, but her mother said not to go to the skating rink Saturday.
Gardner: Uh huh. So it was decided . . .
Patient: It was decided, uh, to cut off her allowance for a week.

The parents are arguing about how to punish a girl who had a temper tantrum. The father suggests cutting off her allowance and the mother prefers that she not be allowed to go to the skating rink the following Saturday. The parents are basically utilizing behavior therapy techniques, that is, negative reinforcement. Of course, there is a place for disciplinary measures, but they do not get to the heart of the problem. As a therapist, I want to go beyond that and not merely foster a method of dealing with temper tantrums that involves suppression and conscious control because of the threat of negative reinforcement.

Gardner: Uh huh. Did that help? Did that help her to remember not to have temper tantrums?

I often use the term *help her remember* or *help him remember* in association with childrens' discussion of disciplinary measures. For example, I might say to a child, "When your parents sent you to your room for a half-hour, did that help you remember not to hit your brother?"

Patient: Yes.

Gardner: But the big question is what did she have a temper tantrum *about?*

Patient: Well, she, she wanted to ride her two-wheeler, but the fender was all broken up. And her father said, "Yeah, we'll have to fix it, but it will be at least a week."

Gardner: Oh, so she was . . .

Patient: She wanted, she wanted to ride it badly.

Gardner: She was upset that she had to wait so long. Was that it?

Patient: Yes.

Gardner: What could she have done instead of having a temper tantrum?

Patient: She could have just accepted it.

Accordingly, as a point of departure for more extensive psychotherapeutic inquiry, I asked the patient what the girl had the temper tantrums *about.* In this way, I hoped to obtain a specific example that would serve as a point of departure for a discussion into the causes of the temper tantrum. The therapist does well to use *concrete examples* rather than *abstractions* when discussing therapeutic issues. In response, the patient gave as an example the girl's broken bike. She was not only upset that she could not ride it but that it would take a week to have it fixed. At this point, I ask the patient, "What could she have done instead of having a temper tantrum?" In this way I introduced the notion of an alternative mode of adaptation to the problem. As mentioned, one of the purposes of therapy is to expand the patient's repertoire of options available for utilization when dealing with life's problems. A broken bicycle presents most children with one of the basic problems of life. In this case, the girl was dealing with it by having a temper tantrum—clearly an inappropriate and maladaptive way of responding to the situation. Rather than immediately suggest to the patient what I would consider to be a preferable mode of adaptation, I tried to elicit his contribution to the solution of this problem.

His response was, "She could just have accepted it." This is certainly a mode of adaptation that can be useful. However, I would not consider it high on the hierarchy of solutions. Rather,

I would only recommend such resignation after all other options have failed. There are certainly times in life when we have to resign ourselves to the fact that there is nothing we can do about a problem. However, I do not generally recommend that as the first solution. It should be the last, after all others have failed. Accordingly, I asked the patient if there were any *other* things she could have done.

> *Gardner:* Okay. Any *other* things she could have done? I think that's part of it.
> *Patient:* . . . (big sighs). . . . I don't know.
> *Gardner:* Anything else? There she was. . . . She wanted to go bike riding . . . and her bike was broken . . . and it would take her father a week to fix it . . . .What else could she have done?
> *Patient:* She could . . . she could have just forgot about it.

The patient had difficulty coming up with another solution. Accordingly, in order to facilitate his coming up with another solution I slowly repeated the problem: "There she was . . . .She wanted to go bike riding . . . and her bike was broken . . . and it would take her father a week to fix it . . . .What else could she have done?" My hope here was that my restatement of the problem might catalyze the formulation of another solution by the patient.

Finally, Andy said, "She could . . . she could have just forgot about it." This response, although somewhat different from the resignation response, is still low on the hierarchy of optimal adaptations. Relegating a problem to the unconscious is certainly a way of adjusting to it. However, it is not a solution that generally involves any gratification, and so the frustrations that generate the reaction of forgetting are likely still to be operative.

> *Gardner:* Well, that's also accepting it. Another thing she could have done is to think about another way she could have some fun. For instance, maybe she could borrow a bicycle from somebody.
> *Patient:* Yeah!
> *Gardner:* Like a neighbor. Or if she had a brother or sister. Then let's say she couldn't borrow a bike from somebody. What else could she have done?

Patient: She could have roller skated.
Gardner: Roller skated. Good! She could have done something else that would be fun. Right? Okay, you get a chip for that. Okay. Now I go.

At this point, I considered the patient to have exhausted all of his possibilities and therefore considered it proper for me to suggest an adaptation myself. And this, too, is an important therapeutic principle. It is only after the therapist has given the patient every opportunity to find solutions himself (herself) that he (she) should suggest modes of adaptation. Accordingly, I suggested that the girl might *borrow* a bicycle from someone (introducing thereby the principle of *substitute gratification*). The patient immediately responded well to this suggestion. However, I did not stop there and again invited the patient to consider what options the girl might have if she could not borrow a bike from someone. He responded, "She could have roller skated." This is certainly a reasonable alternative and allowed the patient himself to contribute to a solution to the problem.

Patient: "What's the best kind of job a person can have? Why? Make believe you are doing that job." I think the best job a person can have is working for a charity drive, like UNICEF, or the American Cancer Society or something like that.
Gardner: Okay. Why is that?
Patient: Because it can help other people who need the help.
Gardner: Uh huh. Right! Right! So you can help other people through the Cancer Society and UNICEF.
Patient: Uh. Try to raise money for treatment for cancer.
Gardner: Right. And UNICEF?
Patient: To raise money for poor people around the world.
Gardner: Uh huh.
Patient: For people who don't have enough food.
Gardner: Do you know what that answer tells me about you?
Patient: What?
Gardner: It tells me that you're the kind of person who's very sensitive to other people's suffering, and who cares a lot about people who are sick, or who are starving, and that's a fine quality to have. And that tells me something about you that's a very admirable trait. Do you know what an admirable trait is?

Patient: No. I don't know what it is.

Gardner: Admirable is something you admire in somebody. You know?

Patient: Yeah.

Gardner: It shows me that you're a thoughtful person who thinks about other people and feels sorry for those who are sick or in pain, and those who are hungry. That's what it tells me about you. Anything you want to say about that?

Patient: I . . . Thank you.

Gardner: You're welcome. Okay. You get a chip for that.

The patient's response was clearly an unusual one for a child of nine-and-a-half. In fact, I cannot recall having had a response to that card that demonstrated so much sensitivity to and sympathy for the sick and the starving. I considered the response to reflect very healthy values, values that can only enhance the self-esteem of the person who has them. Furthermore, I praised Andy for his sensitivity, and he was genuinely touched by my comment. I believe this was an esteem-enhancing experience for him also.

There are some readers, I suspect, who would be quite critical of me at this point for having allowed the game to go on without focusing on what they would consider an extremely important aspect of the patient's response. Specifically, they would criticize me for not having *analyzed* the fact that the patient's response, his benevolent intent notwithstanding, was derived from the fact that he himself had suffered terribly from medical illnesses and that his desire to help others who were sick and deprived stemmed from these experiences. They would suggest that his philanthropy is not as benevolent as it may initially appear, and that he was satisfying vicariously through it his need to minister to his projected self. I am in full agreement that these mechanisms were probably operative in Andy's response. However, I am not in agreement that this should have been analyzed. Every human act has psychodynamics and philanthropic acts are no exception. Because something has psychodynamics is no reason to automatically and reflexively analyze it. Analysis (in therapy at least) should be reserved for *symptoms,* under the theory that analytic insights may contribute to their alleviation. I did not consider Andy's response here to be pathological and therefore did not feel any need to analyze anything. In fact, to have done so might have resulted in a lessened motivation to devote himself to philanthropic acts. There are times when we should not "tamper" with our patients' psyches, and this is one such example.

As mentioned, therapists do well to be quite stringent with regard to praising patients. A common error is to take every opportunity for such praise with the result that they soon lose their value. I generally reserve my compliments for behaviors that truly warrant noncondescending praise, and this was certainly an example of such a situation. The patient beamed when I complimented him. I believe the compliment played a role (admittedly small) in enhancing his feelings of self-worth.

> *Gardner:* My card says, "Say something about your mother that gets you angry." Well, I remember when I was a kid, about nine years old or so. Those were the days that we had radios, but no TV, if you can imagine such a world. There was absolutely no television, which they had invented already, but it wasn't around in everybody's house. And I used to listen to the radio.
>
> My favorite program was *The Lone Ranger*. Have you ever heard of *The Lone Ranger?* (patient nods affirmatively) The Lone Ranger and his Indian friend, Tonto. And I used to love listening to that at night. And I remember on a few occasions that my mother would say to me that I couldn't listen to it until I had finished my job. I had some jobs to do around the house, and I had this homework, and then after I finished that I'd be able to listen to *The Lone Ranger,* and I used to get angry at her for that because . . .
>
> *Patient* (interrupting): Because it was your favorite program.
>
> *Gardner:* It was my favorite program. Right. And then once I got very angry and I remember, uh, screaming and yelling and using bad language at her, and really having a fit, and then she punished me. She wouldn't let me watch it (sic) at all for a couple of days, and I felt really bad about that, and was very angry. . .

As mentioned, I always give an honest answer to the cards in *The Talking, Feeling, and Doing Game.* I usually have some ambivalence when I get a card that instructs me to make comments about members of my family. I believe that the therapist has an obligation to selectively and judiciously reveal things about himself (herself) for the purposes of the therapy. However, one has an obligation to one's family members not to reveal things to others (patients or nonpatients) that are private family matters. What one decides to reveal about oneself is a personal decision; what one reveals about one's family members must take into consideration their needs and right to privacy as well. The criterion I use for determining whether or not I should make such divulgences is this: Would the person about whom information is being divulged object to such disclosures if he (she) were present in the session? If the answer to this question is yes, then I do not divulge the material. If the answer is no, then I will generally divulge it. I have also mentioned how useful I have found the response that relates to some childhood event of mine – an event that occurred when I was at approximately the age of my patient at the time of therapy. This helps strengthen the relationship and enhance the likelihood that the child will become involved in the therapist's response.

Both of these principles were applied in response to the card. My "criticism" of my mother really said nothing particularly critical about her. Rather, it describes a "deficiency" within me. In addition, I related an event that occurred during my childhood, an event to which I suspected the patient could relate. And he definitely did. He was interested in hearing about my childhood experience. Just as children hearing about their parents' experiences strengthens the parent-child bond, a child hearing about a therapist's childhood experiences (when appropriate) can strengthen the therapist-patient relationship. Furthermore, disclosing that I too had my share of "fits" when I was a child was also therapeutic. When a patient has the idea that the therapist is the paragon of mental health and that he (she) is merely a bag of neuroses in comparison, an antitherapeutic situation exists. Selective and judicious divulgence of the therapist's deficiencies can prevent such a deterioration of the therapeutic relationship. At this point, when I spoke about my fit the patient beamed. It was as if he was saying, "I really can't be that bad. Dr. Gardner had such fits also."

> *Patient:* Did you have TV in your home?
> *Gardner:* No, I said there was no TV in most people's homes then.
> *Patient:* Then how come you said "watch it"?
> *Gardner:* Did I say "watch it"?
> *Patient:* Yeah.
> *Gardner:* No, I *listened* to it.
> *Patient:* Oh.
> *Gardner:* That was my mistake. I guess I would have *wished* that I could have watched it, in my thinking back now as a kid, seeing it was really . . .

Andy picked up my error regarding "watching" *The Lone Ranger* on radio, and this in itself can be therapeutic. It makes me human and lessens the likelihood that the patient will idealize me. It can be ego-enhancing for him to benevolently correct my error. It is important for the reader to appreciate that something very important happened here when the patient corrected me. My responding to it in a nonchalant manner provided the patient with a therapeutically beneficial experience. If he was in my position, he would have reacted with self-denigration ("How stupid can I be"). By responding in a relaxed and non-self-deprecatory way, I served as a model for such behavior for the patient. He was also provided with the *living experience* that one can make a mistake and not necessarily castigate oneself for it.

> *Patient:* Did you have that when you finally got a TV? Or did you never get one?
> *Gardner:* Oh, we have TVs now when I got older. But TV sets didn't come, weren't in people's homes, I believe, until the late 1940s, the early 1950s I think. It was after the Second World War. Then they had lots of TV sets around. At any rate, that was one of the things that I was angry at my mother about, her not letting me watch *The Lone Ranger.* But I guess it taught me some lessons about being angry about something. That you don't accomplish much by having a fit. That just makes it . . .
> *Patient:* I know.

Gardner: That just makes it worse.

Patient: I know. I usually have a . . . before I came here, I usually had a lot of them.

Gardner: Uh huh. Do you . . .

Patient: And I got punished for them.

Gardner: Uh huh.

Patient: Usually I got sent up to my room, but I got really angry just for that.

Gardner: Uh huh.

Patient: I wanted to play with my brother and sister and I couldn't because I was upstairs.

Gardner: Oh, I see. You were being punished for a fit?

Patient: Uh huh.

Gardner: And what have you learned here about those fits?

Patient: They couldn't help anything!

Gardner: Uh huh. What's a better way? What's a better thing to do when you're angry?

Patient: Just to, just to . . .

Gardner: What's a better thing to do if you're angry?

Patient: Just to think about . . . like . . . I could be angry. I could watch what I want to watch afterwards, after the punishment.

Gardner: Uh huh.

Patient: Besides, it would be on again.

Gardner: Uh huh. But what if you are angry about something, before you get the punishment, before you have the fit? What's a good way to handle something that bothers you?

Patient: Don't handle it in that way.

Gardner: Uh huh. What's a better way?

Patient: Uh . . . a better way is to talk about why you are angry.

Gardner: Right. Right! And by talking about it, what do you try to do?

Patient: You . . . you try to let out your anger but by not having any fits and talking about it.

Gardner: Right! And then what's the purpose in talking, besides letting out your anger? What else does it do?

Patient: It helps you understand . . .

Gardner: It helps you understand, and anything else?

Patient: Let's see . . .

Gardner: It helps you *solve* the problem. It helps you do something about the problem without having a fit.

Patient: That's right.

The patient spontaneously began talking about his own fits. However, my own discussion of my fits as a child facilitated his talking about his own. I refer to this principle as the "as-long-as-you're-on-the-subject" phenomenon. All therapists have to deal with the problem of getting people to talk about their problems. And for child therapists this problem may be even more formidable. One way of getting a person to talk about a subject is to talk about the *same* subject yourself. And this is what was done here. This switch provided an opportunity to discuss what Andy learned about dealing with his anger. We spoke about the measures to take that would reduce the likelihood of his anger building up to such a level that he would have a temper outburst. We spoke about dealing with problems in the earliest phase by expressing one's resentment at the outset. As mentioned, the patient was very bright and was able to learn these lessons well. He clearly was able to use his intelligence therapeutically.

> *Patient:* My card says, "What is the worst thing a person can do? Show someone doing that thing." Waste their life away. That's what I think.
> *Gardner:* Uh huh. Give me an example, like somebody who would be wasting his or her life away.
> *Patient:* Let's say there were two boys. Their father died, and each got half the will. One boy . . .
> *Gardner* (interrupts): What's a will?
> *Patient:* The *will.*
> *Gardner:* The will . . . the will. Oh, the will when someone dies? Yeah. Yeah.
> *Patient* (nods affirmatively): Each got a thousand dollars.
> *Gardner:* This is a made-up story of yours?
> *Patient:* Yes.
> *Gardner:* Right.
> *Patient:* One person, actually it's a different version of a story from the Bible.
> *Gardner:* Okay.
> *Patient:* The one that Jesus told.
> *Gardner:* Okay.
> *Patient:* Well, one person used it wisely and went and got a job, but the other one just wasted his life away with it, and wasted most of the money having a good time.

Gardner: Uh huh. Then what happened?

Patient: He did a lot of things. But when the money was gone, he lost his friends and had no more friends.

Gardner: Uh huh.

Patient: So he had to turn to be a bad guy.

Gardner: That was a real waste of his life.

Patient: But the other one continued, continued to prosper, and he still used his money wisely.

Gardner: Uh huh.

Patient: To get food . . .

Gardner: Uh huh.

Patient: Clothing.

Gardner: How did he get all that money?

Patient: Put it in a bank and got interest on it.

Gardner: Is that how he . . . ? That was in the Bible?

Patient: No, it wasn't in the Bible.

Gardner (smiling): What was the interest rate in those days?

Patient (laughs): No, I said this is sort of like a modern-day fable.

Gardner: All right. I see. But besides putting the money in the bank and getting interest, did he do anything else?

Patient: Yes, he continued his job.

Gardner: Continued his job. That sounds more like the Bible to me. (therapist laughs)

Patient: Yes. (patient laughs)

Gardner: Uh, anyway, uh, now, so what do we learn from that story?

Patient: That you have only one life to live, and if you waste it, that's it!

Gardner: But some people would say that the second guy really had a great time. He just spent the money and really enjoyed himself, while the first guy went to work. And what's so great about going to work? Some would say that this guy was the wise one. What would you say about that?

Patient: I think they're wrong.

Gardner: Why do you say they're wrong?

Patient: Because if you lose all your money, how can you have a good time when you lose all your money?

Gardner: Let's compare the two guys when they got older. See there was one guy, the first guy, he put his money in the bank—at a good interest we assume—and therefore didn't have much fun when he was young because he wanted to work and he put all his extra money in the bank. Then when he was old, he had a lot of money, but was too old to enjoy it. The second guy, the one who pissed all his money away when he was younger, ends up badly, but so does the first. What about those two guys? During that period of their lives?

Patient: They both were not living their lives wisely. Well, when you put it that way I'm not really sure now.

Gardner: Uh huh.

Patient: Think it was about equal because . . .

Gardner: Why?

Patient: Because that person, the one who saved his money and stuff had a lot of fun when he retired and stuff.

Gardner: I see. So the one who worked was planning for the future. Was that it?

Patient: That's it.

Gardner: Okay. So that he was the smarter guy.

Patient: Uh huh.

Gardner: That's what you're saying?

Patient: Yes.

Gardner: Because he was taking care of his future. He just wasn't only thinking of the present. Is that what you're saying?

Patient: Yes.

Gardner: I would say that there is something else too. It depends upon the kind of job he had. Some people like their work, and some people don't. What about the guy in your story?

Patient: That guy liked his work.

Gardner: Uh huh. What kind of work did he do? What was he doing?

Patient: He was a founder for the ASPCA.

Gardner: A founder? What's a founder? Oh, you mean he started the organization?

Patient: Yes.

Gardner: I assume that this was not what happened in the Bible.

Patient: (laughs)

Gardner: Very good. So he was involved in an organization that took care of animals?

Patient: Yes.

Gardner: I see. Well, that's a very nice thing . . .

Patient: The American Society for the Prevention of Cruelty to Animals!

Gardner: Right. So he did a very noble thing.

Patient: Yes.

Gardner: Do you know what *noble* means?

Patient: I know what it means, but I can't put it into words.

Gardner: Okay. It's very good and kind, and things like that.

Patient: That's what it usually means. Usually I know what it means, but I just can't put it into words.

Gardner: Yes. Sometimes it is hard to define the word that you know what it means. So, actually, though you are comparing the lives of these two guys in different phases of their lives, the guy who was working was still enjoying himself in a different way from the guy who was just splurging with his money. Right? What happened to the guy who splurged his money?

Patient: He was dead in a couple of years.

Gardner: What about your guy who's working? Did he have any fun at all?

Patient: Yes, he had fun.

Gardner: What did he do for fun?

Patient: Well, he had a pet of his own.

Gardner: Uh huh.

Patient: And, and he wanted a dog. And since he took pretty good care of it, in the hunting season the dog returned his gratefulness.

Gardner: By?

Patient: Digging out rabbits out of his hole in the ground so he could shoot them.

Gardner: I see. So he was very helpful. But he had a good time with his dog? Is that what you are saying?

Patient: Yes.

Gardner: I see. So he wasn't just an all-work kind of guy. He recognized that life required a balance of having fun and working at the same time. Is that right?

Patient: He was very smart.

Gardner: It sounds like that. Okay. Very good. You get a chip. That was a good one. Here's a chip for you.

The patient's response to the question about the worst thing a person could do revealed healthy values on the one hand and, in my opinion, a somewhat stringent value system on the other. His story, obviously based on biblical themes, revealed his appreciation that there is a price to be paid for the self-indulgent life. However, I considered his values to be somewhat rigid and self-abnegating. Accordingly, I introduced a little more flexibility in our conversation about his story. I helped the patient appreciate that a more balanced lifestyle might be the more judicious—a lifestyle in which there was room for both work and play. I also reinforced the patient's selection of a benevolent career for the wise brother, namely, the ASPCA. This is another example of the patient's healthy values with regard to giving. Again, I complimented him for the philanthropy and willingness to sacrifice indicated in his response. And this, I hoped, would contribute to the raising of his self-esteem.

> *Gardner:* Okay, now it's my turn. Mine says, "Make believe you're drinking a glass of water." Glugh, glugh, glugh, glugh. You know what?
> *Patient:* What?
> *Gardner:* I have to drink a lot of water.
> *Patient:* How come?
> *Gardner:* A couple of years ago, I had a very painful illness.
> *Patient:* What is it?
> *Gardner:* It's called a kidney stone. Do you know what a kidney is?
> *Patient:* No.
> *Gardner:* Well, I'll tell you. I was in the office here with a patient, with a boy and his mother really. In the middle of the session I started to get terrible cramps. And they were so bad that I had to interrupt the session, and I told the people that I can't go on, I had such pain. And we would have to stop the session, and I became . . .
> *Patient:* Did they understand?
> *Gardner:* Yes. They saw that I couldn't work. It was too painful for me. I was in such pain, and I didn't know what was going on. I had never had any pain like that before, and it was really terrible. And then, finally, after about two hours, I thought about the various possibilities of what it was. And I punched myself lightly over here (therapist points to his back over the kidney area) and I really leaped. And I knew *then* that I probably had a kidney stone.
> *Patient:* How did you know?
> *Gardner:* You see I'm a psychiatrist and I'm also a doctor. A regular doctor. And I figured when that happened . . . I remembered from medical school that that means that I probably had a kidney stone. I didn't know. But certainly it sounded like it. Anyway, I called my doctor and went to the hospital and it was a very painful experience. Uh . . . but it finally passed out. And . . .

Patient: What is a kidney stone anyway?

Gardner: Well, you know the kidneys are up here? (Therapist points to kidney area on his back.)

Patient: Yes.

Gardner: Kidneys. And what the kidney does is take the waste from the blood.

Patient: What . . . it's all blocked up?

Gardner: It filters out waste. You know, your kidney makes your urine.

Patient: Yes.

Gardner: Urine is waste.

Patient: Yes.

Gardner: And waste goes out of your body in your urine when you urinate and go to the bathroom for a bowel movement. That's waste products. The things your body doesn't need.

Patient: Yes.

Gardner: Okay. Now the kidney manufactures the urine, and look what it does. It goes from here (pointing to his back in the kidney region) in the kidney, which is a round thing like that (therapist points to his fist). And the urine goes down this tube called the ureter. (Therapist draws line with finger over anterior surface of his abdomen which follows the path of the ureter.) Then it goes into this thing called the bladder, which is like a ball or sac.

Patient: It's concentrated.

Gardner: Yes, it's concentrated. Very good! The kidney stores if there. It concentrates it and passes it down into the bladder.

Patient: You know what is done with it? When the bladder gets too full, you have to let it out.

Gardner: You let it out. Right! Now the kidney stone is from the kidney. The urine stagnates—it stands there—in certain little places in the kidney. And when that happens it forms stones, which are like little rocks. And then when that rock has to come out, it's very, very painful. It has to go down through the tube called the ureter. And that is very painful. Then the stone goes into the bladder.

Patient: Will I have to have those stones some day?

Gardner: I don't see any reason why.

Patient: Does everyone get them?

Gardner: No. No. I have a special problem with my kidney that makes my kidney make the stones. I mean it's more likely that I'm going to get them than other people. I have that problem. One of the things I have to do is to drink a lot of water; because if I drink a lot of water, then it will lessen the chances that I will get a stone.

Patient: Oh. That's why you have to drink a lot of water.
Gardner: Yeah. Right. That's for me. That's for my kidney. Now let's see. You had a problem too in that same area. Right?

At this point, if the reader hasn't surmised it already, one can see why I discussed my kidney stone problem. It increased the likelihood that the patient would talk directly about his own problems in the same area of his body. We see here yet another manifestation of the "as-long-as-you're-on-the-subject" principle. Furthermore, the divulgence about something personal also served to entrench our relationship.

Patient: Yes.
Gardner: Yep.
Patient: I know what it is.
Gardner: Well, what am I talking about?
Patient: Well, my kidneys . . .
Gardner: Not your kidney. Where was your problem?
Patient: In the bladder I think.
Gardner: No . . . no . . . what are you saying?
Patient: I am saying . . . ask my mom.
Gardner: You know. You know what you had.
Patient: No I don't.
Gardner: You had a problem in that your urine wouldn't come out the right way?
Patient: Uhm.
Gardner: Do you remember that problem?
Patient: Yes.
Gardner: Uh huh. How do things stand with that problem now?
Patient: I didn't like it one bit!
Gardner: What happened with that problem?
Patient: Well, after the operation, they got it back to normal.
Gardner: How is it now?
Patient: Okay.
Gardner: Uh huh. What do you remember about those operations?
Patient (big sigh): The four of them I had in Englewood. The fifth one, the last one, I had in New York.
Gardner: Uh hmm. And what do you remember about the operations?
Patient: What do I remember of it?

Gardner: Uh huh.

Patient: Not much because they were four years ago.

Gardner: Uh huh. How old were you then?

Patient: Five.

Gardner: Uh huh. I see. Do you remember anything about them?

Patient: Uh . . . hmmm.

Gardner: Do you remember anything about them?

Patient: Yes, it was really painful.

Gardner: Uh huh. Very upsetting, huh.

Patient: Yes.

Gardner: Do you still think you are upset about that now?

Patient: No.

Gardner: Do you think about it any more?

Patient: No.

Gardner: Did we talk about . . . did we talk about those operations here?

Patient: Yes.

Gardner: Did you learn anything here about them that was useful? Here? About those operations?

Patient: I don't really think so.

Gardner: You don't really think so. Uh huh. Did you feel worse about it before you came?

Patient: I felt worse about it before I came.

Gardner: Uh huh. Is there anything about anything that happened here to you that made you feel less worse about the operations?

Patient: Yes. When it was over.

Gardner: What?

Patient: When it was over.

Gardner: I don't know what you mean.

Patient: The operations were . . .

Gardner: No, no. I mean about coming here that made you feel less bad about the operations.

Patient: Yes. I remember everybody has to get sick once in a while, so I don't feel so bad about my operations.

Gardner: That's one thing. Right! Another thing is to talk about it. You know, not to be ashamed about it. It's no sin. It's no crime. You know?

Patient: I know.

Gardner: It's not . . . but you're right. I agree with you. Everybody has something. Everybody has some kind of sickness and things that happen to them, but it doesn't make you a terrible person or anything else. You know?

Patient: I know.

Gardner: Do you think less of me because I had this kidney stone? Do you think I was a terrible person for having it?

Patient: No.

Gardner: No? Anything to laugh about, or people to think it's funny or something?

Patient: No.

Gardner: Uh huh. Do you think I think less of you because you had that trouble?

Patient: No.

Gardner: No. Not at all. In fact, I admire you very much. I think you're a fine young man.

Patient: Thank you.

Gardner: And I always think well of and respect you.

Patient (smiling): Thank you.

Gardner: Okay, I'll tell you. Our time is almost up. We want to watch a little bit of this. Okay?

Patient: Okay.

Gardner: So let's see who wins the game. Let's see. How many chips do you have?

Patient: Five.

Gardner: Five? I have three, so you are the winner. Congratulations. (therapist and patient shake hands)

I used the relatively innocuous card "Make believe you're drinking a glass of water" as a point of departure for talking about a problem of mine that was similar to a problem of the patient's. I suspected that this was a good way of getting him to talk about his hypospadias, and my suspicion proved to be true. Talking about my kidney stone provided me with the opportunity to reveal a physical problem of my own, and this, I believe, served the patient well. He and I had something in common. I too knew about pains in that area of the body. I had suffered as had he.

I believe that a factor in the patient's presenting complaint of self-denigration related to his feelings that he was less worthy an individual than others because of his hypospadias and the operative procedures he had suffered in association with its repair. The patient had the experience that I did not look down on him as less worthy a human being because of this problem. Furthermore, my telling him about my kidney stone provided him with the opportunity to see that he himself did not look down on me for having this disorder. This added to my credibility when I said that I did not look down on him and that others were not likely to disparage him because of his hypospadias.

Andy's treatment progressed nicely. He enjoyed a marked reduction in his temper outbursts as well as significant alleviation of his tendency to deprecate himself. His grades improved and he became much more acceptable to friends. I believe the primary factors in his therapeutic improvement were his high intelligence and his winning personality. These attracted me to him and this resulted in his liking me. I also admired his healthy values and I believe my reinforcement of them served to enhance his self-esteem. This enhancement of his feelings of self-worth was another significant factor in his improvement.

MACHISMO

Adolescents are particularly impressed with the value of being macho. "Playing it cool" is "in," whereas anyone who avoids a conflict is viewed as "chicken shit." In our society males, definitely more than females, are unappreciative of the value of the flight reaction. Males in our society are products of a culture that views flight to be a sign of cowardice and fight the only proper reaction to danger. I try to help such youngsters appreciate that the flight reaction is also part of natural survival mechanisms and that all animals in the world utilize each, depending upon the situation. Both serve to preserve life. I try to impress upon the youngster that we human beings somehow have not given proper respect to the flight reaction. I believe that women in our society are much more respectful of it than men.

When demonstrating the point I will often say, "When a rabbit runs away from a wolf, the other animals who observe the rabbit fleeing do not generally call him 'chicken.' " I may describe the appeasement gestures found in certain lower animals. One of the best examples is the one utilized by wolves. When two wolves are fighting, they generally try to bite each other in vulnerable places—especially the neck. In the course of fighting, at a point when it becomes apparent to both which one is going to be the victor, the animal who is on the brink of being killed will turn its neck to such a position that the area of the jugular vein and carotid artery is directly exposed to the jaws of the victorious one. This is generally referred to as an *appeasement gesture*. One would think that the victorious animal would now seize this opportunity to bite the subdued animal in the neck and end the fight instantly. However, he does no such thing. He pulls back and allows the subdued animal to escape. In fact, he cannot do otherwise. His withdrawal is locked into his genetic programming. It is a lifesaving maneuver for the subdued animal; he too has no choice but to utilize the appeasement gesture when he is on the brink of defeat. I try to help the patient appreciate the importance of this maneuver, especially with regard to its lifesaving function. I emphasize that appeasement sometimes enables an individual to avoid a conflict that might result in loss of limb and even life.

The "boys don't cry" dictum is a macho value that is widely prevalent in our society. The notion that it is unmanly to cry is a deep-seated one in our culture. Although the proscription is less rigid for women, the woman who cries is still considered more immature or hysterical than the one who can hold back her tears. The tradition, I believe, is an unfortunate one, because it does not properly respect innate responses. Those who adhere to the principle unnecessarily deprive themselves and their children of an emotional outlet, the inhibition of which contributes to the formation of psychological disorder. One of the effects of the prohibition against crying is that the child who spontaneously bursts into tears is made to feel humiliated and, consequently, his (her) self-esteem is lowered.

The crying prohibition is frequently extended even to a child whose parent or grandparent has just died: "Be brave, don't cry" or "Big boys and girls don't cry." And even if the child is not exposed to such misguided admonitions, he (she) may very well be exposed to subtler remarks: "Mary is taking it so well" or "He's holding up beautifully." Mourning involves a piecemeal desensitization to the pain one feels over the loss of a loved one. Each time one thinks of the deceased, the pain becomes a little more bearable. Each time one cries one feels a little less pained over the loss. To inhibit these reactions (which I believe to be innate) is to prevent a healthy psychological restoration. The persistence of such pent-up emotions prevents the sense of well-being necessary for feeling good about oneself. In addition, if the child feels humiliated and embarrassed over the tears, he (she) suffers an even further lowering of self-esteem.

Children do well, therefore, to see their parents, especially their fathers, cry in appropriate situations. The parent who runs into another room so the children will not observe him (her) cry makes it less likely that they will have a healthy attitude toward crying. Our children learn much from their imitation of us. If the adult is free to cry when the situation warrants it, the child is more likely to act in a similar way.

Although therapy does not usually involve opportunities for the therapist to cry, there are certainly situations in which such crying is appropriate and even desirable. In accordance with the infectiousness of human emotions, there are times when a patient will tell such a sad story that the therapist too may begin to cry. I have had at least a dozen such experiences over the course of the years. Each time I said such things to the patient as "I'm crying too. What you've said is so sad." Or I may not say anything because it is so obvious that I am crying. I have never yet had a patient view me with disdain or consider me to be acting inappropriately with such tears. Obviously, if such episodes occur frequently, then this may represent a defect in the therapist.

In an attempt to provide themselves with a macho image, many youngsters involve themselves in smoking, drinking, and drugs. Although a multiplicity of factors are operative in bringing about these symptoms, one is clearly the attempt to compensate for feelings of low self-worth. Adolescent smokers hope to achieve the image of adult status, and to do so they have to delude themselves into thinking that a cigarette hanging from one's lips can achieve this goal. Furthermore, they have to surround themselves with others who share this delusion, and all concerned must deny the heavy medical price that will inevitably be paid for the utilization of this absurd method for bringing about a specious enhancement of self-worth. The youngster who imbibes alcohol must delude himself into believing that the more alcohol he can hold, the more beers he can "guzzle," or the more recklessly he drives under the influence of alcohol, the more impressive a person he is. He must subscribe to the belief that if he can mosey up to the bar and drink with the best of them, he is indeed a "man." Again, in order to engage in this stupidity, one must surround oneself with a circle of similar fools. Last, the drug addict must bring himself to believe that he is somehow higher and worthier than others who have not thrown off the shackles of a society that has timid and fearful attitudes about the wonders of drugs. Obviously, all this is compensatory and serves to provide a specious sense of self-worth in compensation for deep-seated feelings of inadequacy.

Youngsters who gravitate toward machismo, drinking, alcohol, and drugs as a method for compensating for feelings of inadequacy are less likely to use the educational process to provide them with healthier forms of compensation. Preoccupation with the latest uniform that the macho types wear diverts one from educational pursuits. Hanging around with the macho types, especially in gangs, reduces the likelihood that one will direct oneself to one's studies. Alcohol, tobacco, and drugs all compromise those cognitive abilities necessary for study. Accordingly, anything a therapist can do to help such youngsters see the thinness of their facades and help them to appreciate that they ultimately do not work will thereby help such youngsters with the inevitable educational problems that result from such indulgence.

Clinical Example

The clinical example I provide here is actually of an experience I had with my son Andrew when he was about seven or eight years old. I had taken him to an amusement park. At lunch time the restaurant was quite crowded. Andrew sat down to reserve a table and I went to the counter to buy our hotdogs. There was no particular line and people were crowded about calling out their orders to the people behind the counter. As I was standing there, it became quite clear that the young man serving hotdogs was playing a sadistic game with the customers. He was purposely avoiding giving any recognition to those who came earlier and was randomly accepting orders from the crowd. I, and a number of the other people who were trying to order, became increasingly frustrated and resentful. At one point a newcomer, who was at least three or four inches taller than me, younger, more muscular, and certainly stronger, was immediately offered service by the young sadist behind the counter. The chosen one was there long enough to realize what game was being played and snickered joyfully when he was singled out for immediate attention to his request.

At that point, the anger that had already built up in me to a high level suddenly boiled over, and I yelled to the employee: "You sadistic bastard, you know damn well that that son-of-a-bitch over there just came here. . . ." Before I could say anything else, I suddenly found this "ape" hovering over me, red with rage, screaming at the top of his lungs: "Who the hell do you think you are, calling me a son-of-a-bitch? You take that back. If you don't apologize, I'll beat the shit out of you." The man was ready to lunge at my neck. I had already had two hospitalizations for herniated cervical discs and I immediately recognized that the man could easily injure me for life, and possibly make me a paraplegic. But even if that were not the case, I would have responded in the same way. In a voice loud enough to make a scene that would attract as much attention as possible I responded, *"Sir,* you are correct! I insulted you and I had no business doing so. You have my public apology and these people around here are all witnesses to it." At that point, the man's hands dropped to his side. There was about a 10-second silence, and he walked off and asked for his hotdogs.

I then returned to my seat and said this to Andrew: "Andrew, I want you to always remember what just happened. I hope you'll never forget what you just saw. Most fathers would not have done what I just did. Most fathers would have thought that it would be 'chicken' of them to apologize to that man, especially when their sons were around. They would think that only cowards would apologize in such a situation and that they would be a poor example for their sons. I believe that I set a good example for you by what I just did. There are times when it's smart to fight, and there are other times when it's smart to run away. There are times when it's smart to apologize, and there are times when it's stupid to apologize. This was a time when it was smart to apologize. That man was wrong and he knew he was wrong. I made a mistake too. I shouldn't have called him that name. I could have thought of it all I wanted to, but it was a big mistake to say it. There are lots of crazy people in this world, and you have to be careful, or terrible things could happen to you. You know about all the trouble I've had with my neck. If that man had tried to choke me he might have broken my neck, and he might have even killed me. When I apologized, I saved myself a lot of trouble, and possibly my life."

I believe that my son found this a useful experience. It may be of interest to the reader to know that I, too, found it a useful experience in that I have never again called a stranger a sadist or a son-of-a-bitch. I believe, also, that describing this experience to a patient has therapeutic benefits. It not only communicates a message about the wisdom of flight in certain situations, but does so in a way that is more likely to have clout than a simple statement of the principle. Moreover, it provides an opportunity for communicating to the patient that I, too, am not perfect, I "lost my cool," and that I at times act irrationally. I thereby hope to counteract the risk that the patient will idealize me and suffer the antitherapeutic consequences of this view.

In the context of my discussions on fight and flight I will focus on the macho image that boys and men in our society are encouraged to assume. I will try to help the youngster appreciate that the macho stance—especially when it has become a deep-seated personality pattern—is generally an attempt to compensate for feelings of inadequacy. I try to help the youngster appreciate that true strength does not have to be advertised. Of course, I am working against the powerful influences of society, the military, the advertising industry, women who believe that macho men are more sexually potent, and a variety of other cultural influences. These problems notwithstanding, the therapist does well to try to help youngsters appreciate the futility and absurdity of the macho stance. Rather than using compensatory macho techniques, youngsters do well to subscribe to the principle, attributed to (but certainly not originated by) Theodore Roosevelt: "Speak softly and carry a big stick." Such a stance truly enhances feelings of self-worth.

For younger children certain stories of mine deal directly with this issue. The stories "The Squirrels and the Skunk" and "The Dolphin and the Shark" in my *Dr. Gardner's Fables for Our Times* (Gardner, 1981a) deal with these issues. And the stories "Jeffrey, Julie, and the Cigarettes" and "Jennifer the Scaredy-Cat" in *Dr. Gardner's Stories About the Real World, Vol. II* (Gardner, 1983a) may also prove useful as bibliotherapeutic techniques.

"SMART GIRLS" AND THE "CLASS BRAIN"

Most educators are aware that prior to puberty girls are generally the better students, whereas after puberty boys excel academically. This is in part related to the fact that at any grade level girls are developmentally ahead of their male classmates of the same age. A more important factor in this phenomenon relates to what happens after puberty: the boys start thinking more about careers and the girls about getting married. The specter of living the life of a spinster starts to descend over the heads of many girls during their teens and plays a significant role in their turning away from their studies toward those endeavors, no matter how frivolous, that will enhance their attractiveness to boys. Although she may ultimately get her husband, the girl has paid a heavy price. She has deprived herself of the opportunity to develop in other important areas. And the older she gets, the more bitterly she may come to resent how she has been duped by her parents and others who have supported this foolish misplacement of her values. This tragic situation is one of the leading causes of frustration, disillusionment, and unhappiness in the lives of many women.

It is during the high-school period that some girls start being advised by their well-meaning mothers that they had better not act too intelligent in front of boys lest they scare them away. Or the mother might be a sort of female chauvinist who basically believes that females are smarter than males but that the prudent woman "builds a man's ego" and conducts herself in such a way that he is led to believe that he is the smarter one. In either case the girl is advised to "cool it" regarding her intellectual growth if she is to successfully "get a man." Unfortunately, many, if not most men, *are* so insecure that they would be threatened by a woman who *is* their intellectual equal. So they cooperate with the woman in the latter's intellectual suicide. They gravitate toward women who have not developed their intellectual capacities anywhere near their potential—except in the area of flattering men and "building up their egos." The remedy for this situation, however, does not lie merely in the development of a new generation of women who refuse to play this self-destructive game. Fortunately, as time progresses, an ever-growing number of women are removing themselves from this mold and are going into the job, education, and career world. However, there are still many women who subscribe to the "old school" philosophy to whom my comments apply. This new breed of women has its problems as well. A new breed of men will also have to evolve if these women are to have an ample number of suitable men to relate to on an egalitarian basis (whether in marriage or not). It is in childhood, in the home, and in the school, that the foundation can most effectively be laid down for such new patterns.

Therapists do well to do everything possible to help girls in this category appreciate the injudiciousness of their decision to consciously (or sometimes unconsciously) suppress or ignore their academic attainment because of their awareness that failure to do so might very well result in a diminution of their social popularity. They have to be helped to see how misguided these priorities are and how ultimately they will end up with significant feelings of insecurity as they recognize the disparity between what they are and what they could have been. They have to be helped to appreciate that all of us grow older and that youthful beauty is not permanent. They have to project themselves into the future and ask themselves how they see their lives 20, 30, or 40 years down the line and whether they will be sorry then for the decision to compromise their studies for a little more popularity from a few more inadequate boys.

In some schools a certain amount of stigma is suffered by the better students. Such youngsters are most criticized, of course, by the poorest students, who do so out of jealousy. The bright child may be referred to as a "nurd" or called the "class brain"—often in a pejorative way. Children who are overly sensitive to criticism, who cannot tolerate being different from the majority (no matter how slightly and regardless of the reason), may squelch their academic aspirations and do poorly in school in order to be "one of the boys (or girls)." Such children must be helped to appreciate how they are prostituting themselves and that they are making a terrible sacrifice for a little more popularity. They must be helped to appreciate that the stigma they suffer is the result of secret envy and admiration. They may be helped to maintain their dedication to their studies by more involvement with other academically oriented students. They too must be helped to appreciate that the protection from a lowering of their self-worth that comes from avoidance of studies may seemingly appear judicious at this point. However, if they project themselves into the future, they will appreciate how they ultimately will suffer profound feelings of loss of self-worth as they come to recognize how unfulfilled their lives have become.

HAPPINESS AS A VALUE

We live in a society in which the attainment of *happiness* is considered to be an overriding goal. Parents say, "All I want is that my children should be happy." Fairy tales end with "And they lived happily ever after." People are asked (even by thera- pists), "Do you have a happy marriage?" and, especially in public, people routinely say they have a "happy marriage." People who consider themselves unfortunate enough not to have attained the state of ongoing happiness may feel frustrated and may suffer attendant feelings of low self-worth as they compare themselves to others who they believe have attained this ongoing state of constant euphoria.

As mentioned earlier in this book, there is hardly a school- child who has not been asked to memorize Thomas Jefferson's belief in our inalienable rights to "Life, Liberty and the pursuit of Happiness." Yet there is hardly a person who thinks seriously of the significance of the word *pursuit* in this passage – a word that is vital to its meaning. Jefferson might well have written "Life, Liberty and Happiness," but he was wise enough to appreciate that no person can be guaranteed the right to happiness as it is something that exists, at best, only for short periods and under very special circumstances.

Dr. Geoffrey Osler, a New York City neurologist and a gifted teacher (one of the best I ever had), once suggested that Jefferson should have written "Life, Liberty and the Happiness of Pursuit." Osler's position, which I support, was that the *process of pursuit* of a goal provides our greatest happiness in life. Although life may allow us many periods of happiness, it cannot provide us with a chronic state of happiness. For the sake of completeness (but not, by any means, for the sake of poetic beauty), one could combine what Jefferson and Osler said and guarantee to all men the right to Life, Liberty, the pursuit of Happiness, and the happiness of Pursuit. In short, all should be given the freedom and opportu- nity to enjoy the happiness that can come from pursuing one's goals.

We live in a world where this basic truth is not widely appreciated. People are led to believe that life can be continually happy and that there actually are people who are completely happy. Although no one has ever actually met such a person, everyone has read about them in books and magazines and seen them on movie and television screens. We talk of wanting our children to "be happy." Marriage is supposed to provide us with "happiness." The state of chronic happiness can be obtained, we have come to believe; it's just that something always seems to come along that interferes with our attainment of this elusive goal. And we may die with the feeling of dissatisfaction that life has somehow passed us by and has not given us the degree of happiness that, under better circumstances, we might have enjoyed. There are some who say that the term *happy marriage* is an oxymoron, a contradiction in terms, and that the two preclude one another.

Such an expectation from life, an expectation laid down in childhood by both parents and society at large, helps produce feelings of disillusionment, frustration, and lack of satisfaction with oneself. This was effectively stated many years ago in the film *Lovers and Other Strangers.* A young married man returns to the home of his parents to inform them that he has decided to get a divorce. His distraught parents naturally ask him why. "What has happened?" they imploringly ask. (This and the remaining quotes in this vignette are approximate.) "Nothing special," answers the boy. "I'm just not happy in my marriage, and I want to be happy." In response to this his mother shouts, "If you're going to spend your whole life trying to be happy, you'll be miserable!"

Therapists and parents do best for children to impart to them that life is never perfect. Life inevitably has its frustrations, its struggles, and its grave disappointments. It can also provide, for those who are willing to work for them, intense periods of gratification and even happiness. If we are successful in imparting this view to our children, we will lessen the likelihood that they will suffer from ego-debasing disillusionments about themselves and others. We do well to impress upon them also that the pursuit process may be more important to a sense of ego-enhancement and pleasure than the actual attainment of a goal. Schoolwork, if anything, is one such pursuit. It is a pursuit that starts when the child first begins to learn, during the first few months of life, and should continue throughout the course of life. School is only a segment of one's life where the learning process is formalized.

HEALTHY PLEASURE

When I use the term *healthy pleasure*, I refer to pleasurable experiences that are relatively free of psychopathological elements. Some examples would be a pleasurable response to a beautiful scene, music, dance, or other aesthetic experience. Sexual pleasure in a loving relationship would be another example. Laughing provides healthy pleasure. And relaxation after vigorous physical exercise would be another form. I would also view as healthy pleasure the sense of gratification that comes upon the attainment of a long sought-after goal.

In order to be classified as healthy, the pleasurable experience must be relatively free from psychopathological elements. The euphoria that drug addicts experience (especially in the early stages of their addiction) would be a form of *un*healthy pleasure. I would similarly classify the pleasures that may be derived from any form of drug abuse (as distinguished from a sense of relaxation that may follow the ingestion of small amounts of alcohol). Aristotle believed that "pleasure is the absence of pain." Although I would not go so far as to say that all pleasure can be so viewed, there is no question that the alleviation of pain can provide a pleasurable sensation of relief. And I would include this among the healthy types. When sexual pleasure is used compulsively to serve other purposes, I would consider it among the pathological forms of enjoyment.

I believe that healthy pleasure is a universal antidote to psychogenic pathology. It is esteem-enhancing and thereby serves to reduce the ego-debasing factors that are inextricably involved in most, if not all, forms of psychogenic pathology. However, it is not the universal panacea. It does not *cure* such problems; it only contributes to their alleviation.

Psychotherapeutic Approaches

In the course of the treatment the therapist does well to seize any opportunity in which the child can be encouraged to avail himself (herself) of healthy pleasurable experiences. The therapist should serve as a model for such involvement in the hope that the child will emulate the therapist in this area. The problem for the therapist here relates to the fact that the therapeutic experience may preclude significant amounts of time being spent in such pleasurable activities. The therapist should be providing experiences that a less well trained person cannot. If the child can obtain the same pleasurable experiences from less-trained individuals, or individuals trained in other areas, then the parents should not be seeing the therapist. Not only are therapists generally more costly, but therapists themselves cannot feel gratified professionally when involved in such activities.

There are therapists, for example, whose view of play therapy is that it is simply playing with a child. As mentioned (Gardner, 1986a), I believe that play therapy should be much more *therapy* than *play*. When therapists are involved in a pleasurable activity with the child patient, they should most often, but not necessarily always, be aware of psychodynamic factors that are operative in the interchange so that they may handle whatever goes on in the most therapeutic way. The fact that healthy pleasure is *therapeutic* does not necessarily mean that the experience must be shared with the therapist. A lonely man who forms an affectionate and loving relationship with a woman will find the experience therapeutic. A boy with feelings of inadequacy who, after hard work, excels in Little League baseball is also going to have a therapeutic experience. A child with a neurologically based learning disability who, after special tutoring, is able to function adequately in a regular class will also be therapeutically benefited. In all these cases a therapist's intervention and involvement may not have been necessary. Formal therapy in the consultation room is only one of many therapeutic experiences that a patient may have.

Some of the cards in *The Talking, Feeling, and Doing Game* provide the therapist with the opportunity to engender appreciation of the benefits to be derived from healthy pleasure.

> *Question:* What do you think is the most beautiful thing in the whole world? Why?
> *Response:* One of the most beautiful things in the world is a natural scene. It could be a dawn or a sunset. It could be a

mountain range, a seashore scene, a canyon, or a river. Did you ever stand and look at such a scene? It's one of the most enjoyable things a person can do. It makes one wonder about the glory of the world and the beauties of nature. It can be a marvelous experience.

My own favorite spot is the Grand Canyon in Arizona. It's a deep canyon that has been carved by a river, the Colorado River, over millions years. All the colors of the rainbow are mixed in it. And the scene changes all the time because as the sun moves the colors change. It's a remarkable sight. It's huge and beautiful at the same time. And one of the greatest things to do is to take a hike down into the canyon. It's so deep that you could put the Empire State building on the bottom and the top of the Empire State building would just about reach the top of the canyon. Once I took a helicopter ride into the canyon. We started off a couple of miles to the south of the edge of the canyon and then flew over the treetops. Then, we dipped down into the canyon when we got to the canyon's edge and went down, down, down. The helicopter hovered near the sides and near the bottom. It was one of the most thrilling experiences I've ever had.

There are many other such wonders of the world. You can get new pleasures from different places. There are wondrous things to see in the world. Although you're young now, I hope you'll have many opportunities to enjoy such experiences. Have you ever seen any place like the kinds I have just described?

There are many children who grow up in homes where there is almost a complete absence of aesthetic sensitivity and pleasure from the appreciation of beauty. They are thereby being deprived of one of life's great gratifications and sources of self-esteem enhancement. Introducing the child to such a world and living as a model for the child's involvement in aesthetics can therefore be therapeutic. It will also serve to reduce the child's involvement in unhealthy values such as exhibitionism, materialism, superficiality, artificiality, exploitation, and hypocrisy.

* * *

Question: A boy was laughing. What was he laughing about?

Response: The boy had been in a school play in which he had told some funny jokes and done some funny tricks, including a few stunts. They had made a video tape of the play and now he was watching it. He had a great time during the performance. Practically everyone laughed at his jokes and, at the end of the play, everyone clapped their hands. The whole auditorium applauded him and a few people even stood up and cheered because they were so enthusiastic about his performance. People said such things as, "He's a natural-born comedian," "That kid's really got talent," and "He's going to go places on the stage, you'll see."

They gave the show three times, on a Friday night, a Saturday night, and a Sunday afternoon. And each time he really felt great because he did such a good job. Now he's watching himself perform on a video tape of the show and he's laughing at some of his stunts. It seems kind of strange to watch himself but it also feels very good.

Laughing is one form of healthy pleasure. The attainment of a long sought-after goal can also be salutary. The ego-enhancement that accompanies acclaim for one's efforts is another source of healthy enjoyment. In this response I attempt to engender in the child the desire to pursue such endeavors for the psychological benefit that can be derived from them.

☐ TWENTY

SELF-ESTEEM PROBLEMS OF CHILDREN WITH NEUROLOGICALLY BASED LEARNING DISABILITIES

Although this book focuses on psychogenic problems, some comments about the self-esteem problems of children with neurologically based learning disabilities (NBLD) are warranted and should prove useful for examiners who are treating children whose self-esteem problems may have a neurological component. This is especially the case when the neurological impairment contributes to a learning disability. Although I have mentioned earlier the self-esteem problems of children with NBLD, I will elaborate here on the ways in which the various neurological manifestations contribute to self-esteem problems.

CAUSES OF SELF-ESTEEM PROBLEMS OF NBLD CHILDREN

Parental Contributions

An NBLD child is inevitably a source of disappointment for parents. Healthy parents want their children to be healthy, both physically and emotionally. They want their children to do well in school, to have friends, and to move along the path toward independent adulthood. NBLD children will inevitably disappoint their parents in these important areas. And it is not simply an occasional disappointment; rather, they are reminded daily of the child's impairments. For most parents it is a constant source of heartache. Accordingly, parents of NBLD children cannot provide their youngsters with the positive feedback that enhances self-esteem and pride. Rather, the "reflected appraisals" that such parents provide do the opposite—they contribute to feelings of low self-worth as the child inevitably appreciates their negative feedback. When the NBLD child comes home complaining "The kids all call me stupid," parents are in a much weaker position to reassure the child that such an epithet is unwarranted. If they were to be honest with the child (and preferably they should be), the best they can do is agree with the child that he (she) does indeed exhibit certain intellectual and educational weaknesses, but this does not justify anyone's ridiculing and/or taunting him (her).

Parents who do not tell their NBLD children what is wrong with them can contribute to the children's feeling that they are some kinds of freaks. Children whose disorder is too terrible to talk about cannot but feel that they have the strangest kind of malady—suffered only by the weirdest kinds of people. Honest discussion of the condition, by both parents and therapists, can help lessen this cause of lowered self-worth in NBLD children.

There are parents who, when they first suspect that something is wrong with the child, will deny entirely all manifestations of impairment. Then, when the child's difficulties reach the point where outside consultation becomes crucial, they may try to find a doctor who will tell them that nothing is wrong. They may then embark upon a "doctor shopping syndrome" in which they seek the physician (or other specialist) who will tell them that all previous examiners have misdiagnosed the child's condition and that either nothing is wrong or that some quick cure is readily available. When this inevitably fails, they may continue on the pilgrimage to find yet another doctor who will support their denial mechanisms. Throughout the course of this pilgrimage the children are continually being told, overtly and covertly, that their parents are not satisfied with the way they are and that a quick transformation in the children's total personality is being sought. This too contributes to feelings of low self-worth.

Feeling genuinely needed is another element that contributes to a child's sense of self-respect. One of the criteria that I use to determine if seriously depressed people are suicidal is whether they have the deep conviction (justified or not) that no one in the whole world would miss them if they were dead. People who have such a belief are more likely to kill themselves. Although children are dependent and need their parents, far more than parents need them, children, in order to have a healthy feeling of self-esteem, must still feel that their absence would be painful to their parents. Healthy children in a loving home rarely (if ever) think about their parents' reactions to their absence. This may be an occasional source of concern to the emotionally deprived child. It is often a painful preoccupation of the NBLD child. NBLD children will sense acutely their parents' feelings of not needing them. They cannot help around the household as well as their normal siblings, even younger ones. They do not make others laugh, nor do they produce the inner warm glow of parental pride that their siblings are capable of engendering in their parents. In extreme cases they fully recognize that their parents would be happier if they were indeed dead. And all this cannot but lower feelings of self-worth.

There are parents who will enter into a conspiracy of silence with friends and relatives, the purpose of which is never to let anyone know what's wrong with the child. This program will inevitably fail because the child's deficiencies are generally easily apparent to others. Such children ultimately sense the cover-up and recognize that they have been at the center of a conspiracy of silence. They come to appreciate that they have a disease that is too terrible to talk about and a network of individuals have been party to a conspiracy of silence. This situation cannot but lower feelings of self-worth.

Relationships with Siblings

NBLD children generally have significant problems with their peers, especially those who are not learning disabled.

Typically, the siblings are embarrassed by the odd behavior of the NBLD child, so much so that they may be reluctant to and even avoid entirely having friends come to the home. When such friends do come, the NBLD child may be a significant source of difficulty. The NBLD child is quite lonely and wants to join in with the sibling and his (her) friends. However, because of a wide variety of cognitive, emotional, and developmental difficulties, the NBLD child just does not fit in. The NBLD child may then try to coerce involvement, much to the irritation of the sibling and visitors. Privacy is not respected; rather the child may bang on the sibling's door, giving the visitors no peace until allowed admission. If this continues despite parental discouragement and restraints, the NBLD child's ineptitude and atypical behavior become an irritant to the guests, and they are not likely to return. Furthermore, the frustration and anger engendered in the normal sibling by this situation may not be freely expressed because the parents have induced guilt in the normal sibling over such expression. Or, the sibling may feel sympathetic to the NBLD child and recognize that expression of such anger might be cruel. In either case, the sibling is filled with suppressed rage, which may contribute to the development of a variety of psychopathological symptoms.

Another factor that may contribute to the NBLD child's feelings of low self-worth is the unfavorable comparison that the youngster has with normal sibling(s). I have seen many situations in which the normal child was younger and yet far surpassed the older NBLD sibling in a wide variety of areas. The NBLD child can withdraw and avoid unfavorable comparisons with peers and classmates, but complete avoidance of one's sibling(s) is impossible. This constant confrontation with one's inadequacies also contributes to low self-worth.

Relationships with Peers

The peer situation also inevitably contributes to the NBLD child's feelings of low self-worth. When choosing teammates in sports, NBLD children are usually the last ones to be chosen or may even be told that their involvement is not desired. Obviously, these humiliations lower self-esteem enormously. Coordination deficits, inability to understand the rules of the game, and difficulties in appreciating such concepts as sportsmanship and fair play all contribute to the child's being rejected. The impulsivity and poor self-control of such youngsters may make it difficult for them to hold back in social situations where self-restraint is crucial. Because of their inability to suppress and control responses to taunts, they become easy prey to bullies who recognize that NBLD scapegoats will provide them with the responses they desire, responses such as tantrums, screaming outbursts, crying, and other fits.

In school, as well, NBLD children are recognized as being different from the others. Most often they are in special classes. Although children in these classes are protected from the teasing of their normal classmates while in the schoolroom, they do not enjoy such protection outside the classroom. There, they may be referred to as "ments" and "retards." But even more benevolently they are recognized as "special-ed kids" with the full recognition by themselves and others that their "specialness" is nothing to boast about, nor is it something that others admire. (This is just one of the examples of the fact that euphemisms rarely [if ever] work.)

Even when NBLD children are with other NBLD children, they may not relate well. Sometimes they react much more like younger children who are involved in "parallel play." Specifically, they sit in the same room, each involved in his (her) own little world, not particularly relating with the other children. This is expected among two-to-four-year-olds; it is a source of pain and frustration for parents when older children react similarly. Because of their limited repertoire of ways to interact normally with other children, they may become silly and rambunctious in a manner more appropriate for younger children. Age-inappropriate rambunctiousness and horse play are common, so much so that the parents may have to send the visitor home.

Basically, many of these children just do not know *how* to relate to other children, and it is one of the goals of therapy to help them do so.

Attitudes Toward Their Own Bodies

I have already discussed how children's feelings about their bodies play a role in their development of their self-worth. NBLD children usually have physical concomitants of their learning problems. Their coordination problems cannot but be a source of disappointment as they cannot keep up with their peers in sports and other activities requiring dexterity. Some children have associated congenital anomalies and/or deformities. These may range from the mild and almost unrecognizable to those that are easily recognized by everyone. When minor, these are sometimes referred to as "stigmata," reminiscent of Christ's wounds on the cross. Some examples: atypical eyelids, large or atypically placed ears, atypical head configurations, mild microcephaly or macrocephaly, and atypical stature. Many years ago a well-known child neurologist referred to these children as suffering with the FLK syndrome, an acronym for "Funny Looking Kid syndrome." Obviously, this is not a term that became widely utilized (justifiably so), but it is a statement of these children's atypicality. Obviously, children who have such identifiable differences are likely to be taunted, and this cannot but lower their feelings of self-worth.

Competence

I have already mentioned the important relationship between competence and self-esteem. So important is this relationship that I cannot imagine a person enjoying a feeling of high self-worth who does not simultaneously enjoy actual competence in one or more areas. NBLD children, unfortunately, are likely to be handicapped in this area. In the major areas of functioning they may not be able to exhibit meaningful competence. Their learning difficulties interfere with their achieving a sense of high esteem regarding their academic work. Whereas other poor students may turn to sports to gain ego-enhancement, this route is often not possible for NBLD children because of their coordination and visual-motor weaknesses. Normal children, who do poorly both academically and in sports, may still become highly socialized and enjoy, thereby, the esteem that comes from having many friends. These youngsters, unfortunately, may not even have this route available to them, because of their poor social skills and their inability to appreciate the subtleties of human interaction.

Without competence, the child is not likely to enjoy the ego-enhancement that comes from meaningful and well-directed compliments. Compliments that are not related to any concrete accomplishments can be ego-debasing: "What a fine boy" or "Aren't you a nice girl" causes many children to squirm. They sense that they are being "buttered up" and they may appreciate that they are being insulted as well, because the comment implies that the speaker thinks they are stupid enough to be so taken in. Some NBLD children may actually enjoy such compliments because they are better than nothing. Some may not recognize how artificial these compliments are and so may derive some transient ego-enhancing benefit from them. But others recognize that this kind of compliment is provided because the praiser cannot think of one that is based on some meaningful and actual area of competence.

It is not surprising, then, that the NBLD youngster is over represented in the adolescent and adult drug population. Having no actual areas of competence that they can point to in order to enhance their self-worth, they gravitate toward drugs, which provide specious but transient ego-enhancement. Drugs are attractive also because they provide temporary desensitization to the massive feelings of self-loathing such youngsters suffer because of their failure to have any area of competence or skill. To try to wean such a youngster from drugs without providing some training program in which a true sense of proficiency and mastery can be acquired is futile. Without proficiency in genuine skills, feelings of competence can at best be unstable.

A related problem that contributes to the NBLD children's

feelings of low self-worth is their inability to subscribe meaning-fully to the work ethic. Without the hope of competence, without the feeling of gratification that comes from applying oneself diligently over time, without achieving success, the individual's motivation to pursue a particular task is likely to be diminished enormously. No matter how enthusiastic the encouragers, no matter how committed the child's teachers and trainers are, without meaningful success on the youngster's part, commitment to the work ethic is not likely to take place. There is great wisdom in the old saying, "Nothing succeeds like success." Its opposite, "Nothing fails like failure," is more applicable to the NBLD child.

Another factor operative in one's commitment to the work ethic is the hope for success at the end of one's path. If these children are to be realistic about their ultimate prospects, they have to recognize that the likelihood of success (in the areas considered most important in our society) is extremely poor. Without such hope there can be little (if any) commitment to the work ethic, and there can be no sense of enhanced self-esteem that derives from such commitment. Aleksandrowicz and Alek-sandrowicz (1987) consider impairment in competence to be a central element in the self-esteem problems of NBLD children.

Competition

As mentioned, the ability to be successful in competition is also crucial for one's sense of self-worth. Both normal and NBLD children certainly do well without unhealthy competition, but all of us need the occasional sense of ego-enhancement that comes from success in healthy competition. The NBLD child has little opportunity to enjoy the sense of ego-enhancement that comes from success in the competitive realm. The child may experience some ego-enhancement in special situations, such as the special-ed class. However, most NBLD youngsters recognize that the competition is far less demanding than the traditional and so the award or goal is less valuable and less a source of ego-enhancement. The phenomenon is similar to the "Special Olympics" that handicapped people have. Although the individuals who are successful in these events may enjoy some sense of enhanced self-worth, they inwardly know that they are operating under different rules and so their success does not provide them with the same degree of heightened self-worth. A common maneuver designed to enhance these children's self-worth is to give them medals, trophies, and awards even more easily than they are provided for normal children. Unfortunately, we are living in a world in which such awards are more frequently and easily given than they were in the past. This is a mistake. The idea that the award per se produces the ego-enhancement is erroneous. The more rarely the award is given, the more coveted it becomes, the more difficult it is to obtain, then the greater the likelihood it will engender a high feeling of self-worth. Often, this is lost sight of by those who churn out these awards. Showering youngsters with awards does not work to enhance self-worth, whether it be for the NBLD or the normal child.

Impotence and Self-assertion

NBLD children, because they are less capable in a wide variety of skills and functions, are not as likely to have the same feeling of power over the world as those who are normal. This sense of impotence contributes to their feelings of low self-worth. Furthermore, lacking competence and a sense of power, they are less likely to assert themselves. Accordingly, they are less likely to stand up for their rights, protect themselves from those who would take advantage of them, and achieve other goals that require self-assertion. They are less likely to speak up in the classroom and say that they do not understand what the teacher is saying. Inwardly they often know how ignorant they are about the world, and asking a question publicly is viewed as just another public exposure of their ignorance. There is great wisdom to the ancient aphorism, "Nothing ventured, nothing gained." These children venture less and gain less. Without gains, there is less self-esteem. Children who do not assert themselves may suffer with frustration and pent-up anger associated with their failure to achieve their goals. Pent-up anger also contributes to feelings of low self-worth.

Dependency Problems

As mentioned, overdependent children often have overprotective parents. Professionals who work with NBLD children often tell parents that they are overprotective. I believe that we do well to make a sharp distinction between *over*protection and *extra*protection. NBLD children *need* extra protection because they are not capable of acting as independently as their normal peers. It is only when the parental protectiveness goes beyond what is necessary that the term *overprotective* is warranted. The parent who, under the guise of helping the child with homework, actually does it for him (her), or points out the mistakes so the child can hand in perfect papers, is contributing to the development of overdependency problems and is being overprotective, not just extraprotective. The father who makes the models for the child so that they "look better" is sabotaging the youngster's attempt to gain a feeling of mastery and self-confidence. These parents, although they may produce an immediate sense of specious accomplishment for the child, ultimately undermine the youngster's self-worth in that the child does not gain the competence necessary for genuine self-esteem. Furthermore, these maneuvers entrench the child's dependency on the parent in future activities, thereby perpetuating a situation conducive to the development of low self-worth.

A parent of an NBLD child who does not send the child to day camp—when the child would actually function well in that environment—is depriving the child of the opportunity to gain competence in areas in which the child might succesfully do so. The parents of NBLD children should be there to help, but should be also able to step back and allow the child to function independently when there is any hope that the youngster will be capable of doing so.

Attitudes Toward the Deficiencies

Shakespeare's wisdom is applicable here: "There is nothing either good or bad but thinking makes it so." An important determinant of the NBLD child's self-esteem relates to the youngster's attitude toward his (her) deficiencies. Some youngsters will generalize and consider themselves totally worthless because of their specific (and sometimes isolated) weaknesses. This tendency is likely to be exaggerated in a society that places enormous emphasis on academics, an emphasis that is in part necessary if youngsters are to be capable of functioning in the highly complex industrial society in which we live. As mentioned elsewhere (Gardner, 1987b), many of the children whom we label NBLD have nothing more "wrong" with them than the fact that they are in the 15th to 25th percentile range on bell-shaped curves of academic capability. In an agrarian society, they would have no problem; in an industrialized, Western society they are given the label of disease. And this cannot but contribute to lowered self-worth and cannot but contribute to the tendency of these children to generalize and consider their isolated defects to be manifestations of generalized deformity. Of course, the aforementioned rejections of parents, siblings, and peers all contribute to the tendency to create such generalizations.

It is not surprising, then, that many NBLD children become psychological drop-outs very early in their educational careers. Although they are still sitting in the classroom, and although they are not literally physical drop-outs from school, from the psychological point of view they are effectively drop-outs. Of the many factors operative in this situation, one is their unwillingness to consciously accept and tolerate their deficiencies. Some of them, in a seemingly paradoxical way, have a perfectionistic element in their attitude toward school. Because of their inadequacies, they become intolerant of any manifestation of weaknesses or defect and so do not try at all. For such children one error would be devastating. They may develop the delusion that they could do well if they tried, but choose not to. This position protects them from the ego-debasement that they would suffer if they were to try and consequently be confronted with their weaknesses. They do not have the ego-strength to take the position that no one is perfect and that everyone makes mistakes. Those who follow this principle are unlikely to learn. In contrast, they operate under the delusion that they could be perfect if they tried. Because they don't, they do not enjoy the ego-enhancement that is enjoyed by those who do.

Pathological Adaptations to the Neurological Deficits

The NBLD child may develop a wide variety of psychopathological symptoms that are designed to bolster feelings of low self-worth and/or to deny such feelings. As is true of just about all psychopathological mechanisms, what is initially designed to enhance feelings of self-esteem usually results in lowering self-esteem even further. For example, the unpopular boy who lies to his peers and describes interesting and unusual exploits may enjoy more ego-enhancing attention at first, but as soon as his peers learn of his fabrications (and they invariably do), he suffers more rejection than when he was unpopular but truthful. In addition, even before his friends suspect his lies, he compromises his own dignity by his lying. He is inwardly embarrassed about what he is doing, and this in itself reduces the ego-enhancement he had hoped to achieve.

A common adaptive mechanism used by NBLD children is clowning in the classroom. Not being able to get meaningful attention in the usual ways—such as with good academic performance, friendliness, or skill in sports—the youngster finds that clowning will inevitably attract attention. A boy, for example, who utilizes this maneuver has to blind himself to the fact that he is being laughed *at* much more than he is being laughed *with*. His cognitive impairments make it easier for him to ignore this differentiation. He can therefore delude himself into believing that his classmates' enjoyment of his antics reflects respect. And, if he is rejected in other areas, he may respond with even more harebrained escapades, which further alienate his peers.

The NBLD boy who buys friends with candy and money may experience temporary relief from his loneliness and its associated feelings of worthlessness, but he inwardly knows that his friendships are not true, that they are dependent upon continue bribery, and that he is being exploited. Accordingly, he feels even more inadequate than before. In short, bribery, like all symptoms, is in part a misguided attempt to bolster a lagging self-esteem. What begins as a maneuver to enhance feelings of self-worth ends up lowering them. This, in turn, may stimulate further utilization of the maneuver, resulting in an even greater loss of self-respect.

PSYCHOTHERAPEUTIC APPROACHES

Basic Therapeutic Considerations

Working with NBLD children requires great patience. Because NBLD children often suffer with perceptual impairments (usually visual or auditory), it is often difficult for them to process accurately the therapist's messages. Because their memories are often poor, they do not retain well the therapeutic communications. It behooves therapists, therefore, to determine whether the child has a specific impairment in either auditory or visual processing and/or memory. Therapists then do well to try to utilize the more intact modality(ies) if the child is to profit most effectively from the therapeutic experience. For example, a child with impairments in auditory discrimination and auditory memory not only would have trouble hearing correctly what the therapist says, but would not retain long the therapeutic messages. If, however, the child's visual perception and memory functioned better, the therapist would do well to draw pictures and write down his therapeutic communications. Such graphic communication can be best accomplished in the context of a game. For example, I find drawing figures with typical cartoon-style balloons over each character's head to be useful and attractive to children. We alternate writing in the balloon above each character's head what he (she) is saying. In contrast, the child with impaired visual memory and perception, but intact auditory memory and perception, does far better with verbal interchanges. However, even the more intact faculty may be somewhat impaired. It is only through patient reiteration, through the simultaneous stimulation of the various sensory modalities (sight, hearing, touch, and on occasion smell and taste), that one can expect to "get through." In more recent years I have been encouraging NBLD children to make videotapes of their sessions and review these at home. Videotaped viewing provides a combination of both visual and auditory input, providing thereby the kind of multisensory stimulation that is so important for these children. Because of their memory deficits, the reiteration provided by videotapes can be extremely valuable.

Whatever the therapeutic modality, the therapist does well to exhibit a strong commitment to the work ethic, thereby serving as a model to the child to do so as well. These children have cognitive deficits, and they have learned less than other children. And this is a central factor in their feelings of low self-worth. To the degree that the therapist can encourage compensatory learning, to that degree will the therapist contribute to the enhancement of these children's self-worth.

Circumscribing the Deficits

Children with NBLD tend to generalize and consider themselves totally worthless or loathsome because of their isolated deficits. Everything the therapist can do to help these children put their deficits in proper perspective can be useful toward enhancing their feelings of self-worth. For example, I might relate in a story, "The fox thought that just because *one small part* of his brain wasn't working well (neuroanatomical accuracy has no place in such communications), his *whole* brain was no good and that he couldn't do anything right. This just wasn't so. In fact, he could do most things quite well. It was just that the part of his brain that helped him read was slower in getting things to stick in it, so he had to work harder than most other foxes."

Dealing with Rejections

As mentioned, NBLD children suffer significant rejection, and this is an important factor contributing to their feelings of low self-worth. Such children have to be helped to appreciate that the fact that others reject them does not mean that they are automatically rejectable or unlovable. They have to be helped to appreciate that they are different from many children, but that there are other children like themselves who have similar weaknesses. Meaningful involvements with NBLD peers as well as with adults can provide the child with the verification of this reassurance. Also such involvements provide substitute gratifications to compensate for these rejections. Involving the child in special clubs and organizations for NBLD children can also provide such involvements. The child has to be helped to appreciate, however, that one does not engender love and affection in others by merely existing. One must exhibit qualities that elicit affection. I am not recommending here that the child be taught to mold his (her) personality in accordance with what others may wish, only that a certain amount of accommodation to the likes and dislikes of others is important if one is to "win friends and influence people."

With regard to those who torment the NBLD youngsters, the child must be helped to appreciate that although the weaknesses being ridiculed might very well be present, the taunt is inappropriate and cruel. The youngster has to be helped to appreciate that there is something wrong with a person who would be cruel and sadistic enough to make fun of an individual with a handicap. Furthermore, the child has to be helped to recognize that to the degree that the weaknesses can be rectified and compensated for, to that degree will there be a lessening of the rejections and ridicule. The therapist, however, should not set up unrealistic or unattainable goals in this area, but only encourage the child to work toward those goals that are attainable.

Such children must be helped to appreciate that they are not necessarily what others consider them to be. They must be helped to enrich their own set of criteria for judging their own self-worth. They must be helped to recognize the distortions and fallibilities of others' opinions of them. Parents and therapists can help the youngster gain insight into this process. The mother who says, "Your father doesn't think too much of you because you aren't very good in sports. To your father, sports are the most important thing in the world. There are many others who don't think that any single thing, like sports, is all that important, and they don't put down someone just because he isn't good at sports," is making a healthy statement. Her husband may consider her disloyal, but she has an obligation to her child as well.

Mention has been made of the deep-seated disappointments of the parents of NBLD children. This inevitably contributes to the youngsters' feelings of rejection. Anything the therapist can do to reduce the parental rejection can be useful for the child. I recognize that even the healthiest and most stable parent is not likely to accept everything in the NBLD child; neither will the loving parent generalize and consider the child totally worthless because of certain deficits. Parents who "doctor shop," hide the diagnosis from the child, family, and neighbors, and overprotect or deny the illness all share the basic attitude of not accepting the child for what he (she) is. Parents with inordinately high academic standards, who equate education and intelligence with happiness, will not accept a child who might become a perfectly adequate tradesman or craftsman and, in his (her) own way, have a rewarding life. Such parents are, in effect, saying to the child, "You are a totally worthless person because you aren't smart in school." Parents who put great emphasis on sports or physical prowess may reject the poorly coordinated child whose chances of academic gratification and competence in many other areas are good. These parents, too, may consider their child totally worthless because of his (her) isolated deficits. To the degree that the therapist can help such parents change their attitudes, to that degree will this factor in the child's rejection be reduced.

Tolerating and Accepting Deficiencies

Children with NBLD have to be taught to take a more accepting attitude toward their own weaknesses and tolerate the feelings of low self-worth that come when confronted with them. All of us must learn to do this, but NBLD children more so. The point that no one is perfect and that everyone makes mistakes and has defects must be repeated many times. Often I will comment on my own deficiencies and errors as they occur in the course of my interchanges with the child. For example, if I cannot hear the child (I do have a hearing deficit), I might say, "Please speak a little louder. The nerves inside my ears don't work too well, and I have a little trouble hearing. Just as you have to work harder to learn, I have to work harder to hear." Or, when making a mistake when playing a game, I might remark, "Gee, I missed that one. I'd better pay more attention to the game."

There are NBLD children who are perfectionistic and have unrealistically high standards that would be very difficult, if not impossible, to attain. They are therefore never satisfied with their performance and suffer from chronic feelings of inadequacy. For such children, comments such as these may be helpful: "As long as you think that any grade below A is unacceptable, you'll feel lousy about yourself," or "As long as you feel you have to be the best basketball player in every game in order to be acceptable, you'll feel terrible about yourself."

Behavior That Would Lower Anyone's Self-esteem

When a patient tells me, "I feel lousy about myself," I generally ask, "Are you doing anything that would make anyone feel lousy about himself (herself) were he (she) doing the same thing?" Often, after some thought, I get an affirmative answer, following which I invariably ask for specific examples. The child may be cheating on tests, stealing, or lying excessively. If he (she) has anything approaching a normal conscience, he (she) will feel guilty about these acts. Intrinsic to guilt is self-loathing: "What a terrible person I am for doing all these horrible things." The child in such a situation might be told: "As long as you do those things, you're going to find that you'll feel lousy about yourself." Although the proverbial advice, "Virtue is its own reward," may seem trite, it is most valid.

Pathological Utilization of the Neurological Symptoms

Some children with NBLD use the disorder to rationalize nonaction in areas of competence. They may say, "I am learning disabled, so I can't do anything." The answer to this, of course, should be, "Yes, you are learning disabled, and it is true that there are some things you cannot do as well as others, but that doesn't mean that you can't do *anything* at all. You're trying to cop out." The therapist then does well to address the particular areas in which the youngster is trying to avoid responsibility and not to accept the cop-out. Doing so enhances self-worth. Allowing the youngster to utilize this rationalization will ultimately lower self-worth, as the child is not required to function in areas in which competence has been proven. For example, some NBLD children try to avoid doing household chores with the excuse that they can't do them because of their neurological impairment. Parents of such children are best advised not to indulge such excuses. Requiring the child to participate in and contribute to the household in all the areas in which he (she) is capable not only can reduce the likelihood that this maladaptive reaction will become entrenched but can be ego-enhancing. A healthy part of the child cannot but feel good when he (she) is required to perform the same chores as his (her) normal siblings.

Some NBLD children will consider some of their psychogenic symptoms to be caused by their learning disability and will therefore conclude that they cannot be expected to control them. In my work with such children, I try to clarify (to the degree possible) which symptoms are manifestations of the neurological impairment and which are psychogenic. All psychogenic symptoms should be considered to be under conscious control to some degree, unless strongly proved otherwise (a rare situation). One child insisted that his tendency to withdraw into fantasy and giggle (a state we referred to as his "silliness") was caused by his neurological impairment. Although this was a psychotic manifestation (in a child whose symptoms were otherwise neurotic), I considered it to have a consciously controllable element (which I am sure it did). Although I certainly concerned myself with those factors in his life that were making withdrawal into fantasy more desirable than involvement in reality, at the same time I told stories in which children who were "silly" were laughed at by others, or lost friends, or didn't learn as much as they might have in school.

Some NBLD children consider their medication to be a magic cure. Therapists do well to discourage such a view of medication. They do well to get across the message that the medicine can, at best, be helpful, but that the children themselves must be attentive to their symptoms and recognize that they must use a certain amount of conscious control not to indulge their use. Allowing the child to believe that the medicine is magically helping cannot but lower self-esteem, whereas working toward the goal of controlling the symptoms themselves will enhance the self-esteem of these children. Again, we come here to the work ethic.

A book that I have written to be read by children with NBLD (Gardner, 1973a) has not only helped some children to lessen their tendency to utilize their neurological symptoms, but also to utilize many of the other maladaptive behaviors described in this section.

The Talking, Feeling, and Doing Game

Many of the questions in *The Talking, Feeling, and Doing Game* serve well as points of departure for NBLD children to discuss issues related to self-esteem. For example:

> If you had to be changed into someone else, who would you choose to be? Why?
>
> Suppose two people you knew were talking about you and they didn't know you were listening. What do you think you would hear them saying?
>
> Do you believe that praying for something will make it happen?
>
> Of all the things you learn in school, what do you like learning about the least? Why? If you could live your life all over again, what things would you do differently?
>
> If a fly followed you around for a day and could then talk about you, what would it say?
>
> Who was the best teacher you ever had? Why?

No one is perfect. Everybody has both good and bad parts. Name two bad things about someone you love.

A boy wasn't picked to be on a team. What had happened?

A girl was the only one in the class not invited to a birthday party. Why do you think she wasn't invited?

If the walls of your house could talk, what would they say about your family?

Name two of your good habits. What do you think about each of those habits?

The Mutual Storytelling Technique

When using the mutual storytelling technique with NBLD children, certain aspects and modifications deserve emphasis. Generally, the stories that NBLD children tell are less well organized than those of normal children. Accordingly, the stories are less likely to include the traditional beginning, middle, and end. Therefore, the therapist must try to ascertain a basic underlying theme that will then serve as a basis of his (her) responding story. The lesson or moral that I am usually successful in eliciting from normal children can be a valuable source of information about which of the many psychological themes the story manifests is the most meaningful for the child. NBLD children are less capable of presenting a moral because of their impairments in conceptualizing and abstracting; therefore, this clue to the story's main psychodynamic theme is less frequently elicited from them. In addition, their poor use of pronouns often confuses the listener regarding the antecedents to which the pronouns refer, and it behooves the therapist to interrupt the child for clarification.

There is often an egocentric quality about their storytelling, so that the children may not concern themselves with whether the listener understands them. For example, they may mentally introduce a new character without verbalizing this and may then be surprised that the therapist doesn't understand the particular figure's role. Some backtracking is then warranted if the therapist is to understand what is going on. Such interrupting and clarifying can be therapeutic. It requires these patients to think about the structure and organization of their communications—something that they do not often do. Often these children are allowed to ramble because those to whom they are talking do not wish to go to the trouble of trying to understand them, and they may not therefore appreciate how poorly they communicate. Often I will say to such children, "You know, when you speak, you don't think very much about whether the person you're speaking to can understand you. That's one of the reasons why you have trouble getting along with other people. You need to practice thinking about whether others can understand what you're saying. I'd like you to start practicing *right now* by telling me again the last thing you just spoke about in your story, because I didn't understand it. Now start again at the part where . . . " When making comments such as these, it is important that the therapist's tone be as sympathetic and tolerant as possible.

When therapists relate their own responding stories, they do well to interrupt frequently and ask the child whether he (she) understands what was said. When the story is completed, the therapist does well to ask the child to try to figure out the lesson or moral of the story. As mentioned, NBLD children are less likely to do this well because of their cognitive deficits and may provide a moral that has absolutely nothing to do with the story. Under such circumstances, the therapist should present the moral and then ask the child if he (she) can figure out the relationship between the story and its lesson.

Dramatization of both the child's and the therapist's responding stories can be extremely helpful, especially for NBLD children. This requires a certain freedom on the part of the therapist to "ham it up"—for example, to roll on the floor or to make all kinds of animal sounds. After the completion of a story sequence I might say to the child, "Would you like to make a play about those stories?" If the child expresses interest (and younger children are more likely to be receptive), I might say, "Okay, who do you want to be? The fox or the bear?" After the roles are assigned, we go through all the antics. Therapists who are comfortable enough to regress in this way will have at their disposal an effective therapeutic adjunct of value to all children in treatment, but especially to those with NBLD because of their need for reiteration and multisensory stimulation.

As mentioned, the therapist's strong adherence to the work ethic is crucial to the therapy of these children. Storytelling interchanges provide the opportunity for communications that encourage these children to apply themselves diligently, especially to the learning process. One five-year-old girl with a coordination defect, while playing with the dolls and doll house, had the girl doll fall down the stairs. In response I told a story about a girl who has trouble walking and, as a result, falls down the stairs and hurts herself. Afterwards she practices a long time in order to walk better, and she ends up playing a good game of hopscotch. All this was actively played out with the dolls, much to the patient's enjoyment.

A nine-year-old boy told a story about a football player whose arm is so strong that he throws the football out of the stadium into a nearby football field, where another game is going on. The presence of a second football in the other field causes some interference with the other game; but the ball is returned, and there the story ends. I considered the player's unusual prowess to reflect the patient's desire to possess in fantasy the physical strength he does not have in reality. His grossly inaccurate throw reflects the patient's coordination deficits. However, there are no repercussions following the mishap—a statement of the patient's desire that the world tolerate the untoward consequences of his impairments. In my story, the football player's coach compliments him on his unusual strength, but sadly informs him that he has been placed on probation. He must practice to improves his *aim* or else he will be dropped from the team. His inaccuracy is a source of difficulty not only for his own team, the coach tells him, but for the team in the next stadium as well. So warned, the player practices long and diligently and is reinstated after he has improved.

One nine-year-old boy told a story in which a storekeeper fires two men because of ineptitude. He then suffers a series of reverses and ends up sorry that he had not accepted these workers, their deficiencies notwithstanding. I considered the story to reveal the boy's wish that he be accepted with his deficiencies, regardless of how much inconvenience they cause. He wanted the world to join him in the denial of his impairments—a most unrealistic anticipation. In my story, the storekeeper warns the deficient workers that he cannot afford to keep them if they do not improve. One heeds the warning and works to improve himself; the other asks for help and it is given. In both cases the workers' defects are not tolerated; in both cases the workers rectify their defects in order to be acceptable.

A five-year-old mildly microcephalic girl with a thyroglossal cyst put the toy elephant in front of a small mirror and purposely let it fall down. I considered the play to reveal her desire to avoid confrontation with her defects (not only the cyst, but all others). In my responding story the elephant tells his friends that he doesn't want to look in the mirror because he is very ugly because of a small bump on his neck. His friends (various animals in the jungle) each, in turn, deny that the elephant is ugly just because of the small bump on his neck. They then suggest that he allow a strange animal to look at him, one who has never seen him before, and that he ask that animal if anything looks wrong. The animal sees nothing. The elephant then asks, "Didn't you see that ugly bump on my neck?"

"No," the animal answers, "I didn't notice it until you pointed to it. But even now I can hardly see it. What I did notice was how pretty you are and how nice a person you seem to be."

This is the kind of story I tell to help children circumscribe their defects, put them in proper perspective, and alter their pathological attitudes toward them.

Bibliotherapy

Bibliotherapy can be an important contribution to the treatment of NBLD children. Traditional psychotherapy is very much an oral-aural experience in which the therapist and patient talk with one another. This aspect of the treatment is what is being referred to when children refer to psychotherapists as "talking doctors." For most children with NBLD, mere talking therapy is not going to suffice. They need, more than the rest of us, a multisensory approach, especially one in which the visual elements are also introduced. And this is especially the case for children who have auditory processing problems. Certain books of mine may be particularly useful in this regard. My book for NBLD children (Gardner, 1973a) focuses specifically on the self-esteem problems of these children as well as other related difficulties. My *Stories About the Real World, (Vol. I)* (Gardner, 1972a) and *Vol. II* (Gardner, 1983a) also include reality-oriented stories relevant to the self-esteem problems of children with NBLD. My *Fables for Our Times* (Gardner, 1981a) is basically a series of stories derived from mutual storytelling technique responding stories. Some of these stories may be useful for NBLD children with self-esteem problems. The first chapter of *The Girls and Boys Book About Good and Bad Behavior* (Gardner, 1990) is devoted entirely to self-esteem and the concept is eluded to in various other chapters. Lenkowsky et al. (1987) describe the value of bibliotherapy in the treatment of learning-disabled children.

TWENTY-ONE
SCHOOLS AND SELF-ESTEEM

INTRODUCTION

A discussion of self-esteem problems and their relationship with psychogenic learning disabilities would be incomplete without a detailed discussion of the role of schools, especially as schools relate to the formation of such problems. In recent years, the term *self-esteem* appears frequently in comments and reports of educators, school psychologists, and guidance counselors. There is hardly an aspect of school life in which children's self-esteem is not given serious consideration. Furthermore, in recent years schools have prided themselves on their belief that emphasis on self-esteem has been salutary for students. Although it may be the unpopular thing to say at this point, I believe that the methods that schools have generally used to enhance children's self-worth have resulted in just the opposite, namely, a lowering of self-esteem. And this is the situation at every level, from kindergarten through graduate school, in both public and private schools (although the problem, I believe, is more deep-seated in public schools).

There is no question that we are witnessing a progressive deterioration of educational standards throughout the United

States. Although there certainly are areas in which things have improved in recent years, there is no question that there are more areas in which things have degenerated—so that the overall picture is much more in a downhill than uphill direction. The erosion of standards has occurred at just about every level, from kindergarten through graduate school. No one can deny that there has been a deterioration in the public schools during the last 25 years, certainly in the large cities and probably in suburban and rural communities as well. One compelling verification of this (if one needs it) is the progressive deterioration of Scholastic Aptitude Test (SAT) scores. De Witt (1991) describes the downward trend in average Verbal SAT scores from 431 in 1976 to 422 in 1991. But the numbers here do not reflect the full story. The test has progressively become *easier*. Accordingly, if the test were as rigorous as it was in the past, the deterioration would become even more apparent.

Prof. Richard Askey (1990) of the University of Wisconsin, in a letter to *The New York Times*, compared the kinds of mathematics problems 9th-grade Japanese students must solve to enter the 10th grade with the kinds of mathematics problems American 12th graders take when applying to college. Most of the problems presented to the Japanese students were multi-step problems, requiring a degree of logical reasoning capacity not required of American seniors, most of whose problems were at the one-step level. Askey found that the Japanese students worked at approximately the same level of speed as he did on their problems. The vast majority of his college students were unable to answer the questions solved by 9th-grade Japanese students. The *Education Commission of the States* (Allis, 1991) ranks the United States 10th among the major nations of the world in the number of days per year in which students attend school. Not surprisingly, Japan was first with 243 days whereas the United States had 180. (There were four other countries in which children attended school 200 days or more: West Germany, The Soviet Union, Thailand, and the Netherlands.) Wade (1990) reports that 30 percent of Americans drop out of high school, whereas 90 percent of Japanese children graduate. He also reports that American industry spends an estimated $30 billion a year in remedial education in order to prepare young employees to enter the job market. Here I will discuss what I consider to be some of the important factors operative in bringing about this deplorable situation, factors at the elementary, high school, and college levels.

ELEMENTARY SCHOOL

"All Men Are Created Equal"

Ours is seemingly an egalitarian educational system that assumes that "all children are created equal" and all children should have the opportunity to receive the same educational exposure. This is misguided egalitarianism. The principle blinds itself to the obvious intellectual differences that children exhibit from the time of birth. On the one hand, educators appreciate that every intelligence test has its distribution curve, from the intellectually impaired to the superior. On the other hand, our educational system in the United States does not properly accommodate these differences. I do not claim that there is no appreciation at all of these differences; I only claim that educators do not exhibit enough appreciation of these differences. Although there are special classes for learning-disabled children and technical high schools for those who are not academically inclined, the main thrust and orientation of our educational system is toward preparing youngsters to enter colleges and universities. The ideal presented is that all children should go to college and those who do not achieve this lofty goal bring shame upon themselves and their families. One of the results of this failure to recognize these differences is a significant lowering of the feelings of self-worth of those students who are not intellectually capable of moving along the main stream of American academic orientation, namely, the path that is supposed to end in college (at least). The fact that only about 30 percent of all school children go to college does not seem to affect the general educational thrust that college is the ideal goal.

Most countries have no problem accepting the fact that not

all children should be on a strong academic track. Accordingly, in many countries, somewhere between the ages of nine and eleven, children are divided into three tracks. The highest track ultimately leads to the university. The lowest track ends formal, intense academic training at about age eleven or twelve and then emphasizes various trades and skills. And the middle track is somewhere between the two. Of course, if the child has been placed in the wrong track, there is still a possibility of switching. We would do well in the United States to institute such a system. It would protect many children from significant grief. It would protect many children from the lowering of self-worth that results from our present system. To say that all people should be *treated* equally before the *law* is certainly reasonable. But to say that all are *created* equal is absurd. What is more reasonable to say, as Orwell did in *Animal Farm,* is that "some are more equal than others." Because public statements of such inegalitarianism are considered undemocratic in our society at this time, it is extremely unlikely that such changes will be introduced into our system in the foreseeable future.

Some Causes of School Deterioration

Many factors have contributed to school deterioration in recent years. One relates to teachers' salaries. It is unreasonable to expect that schools can attract high-quality, well-educated individuals when other careers provide much greater pay. In most municipalities garbage men make as much as, if not more than, elementary school teachers. The public sector can generally afford to provide higher salaries than private and parochial schools; yet the public schools seem to be getting the poorest-quality teachers. The more dedicated teachers are willing to take positions for lower salaries in order to work in the more academically stimulating atmosphere of the private and/or parochial schools.

I believe there has been a general diminution in the commitment of teachers to the educational process. I am not claiming that this is true of all teachers, only that the percentage of teachers who are deeply committed to their profession has been sharply reduced in the last 15 to 20 years. One manifestation of this trend is the decreased frequency with which children are required to do homework. Giving children homework most often involves homework for the teacher. And less dedicated teachers are not willing to take on this extra responsibility. In previous years there were many more teachers who were viewed to be somewhat hard-nosed and dictatorial, yet their despotism was benevolent and years later their students were able to look back with gratitude on what they were "forced" to do. Teachers are important models for children. Teachers who have little commitment to the educational process, who are watching the clock throughout the course of the day, who can't wait to get out of the building, are serving as poor models for their students. Accordingly, their students are not likely to learn very much—with a resultant compromise in their feelings of self-worth.

These days, "respect" for the child often involves a degree of permissiveness and indulgence that does not really serve children well in the course of their education. A good educational experience helps the child learn that there are times when one has to do things that may be unpleasant in order to derive future benefits. "Respecting" the child's wish not to endure such discomforts is basically not in the child's best interests. True respect for children involves the *requirement* that they do what is best for them, not the indulgence of their avoidance of reasonable responsibilities.

Another factor operative in the deterioration of the educational system has been the growth of a generation of teachers who themselves have not learned very much during their own educational processes. Often, these are teachers who went to college during the 1960s and 1970s, when students' self-indulgence may have reached an all-time high. Grammar, punctuation, spelling, and foreign languages were dismissed as "irrelevant." Many other subjects that required self-discipline and hard work were also often viewed as irrelevant. Graduates of this era are now teaching our youngsters. Not only do many of these teachers serve as poor models for their students, due to their impaired commitment to the educational process, but they are compromised as well in what they can teach. I routinely ask parents to bring in my child patients' report cards. Often I see egregious errors in grammar, punctuation, and spelling. I have had applicants for secretarial positions whom I would not have even considered hiring because of their ignorance of basic English. They were not people who I felt needed time to adjust to a new job; rather, it might have taken years to get them to reach the point where they could function adequately in a standard secretarial position. They often did not even appreciate how ignorant they were. They did not even recognize that a misspelled word looked misspelled, and so they had no motivation to consult a dictionary for the correct spelling. Obviously, children are not going to learn very much from teachers who don't have the information to teach in the first place. Without learning, there can be little self-worth.

The net effect of these unfortunate trends is that children learn less during their primary and secondary school years—with the result that SAT scores have dropped significantly during the last 15 to 20 years, and many studies have demonstrated that the majority of children are abysmally ignorant of basic facts about history, geography, literature, English, and mathematics. The resultant compromise in what children learn in the course of their academic experience results in a lowered feeling of self-worth.

Report Cards

In recent years educators have operated on the assumption that communicating to children anything about deficiencies is going to be devastating to their self-worth. In order to subscribe to this goal, an elaborate system of subterfuge has grown up, the purpose of which is to hide from children information that might prove "upsetting." Report cards demonstrate well this phenomenon and therapists do well to familiarize themselves with these principles in order to better understand what is going on with patients. The first rule is *Words with a pejorative connotation—no matter how slight—are strictly verboten.* Checks are given, but not crosses. A child may be "good," but no one is "bad." Students may be "right," but not "wrong." "Tests" are no longer given, only "exercises." In many school systems the lowest grade the child can get is NI (needs improvement); there is no such thing as a U (unsatisfactory) or an F (perish the thought and bite your tongue!). I recall one youngster whose school used this marking system: A + + + (excellent), A + + (very good), and A + (passing). There was no grade lower than A +. Presumably, if a child got a zero on every test, he (she) would get an A + average. I don't know who these people think they are fooling; most parents recognized the absurdity of this deceitful marking system.

Another rule that is rigidly adhered to in such reports is one that I call *the rule of the uncompared comparison*. Stated briefly, the rule is this: When describing a child's performance, never make any references — no matter how subtle — to the baseline or standards by which the student's performance is being judged. In this way no accurate information about poor performance will be communicated (since the term *poor* only has meaning in relation to its antithesis, *good*) and so the child will be spared the painful confrontation with his (her) inadequacies. Examples of this are legion: "Jane is doing much better in math." That's the whole sentence. The parent can only wonder, "I guess she must have been doing poorly at first and now she's doing better. Well, that's good to know. But *how poorly* was she doing at first? And *how much better* is she doing now? Was she failing then and passing now? Or was she failing then and still failing now? Did she go from a 10 percent to a 20 percent average (using the now discredited system), from a 30 percent to a 90 percent, or from a 1 percent to a 2 percent?" Or we are told, "Billy is trying much harder in social studies." Again, the same confusion and frustration is produced. We're glad to learn that; but how far have his efforts gotten him? No information at all in that department. The real questions most parents want answered are "Is he passing and failing in comparison to the other kids in the class? Where does he stand? Does he need help? How is he *really* doing?" To spare anyone any hard feelings, no one is told how he is doing. No one's feelings are going to be hurt. All those who do poorly are helped to deny their difficulties. This is supposed to enhance self-esteem. What is enhanced is delusion, procrastination, and the avoidance of painful reality – qualities that have never proven themselves to be particularly effective ways to ultimately enhance anyone's feelings of self-worth or adaptive capacity.

Other devices are commonly used to protect the child from confrontation with inadequacies. Using vague terminology can accomplish this. Words like *slight* and *somewhat* serve this purpose quite well: "Mary is doing somewhat better in spelling" or "Ronald is showing slight improvement in math." Usually improvement is nonexistent or minuscule, and the teacher believes that it would be devastating to the child's "ego" were he (she) told that there was no progress. Another way of accomplishing this is to use a verb form ending in *ing*, in such a way that a vague passage of time is implied: "Bobby is doing fractions," "Gail is still learning the three-times table," or "Malcolm is beginning to learn how to organize his time." No one knows exactly how far these children have gotten in their various pursuits – in fact, one strongly suspects that they have made no progress at all. Another ploy is to avoid focusing at all on academic performance and state, "Virginia is trying very hard" or "Thomas is doing his best." These maneuvers actually do teach children something. They teach them ways to blind themselves to their deficits. In addition, they cannot but lessen the children's respect for the teacher if they sense his (her) duplicity – and they often do.

We need some degree of comparison to ascertain the value of our accomplishments; we cannot judge them in a vacuum. We need some degree of competition to provide us with the esteem enhancement that comes from excelling in comparison to others. It is when exceeding others becomes our primary, if not exclusive, source of ego-enhancement that we get into difficulty. It is then that we are likely to lose the intrinsic satisfactions of the attainment and become so engrossed in competition that we may deprive ourselves of opportunities for other sources of esteem-building. A reasonable degree of excelling others to enhance one's self-worth can be healthy. Used to an excessive degree it becomes dehumanizing, as one's main purpose in life then becomes beating others down. Competition, used in moderation, can spur us on to work more efficiently toward our goals. Used in excess, however, it may become an end in itself and may then lessen the likelihood that we will reach our goals. We may then become more interested in the winning than in the process and the goal, and this lessens our effectiveness in achieving our aim.

The school can and should be a place that teaches healthy competition, in preparation for the competitiveness of adult life. The fact that our society is fiercely competitive is no reason to do away with competition completely, as some would attempt to do. Rather we should tone it down and use it as constructively as possible. Awareness of one's progress and relative position—as compared to others—can be a useful tool in providing students with healthy competitive impetus.

The main purpose of a teacher's rating or feedback system should be to provide students with information about their level of accomplishment as compared to peers and to pinpoint the steps necessary to correct deficiencies. To say "Jimmy has now mastered multiplication up to the six-times table whereas the average student in his grade has, by now, mastered the eight-times table" not only enables everyone to appreciate better the level of accomplishment, but may also serve to encourage Jimmy to work harder to bring up his level. The teacher might add, "Jimmy needs special practice in the seven- and eight-times tables, as well as in the addition of three-digit numbers." In addition, no harm is done, and much is to be gained, by utilizing a grading system (A, B, C, D, and F). High grades provide positive reinforcement and enhance motivation. Because children with low grades may feel disappointed should not be a reason for depriving those with the capacity to get higher grades (via diligence, genetic endowment, and/or personal and family influences) from enjoying the enhanced self-worth that comes with such accomplishment.

HIGH SCHOOL

In their book *What Do Our 17-Year-Olds Know?* Ravitch and Finn (1987) report a study conducted with approximately 18,000 17-year-olds who were selected to reflect the make-up of the U.S.

population as a whole regarding region, sex, race, type of school, and type of community. Some of their findings: Thirty percent of the students did not know that Christopher Columbus reached the New World before 1750. More than 35 percent were not aware that the Watergate scandal took place after 1950. More than 30 percent believed that one consequence of the Spanish-American War was the defeat of the Spanish Armada. Approximately half of the students believed that *Nineteen Eighty-Four* dealt with the destruction of the human race in a nuclear war. Over one-third did not know that Aesop wrote fables. Over 42 percent did not know who Senator Joseph McCarthy was nor for what he became infamous. Seventy percent were unable to identify the Magna Carta. And the book goes on and on with many more examples of the abysmal ignorance of the average American teenager. These findings should not be surprising, considering the kinds of educational programs these youngsters are being provided.

I saw one 9th-grade student recently who had a teacher with a very creative marking system. Students were given three points for each right answer and one point for each wrong answer. Again, the purpose was to protect the self-esteem of those youngsters who got wrong answers. When one thinks about the implications of this system, one gets a good idea about the low depths to which our educational systems have descended. *Under this system two wrong answers equal one right answer.* If one tries to translate this into life's experiences, the results can be devastating. Who would want to go to a physician whose medical school professors marked according to this principle? The implications are that three wrong diagnoses get as much credit as one right diagnosis. Who would want to go to an auto mechanic, lawyer, engineer, architect, accountant, dentist, or anyone else who was trained under such a program? This system, designed to preserve self-esteem, works in just the opposite direction in that the devastating effects of the youngster's failure to learn anything meaningful cannot but lower feelings of self-worth.

One high school youngster in the New York City school system informed me that a new system of multiple choice tests has been recently created that increases the likelihood that every question will be answered correctly. The system works like this: The students are given tests in which they are asked to read a paragraph that is followed by a question with five possible correct answers. The teacher informs the students that they can work more quickly if they look for a particular word that is embedded in the paragraph. That word—which appears only once—could be considered to be like the title of the paragraph in that it epitomizes its meaning. That same word is to be found in one (and only one) of the five questions. Of the five multiple choice questions, only one contains that key word. Not only do the other four not contain that word but, of equal importance, they are completely absurd and irrelevant to the meaning of the paragraph. The students then need not "waste time" reading the paragraph; all they have to do is scan it for the key word that is to be matched with one of the multiple choice responses. Obviously, nothing is being learned here, yet every student is getting extremely high if not perfect scores on examinations. The idea that self-esteem is being preserved by this method is ludicrous.

Some parents bring their adolescents for treatment because of poor academic motivation. Many of these youngsters attend schools where the educational standards are low and where they are automatically moved ahead every year and then dropped off the edge of the system when they complete the twelfth grade. Some, however, are in more demanding high schools, but they still have little commitment to the educational process. Sometimes the youngster's lack of motivation is indeed related to intrafamilial and intrapsychic problems. At other times, the youngster is merely one of a stream of hundreds of thousands who are moving along an educational track that demands little and provides even less. Their teachers are uncommitted and unmotivated, watch the clock, do not give homework (homework for the student is homework for the teacher), and so do not provide models for their students— models of people who are "turned on" by learning.

Whatever the cause of the youngster's impaired academic motivation, I often tell such parents that my treatment is not likely to be successful as long as the youngster knows that, whatever happens, he (she) will still go on to college. I ask them if they have the guts to make a bona fide threat, a threat that will under no circumstances be withdrawn, namely, that if the patient does not show significant improvement in academic motivation, under no circumstances will he (she) go to college for four years of nonlearning and self-indulgence. I advise them to warn the youngster that grades themselves will not be the only criterion used to ascertain whether or not the youngster is deserving of college. This is important because of the grade inflation that exists in our school systems as well as the capacity of youngsters to manipulate their teachers into giving them higher grades. Rather, the criteria that will be used will be SAT scores *and* the parents' own observations of the youngster's commitment to the educational process. It is best to leave this vague. To use as a criterion a certain number of hours of homework per night is not useful because the youngster may easily satisfy this requirement with feigned commitment to homework. I warn the parents that they should not make this threat unless they intend to follow it through. I generally advise them to think about it for a week or two and discuss it in detail before making a decision. I tell them also that they do well to have a specific plan of operation if the youngster does not indeed go to college.

My experience has been that most parents do not make this threat. They just don't have the courage to do it. The notion that their youngster should not go to college is painful, if not impossible, for them to entertain. They would consider it humiliating if their child did not have a "higher education." They do not know how they could face their friends. They point to other youngsters who entered college with the same lack of motivation and then turned around at some point along the program. I agree that such youngsters exist, but my experience has been that they are a minority.

Some parents of unmotivated adolescents believe that the problem lies in the school and the solution is to transfer to another one. This rarely works. I try to emphasize to such parents that the problem lies in the youngster's head and not in the building in which the nonlearning is taking place. Although stories about people such as Abraham Lincoln and others who learned significantly under conditions of privation may seem trite, they should still be told. Again, many parents do not follow my advice, spend their money in a special private school, and still find that the youngster is not particularly motivated. When I see adolescents who are already in the first year of one of these "colleges" and are getting low marks (even with grade inflation and limited standards), I generally advise the parents to tell their youngsters they are no longer going to squander their money on them. I advise them to remove their youngsters from school and have them go out into the workplace for six months or a year and then rethink the whole college decision. After having experiences in the "real world," the youngsters are in a better position to make decisions regarding education vs. other options. In addition, if they are really motivated to go to school, they should be willing to work to contribute toward tuition. Regardless of the affluence of the parents, such youngsters do well to contribute to the payment of a reasonable fraction of their educational expenses. Such a requirement helps separate the truly motivated from the jokers. Unfortunately, most parents with the college disease do not accept this advice. They thereby contribute to the perpetuation of their children's ongoing state of low self-worth.

On occasion, I will see a patient who is a high school or even college dropout who stays at home and does nothing. The parents are not complaining so much about the fact that the youngster is not getting an education (they are long past that point); they are now complaining about the fact that they have a "parasite" on their hands. And indeed they do. The youngster sits around the house all day, watches television, listens to rock music, and gabs with friends. Although in the late teens, the youngster is functioning at the three-year-old level. Most often (but not always) there has been a longstanding history of significant indulgence. This indulgence must be dealt with at the present time. The parents have to be advised to make life tough for such youngsters. No services should be provided. Such youngsters should be required to cook their own meals, purchase their food, do their own laundry, and be made uncomfortable in many other ways. If possible, television sets should be removed, and certainly stereo players. As much as possible, the youngster should be provided with an atmosphere of sensory deprivation. Even telephone services should be restricted and cut off when possible. Otherwise, the youngster is going to sink into a chronic state of morbid dependency on the parents. Again, many of these parents are not capable of following through with these recommendations, so deeply entrenched is their overprotectiveness. Their failure to follow through with these recommendations contributes significantly to the perpetuation of their children's low self-esteem.

COLLEGE

I believe that *most* (but certainly not *all*) colleges in the United States are not serving primarily as educational institutions; rather, they are serving as what I call "winter camps" that alternate with their students' summer recreational (and sometimes work) programs. Most youngsters attending colleges are not really looking for an education, but for another four years of self-indulgence and prolongation of their dependent state. We have a unique disease in the United States, a disease I call *the college disease*. Millions of parents believe that it is crucial that their children attend college. They believe that the schools to which they are sending their children are actually serving educational purposes. When there is a demand for something, there will always be individuals who will be pleased to provide a supply of the item, especially when there is good money to be made in the business. Most colleges in the United States are basically businesses that cater to a gullible population of parents who believe that it is *crucial* that their children (no matter how simple and/or academically unmotivated) have a college education (no matter how specious and inferior).

These institutions have their academic hierarchy, their assistant professors, associate professors, and full professors. They have their college-style buildings (especially red brick and ivy), their alumni associations, their football teams, and their fund-raising campaigns. And they even offer formal courses, the "students" take examinations, and grades are given. Yet the whole scenario does not add up to what can justifiably be referred to as an education. The majority of students are not there to learn; rather they are there primarily to have a good time—which often includes significant indulgence in sex, alcohol, and drugs. What they most often learn are some new sexual techniques, what their tolerance for alcohol is, and perhaps the use of some new drugs that they haven't tried before. They also learn how easy it is to get a college diploma. When the "students" are not engaged in these activities, they go through the motions of attending classes, but little is learned. Grade inflation fosters the delusion that they are learning something and ensures that even those with borderline intelligence will get high grades. Professors are concerned that if they give a student a grade lower than B, then the youngster will have trouble getting into graduate school, and the college's reputation and popularity may thereby suffer. It is rare for someone to "flunk out." And why should they fail? Does one kick a good customer out of the store? If a customer's parents are willing to continue to pay for the services provided, it would be poor business practice and even self- destructive of the college in this highly competitive market to cut off a predictable supply of money because of the student's failure to consume the product being offered.

I am not claiming that *all* the aforementioned criticisms apply to *all* collegiate institutions and *all* students. If I had to give a percentage of those academic institutions in the United States that fit the above description, I would say that it is in the 75 to 80 percent range. As mentioned, these colleges provide many of their students with gratification of pathological dependency needs. Such colleges also serve as a mechanism for transferring dependency from parents to those who administer these institutions. And thwarting college authorities (especially by antisocial behavior and refusal to study) is often a transfer of rebellion from parents to school authorities—a rebellion in which the dependency-denial element is often operative.

When I attended college we generally went from nine a.m. to

five p.m. Monday through Friday, and a half day on Saturday. Most courses met four or five times a week and laboratory courses two to three afternoons a week. It was expected that one would do four or five hours of homework a night. School began the day following Labor Day and continued right through early June. There was a one-week Christmas vacation, possibly a one-week Easter vacation, and of course national holidays. Otherwise we went to school. This is no longer the case. Even in the so-called best colleges and universities, the formal academic program is far less rigorous. Most students average two or three hours a day of classes while professors may only have to come in five to ten hours a week and are otherwise unseen. These days, the academic year, although it may start around Labor Day, generally ends in early May. Some institutions use the Christmas and/or Easter season as an excuse for an extended holiday (two to four weeks). Others have long vacations (lasting two to four weeks) between semesters. Many need no other excuse for a long break than the season (spring or winter vacation). When I attended college, professors were on campus throughout the course of the day, available for help and consultation. Things have vastly changed. Today, it is not uncommon for professors to live at significant distances from the campus and appear only on the days they teach, and often only during the hours when they teach. Otherwise, they are unavailable. Students at these institutions are being short-changed. "Educations" of this kind may cost $15,000 a year or more (just for the basic tuition). Parents and students are being "ripped off."

Recently, a mother of a patient, who teaches at one of the public universities in New York City, related to me an incident that demonstrates well the deterioration of our educational systems, even at the highest level. The woman is a highly intelligent, well-trained, scholarly individual with a Ph.D. in a very demanding field. One day her chairman called her into his office and told her that he was having a problem with her, namely, that too many of her students were failing. He informed her that a 40 percent failure rate was unacceptable. She responded that she was actually being quite generous, and that if she had graded in a more honest way, about 60 percent of her students would fail. He told her that he had sat in on a couple of her classes, knew exactly what the problem was, and considered it easily rectifiable. He then went on to explain to her that she was not giving tests in the "correct" manner. What she was doing was to tell students on Friday, for example, that there would be a test on Monday covering the material in certain chapters of the textbook. This he considered "unfair" to the students. Rather, the "correct" way to give a test was to tell the students on Friday exactly what questions would be asked on Monday. Under the new system, the failure rate dropped from 40 to 20 percent, but even then she found herself being quite generous. Such procedures are a manifestation of the bastardization of the educational system. They make a farce of education and, worse, are a terrible disservice to students. The next step, of course, is merely to tell what questions will be asked and give the answers that will be expected. If one extends this further, one might as well give out (or sell) the diplomas in advance and save everyone a lot of trouble. Again, the idea that these youngsters' self-worth is being preserved is absurd. These students are being ill equipped to function adequately in life and are doomed to suffer with feelings of low self-worth.

Things are even worse at some of the two-year colleges. Many of these institutions merely go through the motions of providing an education and are basically a sham. Students are given textbooks that are seemingly rigorous and demanding, yet in actuality the students are only required to learn a small fraction of what is presented therein. Those in charge recognize the travesty but are party to it, even at the highest levels. A patient of mine, who had just completed his first year at a local community college, proudly told the adolescent group that he was one of the highest students in his class and that he had just been admitted to the academic honor society. In the same sentence he proudly mentioned the name of the honor society, which sounded very much to me like *Phi Beta Kappa*. The members of the group were duly impressed and congratulated him. I was immediately incredulous because I knew that a Phi Beta Kappa key is only awarded to graduates of certain selected four-year colleges. In addition, admission is only possible at the end of the third year of college, and even then only for the superstar students (usually the top 2 percent of the class). It is only after the fourth year that some of the other academic superstars gain admission (usually up to another 8 percent). Accordingly, I asked incredulously if that was the *same* Phi Beta Kappa that I was thinking of, to which he replied, "No, it's not Phi *Beta* Kappa it's Phi *Theta* Kappa." On further inquiry I asked the patient if he appreciated the full implications of the deceit that was being perpetrated by his school on the students, their friends, and families. He somewhat reluctantly agreed that Phi Theta Kappa was indeed a sham and that the school administrators, he was quite sure, appreciated this. He had to admit, as well, that he did not feel good about himself when perpetrating the myth that he held this prestigious academic honor. I pointed out to him that whatever gratifications he may have derived from being among the highest ranked students in his class, and to the degree that he boasted about being in Phi Theta Kappa, to that degree he would lower his self-worth. The selection of this name for the honor society is yet another example of the naiveté of college administrators. If they really believe they are enhancing the self-worth of their students, they are misguided. What they are doing is teaching deceit, false pride, and pathological values – all of which lower self-esteem.

The net result of all this is that students are not getting a bona fide education and are thereby entering into the workplace ill equipped to handle jobs for which they are ostensibly being trained. They also are being deprived of the feelings of accomplishment and high self-worth enjoyed by those who have acquired skills and talents through years of hard labor and dedication. The situation thereby contributes to psychopathology, because feelings of low self-worth are an important contributing factor in the development of psychogenic symptoms. In addition, such bogus education contributes to psychopathic trends (I am not saying gross psychopathy) because of the sanctions the youngsters are given for "cutting corners," taking short-cuts, and otherwise doing shabby work.

At the same time that their education is eroding, the honors that students are receiving become ever easier to acquire. When I graduated from Columbia College in 1952, my recollection is that no more than one percent graduated *summa cum laude*, perhaps another three or four percent *magna cum laude*, and perhaps another five percent *cum laude*. My recollection is that students below the 10 percent level of the class could not hope to acquire any of these honors. In the mid-1980s I attended the Harvard College graduation of one of my children. I noted that the upper 75 percent of the class received one of these honors. In other words, a person could be in the 75th percentile level of the class and would graduate *cum laude*. When I spoke to faculty people about this, I was informed that the school is well aware of its liberal view with regard to bestowing these honors, but that it is justified because it helps students get into graduate school and get better jobs. I am dubious. Those who make these decisions are well aware that cum laude may very well indicate the 50th to 75th percentile of the class and will act accordingly. It serves to compromise the respect for the honor and does Harvard (and other schools who do the same) a disservice. It is one example of the intellectual and moral erosion that has taken place, even at the so-called highest levels of education.

CONCLUSION

Bray (1990) in a *New York Times* article entitled, "Self-Esteem: Hoax or Reality?" comments on the wave of self-esteem enhancing programs that are currently in vogue in schools throughout the country. In the article, she quotes Phyllis Schlafly, president of the Eagle Forum, a politically conservative group based in Alion, Illinois. Although I am not in agreement with some of Ms. Schlafly's political views, I am 100 percent in agreement with her very astute observation of many of these school self-esteem programs: "Instead of teaching them how to read, they are teaching kids how to feel good about being illiterate."

TWENTY-TWO
SELF-ESTEEM FACTORS IN THE DEVELOPMENT OF PSYCHOGENIC PSYCHOPATHOLOGY

Many of the defense mechanisms are called into operation in the service of protecting self-esteem. *Repression* can obliterate from conscious awareness ego-debasing thoughts and feelings. *Reaction formation* protects the individual from the conscious recognition of tendencies that are exactly the opposite of what the individual believes he (she) harbors within, tendencies that would lower self-esteem if they were to be allowed into conscious awareness in their undisguised form. *Rationalization* provides an individual with an acceptable excuse as a replacement for thoughts, feelings, and actions that are unacceptable to the individual and therefore ego-debasing. *Restitution* also assuages ego-debasing guilt. The reparations provide the individual with protection from the esteem-debasing consequences of the unacceptable act. *Regression* allows individuals to remove themselves from anxiety-provoking and potentially ego-degrading experiences. Regressed to the earlier level of development, they avoid facing what they consider to be dangerous and ego-lowering confrontations. *Denial* allows individuals to protect themselves from esteem-lowering experiences by basically deluding themselves into thinking that they do not exist or never existed. And *sublimation* enables an individual to find discharge for esteem-lowering activities through more socially acceptable channels.

It is not difficult to appreciate how dealing with self-esteem operates in the development of most forms of psychogenic psychopathology. Adolescents who abuse drugs do so, in part, to desensitize themselves to the feelings of low self-worth attendant to their life situation. The drugs provide a mechanism for denying reality and drawing one's attention away from the realization of the depth of one's plight (real or imagined). Drugs also provide a sense of euphoria that can compensate for painful feelings of low self-worth (among other painful feelings). Alcohol can serve the same purpose and, like drugs, can also serve to assuage tensions and anxieties that have within them an ego-debasing component.

Although depression, in the adult sense, is not too common in childhood, one aspect of depression that occurs in children is the turning inward of hostility, with associated self-deprecation. Such children, like their adult counterparts, are inhibited in openly expressing their resentments. They turn their anger inward against themselves (a safer target), and their self-flagellation and self-disparagement results in a significant lowering of their self-esteem. Helping such children direct their hostility toward the appropriate source—so that the irritations that are engendering the anger can be more effectively dealt with—can be therapeutic.

I consider guilt to be the feeling of low self-worth that an individual experiences after having performed acts, experienced feelings, or entertained thoughts that the individual has been taught by significant figures in early childhood to be wrong, bad, or sinful. Central to guilt is low self-esteem. The wide variety of symptoms that may be used to deal with guilt are, in a sense, designed to protect an individual from the realization of painful feelings of low self-worth. For example, masochism can serve to reduce guilt: the individual is basically asking for guilt-assuaging punishment. Self-destructive individuals may also have a guilt-reducing factor operative in their symptoms. Suicide may represent the extreme example of an individual's attempt to assuage guilt. Although obsessive-compulsive symptoms may very well have a genetic loading, I believe psychogenic factors are still very much operative. It is not difficult to see how many of these symptoms have a guilt-assuaging element. Many obsessive-compulsive symptoms involve the doing-undoing mechanism in which the guilt over doing something wrong (real or fantasized) is reduced by a magical, guilt-assuaging ritual.

There are other psychogenic disorders of childhood in which the self-esteem element is operative. Oppositional children gain a sense of power and triumph over those whom they thwart, compensating thereby for feelings of inadequacy. Children who shy from human interactions often do so because of the fear of exposure of their inadequacies and weaknesses if they were to involve themselves to a significant degree with other individuals. Children with overanxious disorder do not feel competent to deal with the vicissitudes of life and tend to exaggerate dangers that others take in their stride. Anorexic girls gain an enormous amount of attention from their families in association with their stringent dieting, and such attention can serve to compensate for feelings of low self-worth. Furthermore, the power they gain over the lives of others in association with their eating antics can also serve to provide a specious sense of heightened self-worth. The self-esteem factor is also operative in bulimia. Food serves as a tranquilizer that lessens tensions and anxieties, which are, in part, related to fears of exposure of one's inadequacies, undesirable thoughts and feelings, etc. Girls who feel inadequate to the demands of sexual development may utilize food to produce the obesity that most men find alienating. They thereby protect themselves from sexual overtures that they associate with humiliation, sin, and guilt. Paranoia has within it a compensatory esteem-enhancing component. The paranoid is basically saying, "It is not I who harbors these unacceptable thoughts and feelings. It is he." By the process of projection the paranoid becomes cleansed of guilt-evoking, ego-debasing mental processes (especially hostile and sexual) and, by the process of projection, considers himself (herself) the victim of his own projected impulses. Hysterical youngsters can achieve a degree of esteem-enhancing attention that calmer children do not enjoy. Somatic complaints can also provide the same gratifications.

In short, there is hardly a psychodynamic mechanism in which the self-esteem factor cannot be found to be operative. Of course, these processes are quite complex, and it would be an oversimplification to say that low self-esteem is at the root and the heart of all psychodynamic problems. Although not the funda-mental problem of psychodynamic psychiatry, it certainly has a pervasive influence, and the reader does well to consider this factor when attempting to understand a patient's symptoms.

☐ CONCLUSIONS

It is my hope that the reader by now will be somewhat over-whelmed by the complexity of the low self-esteem problem. It is important that we appreciate its complexity, especially because we are living at a time when programs that promise quick self-esteem enhancement are widespread. Across the nation, classes designed to enhance self-esteem are to be found. They claim cures for drug abuse, alcoholism, and a wide variety of other disorders. Businesses and industry have instituted self-esteem enhancing sessions with the promise that worker motivation, efficiency, and productivity will be enhanced. Williams (1990), in a *New York Times* article entitled "Using Self-Esteem to Fix Society's Ills," states that 42 of 200 companies of the Fortune 500 were offering self-esteem training. Minority groups, as well, have been singled out for such programs, which offer them promise for esteem enhancement in a society in which they are the objects of bias and prejudice. Other programs promise a decrease in teenage pregnancy, antisocial behavior, crime, dependency, and even a reduction in welfare recipients. School districts have introduced self-esteem motivational materials to students. Naturally, companies that sell the books, teaching materials, and other course paraphernalia are flourishing.

The one thing most (if not all) of these programs share in common is their simplicity. Participants are told that massaging one another's shoulders produces relaxation and creates a bond. The good feeling that one experiences in association with such massaging is also said to have a direct effect on self-esteem enhancement. Participants are encouraged to stand up and tell the others about successes they have had in their lives. Breathing techniques are utilized not only as antidotes to stress, depression, and anxiety, but also as an enhancement to self-worth. Participants are presented with flash cards with allegedly esteem-enhancing messages describing how lovable, capable, and desirable the reader is. One of the standard messages is, "It doesn't matter what you do, but who you are." Participants are encouraged to compliment one another, e.g., "You're great," "You're terrific," and "You're just splendid."

Of course, self-esteem "experts" are sprouting up everywhere. To the best of my knowledge, there is no state that has formal licensure or certification for experts in self-esteem. Rather, anyone can consider himself (herself) an expert, and if people are gullible enough to pay that individual money (and there are many gullible people in this world), then the individual is "in business."

I believe these programs are doomed. They are simplistic and appeal to individuals who are looking for quick solutions to the complicated problems of life. Freud was quite antagonistic to Americans and believed that psychoanalysis, especially, would degenerate in America. He believed that Americans did not have the patience for therapeutic techniques that required long-term, in-depth treatment—treatment that attempted to consider the multiplicity of factors operative in human psychological phenomena. The self-esteem craze that we are witnessing today is strong confirmation of Freud's prediction.

Although I consider my self-esteem presentation here to be exhaustive, I do not believe I have completely covered the subject in depth. I have focused primarily on psychological processes that contribute to the development of self-esteem and have described how the failure to take these factors into consideration can result in the development of feelings of low self-worth. Another way of approaching the situation is to consider the role of self-esteem in the development of psychogenic symptoms. This is what Adler did when he concluded that problems in the self-esteem realm are central to the development of most forms of psychogenic psychopathology. He considered low self-esteem to be the primary factor operative when symptoms are formed and that symptoms, more than anything else, result from misguided attempts to compensate for feelings of low self-worth. Although I would not go as far as Adler, I do believe that he made a good point, and it was unfortunate that Freud reacted so negatively to Adler's contributions. My main criticism of Adler, and I have the same criticism of Freud, is that there was too narrow a focus on one factor (albeit an important one) in the development of psychopathology. I believe that Freud overemphasized the sexual factor and Adler the self-esteem factor. I believe that both are right, but that both have somewhat oversimplified. It is my hope that what I have presented here on self-esteem will serve as a derivative contribution of Adler's and complements, as well, those factors in the Freudian contributions that I consider worthy of promulgation.

EPILOGUE

Sometime during the year 1945, when I was in the 9th grade in PS 82 in the Bronx (one of the five boroughs of New York City), I learned about the existence of The Bronx High School of Science. Admission was based purely on one's performance on a citywide test of academic achievement. There were no outreach programs in those days (and there certainly were no outreach programs for Jews). When I learned that I had been accepted for admission, I enjoyed a significant enhancement of my self-esteem, residua of which continue to this day. This was less related to my pride in the accomplishment than to the experiences I had at that school and the enhancement of my general fund of knowledge provided by the setting.

The Latin teacher at Bronx Science was Mr. A. J. Burt. He not only believed that Latin was still a "living language," rumors to the contrary notwithstanding, but that all the romance languages (e.g., Spanish, Italian, and French) were merely "Latin with mistakes." In retrospect, Mr. Burt was a "Latin chauvinist" and did not mention (and I suspect he knew it) that these languages, their "mistakes" notwithstanding, built significantly on their Latin foundation and have enriched humanity enormously. On the first day of second-year Latin we were all given a test to determine what we had learned during the first year. When we returned for the second class, we were all assigned a seat in accordance with our rank on that initial screening examination. The boy (there were no girls at Bronx Science at that time) who ranked highest sat in the first seat of the first row. The number two boy sat in the second seat in the first row. The number three boy sat in the third seat, and so on down the rows so that the boy who was lowest on that test sat in the last seat of the sixth row. Every week we were given a quiz and, of course, there were larger, more inclusive examinations. On the basis of these examinations we were periodically reranked, and our seats were changed in accordance with our class standing.

I still remember Daniel Horowitz, the boy who first occupied the first seat in the first row. To the best of my recollection, he never left that seat throughout the remaining three years. To the best of my recollection, as well, I usually sat in the second or third row. From that vantage point I recall nothing but admiration for Daniel Horowitz. My clear recollection of him, almost 50 years later, is testament to the influence that he had on me. Any jealous resentment I may have felt (and I do not recall any) must have been relegated to the darkest recesses of my unconscious mind by the dazzle of my admiration for him. Furthermore, I do not believe that my self-esteem suffered because I was never able to attain his level of competence in "living Latin." I do not recall suffering with feelings of low self-esteem for never having attained first-row status. I ever aspired to move up the ranks, but I recognized that the *only* way to do so was to study harder and learn more Latin. I recognized also that there were some who were more gifted than I, whose level of competence would be greater than mine no matter how much I studied.

Mr. Burt, I am certain, has long since passed away. I do not know whatever happened to Daniel Horowitz, but I do know that I learned an enormous amount of Latin in Mr. Burt's class, and I have significant residual knowledge of the language to this day. Furthermore, the presence of Daniel Horowitz played an important role in bringing about the enhancement of self-worth that such knowledge produced. Although Daniel Horowitz was very much a living human being, he has served also as a metaphor for all the other Daniel Horowitzes in my life: Maurice Van Besien, Dewitt

Goodman, Michael Sovern, Martin Rosner, Bard Cosman, Stanley Plotkin, Michael Katz, and others. Some of these people are still my friends, others have passed away (Dewitt and Bard are too deeply embedded in my psychic structure ever to be forgotten), and others hardly knew of my existence. The aspirations they have all engendered in me have fueled the labors that have served to enhance significantly my self-esteem.

REFERENCES

Adler, A. A. (1927), *Understanding Human Nature*. Translated by Walter Beran Wolfe. New York: Greenberg Publisher, Inc.

————————— (1938), *Social Interest: A Challenge to Mankind*. Translated by John Linton and Richard Vaughan. London: Faber and Faber, Ltd.

Aleksandrowicz, D. R. and Aleksandrowicz, M. K. (1987), Psychodynamic approach to low self-esteem related to developmental deviations: growing up incompetent. *Journal of the American Academy of Child and Adolescent Psychiatry*, 26(4):583-585.

Allis, S. (1991), Why 180 days aren't enough. *Time*, September 2, 1991, pg. 64ff.

American Heritage Dictionary (1971), Boston: Houghton Mifflin Co.

Arnott, B. and Gushin, J. (1976), Film making as a therapeutic tool. *American Journal of Art Therapy*, 16(1):29-33.

Askey, R. (1990), Letter published in *The New York Times*, July 26, 1990.

Aust, P. H. (1984), Rational-emotive therapy in the school. *Social Work in Education*, 6(2):106-117.

Barth, F. D. (1988), The role of self-esteem in the experience of envy. *The American Journal of Psychoanalysis*, 48(3):198-209.

Beck, A.T. (1967) *Depression: Clinical, Experimental and Therapeutic Aspects*. New York: Harper and Row.

Becker, E. (1973), *The Denial of Death*. New York: The Free Press (A Division of Macmillan Publishing Co., Inc.).

————————— (1975), *Escape from Evil*. New York: The Free Press (A Division of Macmillan Publishing Co., Inc.).

Bellak, L. and Bellak, S. S. (1949), *The Children's Apperception Test.* Larchmont, New York: C.P.S. Co.

Bly, R. (1990), *Iron John: A Book About Men.* Reading, Massachusetts: Addison-Wesley Publishing Company, Inc.

Bray, R. L. (1990), Self-esteem: hoax or reality? *The New York Times,* Education Life, Section 4A, November 4, 1990, pg. 33.

Conn, J. H. (1939), The child reveals himself through play. *Mental Hygiene,* 23(1):1-21.

——————— (1941a), The timid, dependent child. *Journal of Pediatrics,* 19(1):1-2.

——————— (1941b), The treatment of fearful children. *American Journal of Orthopsychiatry,* 11(4):744-751.

——————— (1948), The play-interview as an investigative and therapeutic procedure. *The Nervous Child,* 7(3):257-286.

——————— (1954), Play interview therapy of castration fears. *American Journal of Orthopsychiatry,* 25(4):747-754.

De Witt, K. (1991), Verbal scores hit new low in scholastic aptitude test. *The New York Times,* August 27, 1991, pp. 1ff.

Freud, S. (1909), Analysis of phobia in a five-year-old boy. In: *Collected Papers,* vol. 3, pp. 149-289. New York: Basic Books, Inc., 1959.

Gabel, S. (1984), The draw a story game: an aid in understanding and working with children. *Arts in Psychotherapy,* 11(3):187-196.

Gardner, R. A. (1968), The mutual storytelling technique: Use in alleviating childhood oedipal problems. *Contemporary Psychoanalysis,* 4:161-177.

——————— (1969a), Guilt, Job, and J. B. *Medical Opinion and Review,* 5(2):146-155.

——————— (1969b), The guilt reaction of parents of children with severe physical disease. *American Journal of Psychiatry,* 126:636-644.

——————— (1969c), The game of checkers as a diagnostic and therapeutic tool in child psychotherapy. *Acta Paedopsychiatrica,* 36(5):142-152.

——————— (1969d), Mutual storytelling as a technique in child psychotherapy and psychoanalysis. In *Science and Psychoanalysis,* ed. J. Masserman, vol. XIV, pp. 123-135. New York: Grune and Stratton.

——————— (1970a), The use of guilt as a defense against anxiety. *The Psychoanalytic Review,* 57:124-136.

——————— (1970b), Die Technik des wechselseitigen Geschichtenerzählens bei der Behandlung eines Kindes mit psychogenem Husten. In: *Fortschritte der Psychoanalyse. Internationales Jahrbuch zur Weiterentwicklung der Psychoanalyse,* ed. C. J. Hogrefe, vol. 4, pp. 159-173. Göttingen: Verlag für Psychologie.

_____ (1970c), The mutual storytelling technique: Use in the treatment of a child with post-traumatic neurosis. *American Journal of Psychotherapy*, 24:419-439.

_____ (1971a), *Therapeutic Communication with Children: The Mutual Storytelling Technique*. New York: Jason Aronson, Inc.

_____ (1971b), Mutual storytelling: A technique in child psychotherapy. *Acta Paedopsychiatrica*, 38(9):253-262.

_____ (1972a), *Dr. Gardner's Stories About the Real World*, vol. I. Cresskill, New Jersey: Creative Therapeutics.

_____ (1972b), "Once upon a time there was a doorknob and everybody used to make him all dirty with fingerprints . . ." *Psychology Today*, 5(10):67-92.

_____ (1972c), The mutual storytelling technique in the treatment of anger inhibition problems. *International Journal of Child Psychotherapy*, 1(1):34-64.

_____ (1972d), Little Hans—the most famous boy in the child psychotherapy literature. *International Journal of Child Psychotherapy*, 1(2):24-50.

_____ (1973a), *MBD: The Family Book About Minimal Brain Dysfunction*. Northvale, New Jersey: Jason Aronson, Inc.

_____ (1973b), Psychotherapy of the psychogenic problems secondary to minimal brain dysfunction. *International Journal of Child Psychotherapy*, 2(2):224-256.

_____ (1973c), *The Mutual Storytelling Technique* (audio cassette tapes). Cresskill, New Jersey: Creative Therapeutics.

_____ (1973d), *The Talking, Feeling, and Doing Game*. Cresskill, New Jersey: Creative Therapeutics.

_____ (1974a), La technique de la narration mutuelle d'histo-rettes. *Médicine et Hygi ne* (Geneva), 32:1180-1181.

_____ (1974b), Dramatized storytelling in child psychotherapy. *Acta Paedopsychiatrica*, 41(3):110-116.

_____ (1974c), The mutual storytelling technique in the treatment of psychogenic problems secondary to minimal brian dysfunction. *Journal of Learning Disabilities*, 7:135-143.

_____ (1974d), Psychotherapy of minimal brain dysfunction. In *Current Psychiatric Therapies*, ed. J. Masserman, vol. XIV, pp. 15-21. New York: Grune & Stratton.

_____ (1975a), *Psychotherapeutic Approaches to the Resistant Child*. Northvale, New Jersey: Jason Aronson, Inc.

_____ (1975b), *Psychotherapeutic Approaches to the Resistant Child* (audio cassette tapes). Cresskill, New Jersey: Creative Therapeutics.

_____ (1975c), Techniques for involving the child with MBD in meaningful psychotherapy. *Journal of Learning Disabilities*, 8(5):16-26.

_____ (1975d), Psychotherapy in minimal brain dysfunction. In *Current Psychiatric Therapies*, ed. J. Masserman, vol. XV, pp. 25-38. New York: Grune & Stratton.

_____ (1976), *Psychotherapy with Children of Divorce.* Northvale, New Jersey: Jason Aronson, Inc.

_____ (1977), Children's guilt reactions to parental death: psychodynamics and therapeutic management. *Hiroshima Forum for Psychology,* 4:45-50.

_____ (1979a), Death of a parent. In *Basic Handbook of Child Psychiatry,* ed. J. Noshpitz, vol. IV, pp. 270-283. New York: Basic Books, Inc.

_____ (1979b), Helping children cooperate in therapy. In: *Basic Handbook of Child Psychiatry,* ed. J. Noshpitz, vol. III, pp. 414-433. New York: Basic Books, Inc.

_____ (1979c), Psychogenic difficulties secondary to MBD. In *Basic Handbook of Child Psychiatry,* ed. J. Noshpitz, vol. III, pp. 614-628. New York: Basic Books, Inc.

_____ (1980a), *Dorothy and the Lizard of Oz.* Cresskill, New Jersey: Creative Therapeutics.

_____ (1980b), The mutual storytelling technique. In *The Psychotherapy Handbook,* ed. R. Herink, pp. 408-411. New York: New American Library.

_____ (1980c), What every psychoanalyst should know about minimal brain dysfunction. *Journal of the American Academy of Psychoanalysis,* 8(3):403-426.

_____ (1980d), Minimal brain dysfunction. In *The Child in Normality and Psychopathology,* ed. J. Bemporad, pp. 269-304. New York: Brunner/Mazel, Inc.

_____ (1981a), *Dr. Gardner's Fables for Our Times.* Cresskill, New Jersey: Creative Therapeutics.

_____ (1981b), The mutual storytelling technique and dramatization of the therapeutic communication. In *Drama in Therapy,* ed. G. Schattner and R. Courtney, pp. 211-235. New York: Drama Book Specialists.

_____ (1983a), *Dr. Gardner's Stories About the Real World,* Vol. II. Cresskill, New Jersey: Creative Therapeutics.

_____ (1983b), Treating oedipal problems with the mutual storytelling technique. In *Handbook of Play Therapy,* ed. C. E. Schaefer and K. J. O'Connor, pp. 355-368. New York: John Wiley & Sons, Inc.

_____ (1983c), The talking, feeling, and doing game. In *Handbook of Play Therapy,* ed. C. E. Schaefer and K. J. O'Connor, pp. 259-273. New York: John Wiley & Sons, Inc.

_____ (1984), *Separation Anxiety Disorder: Psychodynamics and*

Psychotherapy. Cresskill, New Jersey: Creative Therapeutics.

_____ (1986a), *The Psychotherapeutic Techniques of Richard A. Gardner.* Cresskill, New Jersey: Creative Therapeutics.

_____ (1986b), The game of checkers in child therapy. In: *Game Play: Therapeutic Uses of Childhood Games,* ed. C. E. Schaefer and S. Reid, pp. 215-232. New York: John Wiley & Sons.

_____ (1986c), The Talking, Feeling, and Doing Game. In *Game Play: Therapeutic Uses of Childhood Games,* ed. C. E. Schaefer and S. Reid, pp. 41-72. New York: John Wiley & Sons.

_____ (1986d), *Child Custody Litigation: A Guide for Parents and Mental Health Professionals.* Cresskill, New Jersey: Creative Therapeutics.

_____ (1987a), *The Parental Alienation Syndrome and the Differentiation Between Fabricated and Genuine Child Sex Abuse.* Cresskill, New Jersey: Creative Therapeutics.

_____ (1987b), *Hyperactivity, The So-Called Attention Deficit Disorder, and The Group of MBD Syndromes.* Cresskill, New Jersey: Creative Therapeutics.

_____ (1988a), *Psychotherapy with Adolescents.* Cresskill, New Jersey: Creative Therapeutics.

_____ (1988b), *The Storytelling Card Game.* Cresskill, New Jersey: Creative Therapeutics.

_____ (1989), *Family Evaluations in Child Custody Mediation, Arbitration, and Litigation.* Cresskill, New Jersey: Creative Therapeutics.

_____ (1990), *The Girls and Boys Book About Good and Bad Behavior.* Cresskill, New Jersey: Creative Therapeutics.

_____ (1991), *The Parents Book About Divorce, Second Edition.* Cresskill, New Jersey: Creative Therapeutics.

Green, A. H. (1980), *Child Maltreatment.* Northvale, New Jersey: Jason Aronson, Inc.

Hoffman, S. and Wizansky, B. (1989), Brief therapeutic intervention using a modified storytelling technique. *International Journal of Short-Term Psychotherapy,* 4:189-194.

Holmes, D. J. (1964), *The Adolescent in Psychotherapy.* Boston: Little, Brown and Company.

Hug-Hellmuth, H. von (1913), *Aus dem Seelenleben des Kindes.* Leipzig, Germany: Deuticke.

Itzak, S. J. (1921), On the technique of child analysis. *International Journal of Psychoanalysis,* 2(3/4):285-305.

Johnson, A. M. (1949), Sanctions for superego lacunae of adolescents. In *Searchlights on Delinquency,* ed. K. R. Eissler, pp. 225-245. New York: International Universities Press.

_____ (1959), Juvenile delinquency. In *American Handbook of Psychiatry*, ed. S. Arieti, vol. I, pp. 844-849. New York: Basic Books, Inc.

Kessler, J. W. (1956), *Psychopathology of Childhood*. Englewood Cliffs, New Jersey: Prentice-Hall, Inc.

Kilpatrick, A. (1986), Some correlates of women's childhood sexual experiences: a retrospective study. *Journal of Sex Research*, 22:221-242.

Legrand, R. Wakefield, H. and Underwager, R. (1989), Alleged behavioral indicators of sexual abuse. *Issues in Child Abuse Accusations*, 1(2):1-5.

Lenkowsky, R. I., Barowsky, E. I., Dayboch, M., and Puccio, L. (1987), Effects of bibliotherapy on the self-concept of learning disabled, emotionally handicapped adolescents in a classroom setting. *Psychological Reports*, 61:483-488.

Lippman, H. S. (1962), *Treatment of the Child in Emotional Conflict*. New York: McGraw Hill, Inc.

Mabee, T. (1986), The provocative reversal (pr) method. *Transactional Analysis Journal*, 16(4):229-233.

Mullahy, P. (1955), *Oedipus Myth and Complex*. New York: Grove Press.

Murray, H. (1936), *The Thematic Apperception Test*. New York: The Psychological Corp.

Nickerson, E. T. (1975), Bibliotherapy: a therapeutic medium for helping children. *Psychotherapy: Theory, Research & Practice*, 12(3):258-261.

Oudshoorn, D. (1979), The behavior technique of Richard Gardner applied to a boy with minimal brain dysfunction. *Tijdschrift Voor Psychotherapie*, 5(5): 235-294.

Poppen, W. A. (1975), Idea Exchange Column. *Elementary School Guidance and Counseling*, 10(1):58-62.

Random House Dictionary of the English Language, Second Edition. New York: Random House, Inc.

Ravitch, D. and Finn, C. E. (1987), *What Do Our 17-Year-Olds Know?* New York: Harper and Row.

Roberts, G. E. (1982), *Roberts Apperception Test for Children*. Los Angeles, California: Western Psychological Services.

Robson, P. J. (1988), Self-esteem—a psychiatric view. *British Journal of Psychiatry*, 153:6-15.

_____ (1989), Development of a new self-report questionnaire to measure self-esteem. *Psychological Medicine*, 19:513-518.

Schooley, C. C. (1974), Communicating with hospitalized children: the mutual storytelling technique. *Journal of Pastoral Care*, 28(2):102-111.

Simon, J. (1982), Love: addiction or road to self-realization, a second look. *The American Journal of Psychoanalysis*, 42(3):253-263.

Solomon, J. C. (1938), Active play therapy. *American Journal of Orthopsychiatry*, 8(3):479-498.

_____ (1940), Active play therapy: further experiences. *American Journal of Orthopsychiatry*, 10(4):763-781.

_____ (1951), Therapeutic use of play. In *An Introduction to Projective Techniques*, ed. H. H. Anderson and G. L. Anderson, pp. 639-661. Englewood Cliffs, New Jersey: Prentice-Hall, Inc.

_____ (1955), Play technique and the integrative process. *American Journal of Orthopsychiatry*, 25(3):591-600.

Stirtzinger, R. M. (1983), Story telling: a creative therapeutic technique. *Canadian Journal of Psychiatry*, 28(7):561-565.

Stone, I. (1971), *Passions of the Mind*. New York: Signet [New American Library, Inc.].

Stone, L. (1985), Sex in the west. *The New Republic*, July 8, 1985, pp. 25-37.

Strom, R. and Strom, S. (1987), Preparing grandparents for a new role. *Journal of Applied Gerontology*, 6(4):476-486.

Strupp, H. H. (1975), Psychoanalysis, "focal psychotherapy," and the nature of the therapeutic influence. *Archives of General Psychiatry*, 32:127–135.

Stubblefield, R. L. (1967), Sociopathic personality disorders I: Antisocial and dyssocial reactions. In *Comprehensive Textbook of Psychiatry*, ed. A. M. Freedman and H. I. Kaplan, pp. 1420-1424. Baltimore: The Williams & Wilkins Co.

Sullivan, H. S. (1953), *The Interpersonal Theory of Psychiatry*. New York: W. W. Norton.

Thomas, A., Chess, S., Birch, H. G., Hertzig, M. E., and Korn, S. (1963), *Behavioral Individuality in Early Childhood*. New York: New York University Press.

Wade, N. (1990), Johnny can't add, Hiroko can. *The New York Times*, July 9, 1990. Section A, editorial page.

Williams, L. (1990), Using self-esteem to fix society's ills. *The New York Times*, March 28, 1990, p. C1ff.

AUTHOR INDEX

573

SUBJECT INDEX

Contamination in therapy, 7,
  49–50, 148
Criticism
  of children by others,
    100–103
Crying, 495–496
  and mourning, 126–127
  and shame, 126–127
Culture
  and adult-child sexuality,
    350–353
  and attitudes regarding the
    body, 136–137
  children feeling needed in an
    affluent vs. deprived, 113
  and machismo, 494
  programs for ethnic groups of,
    144
  romantic love and compliance
    with norms of, 295–296
  and transmission of messages
    down generations, 4–6

Dating, 313–326
  and depression, 324
  group therapy concerning,
    322–324
  helping boys make initial over-
    tures in, 314–320
  and shoplifting, 324–325
  therapy for girls who feel unat-
    tractive in, 320–322
Death of parent
  and mourning, 126–127
Defense mechanisms, 553
Denial, 510, 553, 554
Denial and rationalization
  common adolescent mechanisms
    for, 263–265
  common childhood mechanisms
    for, 260–263
  of deficiencies, 259–265

Dependency
  and neurologically based
    learning disability children,
    518
  romantic love and pathological,
    300
Depression, 425–426, 554
  and dating, 324
Desensitization, 22–23, 77–78, 156,
    515
  regarding self-assertion, 386
Development (child). *See Child
    development*
Disabilities
  neurologically based learning,
    120–121
  psychogenic learning, xx, 378,
    385, 392, 449, 533
Displacement mechanism,
    262–263
Dolls, use of in therapy, 49, 352
Dramatized storytelling, 17–20
  and neurologically based
    learning disability children,
    529–530
Dr. Gardner's Make-Up-a-Story
    Television Program.
    *See Make-Up-a-Story Television
    Program, Dr. Gardner's*
Drug abuse, 154, 156, 496–497,
    554
  and neurologically based
    learning disability children,
    515

Education *see also School and Ac-
    ademic performance*
  effects of conscience abnormali-
    ties on, 128–129
  and neurologically based
    learning disability children,
    513

therapist's response and
responding story to child's
story, 31–34
use of reward chips in, 27,
29–33, 38–39
Storytelling (dramatized). *See Dramatized storytelling*
Stuttering, 82–83
Sublimation, 553–554
Substitute gratification, 479
Suicide, 54–55, 111, 324, 511,
554–555
Symbolization in stories, 6–7, 12,
14, 34

Talking, Feeling, and Doing
Game, 7, 41–51, 96
advantages and disadvantages
of, 48–51
basic format of, 42–45
case example concerning perfectionism, 251–257
in child group and family therapy, 48–49
clinical example regarding
sibling rivalry, 216–217,
220–241
and contamination, 49–50
and dealing with perfectionism,
251–257
example of use involving guilt/
shame, 131–134
and external reinforcements,
184–186
involving competence and self-
esteem, 176–180
involving sexuality and dating,
332–333
and issues concerning competition, 196, 198
and issues concerning
self-assertion, 387–389

and neurologically based
learning disability children,
527–528
and reduction of masturbatory
guilt, 337–338
regarding antisocial behavior
and power, 397–423
regarding parental overprotection and overevaluation,
434–446
and the Storytelling Card Game,
25
technical and therapeutic considerations regarding the,
45–50
use in issues concerning values
and ethics, 450–467,
471–472, 473–494, 506–508
use of reward chips in, 42–44, 47
Teachers
and deterioration of schools,
536–538
Teenagers. *See Adolescents*
Tests for children, use of, 38
Thematic Apperception Test
(TAT), 38
Therapist
admitting own faults in therapy,
250–251, 329–330, 482, 491,
493, 499
and arguing with angry adolescent patients, 427
educational values of, 449–451
identifying with, 471
parents' initial interview with,
310–312
responding story of, 32–33
two types of, 308
and use of concrete examples vs.
abstractions, 477
views of on compliments,
183–184
views on sexuality, 307–313